P9-ELX-959

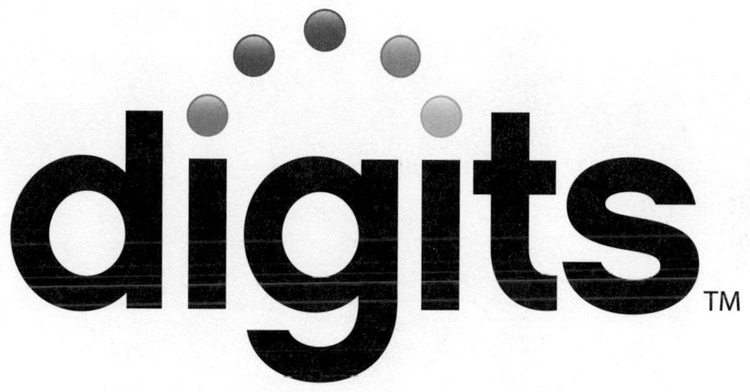

Homework Helper
Grade 7 Volume 1

PEARSON

Boston, Massachusetts • Chandler, Arizona • Glenview, Illinois • Upper Saddle River, New Jersey

Acknowledgments for Illustrations:
Rory Hensley, David Jackson, Jim Mariano, Rich McMahon, Lorie Park, and Ted Smykal

---

ISBN-13: 978-0-13-327631-2
ISBN-10: 0-13-327631-7
3 4 5 6 7 8 9 10 V011 17 16 15 14

Contents

Authors and Advisors

Francis (Skip) Fennell
***digits* Author**
Approaches to mathematics content and curriculum, educational policy, and support for intervention

Dr. Francis (Skip) Fennell is Professor of Education at McDaniel College, and a senior author with Pearson. He is a past president of the National Council of Teachers of Mathematics (NCTM) and a member of the writing team for the Curriculum Focal Points from the NCTM, which influenced the work of the Common Core Standards Initiative. Skip was also one of the writers of the Principles and Standards for School Mathematics.

Art Johnson
***digits* Author**
Approaches to mathematical content and support for English Language Learners

Art Johnson is a Professor of Mathematics at Boston University who taught in public school for over 30 years. He is part of the author team for Pearson's high school mathematics series. Art is the author of numerous books, including Teaching Mathematics to Culturally and Linguistically Diverse Students published by Allyn & Bacon, Teaching Today's Mathematics in the Middle Grades published by Allyn & Bacon, and Guiding Children's Learning of Mathematics, K–6 published by Wadsworth.

Helene Sherman
***digits* Author**
Teacher education and support for struggling students

Helene Sherman is Associate Dean for Undergraduate Education and Professor of Education in the College of Education at the University of Missouri in St. Louis, MO. Helene is the author of Teaching Learners Who Struggle with Mathematics, published by Merrill.

Stuart J. Murphy
***digits* Author**
Visual learning and student engagement

Stuart J. Murphy is a visual learning specialist and the author of the MathStart series. He contributed to the development of the Visual Learning Bridge in enVisionMATH™ as well as many visual elements of the Prentice Hall Algebra 1, Geometry, and Algebra 2 high school program.

Janie Schielack
***digits* Author**
Approaches to mathematical content, building problem solvers,and support for intervention

Janie Schielack is Professor of Mathematics and Associate Dean for Assessment and PreK–12 Education at Texas A&M University. She chaired the writing committee for the NCTM Curriculum Focal Points and was part of the nine-member NCTM feedback and advisory team that responded to and met with CCSSCO and NGA representatives during the development of various drafts of the Common Core State Standards.

Eric Milou
***digits* Author**
Approaches to mathematical content and the use of technology in middle grades classrooms

Eric Milou is Professor in the Department of Mathematics at Rowan University in Glassboro, NJ. Eric teaches pre-service teachers and works with in-service teachers, and is primarily interested in balancing concept development with skill proficiency. He was part of the nine-member NCTM feedback/advisory team that responded to and met with Council of Chief State School Officers (CCSSCO) and National Governors Association (NGA) representatives during the development of various drafts of the Common Core State Standards. Eric is the author of Teaching Mathematics to Middle School Students, published by Allyn & Bacon.

William F. Tate
***digits* Author**
Approaches to intervention, and use of efficacy and research

William Tate is the Edward Mallinckrodt Distinguished University Professor in Arts & Sciences at Washington University in St. Louis, MO. He is a past president of the American Educational Research Association. His research focuses on the social and psychological determinants of mathematics achievement and attainment as well as the political economy of schooling.

> *Pearson tapped leaders in mathematics education to develop* ***digits****. This esteemed author team—from diverse areas of expertise including mathematical content, Understanding by Design, and Technology Engagement—came together to construct a highly interactive and personalized learning experience.*

Grant Wiggins
***digits* Consulting Author**
Understanding by Design

Grant Wiggins is a cross-curricular Pearson consulting author specializing in curricular change. He is the author of Understanding by Design published by ASCD, and the President of Authentic Education in Hopewell, NJ. Over the past 20 years, he has worked on some of the most influential reform initiatives in the country, including Vermont's portfolio system and Ted Sizer's Coalition of Essential Schools.

Randall I. Charles
***digits* Advisor**

Dr. Randall I. Charles is Professor Emeritus in the Department of Mathematics at San Jose State University in San Jose, CA, and a senior author with Pearson. Randall served on the writing team for the Curriculum Focal Points from NCTM. The NCTM Curriculum Focal Points served as a key inspiration to the writers of the Common Core Standards in bringing focus, depth, and coherence to the curriculum.

Jim Cummins
***digits* Advisor**
Supporting English Language Learners

Dr. Jim Cummins is Professor and Canada Research Chair in the Centre for Educational Research on Languages and Literacies at the University of Toronto. His research focuses on literacy development in multilingual school contexts as well as on the potential roles of technology in promoting language and literacy development.

Jacquie Moen
***digits* Advisor**
Digital Technology

Jacquie Moen is a consultant specializing in how consumers interact with and use digital technologies. Jacquie worked for AOL for 10 years, and most recently was VP & General Manager for AOL's kids and teen online services, reaching over seven million kids every month. Jacquie has worked with a wide range of organizations to develop interactive content and strategies to reach families and children, including National Geographic, PBS, Pearson Education, National Wildlife Foundation, and the National Children's Museum.

Welcome to digits

Using the Homework Helper

digits is designed to help you master mathematics skills and concepts in a way that's relevant to you. As the title ***digits*** suggests, this program takes a digital approach. ***digits*** is digital, but sometimes you may not be able to access digital resources. When that happens, you can use the Homework Helper because you can refer back to the daily lesson and see all your homework questions right in the book.

Your Homework Helper supports your work on ***digits*** in so many ways!

The lesson pages capture important elements of the digital lesson that you need to know in order to do your homework.

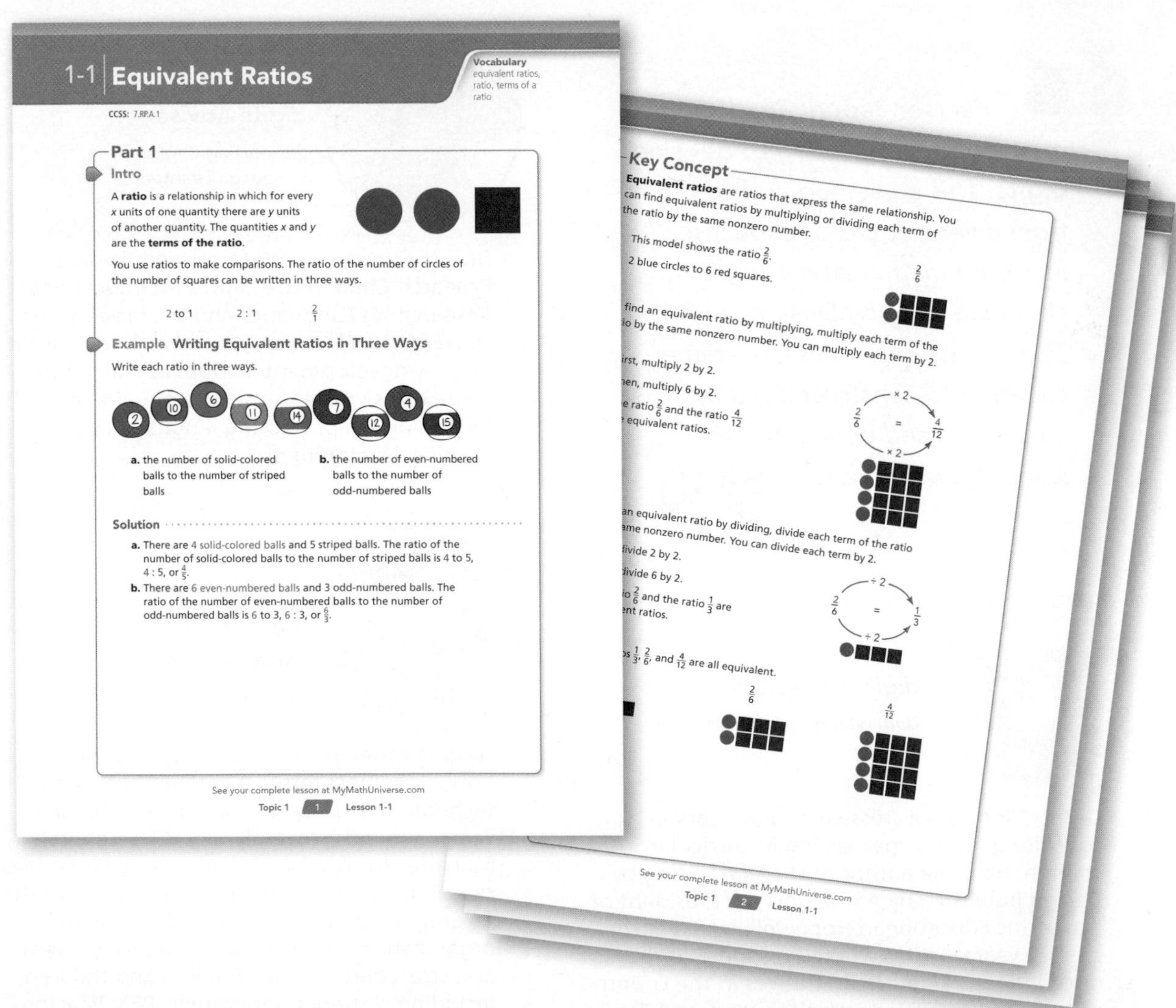

Every lesson in your Homework Helper also includes two pages of homework. The combination of homework exercises includes problems that focus on reasoning, multiple representations, mental math, writing, and error analysis. They vary in difficulty level from thinking about a plan to challenging. The problems come in different formats, like multiple choice, short answer, and open response, to help you prepare for tests.

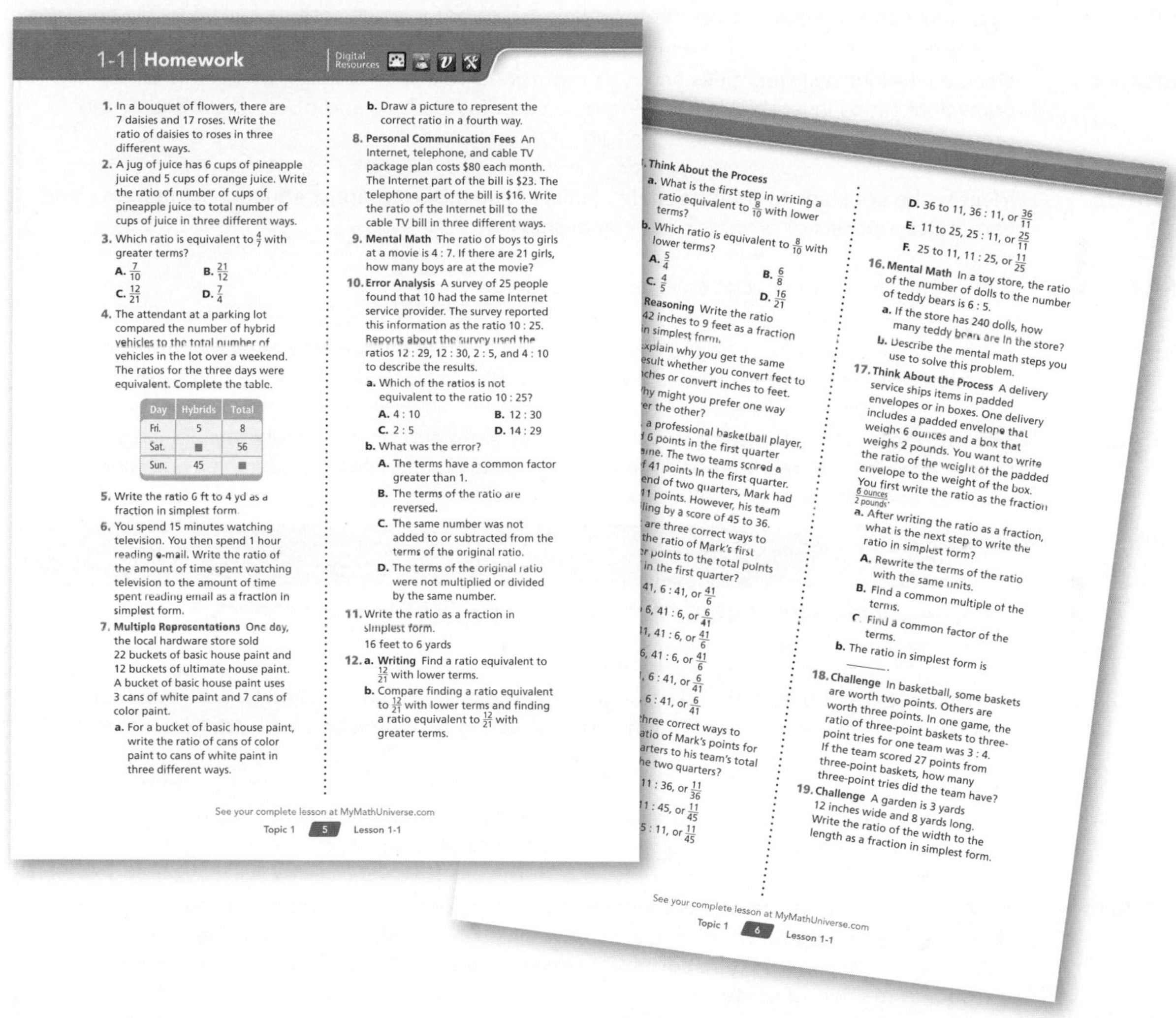

1-1 | Homework

Digital Resources

1. In a bouquet of flowers, there are 7 daisies and 17 roses. Write the ratio of daisies to roses in three different ways.
2. A jug of juice has 6 cups of pineapple juice and 5 cups of orange juice. Write the ratio of number of cups of pineapple juice to total number of cups of juice in three different ways.
3. Which ratio is equivalent to $\frac{4}{7}$ with greater terms?
   A. $\frac{7}{10}$ B. $\frac{21}{12}$
   C. $\frac{12}{21}$ D. $\frac{7}{4}$
4. The attendant at a parking lot compared the number of hybrid vehicles to the total number of vehicles in the lot over a weekend. The ratios for the three days were equivalent. Complete the table.

Day	Hybrids	Total
Fri.	5	8
Sat.	■	56
Sun.	45	■

5. Write the ratio 6 ft to 4 yd as a fraction in simplest form.
6. You spend 15 minutes watching television. You then spend 1 hour reading e-mail. Write the ratio of the amount of time spent watching television to the amount of time spent reading email as a fraction in simplest form.
7. **Multiple Representations** One day, the local hardware store sold 22 buckets of basic house paint and 12 buckets of ultimate house paint. A bucket of basic house paint uses 3 cans of white paint and 7 cans of color paint.
   a. For a bucket of basic house paint, write the ratio of cans of color paint to cans of white paint in three different ways.
   b. Draw a picture to represent the correct ratio in a fourth way.
8. **Personal Communication Fees** An Internet, telephone, and cable TV package plan costs $80 each month. The Internet part of the bill is $23. The telephone part of the bill is $16. Write the ratio of the Internet bill to the cable TV bill in three different ways.
9. **Mental Math** The ratio of boys to girls at a movie is 4 : 7. If there are 21 girls, how many boys are at the movie?
10. **Error Analysis** A survey of 25 people found that 10 had the same Internet service provider. The survey reported this information as the ratio 10 : 25. Reports about the survey used the ratios 12 : 29, 12 : 30, 2 : 5, and 4 : 10 to describe the results.
    a. Which of the ratios is not equivalent to the ratio 10 : 25?
    A. 4 : 10 B. 12 : 30
    C. 2 : 5 D. 14 : 29
    b. What was the error?
    A. The terms have a common factor greater than 1.
    B. The terms of the ratio are reversed.
    C. The same number was not added to or subtracted from the terms of the original ratio.
    D. The terms of the original ratio were not multiplied or divided by the same number.
11. Write the ratio as a fraction in simplest form.
    16 feet to 6 yards
12. a. **Writing** Find a ratio equivalent to $\frac{12}{21}$ with lower terms.
    b. Compare finding a ratio equivalent to $\frac{12}{21}$ with lower terms and finding a ratio equivalent to $\frac{12}{21}$ with greater terms.

See your complete lesson at MyMathUniverse.com

Topic 1 5 Lesson 1-1

Think About the Process
a. What is the first step in writing a ratio equivalent to $\frac{8}{10}$ with lower terms?
b. Which ratio is equivalent to $\frac{8}{10}$ with lower terms?
A. $\frac{5}{4}$ B. $\frac{6}{8}$
C. $\frac{4}{5}$ D. $\frac{16}{21}$

Reasoning Write the ratio 42 inches to 9 feet as a fraction in simplest form.
...xplain why you get the same ...esult whether you convert feet to ...ches or convert inches to feet. ...hy might you prefer one way ...er the other?

...a professional basketball player, ...6 points in the first quarter ...me. The two teams scored a ...f 41 points in the first quarter. ...end of two quarters, Mark had ...11 points. However, his team ...ling by a score of 45 to 36. ...are three correct ways to ...the ratio of Mark's first ...r points to the total points ...in the first quarter?
...41, 6 : 41, or $\frac{41}{6}$
...6, 41 : 6, or $\frac{6}{41}$
...1, 41 : 6, or $\frac{41}{6}$
...6, 41 : 6, or $\frac{41}{6}$
..., 6 : 41, or $\frac{6}{41}$
..., 6 : 41, or $\frac{6}{41}$
...hree correct ways to ...atio of Mark's points for ...arters to his team's total ...he two quarters?
...11 : 36, or $\frac{11}{36}$
...11 : 45, or $\frac{11}{45}$
...5 : 11, or $\frac{11}{45}$

D. 36 to 11, 36 : 11, or $\frac{36}{11}$
E. 11 to 25, 25 : 11, or $\frac{25}{11}$
F. 25 to 11, 11 : 25, or $\frac{11}{25}$

16. **Mental Math** In a toy store, the ratio of the number of dolls to the number of teddy bears is 6 : 5.
    a. If the store has 240 dolls, how many teddy bears are in the store?
    b. Describe the mental math steps you use to solve this problem.
17. **Think About the Process** A delivery service ships items in padded envelopes or in boxes. One delivery includes a padded envelope that weighs 6 ounces and a box that weighs 2 pounds. You want to write the ratio of the weight of the padded envelope to the weight of the box. You first write the ratio as the fraction $\frac{6 \text{ ounces}}{2 \text{ pounds}}$.
    a. After writing the ratio as a fraction, what is the next step to write the ratio in simplest form?
    A. Rewrite the terms of the ratio with the same units.
    B. Find a common multiple of the terms.
    C. Find a common factor of the terms.
    b. The ratio in simplest form is ____.
18. **Challenge** In basketball, some baskets are worth two points. Others are worth three points. In one game, the ratio of three-point baskets to three-point tries for one team was 3 : 4. If the team scored 27 points from three-point baskets, how many three-point tries did the team have?
19. **Challenge** A garden is 3 yards 12 inches wide and 8 yards long. Write the ratio of the width to the length as a fraction in simplest form.

See your complete lesson at MyMathUniverse.com

Topic 1 6 Lesson 1-1

Number	Standard for Mathematical Content
7.RP Ratios and Proportional Relationships	
Analyze proportional relationships and use them to solve real-world and mathematical problems.	
7.RP.A.1	Compute unit rates associated with ratios of fractions, including ratios of lengths, areas and other quantities measured in like or different units.
7.RP.A.2	Recognize and represent proportional relationships between quantities.
7.RP.A.2a	Decide whether two quantities are in a proportional relationship, e.g., by testing for equivalent ratios in a table or graphing on a coordinate plane and observing whether the graph is a straight line through the origin.
7.RP.A.2b	Identify the constant of proportionality (unit rate) in tables, graphs, equations, diagrams, and verbal descriptions of proportional relationships.
7.RP.A.2c	Represent proportional relationships by equations.
7.RP.A.2d	Explain what a point (x, y) on the graph of a proportional relationship means in terms of the situation, with special attention to the points (0, 0) and $(1, r)$ where r is the unit rate.
7.RP.A.3	Use proportional relationships to solve multistep ratio and percent problems. Examples: simple interest, tax, markups and markdowns, gratuities and commissions, fees, percent increase and decrease, percent error.
7.NS The Number System	
Apply and extend previous understandings of operations with fractions to add, subtract, multiply, and divide rational numbers.	
7.NS.A.1	Apply and extend previous understandings of addition and subtraction to add and subtract rational numbers; represent addition and subtraction on a horizontal or vertical number line diagram.
7.NS.A.1a	Describe situations in which opposite quantities combine to make 0. For example, a hydrogen atom has 0 charge because its two constituents are oppositely charged.
7.NS.A.1b	Understand $p + q$ as the number located a distance $\|q\|$ from p, in the positive or negative direction depending on whether q is positive or negative. Show that a number and its opposite have a sum of 0 (are additive inverses). Interpret sums of rational numbers by describing real-world contexts.
7.NS.A.1c	Understand subtraction of rational numbers as adding the additive inverse, $p - q = p + (-q)$. Show that the distance between two rational numbers on the number line is the absolute value of their difference, and apply this principle in real-world contexts.
7.NS.A.1d	Apply properties of operations as strategies to add and subtract rational numbers.
7.NS.A.2	Apply and extend previous understandings of multiplication and division and of fractions to multiply and divide rational numbers.

Number	Standard for Mathematical Content
7.NS The Number System *(continued)*	
Apply and extend previous understandings of operations with fractions to add, subtract, multiply, and divide rational numbers.	
7.NS.A.2a	Understand that multiplication is extended from fractions to rational numbers by requiring that operations continue to satisfy the properties of operations, particularly the distributive property, leading to products such as $(-1)(-1) = 1$ and the rules for multiplying signed numbers. Interpret products of rational numbers by describing real-world contexts.
7.NS.A.2b	Understand that integers can be divided, provided that the divisor is not zero, and every quotient of integers (with non-zero divisor) is a rational number. If *p* and *q* are integers, then $\left(\frac{p}{q}\right) = \frac{(-p)}{q} = \frac{p}{(-q)}$. Interpret quotients of rational numbers by describing real-world contexts.
7.NS.A.2c	Apply properties of operations as strategies to multiply and divide rational numbers.
7.NS.A.2d	Convert a rational number to a decimal using long division; know that the decimal form of a rational number terminates in 0s or eventually repeats.
7.NS.A.3	Solve real-world and mathematical problems involving the four operations with rational numbers.
7.EE Expressions and Equations	
Use properties of operations to generate equivalent expressions.	
7.EE.A.1	Apply properties of operations as strategies to add, subtract, factor, and expand linear expressions with rational coefficients.
7.EE.A.2	Understand that rewriting an expression in different forms in a problem context can shed light on the problem and how the quantities in it are related. For example, $a + 0.05a = 1.05a$ means that "increase by 5%" is the same as "multiply by 1.05."
Solve real-life and mathematical problems using numerical and algebraic expressions and equations.	
7.EE.B.3	Solve multi-step real-life and mathematical problems posed with positive and negative rational numbers in any form (whole numbers, fractions, and decimals), using tools strategically. Apply properties of operations to calculate with numbers in any form; convert between forms as appropriate; and assess the reasonableness of answers using mental computation and estimation strategies.
7.EE.B.4	Use variables to represent quantities in a real-world or mathematical problem, and construct simple equations and inequalities to solve problems by reasoning about the quantities.
7.EE.B.4a	Solve word problems leading to equations of the form $px + q = r$ and $p(x + q) = r$, where *p*, *q*, and *r* are specific rational numbers. Solve equations of these forms fluently. Compare an algebraic solution to an arithmetic solution, identifying the sequence of the operations used in each approach.
7.EE.B.4b	Solve word problems leading to inequalities of the form $px + q > r$ or $px + q < r$, where *p*, *q*, and *r* are specific rational numbers. Graph the solution set of the inequality and interpret it in the context of the problem.

Grade 7 Common Core State Standards *continued*

Number	Standard for Mathematical Content
7.G Geometry	
Draw construct, and describe geometrical figures and describe the relationships between them.	
7.G.A.1	Solve problems involving scale drawings of geometric figures, including computing actual lengths and areas from a scale drawing and reproducing a scale drawing at a different scale.
7.G.A.2	Draw (freehand, with ruler and protractor, and with technology) geometric shapes with given conditions. Focus on constructing triangles from three measures of angles or sides, noticing when the conditions determine a unique triangle, more than one triangle, or no triangle.
7.G.A.3	Describe the two-dimensional figures that result from slicing three- dimensional figures, as in plane sections of right rectangular prisms and right rectangular pyramids.
Solve real-life and mathematical problems involving angle measure, area, surface area, and volume.	
7.G.B.4	Know the formulas for the area and circumference of a circle and use them to solve problems; give an informal derivation of the relationship between the circumference and area of a circle.
7.G.B.5	Use facts about supplementary, complementary, vertical, and adjacent angles in a multi-step problem to write and solve simple equations for an unknown angle in a figure.
7.G.B.6	Solve real-world and mathematical problems involving area, volume and surface area of two- and three-dimensional objects composed of triangles, quadrilaterals, polygons, cubes, and right prisms.
7.SP Statistics and Probability	
Use random sampling to draw inferences about a population.	
7.SP.A.1	Understand that statistics can be used to gain information about a population by examining a sample of the population; generalizations about a population from a sample are valid only if the sample is representative of that population. Understand that random sampling tends to produce representative samples and support valid inferences.
7.SP.A.2	Use data from a random sample to draw inferences about a population with an unknown characteristic of interest. Generate multiple samples (or simulated samples) of the same size to gauge the variation in estimates or predictions.
Draw informal comparative inferences about two populations.	
7.SP.B.3	Informally assess the degree of visual overlap of two numerical data distributions with similar variabilities, measuring the difference between the centers by expressing it as a multiple of a measure of variability.
7.SP.B.4	Use measures of center and measures of variability for numerical data from random samples to draw informal comparative inferences about two populations.
Investigate chance processes and develop, use, and evaluate probability models.	
7.SP.C.5	Understand that the probability of a chance event is a number between 0 and 1 that expresses the likelihood of the event occurring. Larger numbers indicate greater likelihood. A probability near 0 indicates an unlikely event, a probability around $\frac{1}{2}$ indicates an event that is neither unlikely nor likely, and a probability near 1 indicates a likely event.

Number	Standard for Mathematical Content
7.SP Statistics and Probability *(continued)*	
Investigate chance processes and develop, use, and evaluate probability models.	
7.SP.C.6	Approximate the probability of a chance event by collecting data on the chance process that produces it and observing its long-run relative frequency, and predict the approximate relative frequency given the probability.
7.SP.C.7	Develop a probability model and use it to find probabilities of events. Compare probabilities from a model to observed frequencies; if the agreement is not good, explain possible sources of the discrepancy.
7.SP.C.7a	Develop a uniform probability model by assigning equal probability to all outcomes, and use the model to determine probabilities of events.
7.SP.C.7b	Develop a probability model (which may not be uniform) by observing frequencies in data generated from a chance process.
7.SP.C.8	Find probabilities of compound events using organized lists, tables, tree diagrams, and simulation.
7.SP.C.8a	Understand that, just as with simple events, the probability of a compound event is the fraction of outcomes in the sample space for which the compound event occurs.
7.SP.C.8b	Represent sample spaces for compound events using methods such as organized lists, tables and tree diagrams. For an event described in everyday language (e.g., "rolling double sixes"), identify the outcomes in the sample space which compose the event.
7.SP.C.8c	Design and use a simulation to generate frequencies for compound events. For example, use random digits as a simulation tool to approximate the answer to the question: If 40% of donors have type A blood, what is the probability that it will take at least 4 donors to find one with type A blood?

Number	Standard for Mathematical Practice
MP1	Make sense of problems and persevere in solving them.
MP2	Reason abstractly and quantitatively.
MP3	Construct viable arguments and critique the reasoning of others.
MP4	Model with mathematics.
MP5	Use appropriate tools strategically.
MP6	Attend to precision.
MP7	Look for and make use of structure.
MP8	Look for and express regularity in repeated reasoning.

1-1 Equivalent Ratios

Vocabulary
equivalent ratios, ratio, terms of a ratio

CCSS: 7.RP.A.1

Part 1

Intro

A **ratio** is a relationship in which for every *x* units of one quantity there are *y* units of another quantity. The quantities *x* and *y* are the **terms of the ratio**.

You use ratios to make comparisons. The ratio of the number of circles of the number of squares can be written in three ways.

2 to 1 2 : 1 $\frac{2}{1}$

Example Writing Equivalent Ratios in Three Ways

Write each ratio in three ways.

a. the number of solid-colored balls to the number of striped balls

b. the number of even-numbered balls to the number of odd-numbered balls

Solution

a. There are 4 solid-colored balls and 5 striped balls. The ratio of the number of solid-colored balls to the number of striped balls is 4 to 5, 4 : 5, or $\frac{4}{5}$.

b. There are 6 even-numbered balls and 3 odd-numbered balls. The ratio of the number of even-numbered balls to the number of odd-numbered balls is 6 to 3, 6 : 3, or $\frac{6}{3}$.

Key Concept

Equivalent ratios are ratios that express the same relationship. You can find equivalent ratios by multiplying or dividing each term of the ratio by the same nonzero number.

This model shows the ratio $\frac{2}{6}$.

2 blue circles to 6 red squares.

$\frac{2}{6}$

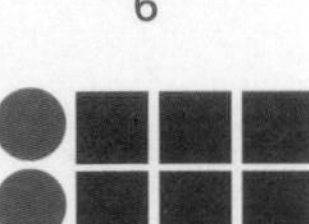

To find an equivalent ratio by multiplying, multiply each term of the ratio by the same nonzero number. You can multiply each term by 2.

First, multiply 2 by 2.

Then, multiply 6 by 2.

The ratio $\frac{2}{6}$ and the ratio $\frac{4}{12}$ are equivalent ratios.

$$\frac{2}{6} \xrightarrow{\times 2} = \frac{4}{12}$$

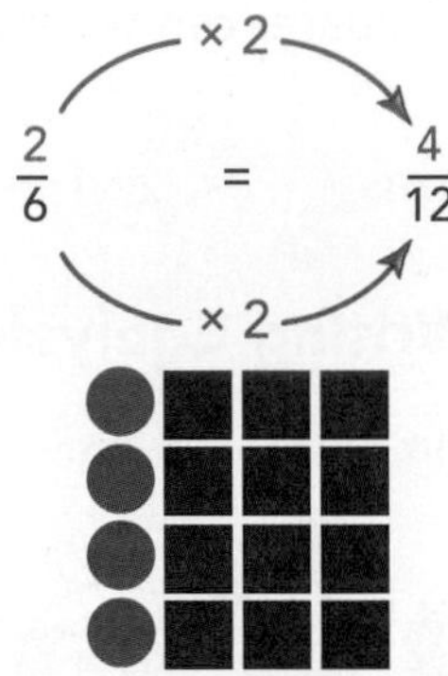

To find an equivalent ratio by dividing, divide each term of the ratio by the same nonzero number. You can divide each term by 2.

First, divide 2 by 2.

Then, divide 6 by 2.

The ratio $\frac{2}{6}$ and the ratio $\frac{1}{3}$ are equivalent ratios.

$$\frac{2}{6} \xrightarrow{\div 2} = \frac{1}{3}$$

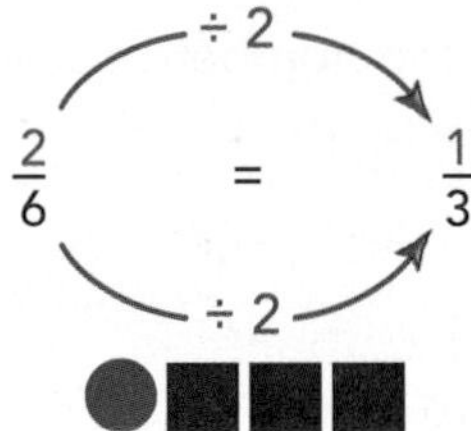

So, the ratios $\frac{1}{3}$, $\frac{2}{6}$, and $\frac{4}{12}$ are all equivalent.

$\frac{1}{3}$

$\frac{2}{6}$

$\frac{4}{12}$

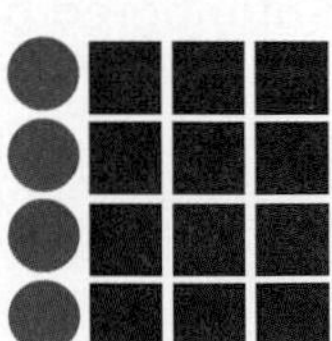

Part 2

Example Finding Equivalent Ratios

You volunteer at an animal shelter and need to order supplies. You know that the ratio of kitten supplies to adult cat supplies for each category is equivalent. Use the information to complete the table.

PET SUPPLIES

SUPPLY	KITTEN	ADULT CAT
Food (bags)		8
Treats (bags)	42	56
Food (cans)	126	

Solution

The ratio $\frac{\text{number of bags of kitten food}}{\text{number of bags of adult cat food}}$ is equivalent to the ratio $\frac{\text{number of bags of kitten treats}}{\text{number of bags of adult cat treats}}$.

Find the ratio equivalent to $\frac{42}{56}$ with a denominator of 8.

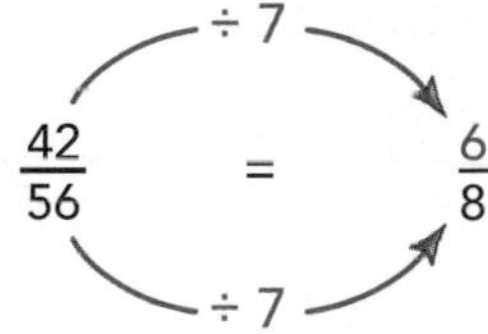

The ratio $\frac{\text{number of bags of kitten food}}{\text{number of bags of adult cat food}}$ is equivalent to the ratio $\frac{\text{number of bags of kitten treats}}{\text{number of bags of adult cat treats}}$.

Find the ratio equivalent to $\frac{42}{56}$ with a numerator of 126.

PET SUPPLIES

SUPPLY	KITTEN	ADULT CAT
Food (bags)	6	8
Treats (bags)	42	56
Food (cans)	126	168

$$\frac{42}{56} = \frac{126}{168} \quad (\times 3)$$

Part 3

Intro

Equivalent ratios have the same simplest form. To write a ratio in simplest form, first write it as a fraction. Then divide the numerator and the denominator by their greatest common factor (GCF).

When the two terms of a ratio have the same unit of measure, the units cancel out.

$$\frac{30 \text{ min}}{1 \text{ hr}} = \frac{30 \text{ min}}{60 \text{ min}} = \frac{1 \cancel{\text{min}}}{2 \cancel{\text{min}}} = \frac{1}{2}$$

÷ 30

÷ 30

1 hr = 60 mins.

Example Comparing Lengths Using Ratios

You make a banner 6 ft long to hang behind the desk at the animal shelter. Your friend makes a banner 6 yd long to hang on the outside of the building. Write the ratio of the length of your banner to the length of your friend's banner as a fraction in simplest form.

Solution

Method 1

Convert yards to feet.

$$\frac{6 \text{ ft}}{6 \text{ yd}} = \frac{6 \text{ ft}}{6 \cancel{\text{yd}} \times \frac{3 \text{ ft}}{1 \cancel{\text{yd}}}}$$

$$= \frac{6 \text{ ft}}{18 \text{ ft}}$$

$$= \frac{6 \text{ ft} \div 6}{18 \text{ ft} \div 6}$$

$$= \frac{1 \cancel{\text{ft}}}{3 \cancel{\text{ft}}}$$

$$= \frac{1}{3}$$

There are 3 feet in 1 yard.

Divide by GCF.

Method 2

Convert feet to yards.

$$\frac{6 \text{ ft}}{6 \text{ yd}} = \frac{6 \cancel{\text{ft}} \times \frac{1 \text{ yd}}{3 \cancel{\text{ft}}}}{6 \text{ yd}}$$

$$= \frac{2 \text{ yd}}{6 \text{ yd}}$$

$$= \frac{2 \text{ yd} \div 2}{6 \text{ yd} \div 2}$$

$$= \frac{1 \cancel{\text{yd}}}{3 \cancel{\text{yd}}}$$

$$= \frac{1}{3}$$

The ratio of the length of your banner to the length of your friend's banner is $\frac{1}{3}$.

Digital Resources    

1. In a bouquet of flowers, there are 7 daisies and 17 roses. Write the ratio of daisies to roses in three different ways.

2. A jug of juice has 6 cups of pineapple juice and 5 cups of orange juice. Write the ratio of number of cups of pineapple juice to total number of cups of juice in three different ways.

3. Which ratio is equivalent to $\frac{4}{7}$ with greater terms?

A. $\frac{7}{10}$ **B.** $\frac{21}{12}$

C. $\frac{12}{21}$ **D.** $\frac{7}{4}$

4. The attendant at a parking lot compared the number of hybrid vehicles to the total number of vehicles in the lot over a weekend. The ratios for the three days were equivalent. Complete the table.

Day	Hybrids	Total
Fri.	5	8
Sat.	■	56
Sun.	45	■

5. Write the ratio 6 ft to 4 yd as a fraction in simplest form.

6. You spend 15 minutes watching television. You then spend 1 hour reading e-mail. Write the ratio of the amount of time spent watching television to the amount of time spent reading email as a fraction in simplest form.

7. Multiple Representations One day, the local hardware store sold 22 buckets of basic house paint and 12 buckets of ultimate house paint. A bucket of basic house paint uses 3 cans of white paint and 7 cans of color paint.

a. For a bucket of basic house paint, write the ratio of cans of color paint to cans of white paint in three different ways.

b. Draw a picture to represent the correct ratio in a fourth way.

8. Personal Communication Fees An Internet, telephone, and cable TV package plan costs $80 each month. The Internet part of the bill is $23. The telephone part of the bill is $16. Write the ratio of the Internet bill to the cable TV bill in three different ways.

9. Mental Math The ratio of boys to girls at a movie is 4 : 7. If there are 21 girls, how many boys are at the movie?

10. Error Analysis A survey of 25 people found that 10 had the same Internet service provider. The survey reported this information as the ratio 10 : 25. Reports about the survey used the ratios 12 : 29, 12 : 30, 2 : 5, and 4 : 10 to describe the results.

a. Which of the ratios is not equivalent to the ratio 10 : 25?

A. 4 : 10 **B.** 12 : 30

C. 2 : 5 **D.** 14 : 29

b. What was the error?

A. The terms have a common factor greater than 1.

B. The terms of the ratio are reversed.

C. The same number was not added to or subtracted from the terms of the original ratio.

D. The terms of the original ratio were not multiplied or divided by the same number.

11. Write the ratio as a fraction in simplest form.

16 feet to 6 yards

12. a. Writing Find a ratio equivalent to $\frac{12}{21}$ with lower terms.

b. Compare finding a ratio equivalent to $\frac{12}{21}$ with lower terms and finding a ratio equivalent to $\frac{12}{21}$ with greater terms.

13. Think About the Process

a. What is the first step in writing a ratio equivalent to $\frac{8}{10}$ with lower terms?

b. Which ratio is equivalent to $\frac{8}{10}$ with lower terms?

A. $\frac{5}{4}$ **B.** $\frac{6}{8}$

C. $\frac{4}{5}$ **D.** $\frac{16}{21}$

14. a. Reasoning Write the ratio 42 inches to 9 feet as a fraction in simplest form.

b. Explain why you get the same result whether you convert feet to inches or convert inches to feet.

c. Why might you prefer one way over the other?

15. Mark, a professional basketball player, scored 6 points in the first quarter of a game. The two teams scored a total of 41 points in the first quarter. At the end of two quarters, Mark had scored 11 points. However, his team was trailing by a score of 45 to 36.

a. What are three correct ways to write the ratio of Mark's first quarter points to the total points scored in the first quarter?

A. 6 to 41, 6 : 41, or $\frac{41}{6}$

B. 41 to 6, 41 : 6, or $\frac{6}{41}$

C. 6 to 41, 41 : 6, or $\frac{41}{6}$

D. 41 to 6, 41 : 6, or $\frac{41}{6}$

E. 6 to 41, 6 : 41, or $\frac{6}{41}$

F. 41 to 6, 6 : 41, or $\frac{6}{41}$

b. What are three correct ways to write the ratio of Mark's points for the two quarters to his team's total points for the two quarters?

A. 11 to 36, 11 : 36, or $\frac{11}{36}$

B. 11 to 45, 11 : 45, or $\frac{11}{45}$

C. 45 to 11, 45 : 11, or $\frac{11}{45}$

D. 36 to 11, 36 : 11, or $\frac{36}{11}$

E. 11 to 25, 25 : 11, or $\frac{25}{11}$

F. 25 to 11, 11 : 25, or $\frac{11}{25}$

16. Mental Math In a toy store, the ratio of the number of dolls to the number of teddy bears is 6 : 5.

a. If the store has 240 dolls, how many teddy bears are in the store?

b. Describe the mental math steps you use to solve this problem.

17. Think About the Process A delivery service ships items in padded envelopes or in boxes. One delivery includes a padded envelope that weighs 6 ounces and a box that weighs 2 pounds. You want to write the ratio of the weight of the padded envelope to the weight of the box. You first write the ratio as the fraction $\frac{6 \text{ ounces}}{2 \text{ pounds}}$.

a. After writing the ratio as a fraction, what is the next step to write the ratio in simplest form?

A. Rewrite the terms of the ratio with the same units.

B. Find a common multiple of the terms.

C. Find a common factor of the terms.

b. The ratio in simplest form is _______.

18. Challenge In basketball, some baskets are worth two points. Others are worth three points. In one game, the ratio of three-point baskets to three-point tries for one team was 3 : 4. If the team scored 27 points from three-point baskets, how many three-point tries did the team have?

19. Challenge A garden is 3 yards 12 inches wide and 8 yards long. Write the ratio of the width to the length as a fraction in simplest form.

1-2 Unit Rates

Vocabulary
rate, unit price, unit rate

CCSS: 7.RP.A.1

Key Concept

A **rate** is a ratio that compares quantities measured in different units. A **unit rate** is the rate for one unit of a given quantity. When a unit rate is written as a fraction, the denominator is 1 unit. The 1 in a unit rate is read as "per."

If a car travels 120 mi on 4 gal of gasoline, then the rate is $\frac{120 \text{ mi}}{4 \text{ gal}}$.

The unit rate is $\frac{30 \text{ mi}}{1 \text{ gal}}$, or 30 miles per gallon.

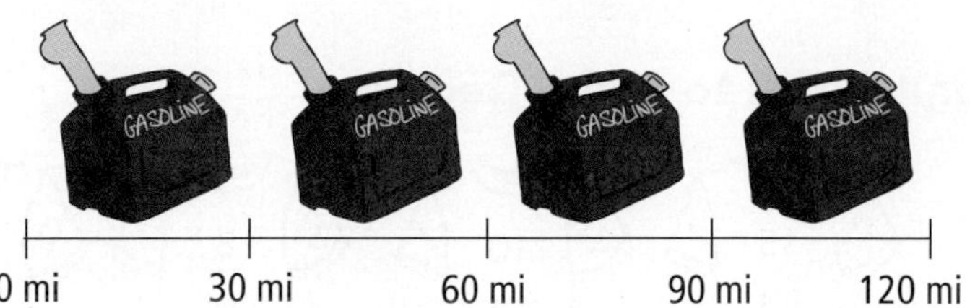

Part 1

Example Finding Unit Rates

A lobster molts, or sheds its shell, 20 times over a period of 5 years. How many times per year does the lobster molt?

Solution

The ratio of the number of molts to the number of years is $\frac{20 \text{ molts}}{5 \text{ years}}$.

Divide by 5 to find the number of molts per year.

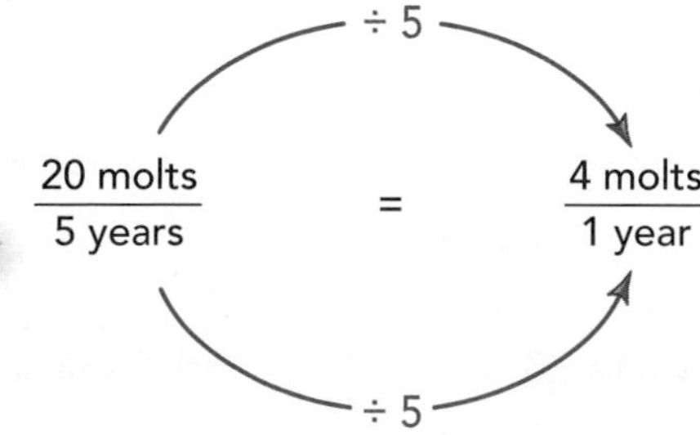

The unit rate is $\frac{4 \text{ molts}}{1 \text{ year}}$, or 4 molts per year.

The lobster molts 4 times per year.

Part 2

Intro

A **unit price** is a unit rate that gives the price of one item, or the price per item.

Rate:

$25 for 4 tickets

$\frac{\$25}{4 \text{ tickets}}$

Unit Price:

$6.25 for 1 ticket

$\frac{\$6.25}{1 \text{ ticket}}$, or $6.25 per ticket

Example Using Unit Rates to Make Decisions

Your class is tie-dying T-shirts to sell for a fundraiser. You are in charge of buying the plain T-shirts. Which package is the best buy? Which package is the worst buy?

Solution

Find the unit price for each package. The best buy has the lowest price per T-shirt. The worst buy has the highest price per T-shirt.

12 T-shirts for $39.00

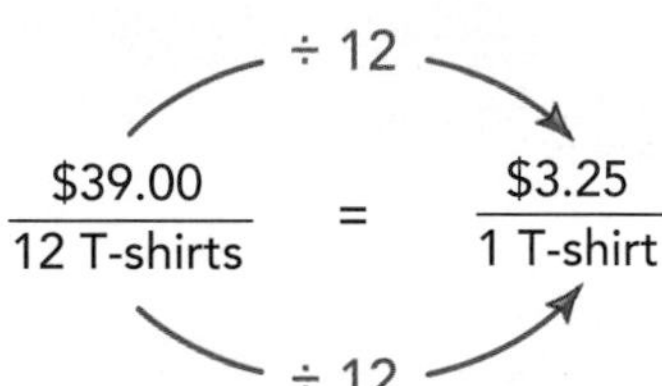

$$\frac{\$39.00}{12 \text{ T-shirts}} = \frac{\$3.25}{1 \text{ T-shirt}} \quad (\div 12)$$

The unit price is $3.25 per T-shirt.

8 T-shirts for $27.20

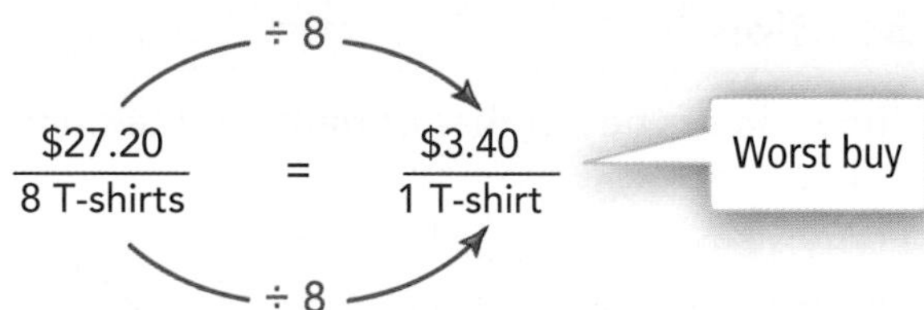

$$\frac{\$27.20}{8 \text{ T-shirts}} = \frac{\$3.40}{1 \text{ T-shirt}} \quad (\div 8)$$

Worst buy

The unit price is $3.40 per T-shirt.

15 T-shirts for $47.25

$$\frac{\$47.25}{15 \text{ T-shirts}} = \frac{\$3.15}{1 \text{ T-shirt}} \quad (\div 15)$$

The unit price is $3.15 per T-shirt.

10 T-shirts for $29.90

$$\frac{\$29.90}{10 \text{ T-shirts}} = \frac{\$2.99}{1 \text{ T-shirt}} \quad (\div 10)$$

Best buy

The unit price is $2.99 per T-shirt.

Part 3

Intro

The Know-Need-Plan graphic organizer is a tool that can help you make sense of problems.

Organizing what you know and what you need can make it easier to form a plan.

Suppose a water pump moves 330 gal of water in 22 min. How many gallons of water does the pump move in 39 min?

Know
The number of gallons of water a water pump moves in 22 min

Need
The number of gallons of water the pump moves in 39 min

Plan
Find the unit rate of gallons per minute. Then use the unit rate to find the amount of water moved in 39 min.

Example Using Unit Rates to Find Information

Astronauts have different nutritional needs in space than on Earth. An astronaut's diet contains 18 mg of iron for 2 days. How many milligrams of iron should the astronaut's diet contain for 9 days?

Solution

Know
The quantity of iron for 2 days

Need
The quantity of iron for 9 days

Plan
Find the unit rate of iron per day. Then use the unit rate to find the quantity of iron for 9 days.

continued on next page >

Part 3

Solution continued

First, find the unit rate in milligrams per day.

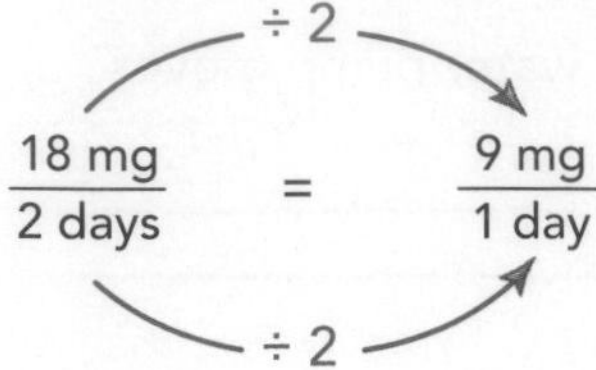

Then use the unit rate to find the number of milligrams of iron the astronaut's diet should contain for 9 days.

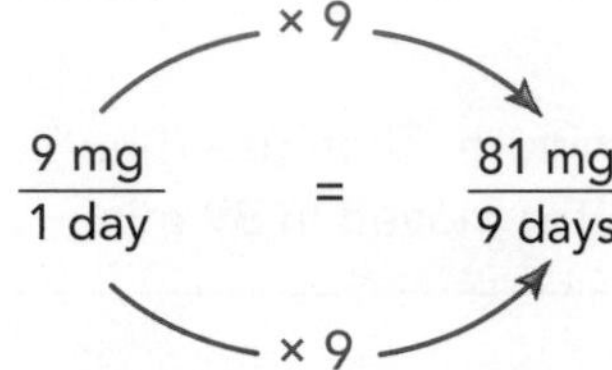

The astronaut's diet should contain 81 mg of iron for 9 days.

Digital Resources   

1. An airplane on autopilot took 5 hours to travel 3,475 kilometers. What is the unit rate for kilometers per hour?
2. What is the unit rate for meters per second if a car travels 374 meters in 17 seconds?
3. In a week, 12 hens laid 48 eggs. What is the unit rate for eggs per hen?
4. A package of 5 pairs of insulated gloves costs $29.45. What is the unit price of the pairs of gloves?
5. You want to buy some rice. A 7-ounce package costs $2.59. A 12-ounce package costs $4.56. An 18-ounce package costs $6.30. Which package is the best buy?
6. Population density is the number of people per unit of area. The population density of a certain region is 60 people per square kilometer. If the region covers 23 square kilometers, what is the population of the region?
7. A store sells 12 cans of soup for $15. How much would it cost you to buy 7 cans of soup?
8. **a.** What is the unit rate for miles per gallon if you travel 460 miles on 20 gallons of fuel?
   b. Describe another unit rate that you could find for this situation.
   c. Explain the meaning of that unit rate.
9. **Writing** During a thunderstorm yesterday, 600 millimeters of rain fell in 30 minutes.
   a. What is the unit rate for millimeters per minute?
   b. Describe a situation in which it would be useful to know this unit rate.
   c. Explain why the unit rate would be useful.
10. **Error Analysis** A contractor purchases 7 dozen pairs of padded work gloves for $103.32. He incorrectly calculates the unit price at $14.76 per pair for the expense report.
    a. What is the correct unit price?
    b. Why is the contractor's unit price incorrect?
    A. The contractor uses subtraction rather than division to find the unit price.
    B. The contractor uses multiplication rather than division to find the unit price.
    C. The contractor's unit price is per glove, not per pair of gloves.
    D. The contractor's unit price is per dozen pairs, not per pair of gloves.
11. **Fundraising** The track team needs new uniforms. The students plan to sell plush toy tigers (the school mascot) for $5 each. The students find three companies online that sell stuffed mascots. Company A sells 12 tigers for $33.24. Company B sells 16 tigers for $44.80. Company C charges $41.10 for 15 tigers. Which company has the best buy?
12. **Reasoning** A store sells a package of 25 trading cards for $5.25.
    a. Explain how you can tell that the unit price per card is less than $1.
    b. What is the unit price per card?
13. **Estimation** A car takes 55.3 seconds to travel 1 mile.
    a. How long does it take the car to travel 5.8 miles? Round to the nearest whole number to find the estimated answer.
    b. Find the exact answer.
14. **Think About the Process** At a little-known vacation spot, taxi fares are a bargain. A 36-mile taxi ride takes 42 minutes and costs $25.20. You want to find the cost of a 47-mile taxi ride. What unit price do you need?

15. Some people advise that in very cold weather, you should keep the gas tank in your car more than half full. Irene's car had 6.1 gallons in the 15-gallon tank on the coldest day of the year. Irene filled the tank with gas that cost $3.80 per gallon. How much did Irene spend on gas?

16. A nursery owner buys 5 panes of glass to fix some damage to her greenhouse. The 5 panes cost $14.25. Unfortunately, she breaks 2 more panes while repairing the damage. What is the cost of another 2 panes of glass?

17. **Think About the Process** At a supermarket, a 6-ounce bottle of brand A salad dressing costs $1.56. A 14-ounce bottle costs $3.36. A 20-ounce bottle costs $5.60.

   a. What unit prices do you need to know to find the best buy?

   A. The unit prices per bottle

   B. The unit prices per bottle and per ounce

   C. The unit prices per ounce

   D. The unit prices per dollar

   b. Which size bottle is the best buy?

18. **Challenge** A warehouse store sells 5.5-ounce cans of tuna in packages of 6. A package of 6 cans costs $9.24. The store also sells 6.5-ounce cans of the same tuna in packages of 3. A package of 3 cans costs $4.68. The store sells 3.5-ounce cans in packages of 4 cans for $4.48. Which package is the best buy?

19. **Challenge** An arts academy requires there to be 3 teachers for every 75 students and 6 tutors for every 72 students.

   a. How many students does the academy have per teacher?

   b. How many students does the academy have per tutor?

   c. How many tutors does the academy need if it has 120 students?

1-3 Ratios with Fractions

CCSS: 7.RP.A.1

Part 1

Intro

You can have a ratio where one term is a fraction. Simplify these ratios by finding an equivalent ratio where both terms are whole numbers.

Multiply each term of the ratio by the denominator of the fraction. Then write the ratio in simplest form.

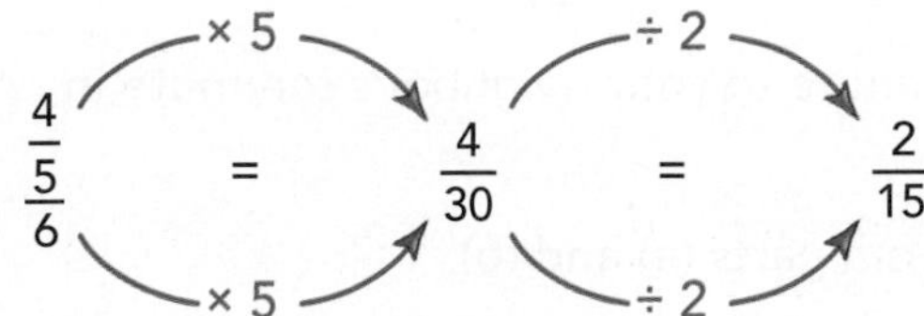

$$\frac{\frac{4}{5}}{6} \overset{\times 5}{=} \frac{4}{30} \overset{\div 2}{=} \frac{2}{15}$$

The ratio $\frac{\frac{4}{5}}{6}$ written in simplest form is $\frac{2}{15}$.

Example **Writing Ratios as Fractions**

Your neighbor commutes 12 mi to work. You commute $\frac{9}{10}$ mi to school.

a. Write the ratio of your neighbor's commute to your commute as a fraction in simplest form.

b. Write the ratio of your commute to your neighbor's commute as a fraction in simplest form.

c. How are the ratios from parts (a) and (b) related?

Solution

a. The ratio of your neighbor's commute to your commute is $\frac{12 \text{ mi}}{\frac{9}{10} \text{ mi}}$.

Multiply each term of the ratio by 10.

Divide each term of the ratio by the GCF.

$$\frac{12 \text{ mi}}{\frac{9}{10} \text{ mi}} \overset{\times 10}{=} \frac{120 \text{ mi}}{9 \text{ mi}} \overset{\div 3}{=} \frac{40 \cancel{\text{ mi}}}{3 \cancel{\text{ mi}}} = \frac{40}{3}$$

continued on next page >

Part 1

Solution continued

The ratio of your neighbor's commute to your commute in simplest form is $\frac{40}{3}$.

b. The ratio of your commute to your neighbor's commute is $\frac{\frac{9}{10}\text{ mi}}{12\text{ mi}}$.

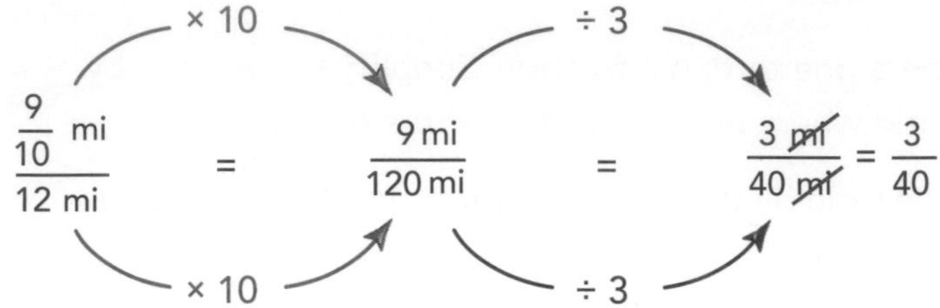

$$\frac{\frac{9}{10}\text{ mi}}{12\text{ mi}} = \frac{9\text{ mi}}{120\text{ mi}} = \frac{3\text{ mi}}{40\text{ mi}} = \frac{3}{40}$$

The ratio of your commute to your neighbor's commute in simplest form is $\frac{3}{40}$.

c. Compare the ratios from parts (a) and (b).

The ratios $\frac{40}{3}$ and $\frac{3}{40}$ are reciprocals.

Key Concept

You can also have ratios where both terms are fractions. Simplify these ratios by finding an equivalent ratio where both terms are whole numbers.

Multiply each term of the ratio by the least common multiple (LCM) of the denominators of the fractions. Then write the ratio in simplest form.

Suppose you have the ratio $\frac{\frac{3}{4}}{\frac{6}{7}}$.

To simplify the ratio, multiply each term by the least common multiple (LCM) of the denominators of the two fractions. The LCM of 4 and 7 is 28. Multiply each term of the ratio by 28.

$\frac{3}{4} \times 28 = 21$ $\qquad\qquad$ $\frac{6}{7} \times 28 = 24$

Now, to simplify the fraction, divide by the greatest common factor (GCF) of the numerator and denominator. The GCF of 21 and 24 is 3. Divide each term of the ratio by 3.

$$\frac{\frac{3}{4}}{\frac{6}{7}} \xrightarrow{\times 28} \frac{21}{24} \xrightarrow{\div 3} \frac{7}{8}$$

The ratio $\frac{\frac{3}{4}}{\frac{6}{7}}$ written in simplest form is $\frac{7}{8}$.

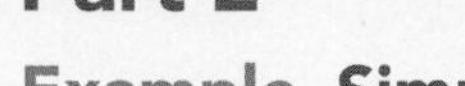

Part 2

Example Simplifying Ratios with Fractional Terms

Determine whether each statement is *true* or *false*.

a. The ratio $\frac{\frac{2}{3}\text{ ft}^2}{\frac{1}{5}\text{ ft}^2}$ is equivalent to $\frac{10}{3}$.

b. The ratio $\frac{\frac{4}{5}\text{ km}^2}{\frac{6}{7}\text{ km}^2}$ is equivalent to $\frac{14}{15}$.

c. The ratio $\frac{\frac{4}{3}\text{ in}^2}{\frac{8}{9}\text{ in}^2}$ is equivalent to $\frac{2}{3}$.

Solution

a.

The LCM of 3 and 5 is 15.

$$\frac{\frac{2}{3}\text{ ft}^2}{\frac{1}{5}\text{ ft}^2} \underset{\times 15}{\overset{\times 15}{=}} \frac{10\text{ ft}^2}{3\text{ ft}^2} = \frac{10}{3}$$

The ratio $\frac{\frac{2}{3}}{\frac{1}{5}}$ is equivalent to $\frac{10}{3}$. The statement is *true*.

b.

The LCM of 5 and 7 is 35.

The GCF of 28 and 30 is 2.

$$\frac{\frac{4}{5}\text{ km}^2}{\frac{6}{7}\text{ km}^2} \underset{\times 35}{\overset{\times 35}{=}} \frac{28\text{ km}^2}{30\text{ km}^2} \underset{\div 2}{\overset{\div 2}{=}} \frac{14\text{ km}^2}{15\text{ km}^2} = \frac{14}{15}$$

The ratio $\frac{\frac{4}{5}}{\frac{6}{7}}$ is equivalent to $\frac{14}{15}$. The statement is *true*.

continued on next page >

Part 2

Solution continued

c.

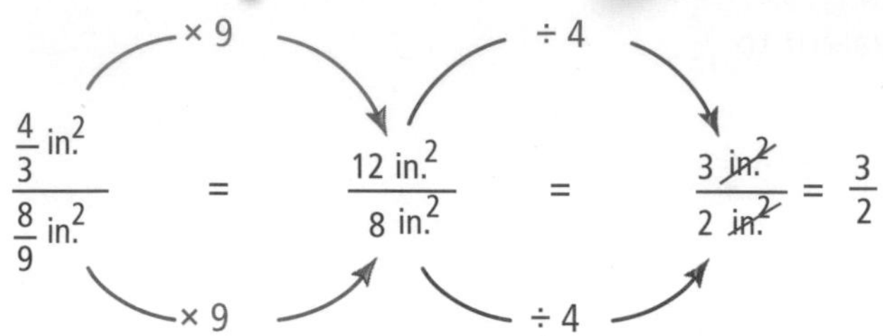

$$\frac{\frac{4}{3}\text{ in.}^2}{\frac{8}{9}\text{ in.}^2} = \frac{12\text{ in.}^2}{8\text{ in.}^2} = \frac{3\text{ in.}^2}{2\text{ in.}^2} = \frac{3}{2}$$

The ratio $\frac{\frac{4}{3}}{\frac{8}{9}}$ is equivalent to $\frac{3}{2}$, not $\frac{2}{3}$. The statement is *false*.

Part 3

Example Writing Ratios with Mixed Numbers

A professional football field is $53\frac{1}{3}$ yards wide. Find the ratio of the width of the actual field to the width of the field in the poster as a fraction in simplest form.

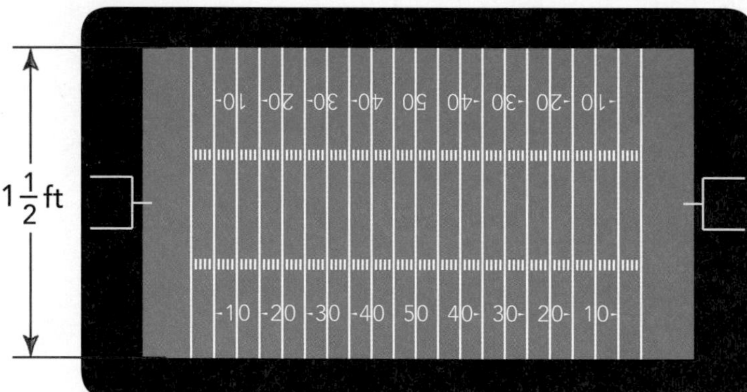

Solution

First, convert yards to feet.

$$53\frac{1}{3}\text{ yd} = \frac{160}{3}\text{ yd} \times \frac{3\text{ ft}}{1\text{ yd}}$$
$$= 160\text{ft}$$

There are 3 feet in 1 yard.

continued on next page >

Part 3

Solution continued

Then find the ratio of the width of the actual field to the width of the field in the poster as a fraction in simplest form.

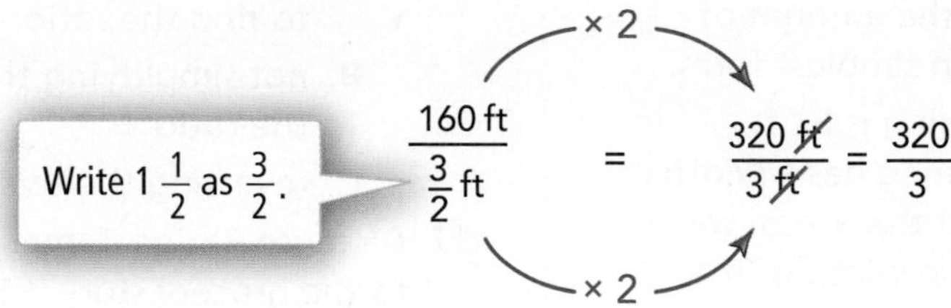

The ratio of the width of the actual field to the width of the field in the poster is $\frac{320}{3}$.

1. Write the ratio $\frac{2}{3}$ to 8 as a fraction in simplest form.
2. A recipe includes 8 cups of flour and $\frac{2}{3}$ cup of sugar. Write the ratio of the amount of flour to the amount of sugar as a fraction in simplest form.
3. The width of a building is 51 ft. A model of the building has a width of $\frac{6}{7}$ ft. Find the ratio of the actual width of the building to the width of the model as a fraction in simplest form.
4. Write the ratio $\frac{\frac{4}{9}}{\frac{5}{9}}$ in simplest form.
5. Write the ratio $\frac{\frac{1}{7}\text{ yd}}{\frac{3}{5}\text{ yd}}$ in simplest form.
6. Write the ratio $\frac{\frac{4}{5}\text{ cm}^2}{\frac{10}{17}\text{ cm}^2}$ in simplest form.
7. You mix $3\frac{1}{2}$ quarts of juice with $5\frac{1}{4}$ quarts of ginger ale to make fruit punch. What is the ratio of the amount of juice to the amount of ginger ale in simplest form?
8. A model of a famous statue is $2\frac{1}{2}$ inches tall. The actual statue is $6\frac{2}{3}$ feet tall. What is the ratio of the height of the model to the height of the actual statue in simplest form?
9. a. **Writing** Write the ratio $\frac{\frac{2}{3}\text{ lb}}{\frac{4}{5}\text{ lb}}$ in simplest form.
   b. Is there more than one way to get the simplest form? Explain.
10. a. **Reasoning** Write the ratio $\frac{\frac{2}{3}}{\frac{1}{5}}$ in simplest form.
   b. How is the simplest form of the ratio $\frac{\frac{2}{3}}{\frac{1}{5}}$ related to the simplest form of the ratio $\frac{\frac{1}{5}}{\frac{2}{3}}$? Explain.
11. **Error Analysis** A covered bridge is $6\frac{2}{3}$ yards long. In a painting for sale at a gallery, the bridge is $1\frac{1}{4}$ feet long. A customer wants to know the ratio of the length of the bridge in the painting to the actual length of the bridge. One salesperson says the ratio in simplest form is $\frac{3}{16}$. Another salesperson says the ratio in simplest form is $\frac{1}{16}$.
   a. Which ratio is correct?
   b. What error leads to the incorrect ratio?
      A. using terms with different units to find the ratio
      B. not simplifying the terms of the ratio
      C. reversing the terms of the ratio
12. **Distance Ratios** Tamar travels $\frac{8}{9}$ mile to the grocery store. Melkon travels 4 miles to the grocery store.
   a. Write the ratio of the distance Melkon travels to the distance Tamar travels as a fraction in simplest form.
   b. Write the ratio of the distance Tamar travels to the distance Melkon travels as a fraction in simplest form.
13. **Mental Math** Write the ratio $\frac{6}{7}$ to 8 as a fraction in simplest form.
14. Marcial spends $\frac{4}{5}$ hour drawing on Monday. He spends a total of 6 hours drawing from Tuesday to Friday and a total of 2 hours on Saturday and Sunday. Write the ratio of the time Marcial spends drawing on Monday to the time he spends drawing the rest of the week as a fraction in simplest form.
15. A length of a tunnel on a construction plan is $3\frac{1}{2}$ feet long. The actual tunnel is to be $51\frac{1}{3}$ yards long. What will be the ratio, in simplest form, of the length of the actual tunnel to the length on the construction plan?
16. **Think About the Process** You have to write a ratio equivalent to $\frac{\frac{4}{5}}{\frac{10}{11}}$ where both terms are whole numbers.
   a. By what number can you first multiply each fraction to get a ratio where both terms are whole numbers?
      A. 40 B. 55
      C. 10 D. 11
   b. Write the ratio in simplest form.

17. Think About the Process To write the ratio $\frac{9\frac{1}{3}}{1\frac{1}{5}}$ in simplest form, you rewrite the mixed numbers as improper fractions.

a. What is the next step to write the ratio in simplest form? Select the correct terms to complete the following sentence.

Multiply each term of the ratio by the greatest common factor/least common multiple of the denominators/numerators of the fractions.

b. What is the ratio in simplest form?

18. Challenge The surface of a computer chip is a rectangle with length $\frac{7}{32}$ inch and width $\frac{1}{16}$ inch.

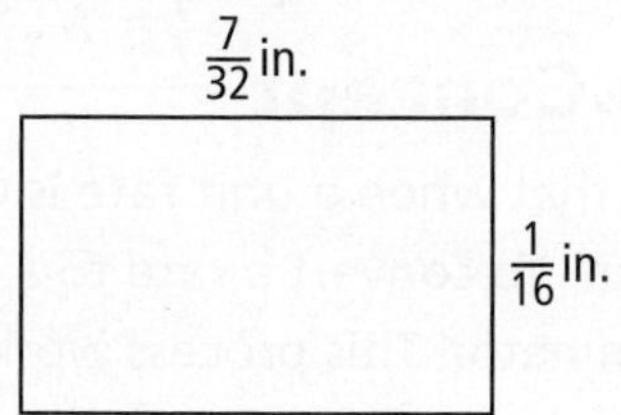

(Figure is not to scale)

a. Write the ratio of the length of the rectangle to the perimeter of the rectangle as a fraction in simplest form.

b. Write the ratio of the width to the perimeter as a fraction in simplest form.

19. Challenge A square garden has side length $6\frac{4}{9}$ yards. A square flower bed measures $7\frac{1}{4}$ feet on each side.

a. What is the ratio of the side length of the garden to the side length of the flower bed in simplest form?

b. What is the ratio of the area of the garden to the area of the flower bed?

1-4 Unit Rates With Fractions

CCSS: 7.RP.A.1

Key Concept

Recall that when a unit rate is written as a fraction, the denominator is 1 unit. To convert a rate to a unit rate, divide each term by the denominator. This process works even if the denominator of the rate is a fraction.

Suppose you walk $\frac{3}{2}$ mi in $\frac{3}{4}$ h.
Write this rate as a fraction.

$$\frac{\frac{3}{2}\text{ mi}}{\frac{3}{4}\text{ h}}$$

To convert this rate to a unit rate, divide each term by the denominator. Remember, dividing by a fraction is the same as multiplying by its reciprocal.

$$\frac{\frac{3}{2}\text{ mi}}{\frac{3}{4}\,h} \xrightarrow{\div \frac{3}{4}} \frac{\frac{3}{2} \times \frac{4}{3}\text{ mi}}{\frac{3}{4} \times \frac{4}{3}\,h}$$

Now, simplify.
Your unit rate is 2 miles per hour.

$$\frac{\frac{3}{2}\text{ mi}}{\frac{3}{4}\,h} \xrightarrow{\div \frac{3}{4}} \frac{2\text{ mi}}{1\,h}$$

Part 1

Example Finding Unit Rates Using Fractions

A recipe calls for $\frac{3}{4}$ c of dry milk powder to make 6 dog biscuits. How many cups of milk powder do you need per dog biscuit?

Solution

Write the rate. Divide by the denominator to find the unit rate.

Remember that dividing by a number is the same as multiplying by its reciprocal.

continued on next page >

Part 1

Solution continued

Divide by the denominator, 6, to find the unit rate.

$$\frac{\frac{3}{4}\text{ c}}{6\text{ biscuits}} = \frac{\frac{3}{4} \div 6\text{ c}}{1\text{ biscuit}}$$

(÷ 6 applied to numerator and denominator)

Now simplify. Divide 3 and 6 by their greatest common factor, 3.

$$= \frac{\frac{\cancel{3}^{1}}{4} \times \frac{1}{\cancel{6}_{2}}\text{ c}}{1\text{ biscuit}}$$

Now, multiply.

$$= \frac{\frac{1}{8}\text{ c}}{1\text{ biscuit}}$$

You need $\frac{1}{8}$ c of dry milk per biscuit.

Part 2

Example Converting Unit Rates Using Fractions

Write each rate as a unit rate.

a. $\frac{\frac{1}{2}\text{ mi}}{\frac{1}{4}\text{ h}}$ **b.** $\frac{\frac{7}{10}\text{ ft}}{\frac{1}{5}\text{ s}}$ **c.** $\frac{\frac{4}{5}\text{ km}}{\frac{2}{3}\text{ min}}$ **d.** $\frac{\frac{15}{4}\text{ m}}{\frac{5}{6}\text{ min}}$

Solution

Divide each ratio by its denominator to find an equivalent ratio with a denominator of 1 unit.

a.

$$\frac{\frac{1}{2}\text{ mi}}{\frac{1}{4}\text{ h}} = \frac{\frac{1}{2} \div \frac{1}{4}\text{ mi}}{1\text{ h}}$$

(÷ $\frac{1}{4}$ applied to numerator and denominator)

$$= \frac{\frac{1}{\cancel{2}_{1}} \times \cancel{4}_{2}\text{ mi}}{1\text{ h}}$$

$$= \frac{2\text{ mi}}{1\text{ h}}$$

$$= 2\text{ mi/h}$$

The unit rate is 2 miles per hour.

b.

$$\frac{\frac{7}{10}\text{ ft}}{\frac{1}{5}\text{ s}} = \frac{\frac{7}{10} \div \frac{1}{5}\text{ ft}}{1\text{s}}$$

(÷ $\frac{1}{5}$ applied to numerator and denominator)

$$= \frac{\frac{7}{{}_{2}\cancel{10}} \times \cancel{5}_{1}\text{ ft}}{1\text{ s}}$$

$$= \frac{\frac{7}{2}\text{ ft}}{1\text{ s}}$$

$$= \frac{7}{2}\text{ ft/s}$$

The unit rate is $3\frac{1}{2}$ feet per second.

continued on next page >

Part 2

Solution continued

c.

$$\frac{\frac{4}{5}\text{ km}}{\frac{2}{3}\text{ min}} = \frac{\frac{4}{5} \div \frac{2}{3}\text{ km}}{1\text{ min}} \qquad (\div \tfrac{2}{3})$$

$$= \frac{\frac{\not{4}^{2}}{5} \times \frac{3}{\not{2}_{1}}\text{ km}}{1\text{ min}}$$

$$= \frac{\frac{6}{5}\text{ km}}{1\text{ min}}$$

$$= \frac{6}{5}\text{ km/min}$$

The unit rate is $1\frac{1}{5}$ kilometers per minute.

d.

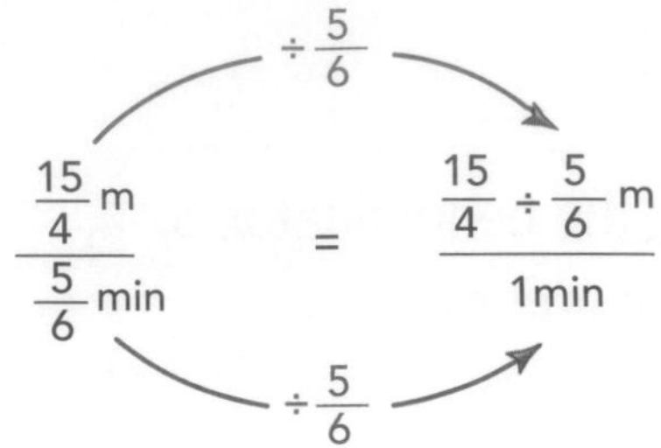

$$\frac{\frac{15}{4}\text{ m}}{\frac{5}{6}\text{ min}} = \frac{\frac{15}{4} \div \frac{5}{6}\text{ m}}{1\text{min}} \qquad (\div \tfrac{5}{6})$$

$$= \frac{\frac{\not{15}^{3}}{\not{4}_{2}} \times \frac{\not{6}^{3}}{\not{5}_{1}}\text{ m}}{1\text{ min}}$$

$$= \frac{\frac{9}{2}\text{ m}}{1\text{ min}}$$

$$= \frac{9}{2}\text{ m/min}$$

The unit rate is $4\frac{1}{2}$ meters per minute.

Part 3

Example Using Unit Rates to Solve Real-World Problems

You are running a fuel economy study. Which car can travel the greater distance on 1 gal of gasoline?

Solution

Find the unit rate of miles per gallon for each car. The car with the greater unit rate is the car that can travel the greater distance on 1 gal of gasoline.

continued on next page >

Part 3

Solution continued

Car A travels $18\frac{2}{5}$ mi, or $\frac{92}{5}$ mi.

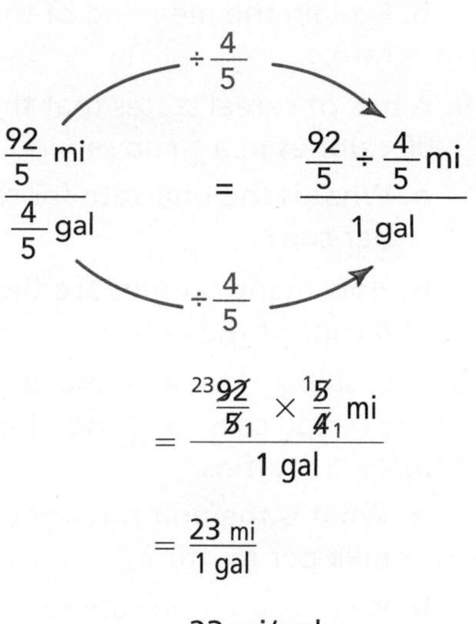

$$\frac{\frac{92}{5}\text{ mi}}{\frac{4}{5}\text{ gal}} = \frac{\frac{92}{5} \div \frac{4}{5}\text{ mi}}{1\text{ gal}}$$

$$= \frac{\frac{\cancel{92}^{23}}{\cancel{5}_1} \times \frac{\cancel{5}^1}{\cancel{4}_1}\text{ mi}}{1\text{ gal}}$$

$$= \frac{23\text{ mi}}{1\text{ gal}}$$

$$= 23\text{ mi/gal}$$

Car B travels $28\frac{1}{2}$ mi, or $\frac{57}{2}$ mi.

$$\frac{\frac{57}{2}\text{ mi}}{\frac{5}{4}\text{ gal}} = \frac{\frac{57}{2} \div \frac{5}{4}\text{ mi}}{1\text{ gal}}$$

(numerator and denominator each $\div \frac{5}{4}$)

$$= \frac{\frac{57}{\cancel{2}_1} \times \frac{\cancel{4}^2}{5}\text{ mi}}{1\text{ gal}}$$

$$= \frac{\frac{114}{5}\text{ mi}}{1\text{ gal}}$$

$$= 22\frac{4}{5}\text{ mi/gal}$$

Car A has a unit rate of 23 miles per gallon. Car B has a unit rate of $22\frac{4}{5}$ miles per gallon.

Car A can travel a greater distance on 1 gal of gas.

1. Harry is bundling magazines to recycle. He notices that 4 magazines weigh $\frac{3}{8}$ pound in all and that the magazines all weigh the same amount. What is the unit rate for pounds per magazine?
2. Leo reads 13 pages in $\frac{1}{3}$ hour.
   a. What is the unit rate for pages per hour?
   b. What is the unit rate for hours per page?
3. Write the rate $\frac{\frac{1}{7}\text{ inch}}{\frac{1}{14}\text{ minute}}$ as a unit rate.
4. a. Write $\frac{\frac{7}{3}\text{ miles}}{\frac{4}{9}\text{ hour}}$ as a unit rate.
   b. Describe a situation that would use this unit rate.
5. A bicyclist rides $\frac{1}{5}$ mile in $\frac{1}{65}$ hour. Write this rate as a unit rate.
6. Yesterday, Grace drove $38\frac{1}{2}$ miles. She used $1\frac{1}{4}$ gallons of gasoline. What is the unit rate for miles per gallon?
7. You are running a fuel economy study. One of the cars you find is blue. It can travel $35\frac{1}{2}$ miles on $1\frac{1}{4}$ gallons of gasoline. Another car is red. It can travel $27\frac{1}{5}$ miles on $\frac{4}{5}$ gallon of gasoline.
   a. What is the unit rate for miles per gallon for the blue car?
   b. What is the unit rate for miles per gallon for the red car?
   c. Which car could travel the greater distance on 1 gallon of gasoline?
8. **Writing** A store sells two kinds of candles, scented and unscented. The scented candles burn $\frac{1}{8}$ inch in $\frac{1}{4}$ hour. The unscented candles burn $\frac{1}{9}$ inch in $\frac{1}{3}$ hour.
   a. What is the unit rate for inches burned per hour for the scented candles?
   b. What is the unit rate for inches burned per hour for the unscented candles?
   c. Which kind of candle burns more in an hour?
   d. Show how to find the unit rate of hours per inch for each kind of candle.
   e. Explain the meaning of this unit rate.
9. A box of cereal states that there are 90 calories in a $\frac{3}{4}$-cup serving.
   a. What is the unit rate for calories per cup?
   b. How many calories are there in 4 cups of the cereal?
10. **Reasoning** Hannah is making muffins. The recipe calls for $\frac{2}{3}$ cup of milk to make 8 muffins.
    a. What is the unit rate for cups of milk per muffin?
    b. What is the unit rate for muffins per cup of milk?
    c. Show or describe at least two ways to find the unit rate for muffins per cup of milk.
11. **Think About the Process** There was a long rainstorm last week. In the first 4 hours, $\frac{2}{3}$ inch of rain fell. To find the unit rate for inches per hour, the first step is to write the rate as shown below.

$$\frac{\frac{2}{3}\text{ inch}}{4\text{ hour}}$$

    a. What is the next step?
       A. Divide both terms by 4.
       B. Multiply both terms by $\frac{2}{3}$.
       C. Divide both terms by $\frac{2}{3}$.
       D. Multiply both terms by 4.
    b. What is the unit rate for inches per hour?
    c. What is the unit rate for hours per inch?

12. **Error Analysis** Henry incorrectly said the rate $\frac{\frac{1}{5}\text{ pound}}{\frac{1}{20}\text{ quart}}$ can be written as the unit rate $\frac{1}{100}$ pound per quart.

a. What is the correct unit rate?

b. What was Henry's likely error?

A. He multiplied both terms by the numerator. He should have multiplied both terms by the denominator.

B. He divided both terms by the numerator. He should have divided both terms by the denominator.

C. He divided both terms by the denominator. He should have multiplied both terms by the denominator.

D. He multiplied both terms by the denominator. He should have divided both terms by the denominator.

13. **Open-Ended** Graham drove $42\frac{1}{3}$ miles in $1\frac{1}{3}$ hours.

a. What is the unit rate for miles per hour?

b. Describe a situation in which the unit rate would be easier to work with than the given rate.

14. A robot can complete 8 tasks in $\frac{5}{6}$ hour.

a. What is the unit rate for hours per task?

b. What is the unit rate for tasks per hour?

c. Explain why it might be important to know each of these unit rates.

15. A certain blueprint shows two fences. Fence A is $1\frac{1}{2}$ feet long but is $1\frac{4}{5}$ inches long on the blueprint.

a. What is the unit rate for inches per foot on this blueprint?

b. If fence B is 5 feet long, how long is fence B on the blueprint?

16. **Think About the Process** Rob is putting soil into planters that are all the same size. He wants to put the same amount of soil into each planter. After a while, he finds that he has used $7\frac{1}{4}$ kilograms of dirt to fill $2\frac{1}{2}$ planters. To find how much dirt is in each full planter, he sets up the rate shown below.

$$\frac{7\frac{1}{4}\text{ kilograms}}{2\frac{1}{2}\text{ planters}}$$

a. What should Rob do to find the unit rate for kilograms per planter?

A. Divide both terms by $\frac{5}{2}$.

B. Divide both terms by $\frac{29}{4}$.

C. Multiply both terms by $\frac{5}{2}$.

D. Multiply both terms by $\frac{29}{4}$.

b. What is the unit rate?

17. **Challenge** Josh plans to make birdhouses to sell at a craft fair. He has a sample of the wood he wants to use. The sample has area $\frac{1}{5}$ square foot and weighs $\frac{1}{2}$ pound. The local hardware store sells the wood only by the square yard. There are 9 square feet in 1 square yard.

a. What is the unit rate for pounds of the wood per square yard?

b. If Josh needs 3 square yards of the wood in all, how many pounds of the wood does he need?

18. **Challenge** Yesterday, Noah ran $2\frac{1}{2}$ miles in $\frac{3}{5}$ hour. Emily ran $3\frac{3}{4}$ miles in $\frac{5}{6}$ hour. Anna ran $3\frac{1}{2}$ miles in $\frac{3}{4}$ hour.

a. What was the unit rate for miles per hour for Noah?

b. What was the unit rate for miles per hour for Emily?

c. What was the unit rate for miles per hour for Anna?

d. Who ran the fastest?

e. Describe two ways you can find who ran the fastest.

1-5 Problem Solving

CCSS: 7.RP.A.1

Part 1

Example Using Ratios to Solve Real-World Problems

a. What is the ratio of the length of the tile to the length of the board?

b. What is the ratio of the area of the tile to the area of the board?

c. How many tiles will fit on the board without overlapping?

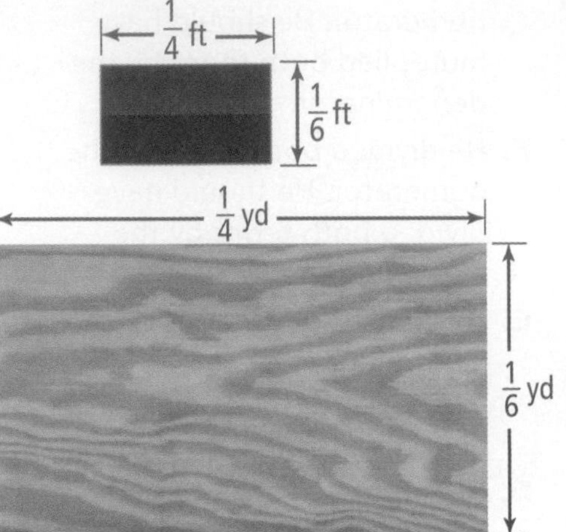

Solution

a. Find the length of the board in terms of feet.

$$\frac{1}{4}\text{ yd} \times \frac{3\text{ ft}}{1\text{ yd}} = \frac{3}{4}\text{ ft}$$

The length of the board is $\frac{3}{4}$ ft, and the length of the tile is $\frac{1}{4}$ ft.

$$\frac{\frac{1}{4}\text{ ft}}{\frac{3}{4}\text{ ft}} = \frac{1}{3}$$

× 4 (numerator), × 4 (denominator)

The ratio of the length of the tile to the length of the board is $\frac{1}{3}$.

b. $A = \frac{1}{6}\text{ ft} \cdot \frac{1}{4}\text{ ft}$

$= \frac{1}{24}\text{ ft}^2$

$A = \frac{3}{4}\text{ ft} \cdot \frac{1}{2}\text{ ft}$

$= \frac{3}{8}\text{ ft}^2$

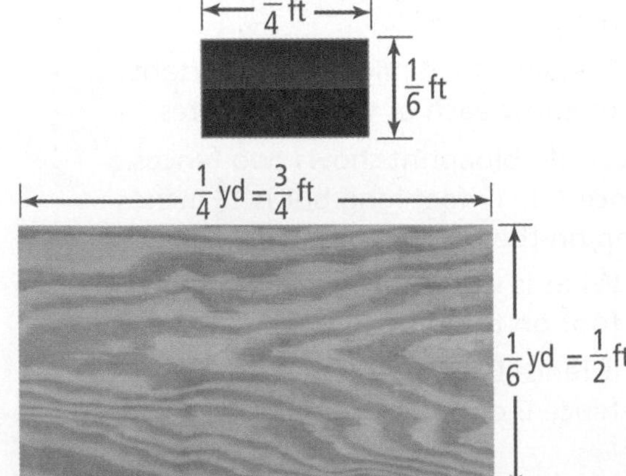

continued on next page >

Part 1

Solution continued

$$\frac{\frac{1}{24}\text{ ft}^2}{\frac{3}{8}\text{ ft}^2} = \frac{1}{9}$$

(× 24 top and bottom)

The ratio of the area of the tile to the area of the board is $\frac{1}{9}$.

c. Since the ratio of the length of the tile to the length of the board is $\frac{1}{3}$, the board is three times as long as the tile. So 3 tiles can fit along the length of the board.

Since the ratio of the width of the tile to the width of the board is $\frac{1}{3}$, the board is three times as wide as the tile. So 3 tiles can fit along the width of the board.

So $3 \cdot 3$, or 9 tiles can fit on the board.

Part 2

Example Comparing Unit Rates to Solve Real-World Problems

On Monday, you and your dog run to a park $2\frac{1}{4}$ mi from your house.

It takes you and your dog 18 min to run to the park and 24 min to run home from the park.

On Tuesday, you run the entire $4\frac{1}{2}$ mi at a constant speed of $6\frac{1}{4}$ mi/h.

On which day did your run take less time?

Solution

Method 1 Find the number of minutes that your run took on Tuesday.

On Tuesday, you ran $4\frac{1}{2}$ mi at a constant speed of $6\frac{1}{4}$ mi/h. You can rewrite $4\frac{1}{2}$ mi as $\frac{9}{2}$ mi and $6\frac{1}{4}$ mi/h as $\frac{\frac{25}{4}\text{ mi}}{1\text{ h}}$. Note that $\frac{\frac{25}{4}\text{ mi}}{1\text{ h}}$ is equivalent to $\frac{25\text{ mi}}{4\text{ h}}$.

Use the equation $d = rt$.

$$d = rt$$

$$\frac{9}{2}\text{ mi} = \frac{25\text{ mi}}{4\text{ h}} \cdot t$$

Substitute $\frac{9}{2}$ mi for d and $\frac{25\text{ mi}}{4\text{ h}}$ for r.

$$\frac{9}{2}\text{ mi} \div \frac{25\text{ mi}}{4\text{ h}} = \frac{25\text{ mi}}{4\text{ h}} \div \frac{25\text{ mi}}{4\text{ h}} \cdot t$$

continued on next page >

Part 2

Solution continued

$$\frac{9}{_1 2}\cancel{\text{mi}} \cdot \frac{^2\cancel{4}\text{h}}{25\ \cancel{\text{mi}}} = \frac{^1\cancel{25}\ \cancel{\text{mi}}}{_1\cancel{4}\cancel{\text{h}}} \cdot \frac{^1\cancel{4}\cancel{\text{h}}}{_1\cancel{25}\cancel{\text{mi}}} \cdot t$$

$$\frac{18}{25}\text{ h} = t$$

Find $\frac{18}{25}$ h in terms of minutes.

$$\frac{18}{25}\text{ h} = \frac{18}{_5\cancel{25}}\cancel{\text{h}} \cdot \frac{^{12}\cancel{60}\text{ min}}{1\cancel{\text{h}}}$$

$$= \frac{216}{6}\text{ min, or } 43.2\text{ min}$$

On Monday, your run took 18 + 24, or 42 min. On Tuesday, your run took 43.2 min. Your run took less time on Monday.

Method 2 Find the distance you would have run on Tuesday if you ran for 42 min at a constant speed of $6\frac{1}{4}$ mi/h.

If your run took less time on Tuesday, then you would have run $4\frac{1}{2}$ mi in less than 42 min. Use the equation $d = rt$.

Since the speed is in terms of miles per hour, express 42 min in hours.

$$42\text{ min} = {}^7\cancel{42}\ \cancel{\text{min}} \cdot \frac{1h}{_{10}\cancel{60}\ \cancel{\text{min}}}$$

$$= \frac{7}{10}\text{ h}$$

You can rewrite $6\frac{1}{4}$ mi/h as $\frac{\frac{25}{4}\text{ mi}}{1\text{ h}}$. Note that $\frac{\frac{25}{4}\text{ mi}}{1\text{ h}}$ is equivalent to $\frac{25\text{ mi}}{4\text{ h}}$.

$$d = rt$$

$$= \frac{25\text{ mi}}{4\text{ h}} \cdot \frac{7}{10}\text{ h}$$

$$= \frac{^5\cancel{25}\text{ mi}}{4\cancel{\text{h}}} \cdot \frac{7}{_2\cancel{10}}\cancel{\text{h}}$$

$$= \frac{35}{8}\text{ mi, or } 4\frac{3}{8}\text{ mi}$$

Substitute $\frac{25\text{ mi}}{4\text{ h}}$ for r and $\frac{7}{10}$ for t.

On Tuesday, you ran $4\frac{3}{8}$ mi in 42 min.

$$4\frac{3}{8}\text{ mi} < 4\frac{1}{2}\text{ mi}$$

On Tuesday, you ran fewer miles in 42 min than on Monday. Your run took less time on Monday.

Part 3

Example Using Ratios to Solve Real-World Problems

You and your friends are making 4 different batches of the same soup. How much of each ingredient do you need to complete each batch?

Soup Recipe

Batch	Broth (cups)	Rice (cups)	Total (cups)
A	$1\frac{7}{8}$		
B	$3\frac{3}{4}$	$\frac{3}{4}$	
C		$1\frac{7}{8}$	
D			18

Solution

From Batch B, you know that the ratio of cups of rice to cups of broth is $\frac{\frac{3}{4}}{3\frac{3}{4}}$.

For Batch A, you know a quantity of broth and need to find a quantity of rice. Find an equivalent ratio with a denominator of $1\frac{7}{8}$.

$\frac{\frac{3}{4}}{3\frac{3}{4}}$ — $3\frac{3}{4} = \frac{15}{4}$

First, divide each term of the ratio by $\frac{15}{4}$ to get a denominator of 1.

$$\frac{\frac{3}{4}}{\frac{15}{4}} = \frac{\frac{3}{4} \div \frac{15}{4}}{\frac{15}{4} \div \frac{15}{4}}$$

(÷ $\frac{15}{4}$ on top and bottom)

Dividing by $\frac{15}{4}$ is the same as multiplying by $\frac{4}{15}$.

$$\frac{\frac{3}{4}}{\frac{15}{4}} = \frac{\frac{3}{4} \times \frac{4}{15}}{\frac{15}{4} \times \frac{4}{15}}$$

(÷ $\frac{15}{4}$ on top and bottom)

Simplify each expression in the ratio.

$$\frac{\frac{3}{4}}{\frac{15}{4}} = \frac{\frac{1}{5}}{1}$$

(÷ $\frac{15}{4}$ on top and bottom)

continued on next page >

Part 3

Solution continued

So, you need $\frac{1}{5}$ cup of rice per cup of broth.

Now, multiply each term of the ratio by $1\frac{7}{8}$.

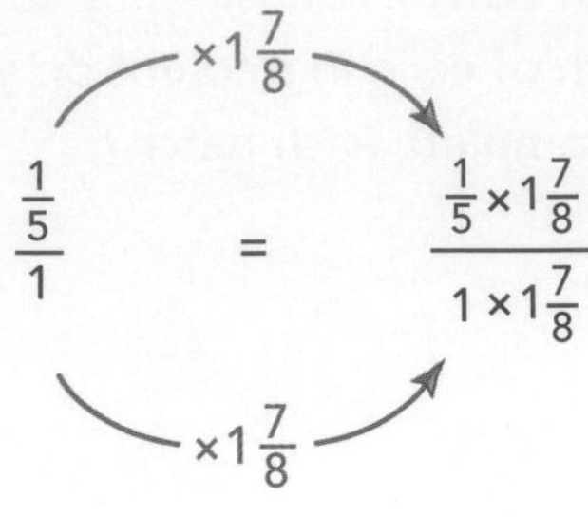

Then, simplify.

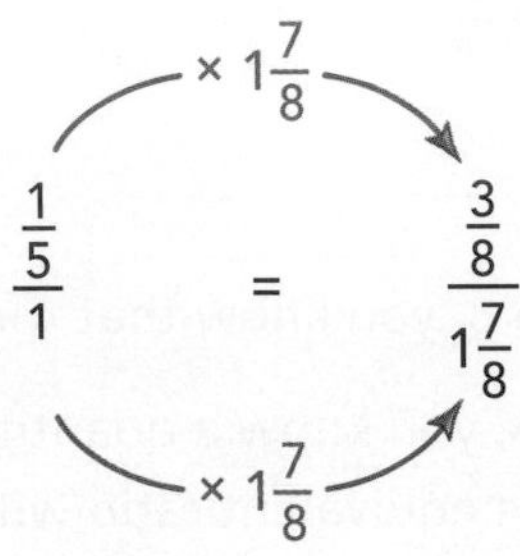

A ratio equivalent of $\frac{\frac{3}{4}}{\frac{15}{4}}$ is $\frac{\frac{3}{8}}{1\frac{7}{8}}$.

For Batch A, when you use $1\frac{7}{8}$ cups of broth, you need $\frac{3}{8}$ of a cup of rice.

For Batch C, you know a quantity of rice and need to find a quantity of broth. Use the ratio of rice to broth from Batch B. Find an equivalent ratio with a numerator of $1\frac{7}{8}$.

First, divide each term of the ratio by $\frac{3}{4}$ to get a numerator of 1.

$$\frac{\frac{3}{4}}{\frac{15}{4}} = \frac{\frac{3}{4} \div \frac{3}{4}}{\frac{15}{4} \div \frac{3}{4}}$$

Dividing by $\frac{3}{4}$ is the same as multiplying by $\frac{4}{3}$.

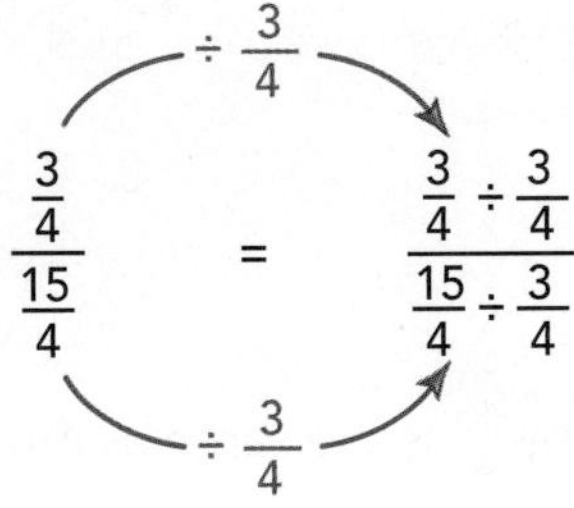

Simplify each expression in the ratio.

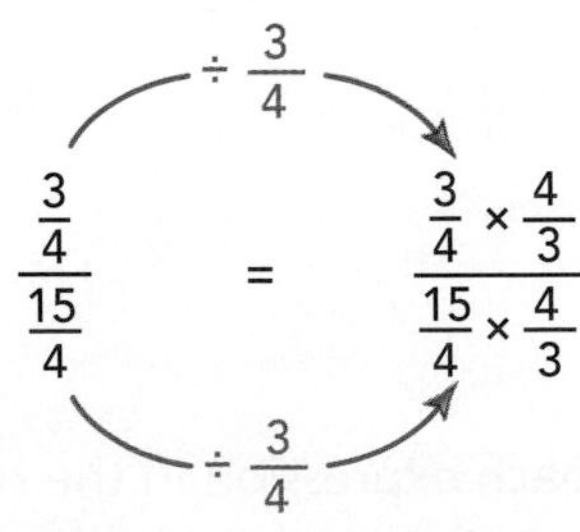

continued on next page >

Part 3

Solution continued

You need 1 cup of rice for every 5 cups of broth.

Now, multiply each term of the ratio by $1\frac{7}{8}$.

$$\frac{1}{5} = \frac{1 \times 1\frac{7}{8}}{5 \times 1\frac{7}{8}} \quad (\times 1\tfrac{7}{8})$$

Then, simplify.

$$\frac{1}{5} = \frac{1\frac{7}{8}}{9\frac{3}{8}} \quad (\times 1\tfrac{7}{8})$$

A ratio equivalent of $\frac{\frac{3}{4}}{\frac{15}{4}}$ is $\frac{1\frac{7}{8}}{9\frac{3}{8}}$.

For Batch C, when you use $1\frac{7}{8}$ cups of rice, you need $9\frac{3}{8}$ cups of broth.

For Batch D, you want a total of 18 cups. You need 1 cup of rice for every 5 cups of broth. That is a total of 6 cups.

Since $6 \cdot 3 = 18$, find a ratio equivalent to $\frac{1}{5}$ by multiplying each term by 3.

$$\frac{1}{5} = \frac{1 \times 3}{5 \times 3} \quad (\times 3)$$

Then, simplify.

$$\frac{1}{5} = \frac{3}{15} \quad (\times 3)$$

For Batch D, if you want a total of 18 cups of soup, you need 3 cups of rice and 15 cups of broth.

Now that you know how much rice and broth you need for each batch, you can add to find the total number of cups for each batch.

Soup Recipe

Batch	Broth (Cups)	Rice (Cups)	Total (Cups)
A	$1\frac{7}{8}$	$\frac{3}{8}$	$2\frac{1}{4}$
B	$3\frac{3}{4}$	$\frac{3}{4}$	$4\frac{1}{2}$
C	$9\frac{3}{8}$	$1\frac{7}{8}$	$11\frac{1}{4}$
D	15	3	18

1-5 | Homework

Digital Resources   

1. An artist is using tiles and boards for a project. A tile has length $\frac{2}{3}$ ft and width $\frac{2}{3}$ ft. A board has length $\frac{1}{2}$ yd and width $\frac{1}{2}$ yd.
   a. What is the ratio of the length of the tile to the length of the board?
   b. What is the ratio of the area of the tile to the area of the board?
2. Diana is going camping with her family. Their campsite is $\frac{3}{4}$ mile away. They walk at a steady speed of $1\frac{1}{8}$ mi/h. How many minutes will it take them to get to the campsite?
3. A recipe calls for $\frac{1}{2}$ cup of ingredient A for every $1\frac{2}{3}$ cups of ingredient B. You use 4 cups of ingredient A. How many cups of ingredient B do you need?
4. **Reasoning** A carpenter uses $9\frac{1}{2}$ ft of cedar for every $5\frac{2}{3}$ ft of redwood for a construction project.
   a. If the carpenter uses $4\frac{3}{4}$ ft of cedar, how much redwood does he need?
   b. Is there more than one way to find the amount of redwood? Explain.
5. Al made a tree house last summer. He started by making a model. The model included a window with height $\frac{1}{3}$ in. and width $\frac{1}{6}$ in. The actual tree house window had height $\frac{1}{2}$ yd and width $\frac{1}{4}$ yd. Al incorrectly said that the ratio of the height of the window in the model to the height of the window in the tree house was $\frac{2}{3}$.
   a. What was the correct ratio?
   b. What was Al's likely error?
      A. He found the ratio of the widths instead of the ratio of the heights.
      B. He found the ratio of height to width for one window instead of the ratio of the heights.
      C. He reversed the order of the terms of the ratio.
      D. He did not convert one of the units before finding the ratio.
6. An architect makes a model of a new house. The model shows a tile patio in the backyard. In the model, each tile has length $\frac{1}{3}$ in. and width $\frac{1}{6}$ in. The actual tiles have length $\frac{1}{4}$ ft and width $\frac{1}{8}$ ft.
   a. What is the ratio of the length of a tile in the model to the length of an actual tile?
   b. What is the ratio of the area of a tile in the model to the area of an actual tile?
   c. Describe two ways to find each ratio.
7. Timothy gets a phone call from some of his friends. They say they will be at the library in 40 min and ask him to meet them there. He decides to walk to the library which is $\frac{5}{8}$ mi away. He walks at a steady speed of $1\frac{1}{4}$ mi/h.
   a. Will he get there before his friends?
   b. Describe three ways you could solve this problem.
8. An object is traveling at a steady speed of $10\frac{1}{10}$ km/h.
   a. How long will it take the object to travel $4\frac{9}{10}$ km? Round to the nearest integer to find the estimated answer.
   b. Find the exact answer.

See your complete lesson at MyMathUniverse.com

9. Think About the Process On Thursday you biked to a playground $2\frac{1}{3}$ mi from your house. It took you 13 min to bike there and 11 min to bike back home. On Friday you biked the entire $4\frac{2}{3}$ mi at a constant speed of $12\frac{1}{2}$ mi/h.

a. What must you do to compare the times it took to go to and from the playground each day?

A. Add to find Friday's time. Solve $d = rt$ for t to find Thursday's time.

B. Add to find Thursday's time. Solve $d = rt$ for t to find Friday's time.

C. Add to find Thursday's time. Solve $d = rt$ for t twice, and then add, to find Friday's time.

D. Add twice to find Friday's time. Solve $d = rt$ for t to find Thursday's time.

b. How many minutes did your bike ride take on Thursday?

c. How many minutes did your bike ride take on Friday?

d. On which day did it take less time?

10. Last week, Andy decided to get his favorite photograph enlarged to make a poster. When he got the poster enlarged, there was a mark on it. The mark, which had length $\frac{1}{2}$ ft and width $\frac{3}{8}$ ft, came from a mark on the photograph that had length $\frac{2}{3}$ in. and width $\frac{1}{2}$ in. Find the ratio of the length of the mark on the photograph in inches to the length of the mark on the poster in inches.

11. A recipe calls for $3\frac{1}{2}$ teaspoons of mustard seeds, 10 cups of tomato sauce, and $11\frac{1}{4}$ cups of beans. You use $6\frac{2}{3}$ cups of tomato sauce.

a. How many teaspoons of mustard seeds do you need?

b. How many cups of beans do you need?

12. Think About the Process For every $\frac{4}{5}$ mile Shandra runs, she walks $2\frac{2}{5}$ miles. Suppose Shandra plans to run $1\frac{3}{10}$ miles. To find how far Shandra should walk, she first writes the ratio $\frac{\frac{4}{5}}{\frac{12}{5}}$.

a. What is the next step?

A. Find an equivalent ratio with denominator $\frac{13}{10}$.

B. Find an equivalent ratio with numerator $\frac{4}{5}$.

C. Find an equivalent ratio with numerator $\frac{13}{10}$.

b. How far should Shandra walk?

13. Challenge Ari, Beth, and Cindy each went for a walk yesterday afternoon. Ari walked $2\frac{3}{4}$ mi at a constant speed of $2\frac{1}{2}$ mi/h. Beth walked $1\frac{3}{4}$ mi at a constant speed of $1\frac{1}{4}$ mi/h. Cindy walked for 1 hour and 21 minutes at a constant speed of $1\frac{1}{8}$ mi/h. List the three people in order of the times they spent walking from least time to greatest time.

14. Challenge The table lists recommended amounts of food to order for 25 party guests. Nathan and Amanda are hosting a graduation party for 40 guests. They know there will also be guests stopping by who may have come from other parties. For ordering purposes, they will count each of the "drop-in" guests as half a guest. How much of each food item should Nathan and Amanda order for a graduation party with 45 drop-in guests?

Party Food

Item	Amount
Fried Chicken	24 pieces
Deli Meats	$3\frac{2}{3}$ pounds
Lasagna	$10\frac{3}{4}$ pounds

2-1 Proportional Relationships and Tables

Vocabulary
proportional relationship

CCSS: 7.RP.A.2, 7.RP.A.2a

Key Concept

Two quantities *x* and *y* have a **proportional relationship** if *y* is always a constant multiple of *x*. A relationship is proportional if it can be described with equivalent ratios.

When there are 2 circles, there is 1 square. The ratio of circles to squares is 2 to 1.

$\frac{2}{1}$

When there are 4 circles, there are 2 squares. The ratio of circles to squares is 4 to 2, or 2 to 1.

$\frac{4}{2} = \frac{2}{1}$

When there are 6 circles, there are 3 squares. The ratio of circles to squares is 6 to 3, or 2 to 1.

$\frac{6}{3} = \frac{2}{1}$

Each ratio $\frac{\text{number of circles}}{\text{number of squares}}$ is equivalent to $\frac{2}{1}$.

There are two times as many circles as squares.

There is a proportional relationship between the number of circles and the number of squares.

See your complete lesson at MyMathUniverse.com

Part 1

Example Determining Whether Relationships are Proportional Using Tables

The diagram shows a series of squares drawn on graph paper. The side length and perimeter of each square are labeled.

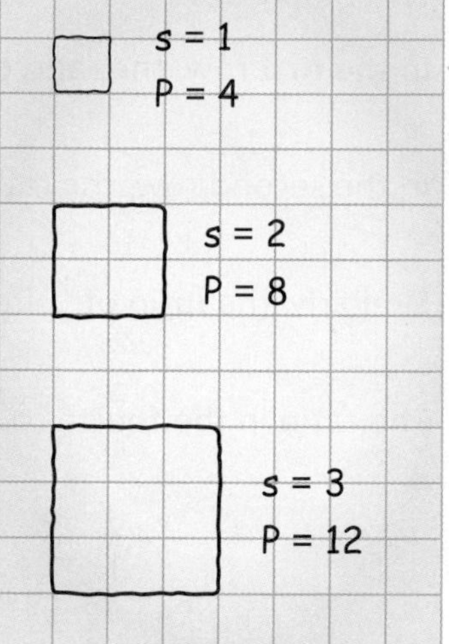

Use the diagram to complete the table. Draw the next few squares as needed. Write all the ratios in simplest form.

Side length	1	2	3		5	
Perimeter	4			16		24
Ratio $\frac{\text{perimeter}}{\text{side length}}$		$\frac{8}{2} = \frac{4}{1}$				

Is the relationship between the perimeter and side length of a square proportional? How do you know?

Solution

Side length	1	2	3	4	5	6
Perimeter	4	8	12	16	20	24
Ratio $\frac{\text{perimeter}}{\text{side length}}$	$\frac{4}{1}$	$\frac{8}{2} = \frac{4}{1}$	$\frac{12}{3} = \frac{4}{1}$	$\frac{16}{4} = \frac{4}{1}$	$\frac{20}{5} = \frac{4}{1}$	$\frac{24}{6} = \frac{4}{1}$

Each ratio is equivalent to $\frac{4}{1}$.

Since all the ratios are equivalent, the relationship between side length and perimeter of a square is proportional.

Part 2

Intro

A table can be used to show a proportional relationship between two quantities.

In the first row, the ratio of $\frac{y}{x}$ is $\frac{2}{1}$.

In the second row, the ratio of $\frac{y}{x}$ is $\frac{4}{2}$ or $\frac{2}{1}$.

Similarly, the ratio of $\frac{y}{x}$, in the third row, is $\frac{6}{3}$ or $\frac{2}{1}$.

The ratio in the fourth row is $\frac{8}{4}$, which also equals $\frac{2}{1}$.

x	y
1	2
2	4
3	6
4	8

$$\frac{y}{x} : \frac{2}{1}$$

$$\frac{4}{2} = \frac{2}{1}$$

$$\frac{6}{3} = \frac{2}{1}$$

$$\frac{8}{4} = \frac{2}{1}$$

Each ratio $\frac{y}{x}$ is equivalent to $\frac{2}{1}$.

x	y
1	$2(1) = 2$
2	$2(2) = 4$
3	$2(3) = 6$
4	$2(4) = 8$

Each y value is twice the corresponding x value.

The table shows a proportional relationship between x and y.

Example Determining Whether Relationships Are Proportional Using Tables

Determine whether each table shows a proportional relationship between x and y.

a.

x	y
8	4
6	3
$\frac{1}{2}$	$\frac{1}{4}$
11	$5\frac{1}{2}$

b.

x	y
3	9
12	36
$\frac{4}{9}$	$\frac{4}{3}$
$1\frac{1}{3}$	4

c.

x	y
8	4
7	3
6	2
5	1

continued on next page >

Part 2

Example continued

Solution

a.

x	y	Ratio $\frac{y}{x}$
8	4	$\frac{4}{8} = \frac{1}{2}$
6	3	$\frac{3}{6} = \frac{1}{2}$
$\frac{1}{2}$	$\frac{1}{4}$	$\frac{\frac{1}{4}}{\frac{1}{2}} = \frac{1}{2}$
11	$5\frac{1}{2}$	$\frac{5\frac{1}{2}}{11} = \frac{1}{2}$

The ratio $\frac{y}{x}$ for each row of the table is equivalent to $\frac{1}{2}$.

$\frac{\frac{1}{4}}{\frac{1}{2}} = \frac{1}{4} \cdot \frac{2}{1}$

The table does show a proportional relationship between x and y.

b.

x	y	Ratio $\frac{y}{x}$
3	9	$\frac{9}{3} = \frac{3}{1}$
12	36	$\frac{36}{12} = \frac{3}{1}$
$\frac{4}{9}$	$\frac{4}{3}$	$\frac{\frac{4}{3}}{\frac{4}{9}} = \frac{3}{1}$
$1\frac{1}{3}$	4	$\frac{\frac{4}{1}}{1\frac{1}{3}} = \frac{3}{1}$

The ratio $\frac{y}{x}$ for each row of the table is equivalent to $\frac{3}{1}$.

$\frac{\frac{4}{1}}{1\frac{1}{3}} = \frac{4}{1} \cdot \frac{3}{4}$

The table does show a proportional relationship between x and y.

continued on next page >

Part 2

Solution continued

c.

x	y	Ratio $\frac{y}{x}$
8	4	$\frac{4}{8} = \frac{1}{2}$
7	3	$\frac{3}{7}$
6	2	$\frac{2}{6} = \frac{1}{3}$
5	1	$\frac{1}{5}$

the ratios $\frac{y}{x}$ for the rows of the table are *not* equivalent.

The table does *not* show a proportional relationship between x and y.

Part 3

Example Using Tables and Proportional Relationships to Solve Real-World Problems

The table shows the costs for four different photocopying jobs. Is there a proportional relationship between the number of copies and the cost? How do you know?

Photocopy Costs

Number of Copies	Cost ($)
150	18
225	27
550	55
1,050	84

continued on next page >

Part 3

Example continued

Solution

Photocopy Costs

Number of Copies	Cost ($)	$\frac{\text{Cost}}{\text{Number of copies}}$
150	18	$\frac{\$18}{150 \text{ copies}} = \$.12$ per copy
225	27	$\frac{\$27}{225 \text{ copies}} = \$.12$ per copy
550	55	$\frac{\$55}{550 \text{ copies}} = \$.10$ per copy
1,050	84	$\frac{\$84}{1{,}050 \text{ copies}} = \$.08$ per copy

The ratios $\frac{\text{Cost}}{\text{Number of Copies}}$ for the rows of the table are not equivalent.

Not the same unit price

The price per copy decreases as the number of copies increases. There is *not* a proportional relationship between the number of copies and the cost.

1. The amount of time Gareth spends studying and his test scores have a proportional relationship. Complete the table.

Test Scores

Hours Studying	2	3	4
Test Score	46	69	92
Ratio $\frac{\text{Test Score}}{\text{Hours Studying}}$	$\frac{46}{2} = \frac{23}{1}$	■	■

2. Decide whether the table shows a proportional relationship between x and y.

x	2	4	7	10
y	4	16	49	100

3. Decide whether the table shows a proportional relationship between x and y.

x	y
30	150
$\frac{1}{6}$	$\frac{5}{6}$
199	995
$\frac{2}{15}$	$\frac{2}{3}$

4. Each morning at a pet store, Jill puts gerbil food in the cage according to how many gerbils there are. The table shows the amounts of food for different numbers of gerbils. Decide if the relationship between the number of gerbils and the amount of food is proportional.

Pet Food

Gerbils	Food (grams)
4	62
7	108.5
8	124
11	170.5

5. **Writing** A wholesale club sells eggs by the dozen.

Cost of Dozens of Eggs

Dozen	Cost ($)
6	21
8	28
10	35
14	49

a. Does the table show a proportional relationship between the number of dozens of eggs and the cost?

b. Which ratio would be more useful to someone going to the wholesale club, $\frac{\text{cost}}{\text{dozen}}$ or $\frac{\text{dozen}}{\text{cost}}$? Explain.

6. **Think About the Process** The number of songs on a CD and the length of the CD have a proportional relationship.

a. Which operation should you use to find the ratios?

A. Multiplication **B.** Subtraction
C. Division **D.** Addition

For parts (b) through (d), complete the table.

Lengths of CDs

Number of Songs	10	12	b. ■
Length (Minutes)	55	66	77
Ratio $\frac{\text{Length}}{\text{Songs}}$	c. ■	d. ■	$5\frac{1}{2}$

7. a. **Reasoning** Decide whether the table shows a proportional relationship between x and y.

x	4	5	6	10
y	64	125	216	1,000
Ratio $\frac{y}{x}$	?	?	?	?

b. Explain whether you can use the table to find the value of y when $x = 11$.

8. Error Analysis The table shows a proportional relationship between x and y. Dimitrios and Katerina have to complete the table. Katerina incorrectly says the ratio $\frac{y}{x}$ is $\frac{1}{10}$.

a. Complete the table.

x	y	Ratio $\frac{y}{x}$
3	30	■
5	50	■
7	70	■
9	90	■

b. What error did Katerina likely make?

9. Think About the Process Kendall earns extra money by raking yards in the fall. The table shows the number of yards she rakes each day and the hours she spends raking them.

Ranking Yards

Yards	Hours	Ratio $\frac{\text{Hours}}{\text{Yards}}$
8	5	?
5	4	?
4	5	?
3	4	?

a. What is the first step in deciding whether the relationship between the number of yards and the hours spent raking is proportional?

A. Finding the total number of days Kendall rakes leaves

B. Finding the ratio for each row in the table

C. Comparing the ratios in the table

D. Simplifying each ratio in the table

b. Is the relationship between the number of yards and the hours spent raking proportional?

10. Open-Ended The lengths and widths of four rectangles have a proportional relationship.

a. Complete the table.

Dimensions of Rectangle

Length	2	3	4	■
Width	14	■	28	35
Ratio $\frac{\text{Width}}{\text{Length}}$	■	$\frac{7}{1}$	■	$\frac{7}{1}$

b. Draw and label two rectangles with lengths and widths that have the same proportional relationship.

11. The table shows a proportional relationship between x and y. Complete the table.

x	13	$\frac{1}{4}$	11
y	$3\frac{1}{4}$	■	■
Ratio $\frac{y}{x}$	■	$\frac{1}{4}$	■

12. Decide whether the table shows a proportional relationship between x and y.

x	y
19	$3\frac{4}{5}$
$\frac{4}{5}$	$\frac{4}{25}$
5	$\frac{1}{5}$
13	$2\frac{3}{5}$

13. Challenge You are head of the city's Street Department. During snowstorms, you send out the trucks to do the plowing. The amount of snow and the number of trucks are shown in the table.

Amount of Snowfall

Snow (in.)	Trucks
6	15
8	20
12	30
18	45

a. Decide if the relationship between the amount of snow and the number of trucks is proportional.

b. For a 23-in. snowfall, how many trucks would you send out? Explain.

2-2 Proportional Relationships and Graphs

CCSS: 7.RP.A.2, Also 7.RP.A.2d

Key Concept

A graph can be used to show a proportional relationship between two quantities.

The table shows a proportional relationship between time and the number of heartbeats. Each row of the table can be represented as a ratio.

Resting Heart Rate

Time (s)	Heartbeats
4	6
6	9
10	15
12	18

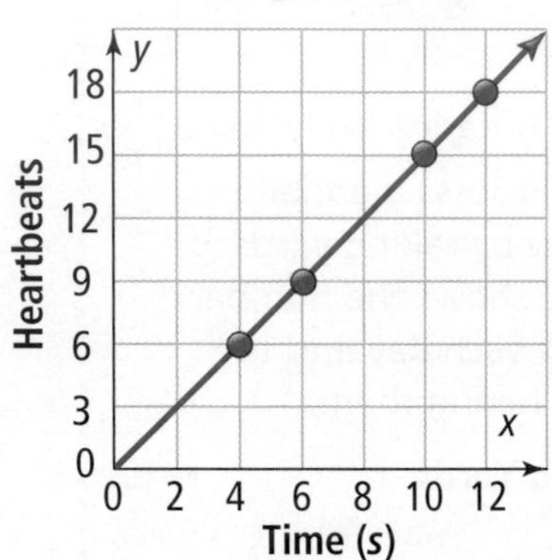

Each ratio can also be represented as a point on a graph. Draw a line through all of the points. Each *y*-value is $\frac{3}{2}$ times the *x*-value. This means that every time the *x*-value increases by 2, the *y*-value increases by 3.

Notice that the line passes through the origin. A graph that represents a proportional relationship is a straight line passing through the origin.

Part 1

Example Recognizing Proportional Relationships from Graphs

Does each graph show a proportional relationship between x and y?

a.

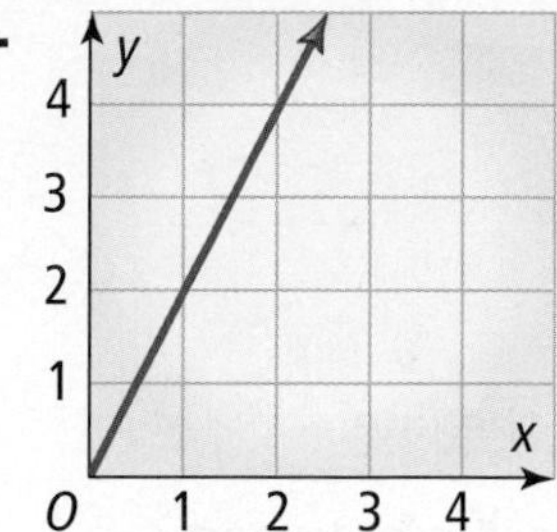

b.

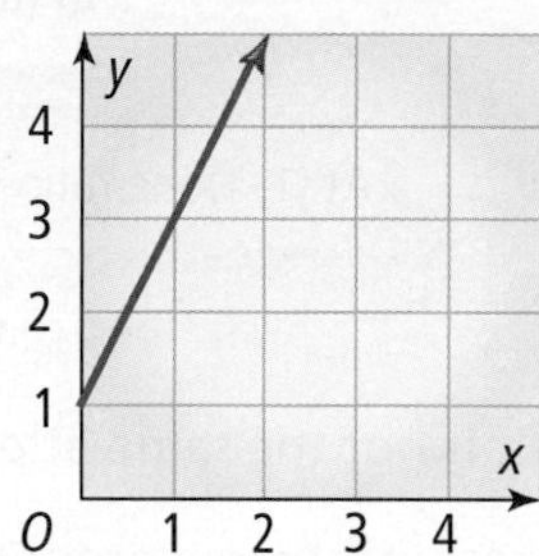

c.

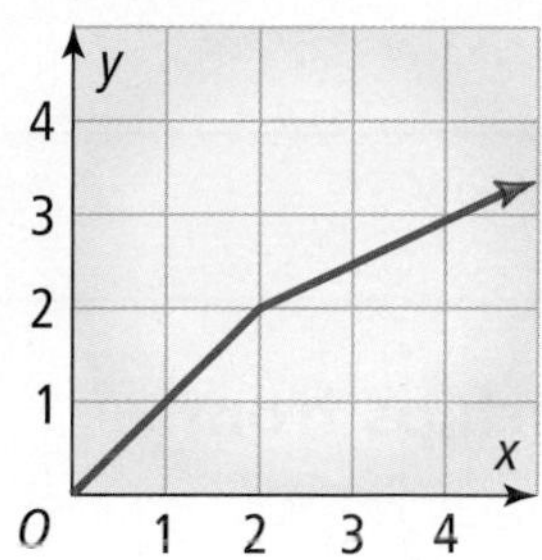

Solution

a.

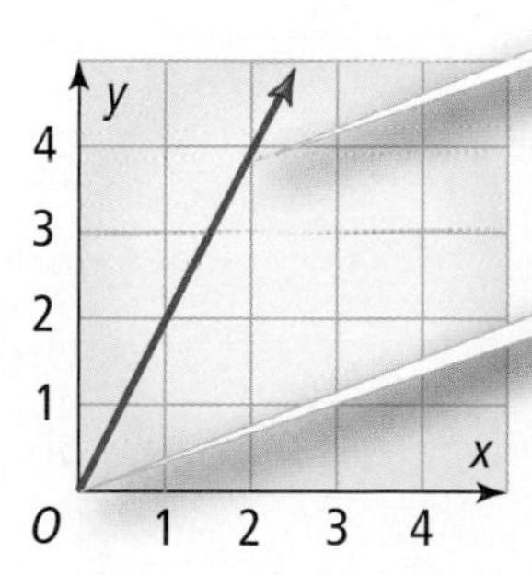

Yes, the graph shows a proportional relationship between x and y.

b.

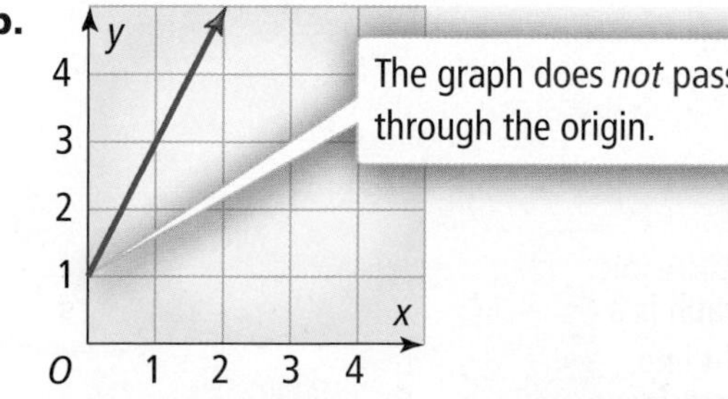

No, the graph does *not* show a proportional relationship between x and y.

continued on next page >

Part 1

Solution continued

c.

At (4, 3) the ratio is $\frac{y}{x} = \frac{3}{4}$.

At (1, 1) the ratio is $\frac{y}{x} = \frac{1}{1}$.

The ratio of y to x is *not* the same at every point on the line.

No, the graph does *not* show a proportional relationship between x and y.

Part 2

Example Recognizing Proportional Relationships from Equations

Does the equation $y = 6x$ show a proportional relationship between x and y? Explain.

Solution

Step 1 Make a table of values.

x	y
0	0
1	6
2	12
3	18
4	24

Step 2 Graph the points. Draw a line through the points.

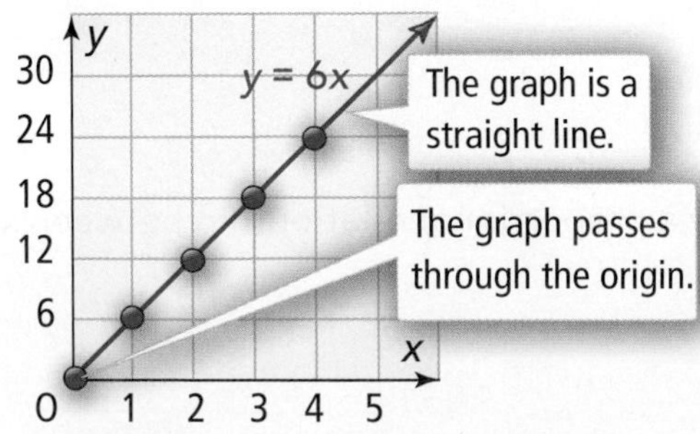

continued on next page >

Part 2

Solution continued

The graph of the equation $y = 6x$ is a graph of a straight line that passes through the origin. The graph shows a relationship where y is 6 times x.

Yes, the equation $y = 6x$ shows a proportional relationship between x and y.

Part 3

Example Interpreting Graphs of Proportional Relationships

The graph shows a proportional relationship between time and the distance run by a cheetah.

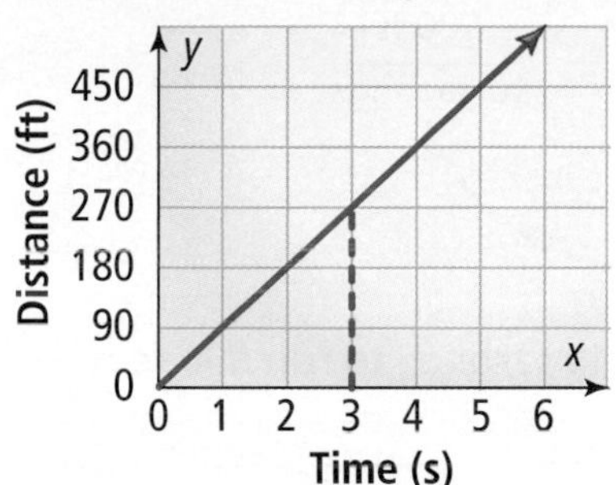

a. What does the point (1, 90) represent?

b. What does the point (0, 0) represent?

c. How far did the cheetah run in 3 seconds?

d. Assuming the cheetah continues to run at the same speed, how long would it take the cheetah to run 900 ft?

Solution

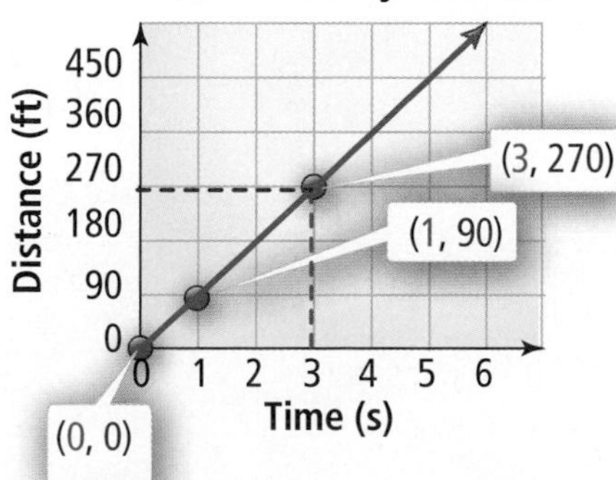

a. The x-axis shows time and the y-axis shows distance. The point (1, 90) represents 90 feet traveled in 1 second. This point also represents the unit rate 90 ft per second.

continued on next page >

Part 3

Solution continued

b. The *x*-axis shows time and the *y*-axis shows distance. The point (0, 0) represents 0 feet traveled in 0 seconds.

c. To find how far the cheetah traveled in 3 seconds, locate the point on the line with an *x*-coordinate of 3. The *y*-coordinate shows the distance traveled. The point (3, 270) is on the line, so the cheetah traveled 270 feet in 3 seconds.

d. Find the rate equivalent to $\frac{90 \text{ ft}}{1 \text{ second}}$ with a numerator of 900 ft.

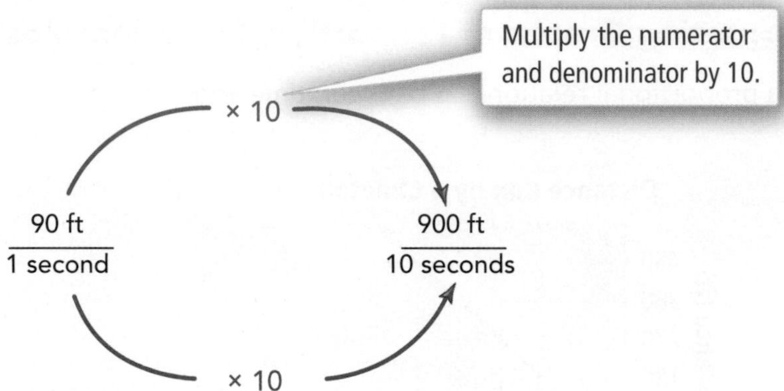

It would take the cheetah 10 seconds to run 900 feet.

Digital Resources  

1. Which of the graphs shows a proportional relationship?

A. 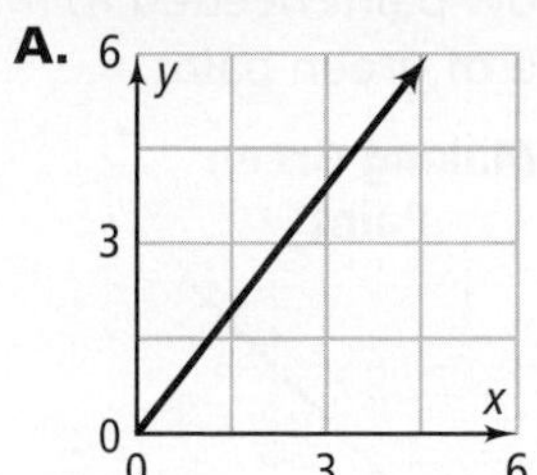

B. 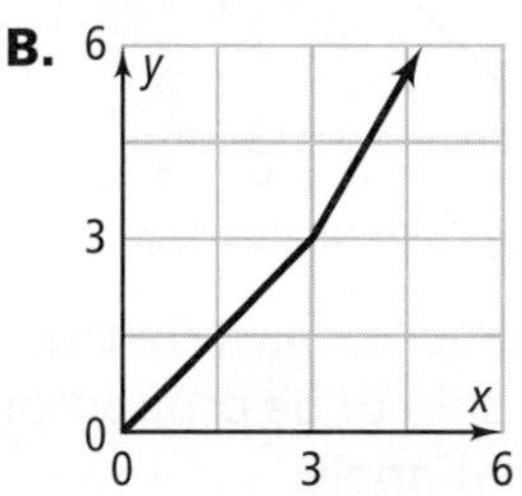

C. 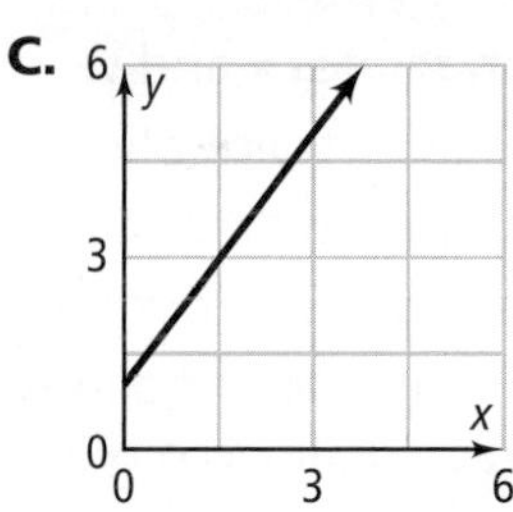

2. Does the graph show a proportional relationship between x and y?

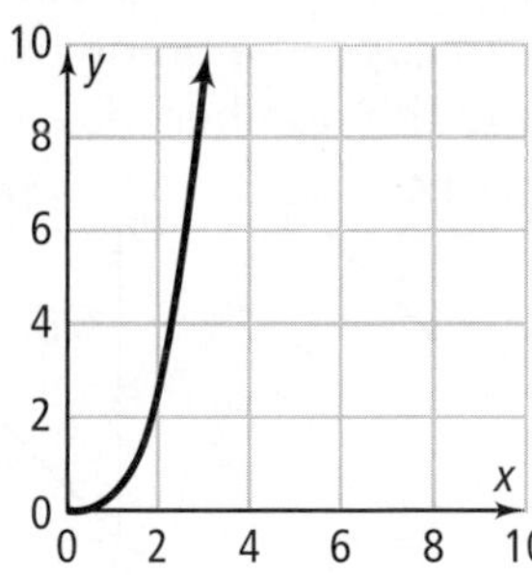

A. No, because the graph does not pass through the origin.

B. Yes, because the graph passes through the origin.

C. Yes, because the graph is a straight line.

D. No, because the graph is not a straight line.

3. The graph shows a proportional relationship between time and number of boxes a machine packages. How many boxes does the machine package in 4 minutes?

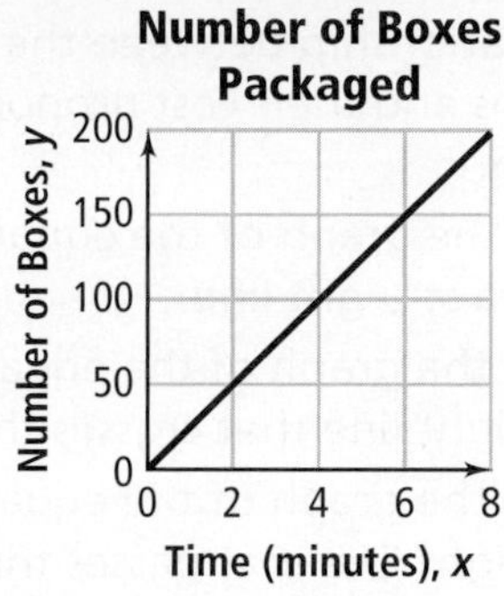

4. A baker likes to make cookies. The graph shows a proportional relationship between cups of flour used and number of cookies made.

a. What does the point (0,0) represent? Select all that apply.

A. The unit rate is 0 cups of flour per cookie.

B. The baker makes 0 cookies with 0 cups of flour.

C. The baker needs 0 cups of flour to make 0 cookies.

D. The unit rate is 0 cookies per cup of flour.

b. What does the point (1,18) represent? Select all that apply.

A. The unit rate is 18 cookies per cup of flour.

B. The baker needs 18 cups of flour to make 1 cookie.

C. The baker makes 18 cookies with 1 cup of flour.

D. The unit rate is 18 cups of flour per cookie.

5. The equation $y = 50 + 13x$ represents the cost, y, to manufacture x items. Is the relationship between the number of items and their cost proportional? Explain.
   A. No, the graph of the equation is not a straight line.
   B. Yes, the graph of the equation is a straight line that crosses the y-axis.
   C. Yes, the graph of the equation is a straight line that passes through the origin.
   D. No, the graph of the equation does not pass through the origin.

6. The cost for a ticket to a museum is $13.
   a. Write an equation that represents the cost, y, for x tickets.
   b. Does the equation represent a proportional relationship?
      A. Yes, the graph of the equation is a straight line that passes through the origin.
      B. No, the graph of the equation is not a straight line.
      C. Yes, the graph is a straight line that does not pass through the origin.
      D. No, the graph of the equation does not pass through the origin.

7. **Think About the Process** The relationship between x and y is represented by the equation $y = 10x$.
   a. How can you decide if the equation represents a proportional relationship?
   b. Does $y = 10x$ represent a proportional relationship between x and y?

8. **Think About the Process** The graph shows the proportional relationship between gallons of blue paint and gallons of yellow paint needed to make a certain shade of green paint.

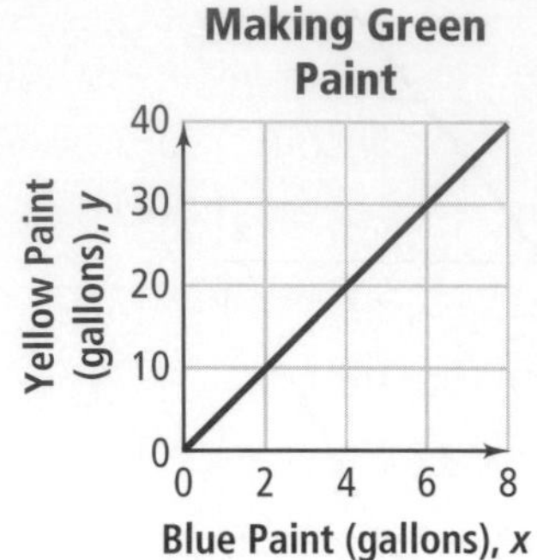

   a. Which statements must be true for the relationship to be proportional? Select all that apply.
      A. The graph relates x and y.
      B. The graph is a straight line.
      C. The graph passes through (0,0).
      D. The graph passes through (5,1).
   b. What is the unit rate of gallons of yellow paint to gallons of blue paint?

9. **Challenge** Each graph shows the proportional relationship between the number of cups of a brand of breakfast cereal and the number of calories.

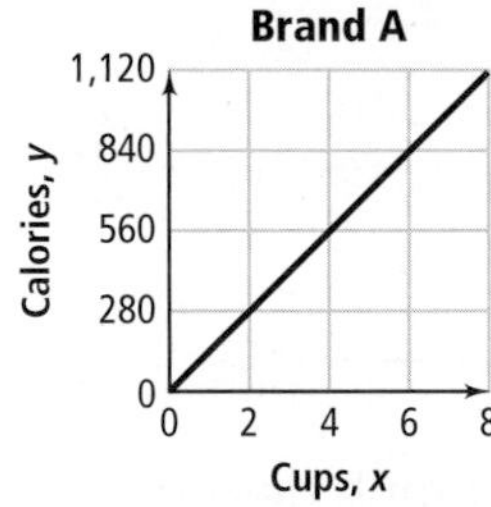

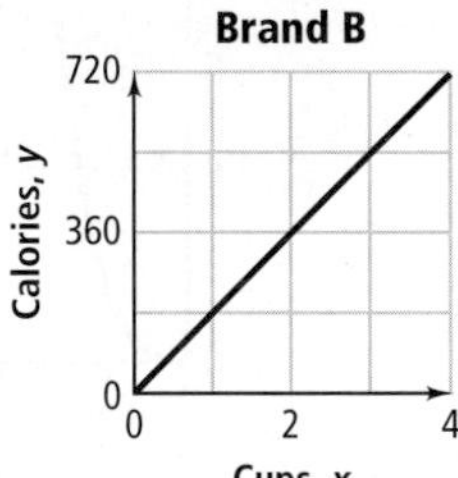

   a. What is the unit rate of calories per cup for Brand A?
   b. What is the unit rate of calories per cup for Brand B?
   c. Which brand has fewer calories per cup?
   d. If the unit rates for the two relationships are different, one graph should appear to rise faster than the other. Explain why the graphs appear to rise at the same rate.

2-3 Constant of Proportionality

Vocabulary
constant of proportionality

CCSS: 7.RP.A.2, 7.RP.A.2b, Also 7.NS.A.2d

Key Concept

Recall that two quantities x and y have a proportional relationship if y is always a constant multiple of x. This constant multiple $\frac{y}{x}$ is called the **constant of proportionality**.

If x and y have different units, then the constant of proportionality can be written as a unit rate.

Each brick shown has a length of 20 cm. The proportion total length of one brick to the number of bricks is 20 to 1, so the unit rate is 20. The proportion remains the same as bricks are added. The final proportion is 100 to 5, so the unit rate is still 20.

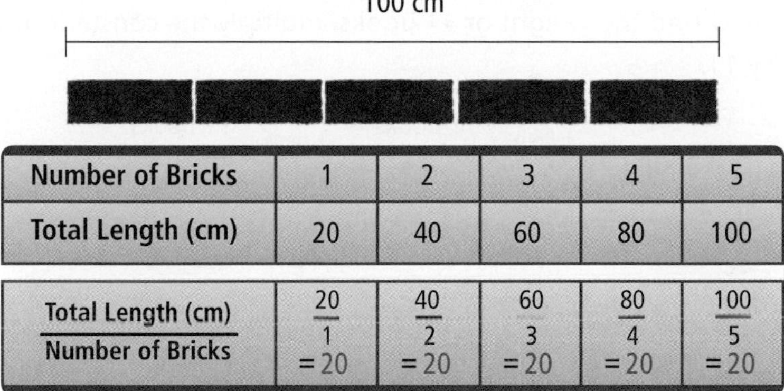

Number of Bricks	1	2	3	4	5
Total Length (cm)	20	40	60	80	100

$\frac{\text{Total Length (cm)}}{\text{Number of Bricks}}$	$\frac{20}{1} = 20$	$\frac{40}{2} = 20$	$\frac{60}{3} = 20$	$\frac{80}{4} = 20$	$\frac{100}{5} = 20$

The constant of proportionality is 20 cm per brick.

Part 1

Example Finding Constants of Proportionality

The weight of the stack depends on the number of books in the stack. Identify the constant of proportionality for this situation. Then use the constant of proportionality to find the weight of 11 books.

Solution

The constant of proportionality is the ratio $\frac{y}{x}$ where x is the independent variable and y is the dependent variable.

continued on next page >

Part 1

Solution continued

Here the independent variable is the number of books and the dependent variable is the weight of the stack.

$$\text{constant of proportionality} = \frac{\text{weight of stack}}{\text{number of books}}$$

$$= \frac{15.75 \text{ lb}}{9 \text{ books}}$$

A stack of 9 books weighs 15.75 lb.

$$= 1.75 \text{ lb per book}$$

The constant of proportionality is 1.75 lb per book.

The constant of proportionality is a unit rate that gives the weight per book. So to find the weight of 11 books, multiply the constant of proportionality by 11.

$$\frac{1.75 \text{ lb}}{1 \text{ book}} \cdot 11 \text{ books} = \frac{1.75 \text{ lb}}{1 \cancel{\text{book}}} \cdot 11 \cancel{\text{books}}$$

$$= 19.25 \text{ lb}$$

The weight of 11 books is 19.25 lb.

Part 2

Example Comparing Constants of Proportionality

You have a recipe that calls for 2 cups of flour to make 3 dozen cookies. Your friend has a cookie recipe that calls for 3 cups of flour to make 60 cookies. Are the constants of proportionality the same for the two recipes? Are the recipes for the same cookie? How do you know?

Solution

Since the number of cookies made depends on the amount of flour used, the constant proportionality is the ratio of the number of cookies to the amount of flour.

$$\text{constant of proportionality} = \frac{\text{number of cookies}}{\text{amount of flour}}$$

3 dozen = 36

You: $\text{constant of proportionality} = \frac{36 \text{ cookies}}{2 \text{ cups flour}}$

$$= 18 \text{ cookies per cup of flour}$$

Your friend: $\text{constant of proportionality} = \frac{60 \text{ cookies}}{3 \text{ cups flour}}$

$$= 20 \text{ cookies per cup of flour}$$

Your recipe has a constant of proportionality of 18 cookies per cup of flour. Your friend's recipe has a constant of proportionality of 20 cookies per cup of flour.

continued on next page >

Part 2

Solution continued

The recipes do *not* have the same constant of proportionality since each recipe makes a different number of cookies per cup of flour. This means the recipe are *not* for the same cookie.

Part 3

Example Using Constants of Proportionality

The table shows the amount of money raised based on the number of tickets sold for a charity concert.

Charity Fundraiser

Tickets Sold	Money Raised ($)
160	3,600
500	11,250
750	16,875
1,600	36,000

a. Does the table show a constant of proportionality? If so, what is the constant of proportionality for this situation?

b. You can sell no more than 2,500 tickets for the concert. Find the maximum amount of money the fundraiser can raise.

Solution

a. First determine if the table shows a proportional relationship between the amount of money raised and the number of tickets sold.

Charity Fundraiser

Tickets Sold	Money Raised ($)	$\frac{\text{Money Raised (\$)}}{\text{Tickets Sold}}$
160	3,600	$\frac{3,600}{160} = 22.50$
500	11,250	$\frac{11,250}{500} = 22.50$
750	16,875	$\frac{16,875}{750} = 22.50$
1,600	36,000	$\frac{36,000}{1,600} = 22.50$

The amount of money raised depends on the number of tickets sold.

For each row, the ratio of the money raised to tickets sold is $22.50 per ticket.

The table shows a proportional relationship between the amount of money raised and the number of tickets sold.

continued on next page >

Part 3

Solution continued

$$\text{constant of proportionality} = \frac{\text{Money Raised}}{\text{Tickets Sold}}$$
$$= \$22.50 \text{ per ticket}$$

The constant of proportionality is $22.50 per ticket.

b. The maximum number of tickets that can be sold is 2,500. To find the maximum amount of money that can be raised, multiply the constant of proportionality by 2,500.

$$\frac{\$22.50}{1 \cancel{\text{ticket}}} \cdot 2{,}500 \cancel{\text{tickets}} = \$56{,}250$$

The maximum amount of money that can be raised is $56,250.

Part 4

Example Finding Constants of Proportionality From Graphs

The graph shows the number of times a male hummingbird beats its wing based on time.

a. What is the constant of proportionality for this situation?

b. What does the point (1, 80) represent?

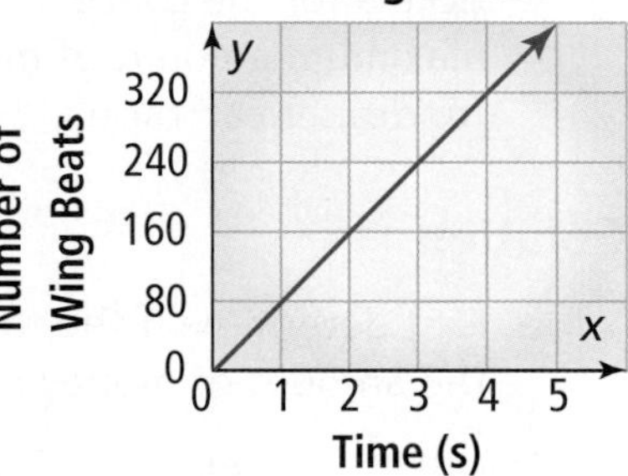

Solution

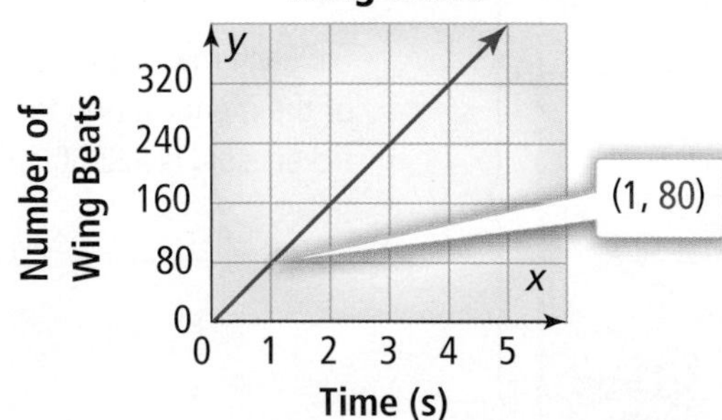

The graph shows a proportional relationship between time and the number of wing beats since the graph is a straight line passing through the origin.

a. The number of wing beats depends on time. To find the constant of proportionality, choose any point (x, y) on the graph except the origin and find the ratio $\frac{y}{x}$.

continued on next page >

Part 4

Solution continued

Use the point (1, 80).

$$\text{constant of proportionality} = \frac{y}{x}$$
$$= \frac{80}{1}$$

The constant of proportionality is 80 wing beats per second.

b. The point (1, 80) represents 80 wing beats in 1 second. This point represents the unit rate, 80 wing beats per second. This point also represents the constant of proportionality.

1. The variable y is in a proportional relationship with x. The number of squares represents an x value. The number of ovals represents the corresponding y value. Identify the constant of proportionality.

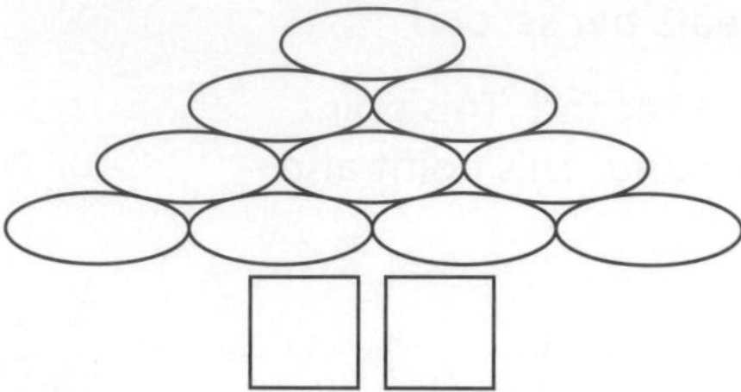

2. Suppose the relationship between x and y is proportional. When x is 6, y is 78. Identify the constant of proportionality of y to x.

3. Since a middle school opened, the girls' basketball team has had the same record every season. The team has won a total of 169 games while losing only 13 games. Find the constant of proportionality of wins to losses.

4. Does the table show a proportional relationship? If so, what is the constant of proportionality of y to x?

x	5	6	7	8
y	90	108	126	144

5. The distance a jet aircraft flies has a proportional relationship with its number of hours in flight. The table shows the number of miles flown for a number of hours in flight.

Passenger Jet Travel

Hours	2	3	4	5
Miles	840	1,260	1,680	2,100

a. Find the constant of proportionality.

b. How long will the jet take to travel 4,620 miles?

6. The height of a stack of DVD cases is in a proportional relationship to the number of cases in the stack. A stack of 6 cases and its height are shown.

Golden Oldies, 2005
Golden Oldies, 2004
Golden Oldies, 2003
Golden Oldies, 2002
Golden Oldies, 2001
Golden Oldies, 2000

The height of 6 DVD cases is 114 mm.

a. What is the constant of proportionality in millimeters per DVD case?

b. What is the height of 13 DVD cases in millimeters?

7. Estimation The graph shows the number of calories burned while running. Estimate the constant of proportionality of calories burned to time spent running.

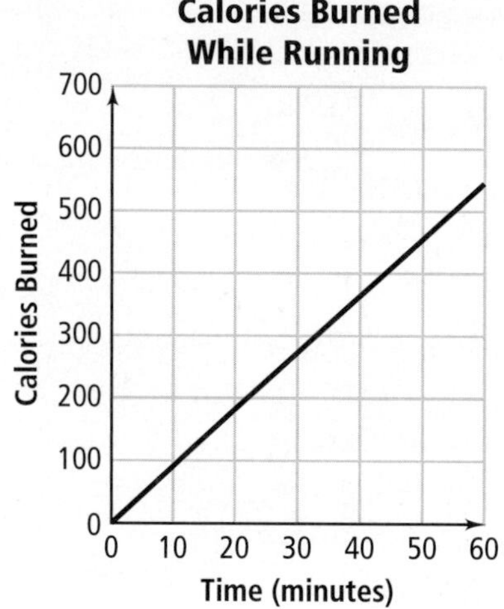

a. The constant of proportionality is about how many calories per minute?

b. What does the point (35, 315) represent?

A. 315 calories burned in 35 minutes

B. 35 calories burned in 315 minutes

C. 315 calories burned in 1 minute

8. Writing Suppose the relationship between x and y is proportional. When x is 29, y is 275.5.

a. Find the constant of proportionality of y to x.

b. Use the constant of proportionality to find x when y is 408.5.

c. Explain how you can tell a relationship that is proportional from a relationship that is not proportional.

9. Think About the Process The width of a row of identical townhouses is in a proportional relationship with the number of townhouses. The diagram suggests a row of 5 townhouses and gives their total width.

The width of 5 townhouses is 95 ft.

a. Which operation should you use to find the constant of proportionality?

A. Addition

B. Division

C. Subtraction

D. Multiplication

b. What is the constant of proportionality in feet per townhouse?

c. What is the width of 9 townhouses in feet?

10. Think About the Process

m	4.5	5.5	6.5	7.5
n	225	275	325	375

a. How can you tell that the table shows a proportional relationship?

A. The value of n is always m minus a constant.

B. The value of n is always m plus a constant.

C. The value of n is always m times a constant.

b. What is the constant of proportionality of n to m?

c. If $m = 13$, what is n?

11. Error Analysis You and a friend look at the graph. Your friend incorrectly says the constant of proportionality of y to x is $\frac{1}{18}$.

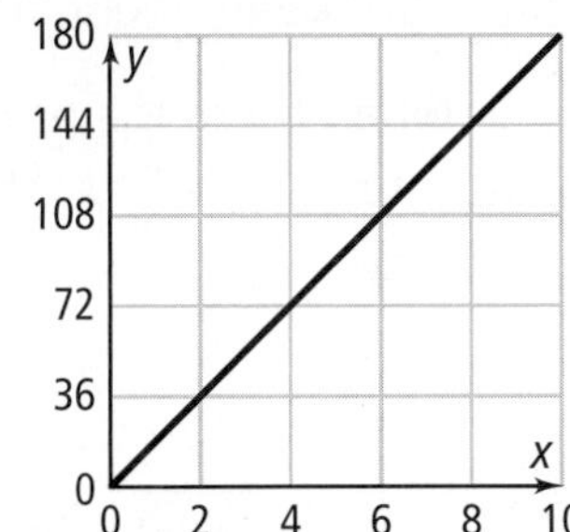

a. Find the correct constant of proportionality.

b. What is your friend's likely error?

A. Your friend found $x - y$.

B. Your friend found $x \cdot y$.

C. Your friend found $\frac{x}{y}$.

D. Your friend found $x + y$.

12. Challenge A city has two paint supply stores. Store A sells 2-gallon containers of paint. Each container covers 680 square feet for $58. Store B sells paint only by the quart. Each quart sells for $7.25 and covers 85 square feet. At each store, the cost of paint is in a proportional relationship to the amount of paint.

a. Find the constant of proportionality for Store A.

b. At which store is paint a better buy? (Hint: 4 quarts = 1 gallon)

A. Paint is of equal value at both stores.

B. Store B

C. Store A

2-4 Proportional Relationships and Equations

Vocabulary
proportion

CCSS: 7.RP.A.2, 7.RP.A.2b, 7.RP.A.2c

Key Concept

You have used tables and graphs to represent proportional relationships. An equation can also describe a proportional relationship between two variables.

Recall that when there is a proportional relationship between x and y, y is a constant multiple of x. This constant multiple is the constant of proportionality.

$$y = mx$$

Constant of proportionality, $\frac{y}{x}$

Since the value of y depends on the value of x, y is the dependent variable and x is the independent variable.

Part 1

Example Understanding Equations Representing Proportional Relationships

Your friend uses the equation $y = 8.5x$ to calculate the total cost y in dollars for x movie tickets.

a. What is the constant of proportionality shown in the equation?
b. What does the constant of proportionality represent in this situation?
c. How much will 13 movie tickets cost?

Solution

a. $y = 8.5x$

$8.5 = \frac{y}{x}$

The constant of proportionality is $8.50 per ticket.

b. The constant of proportionality represents the unit cost, or the price, y, per movie ticket, x.

c. To find how much 13 movie tickets will cost, substitute 13 for x.

	$y = 8.5x$
Substitute 13 for x.	$= 8.5(13)$
Multiply.	$= 110.5$

It will cost $110.50 for 13 movie tickets.

Part 2

Example Identifying Equations of Proportional Relationships

a. A certain vegetable dip contains 60 Calories per serving. What equation represents the number of Calories y in x servings of dip?

b. At a telethon, a volunteer can take 60 calls in 5 h. What equation represents the number of calls y a volunteer can take in x hours?

c. A machine can make 60 keys in 12 min. What equation represents the number of keys y made in x minutes?

Solution

Find each unit rate. Then use the unit rate to write an equation.

a. Let y = the number of Calories. Let x = the number of servings. The unit rate is 60 Calories per serving.

$$y \text{ Calories} = \frac{60 \text{ Calories}}{1 \not{\text{serving}}} \cdot x \not{\text{servings}}$$

$$y \text{ Calories} = \frac{60 \text{ Calories}}{1} \cdot x$$

The label "Calories" appears on both sides of the equation.

$$y \not{\text{Calories}} \cdot \frac{1}{\not{\text{Calories}}} = \frac{60 \not{\text{Calories}}}{1} \cdot x \cdot \frac{1}{\not{\text{Calories}}}$$

$$y = 60 \cdot x$$

$$y = 60x$$

b. Let y = the number of calls. Let x = the number of hours.

$\frac{60 \text{ calls}}{5 \text{ hours}}$ = 12 calls per hour. The unit rate is 12 calls per hour.

$$y \text{ calls} = \frac{12 \text{ calls}}{1 \not{\text{hour}}} \cdot x \not{\text{hours}}$$

$$y \text{ calls} = \frac{12 \text{ calls}}{1} \cdot x$$

The label "calls" appears on both sides of the equation.

$$y \not{\text{calls}} \cdot \frac{1}{\not{\text{calls}}} = \frac{12 \not{\text{calls}}}{1} \cdot x \cdot \frac{1}{\not{\text{calls}}}$$

$$y = 12 \cdot x$$

$$y = 12x$$

c. Let y = the number of keys. Let x = the number of minutes.

$\frac{60 \text{ keys}}{12 \text{ min}}$ = 5 keys per minute. The unit rate is 5 keys per minute.

$$y \text{ keys} = \frac{5 \text{ keys}}{1 \not{\text{min}}} \cdot x \not{\text{min}}$$

$$y \text{ keys} = \frac{5 \text{ keys}}{1} \cdot x$$

The label "keys" appears on both sides of the equation.

$$y \not{\text{keys}} \cdot \frac{1}{\not{\text{keys}}} = \frac{5 \not{\text{keys}}}{1} \cdot x \cdot \frac{1}{\not{\text{keys}}}$$

$$y = 5 \cdot x$$

$$y = 5x$$

See your complete lesson at MyMathUniverse.com

Part 3

Intro

When you travel to another country, you often need to exchange U.S. dollars for the local currency. When you exchange money, you receive the equivalent amount in local currency based on the exchange rate. An exchange rate is an example of a constant of proportionality.

Recently, the exchange rate for U.S. dollars to Indian rupees was 1 dollar = 45 rupees. The constant of proportionality is 45 rupees per dollar.

Example Writing Equations for Proportional Relationships

You are going on a trip to Spain. When you ask for the exchange rate, your bank shows you the table. Write an equation you can use to find how many euros y you will receive in exchange for x U.S. dollars.

Currency Exchange

U.S. Dollars($)	Euros(€)
50	37.50
100	75
120	90
175	131.25

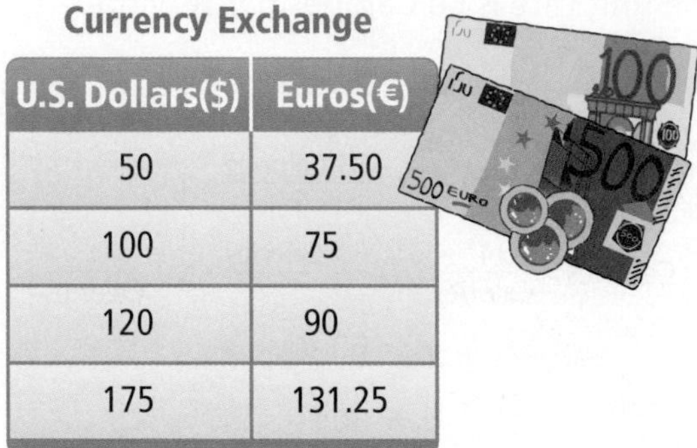

Solution

The number of euros, y, you receive depends on the number of U.S. dollars, x, you exchange.

Currency Exchange

U.S. Dollars ($)	Euros (€)	$\frac{\text{Euros}}{\text{U.S. Dollars}}$
50	37.50	$\frac{37.50}{50} = 0.75$
100	75	$\frac{75}{100} = 0.75$
120	90	$\frac{90}{120} = 0.75$
175	131.25	$\frac{131.25}{175} = 0.75$

Each row shows the unit rate of 0.75 euros per U.S. dollar.

There is a proportional relationship between U.S. dollars and euros.

The constant of proportionality is the unit rate of euros per U.S. dollar, or 0.75.

The equation is $y = 0.75x$.

continued on next page >

Part 3

Solution continued

Check

In the equation, x represents the number of U.S. dollars and y represents the number of euros.

Let $x = 50$.	Let $x = 100$.	Let $x = 120$.	Let $x = 175$.
$y = 0.75(50)$	$y = 0.75(100)$	$y = 0.75(120)$	$y = 0.75(175)$
$= 37.50$ ✓	$= 75$ ✓	$= 90$ ✓	$= 131.25$ ✓

Part 4

Intro

A **proportion** is an equation stating that two ratios are equal. You can use a proportion to solve a problem. Solving a proportion is similar to finding an equivalent ratio.

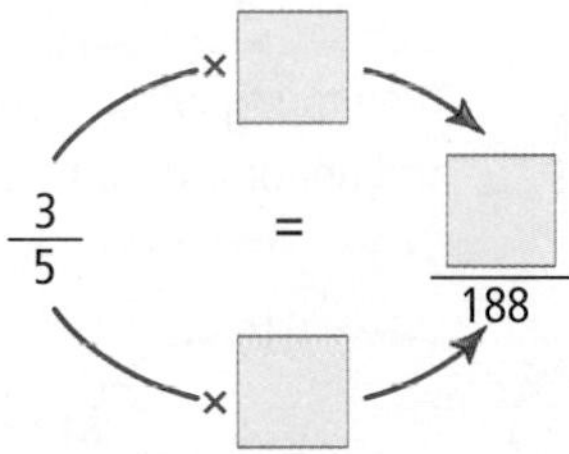

In the average adult male, for each 5 lb of body weight about 3 lb is water. How much of a 188-lb adult male is water?

Set up a proportion. $\frac{3}{5} = \frac{w}{188}$ ← Water (lb) / ← Body Weight (lb)

Multiply each side of the equation by 188. $\frac{3}{5}(188) = \frac{w}{188}(188)$

Simplify. $\frac{564}{5} = w$

$112.8 = w$

About 112.8 lb of a 188-lb adult male is water.

Example Solving Proportion Problems

In a local soccer league, the ratio of goalies to the total number of players on a team is about 2 to 30. If the league has 915 players, about how many goalies are there?

continued on next page >

Part 4

Example continued

Solution

Method 1 Use a proportion. Let x = the total number of goalies in the league.

Use the ratio $\frac{\text{number of goalies}}{\text{total number of players}}$.	$\frac{2}{30} = \frac{x}{915}$
Multiply each side by 915.	$\frac{2}{30} \cdot (915) = \frac{x}{915} \cdot (915)$
Simplify.	$\frac{1{,}830}{30} = x$
	$61 = x$

There are about 61 goalies in the league.

Method 2 Use an equivalent ratio.
Find an equivalent ratio $\frac{2}{30}$ with a denominator of 915.

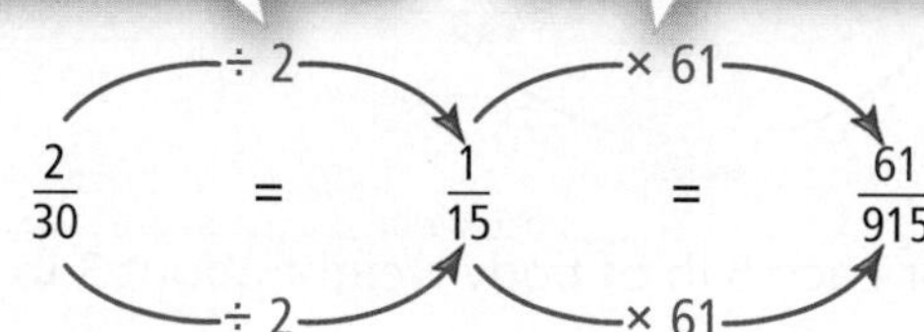

$$\frac{2}{30} \underset{\div 2}{\overset{\div 2}{=}} \frac{1}{15} \underset{\times 61}{\overset{\times 61}{=}} \frac{61}{915}$$

The ratio $\frac{61}{915}$ is equivalent to $\frac{2}{30}$.

There are about 61 goalies in the league.

1. The equation $y = \frac{5}{7}x$ describes a proportional relationship between x and y. What is the constant of proportionality?
2. The equation $P = 3s$ represents the perimeter P of an equilateral triangle with side length s. What is the perimeter of an equilateral triangle with side length 4 ft?
3. You bike 11.2 miles in 1.4 hours at a steady rate. What equation represents the proportional relationship between the x hours you bike and the distance y in miles that you travel?
4. Marco needs to buy some cat food. At the nearest store, 3 bags of cat food cost $15.75. How much would Marco spend on 5 bags of cat food?
5. An arts and crafts store sells sheets of stickers. Use the table to write an equation you can use to find the total cost y in dollars for x sheets of stickers.

Costs of Stickers

Number of Sheets (x)	Cost in Dollars (y)
3	6.15
5	10.25
13	26.65
19	38.95

6. Jane likes to exercise daily. The table shows the number of calories y she burns by exercising steadily for x minutes. How many calories would she burn by exercising for 29 minutes?

Calories Burned

Time in Minutes (x)	Calories Burned (y)
20	220
25	275
30	330
40	440

7. Solve the proportion $\frac{22}{24} = \frac{t}{84}$.

8. In a certain chemical, the ratio of zinc to copper is 3 to 16. A jar of the chemical contains 320 grams of copper. How many grams of zinc does it contain?
9. **Mental Math** Professional chefs usually measure ingredients by weight rather than by volume. A recipe calls for 2 ounces of flour for every 3 ounces of sugar.
   a. If you are a chef and you use 12 ounces of sugar, how many ounces of flour should you use?
   b. Explain how you can use mental math to find the answer. Explain why a chef might need mental math to find an answer like this.
10. **Writing** Ann's car can go 228 miles on 6 gallons of gas. During a drive last weekend, Ann used 7 gallons of gas.
    a. How far did she drive?
    b. Explain how the problem changes if you were given the distance Ann drove last weekend instead of how much gas she used.
11. **Reasoning** The equation $y = 6.41x$ describes a proportional relationship between x and y.
    a. What is the constant of proportionality?
    b. Explain why your answer is called the "constant of proportionality."
12. **Multiple Representations** The proportions $\frac{a}{b} = \frac{c}{d}$ and $\frac{b}{a} = \frac{d}{c}$ are called equivalent proportions.
    a. Find a proportion equivalent to $\frac{3}{7} = \frac{9}{x}$.

    A. $\frac{7}{3} = \frac{9}{x}$ **B.** $\frac{7}{3} = \frac{x}{9}$

    C. $\frac{7}{9} = \frac{x}{3}$ **D.** $\frac{7}{x} = \frac{9}{3}$

    b. What is the solution of the proportion?
    c. Explain why, based on this example, solving an equivalent proportion can be useful.

13. Error Analysis Roberto incorrectly said that the solution of the proportion $\frac{4}{5} = \frac{x}{7}$ is $\frac{4}{35}$.

a. What is the correct solution?

b. What error did Roberto likely make?

A. He multiplied each side of the equation by 7.

B. He multiplied the left side of the equation by 7, but divided the right side by 7.

C. He divided each side of the equation by 7.

D. He multiplied the right side of the equation by 7, but divided the left side by 7.

14. Buying Posters Ann uses the equation $y = 8.25x$ to calculate the total cost y in dollars for x posters. How much would she spend on 4 posters?

15. Multiple Representations Irene is a chemist. Yesterday, she combined 250 mL of water with 750 mL of acid to make 1,000 mL of a solution. Today, she wants to make 1,800 mL of the same solution.

a. Which two of these proportions could Irene solve to find the amount of water she needs?

A. $\frac{1{,}000}{750} = \frac{1{,}800}{x}$

B. $\frac{1{,}000}{250} = \frac{1{,}800}{x}$

C. $\frac{250}{1{,}000} = \frac{x}{1{,}800}$

D. $\frac{750}{1{,}000} = \frac{x}{1{,}800}$

b. How much water does she need?

16. Think About the Process A machine can make 56 parts in 4 hours. It can also make 70 parts in 5 hours.

a. Which of these rates could you use to write an equation of the form $y = mx$ that represents the number of parts y the machine can make in x hours? Select all that apply.

A. $\frac{70 \text{ parts}}{5 \text{ hours}}$ **B.** $\frac{70 \text{ parts}}{4 \text{ hours}}$

C. $\frac{56 \text{ parts}}{5 \text{ hours}}$ **D.** $\frac{56 \text{ parts}}{4 \text{ hours}}$

b. What equation represents the number of parts y the machine can make in x hours?

17. Think About the Process Water is steadily dripping from a faucet into a bowl. You want to write an equation that represents the number of milliliters y of water in the bowl after x seconds.

Water from Dripping Faucet

Time in Seconds (x)	Milliliters in Bowl (y)
20	320
35	560
45	720
60	960

a. What is the unit rate for milliliters per second?

b. What is the equation?

18. Challenge A car is traveling at a steady speed. It travels $2\frac{1}{3}$ miles in $3\frac{1}{2}$ minutes.

a. How far will it travel in 34 minutes?

b. How far will it travel in 1 hour?

2-5 Maps and Scale Drawings

Vocabulary
scale, scale drawing

CCSS: 7.G.A.1

Key Concept

A **scale drawing** is an enlarged or reduced drawing of an object that is proportional to the actual object.

A **scale** is the ratio that compares a length in a scale drawing to the corresponding length in the actual object.

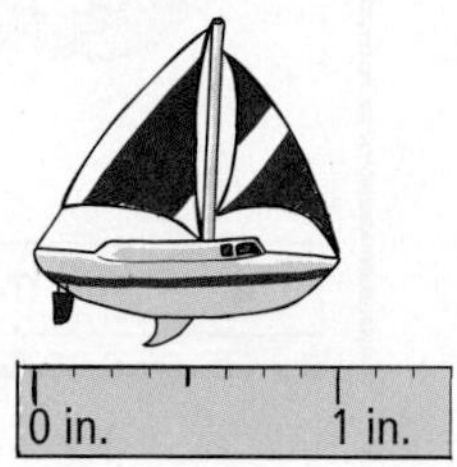

A 1 in.-long scale drawing is made of a 15 ft boat. The scale can be written as:

1 in. : 15 ft or 1 in. = 15 ft

Drawing

Actual

Part 1

Intro

You can use a scale to find an actual distance given a scale drawing. You can also use a scale to make a scale drawing given an actual distance.

Consider the scale 1 in. = 15 ft. You can write two different ratios.

$\frac{1 \text{ in.}}{15 \text{ ft.}}$

Use when you know the actual distance and want the scale drawing distance.

$\frac{15 \text{ ft.}}{1 \text{ in.}}$

Use when you know the scale drawing distance and want the actual distance.

Part 1

Example Using Maps and Keys

The American Golden-Plovers migrate from Nova Scotia to South American every fall. The map shows the route that the birds fly. About how long is the migration?

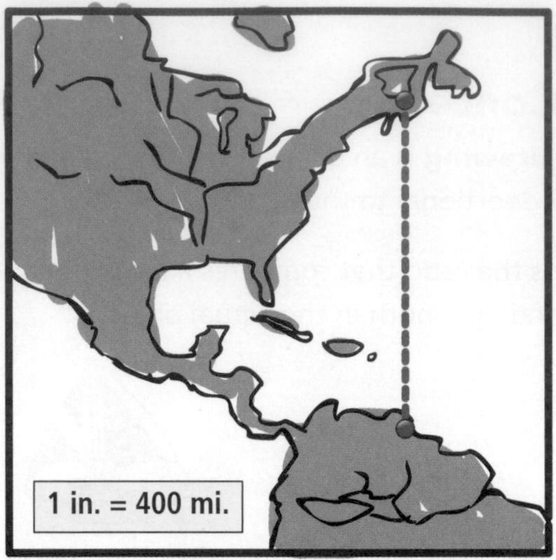

Solution

The distance on the map is 6 in.

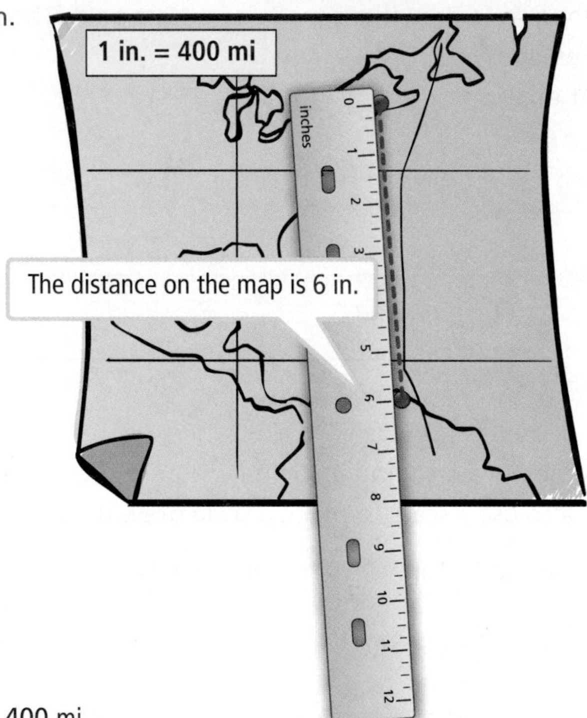

The scale of the map is 1 in. = 400 mi.

The scale can be represented as either

$$\frac{400 \text{ mi}}{1 \text{ in.}} \text{ or } \frac{1 \text{ in.}}{400 \text{ mi}}$$

You want to find the actual distance, so use $\frac{400 \text{ mi}}{1 \text{ in.}}$.

To find the actual distance of the migration, multiply this scale by the distance of the migration on the map.

$$\frac{400 \text{ mi}}{1 \cancel{\text{in.}}} \cdot 6 \cancel{\text{in.}} = 2{,}400 \text{ mi}$$

The migration is about 2,400 mi.

Part 2

Intro

There is a proportional relationship between a scale drawing and the actual object. The scale is the constant of proportionality.

You can write an equation to represent this relationship.

Consider the scale 1 in. = 15 ft. You can write two different equations.

$y = \frac{1 \text{ in.}}{15 \text{ ft}}x$

Use when you know the actual distance and want the scale drawing distance.

$y = \frac{15 \text{ ft}}{1 \text{ in.}}x$

Use when you know the scale drawing distance and want the actual distance.

Example Finding Actual Measurements from Scale Drawings

You make a scale drawing of a rectangular billboard for an aquarium. You can use a scale of 1 in. = 1.5 ft. What are the dimensions of the actual billboard? What is the area of the actual billboard?

Solution

Know

- The scale drawing is 8 in. by 16 in.
- The scale $\frac{\text{length of actual object}}{\text{length of scale drawing}} = \frac{1.5 \text{ ft}}{1 \text{ in.}}$

Need

The height, width, and area of the actual billboard.

Plan

Use the equation $y = 1.5x$, where x = a length (in inches) of the scale drawing and y = the corresponding length (in feet) of the actual billboard. Multiply the actual height and width to find the area of the billboard.

continued on next page >

Part 2

Solution continued

Step 1 Find the actual height and width of the billboard.

The drawing is 8 in. high.

Let $x = 8$.

Find y, the actual height of the billboard.

$y = 1.5x$

Substitute 8 for x. $= 1.5(8)$

Multiply. $= 12$

The actual height of the billboard is 12 ft.

The drawing is 16 in. wide.

Let $x = 16$.

Find y, the actual width of the billboard.

$y = 1.5x$

Substitute 16 for x. $= 1.5(16)$

Multiply. $= 24$

The actual width of the billboard is 24 ft.

The dimensions of the billboard are 12 ft by 24 ft.

Step 2 Find the area of the billboard.

The billboard is a rectangle. The area of the billboard is (12 ft)(24 ft) = 288 ft^2.

Part 3

Example Finding Dimensions of Scale Drawings

You are making a map of the United States. The map uses a scale of about 1 cm = 100 mi. You want to use a scale of about 2 cm = 125 mi. What will be the dimensions of Kansas on your map?

2.1 cm

Kansas

4 cm

continued on next page >

Part 3

Example continued

Solution

Step 1 Find the actual dimensions of Kansas.

Every centimeter on the map represents 100 mi. Multiply each dimension on the map by $\frac{100 \text{ mi}}{1 \text{ cm}}$ to find the actual distance.

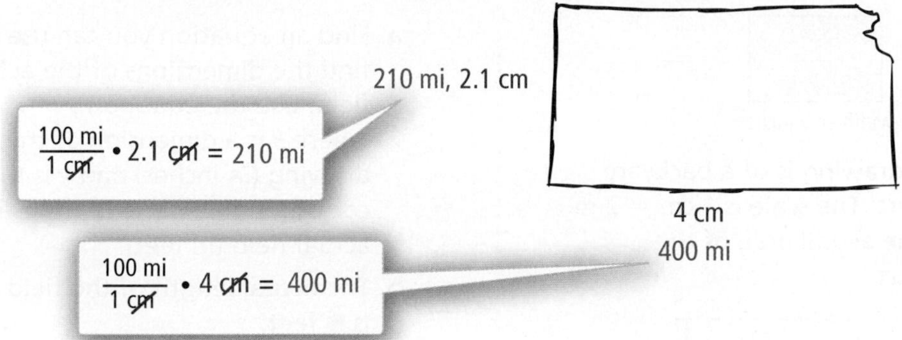

Step 2 Find the dimensions of Kansas on your map using your scale $\frac{2 \text{ cm}}{125 \text{ mi}}$.

$\frac{2 \text{ cm}}{125 \cancel{\text{mi}}} \cdot 400 \cancel{\text{mi}} = 6.4 \text{ cm}$ — The width of Kansas on your map

$\frac{2 \text{ cm}}{125 \cancel{\text{mi}}} \cdot 210 \cancel{\text{mi}} = 3.36 \text{ cm}$ — The height of Kansas on your map

On your map, Kansas will be about 6.4 cm wide and 3.36 cm high.

Digital Resources    

1. On a map, 1 inch equals 5 miles. Two cities are 8 inches apart on the map. What is the actual distance between the cities?

2. You make a scale drawing of a banner for a school dance. You use a scale of 1 inch = 3 feet. What is the actual width of the banner?

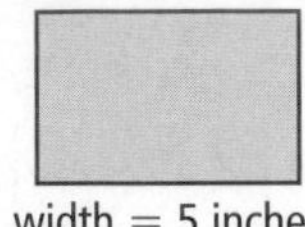

3. The scale drawing is of a backyard tennis court. The scale is 1 cm = 2 m. What is the actual area of the tennis court?

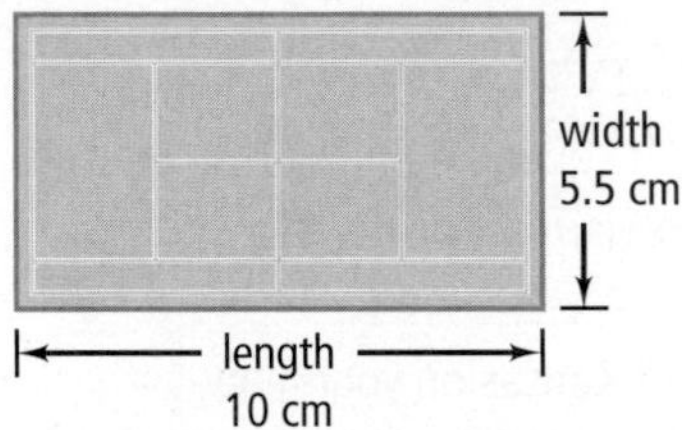

4. **Writing** The drawing below of a swimming pool has a scale of 1 inch = 3 meters.

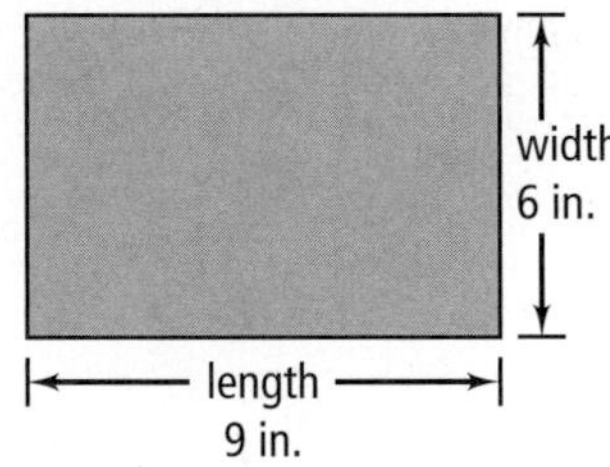

   a. Find the dimensions of another drawing of this swimming pool with a scale of 2 inches = 5 meters.

   b. How many different scales are available to use for a scale drawing? Why could one scale be more useful than another?

5. **Think About the Process** The scale for the drawing of a rectangular playing field is 2 inches = 5 feet.

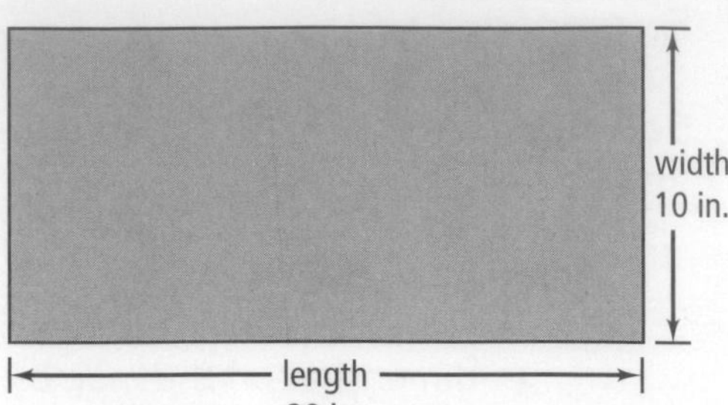

   a. Find an equation you can use to find the dimensions of the actual field. Use the equation $y = ■ x$, where x is a dimension of the scale drawing (in inches) and y is the corresponding dimension of the actual field (in feet).

   b. The actual length of the field is ■ feet.

   c. The actual width of the field is ■ feet.

6. **Think About the Process** The blueprint of a concrete patio has a scale of 2 in. = 3 ft. You want to find the dimensions of a new blueprint of the patio with a scale of 4 in. = 5 ft.

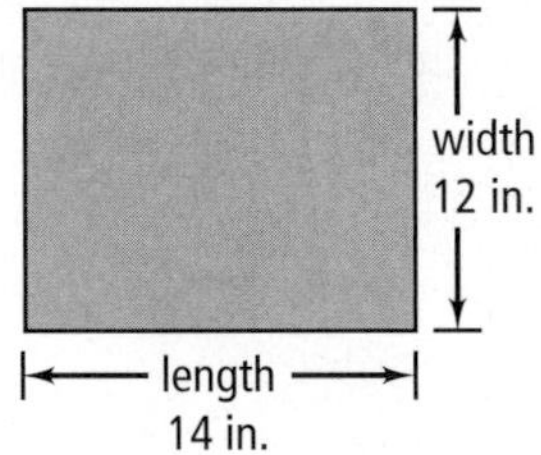

   a. What is the first step in finding the dimensions of the new scale?

   A. Multiply each dimension on the scale drawing by $\frac{2\text{ in.}}{3\text{ ft}}$ to find the actual dimension of the patio.

   B. Multiply each dimension on the scale drawing by $\frac{5\text{ ft}}{4\text{ in.}}$ to find the actual dimension of the patio.

   C. Multiply each dimension on the scale drawing by $\frac{3\text{ ft}}{2\text{ in.}}$ to find the actual dimension of the patio.

   b. The length of the blueprint with the new scale is ■ in.

   c. The width of the blueprint with the new scale is ■ in.

7. Error Analysis On the floor plan, 1 in. represents 2 ft. Tony calculates the actual length of the kitchen to be 2 ft.

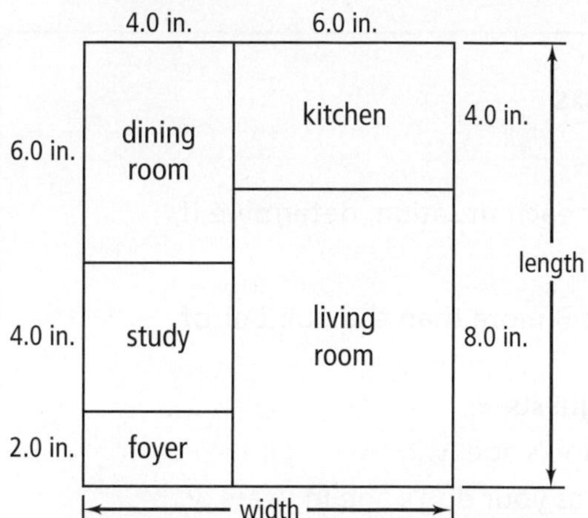

a. What is the actual length of the kitchen?

b. What error did Tony likely make?

A. He multiplied 4.0 in. by the ratio $\frac{1 \text{ in.}}{2 \text{ ft}}$ and did not consider the units.

B. He multiplied 4.0 in. by the ratio $\frac{1 \text{ in.}}{2 \text{ ft}}$.

C. He divided 4.0 in. by the ratio $\frac{1 \text{ in.}}{2 \text{ ft}}$ and did not consider the units.

c. Explain how you could have recognized that Tony's result was likely an error.

8. Multiple Representations On a map, 2 inches equals 180 miles. The distance that a family travels is 6.5 inches on the map.

a. Which two ratios represent the scale of the map?

A. $\frac{2 \text{ miles}}{6.5 \text{ inches}}$ **B.** $\frac{6.5 \text{ miles}}{2 \text{ inches}}$

C. $\frac{180 \text{ miles}}{2 \text{ inches}}$ **D.** $\frac{6.5 \text{ inches}}{180 \text{ miles}}$

E. $\frac{180 \text{ miles}}{6.5 \text{ inches}}$ **F.** $\frac{2 \text{ inches}}{180 \text{ miles}}$

b. What is the actual distance the family travels?

9. Estimation A 12-foot wall measures 2.75 inches on a scale drawing. In the drawing, a second wall is 9 inches long. Estimate the actual length of the second wall.

10. The distance between City A and City B is 200 miles. A length of 1.9 feet represents this distance on a certain wall map. City C and City D are 3.8 feet apart on this map. What is the actual distance between City C and City D?

11. The map shows the distance between two towns A and B.

The gridlines are spaced 1 in. apart

$1 \text{ in.} = 3\frac{1}{4} \text{ km}$

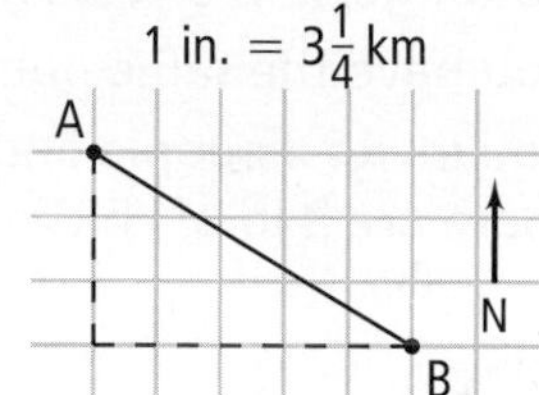

a. What is the actual distance from north to south?

b. What is the actual distance from east to west?

12. Challenge If installed carpet costs $1.50 per square foot, how much will it cost to carpet the entire living room floor of the cabin?

The gridlines are spaced 1 in. apart

1 inch = 4 feet

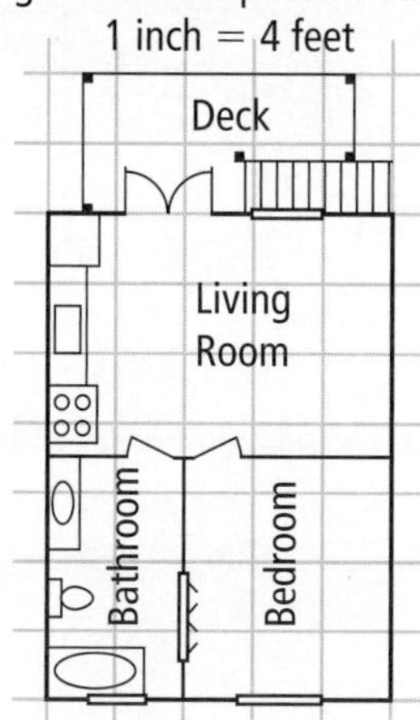

2-6 Problem Solving

CCSS: 7.G.A.1, Also 7.RP.A.2, 7.RP.A.2a, 7.RP.A.2b, 7.RP.A.2c, 7.RP.A.2d

Part 1

Example Determining If Relationships Are Proportional

You are throwing your dog a birthday party. For each situation, determine if the relationship between x and y is proportional.

a. You buy a number of dog bones, y, that is 3 more than the number of dogs, x, that you invite.

b. You have twice as many party hats, y, as guests, x.

c. Your age, x, is 8 years greater than your dog's age, y.

d. You have the same number of candles, x, as your dog's age in years, y.

e. You invite x people and cook y lb of chicken. For every 4 invitees, there are 3 lb of chicken.

Solution

a. You buy a number dog bones y that is 3 more than the number of dogs x you invite.

$y = x + 3$

x	y	Ratio $\frac{y}{x}$
1	4	$\frac{4}{1}$
2	5	$\frac{5}{2}$
3	6	$\frac{6}{3} = \frac{2}{1}$
4	7	$\frac{7}{4}$

The ratio $\frac{y}{x}$ for each row is *not* equivalent.

The relationship is not proportional.

continued on next page >

Part 1

Solution continued

b. You have twice as many party hats y as guests x.

Words Twice as many party hats y as guests x

Equation $y = 2x$

The constant of proportionality is 2.

The relationship is proportional.

c. Your age x is 8 years greater than your dog's age y.

$x = y + 8$

x	y	Ratio $\frac{x}{y}$
9	1	$\frac{9}{1}$
10	2	$\frac{10}{2} = \frac{5}{1}$
11	3	$\frac{11}{3}$
12	4	$\frac{12}{4} = \frac{3}{1}$

The ratio $\frac{x}{y}$ for each row is *not* equivalent.

The relationship is not proportional.

d. You have the same number of candles x as your dog is years old y.

Words Same number of candles x as your dog is years old y

Equation $y = x$

The constant of proportionality is 1.

The relationship is proportional.

continued on next page >

Part 1

Solution continued

e. You invite x people and cook y pounds of chicken. For every 4 invitees, there are 3 lb of chicken.

When x increases by 4, y increases by 3.

x	y	Ratio $\frac{y}{x}$
4	3	$\frac{3}{4}$
8	6	$\frac{6}{8} = \frac{3}{4}$
12	9	$\frac{9}{12} = \frac{3}{4}$
16	12	$\frac{12}{16} = \frac{3}{4}$

The ratio $\frac{y}{x}$ for each row is equivalent to $\frac{3}{4}$.

The relationship is proportional.

Part 2

Example Using Scale Drawings

The blueprint is a scale drawing of an apartment. Could a bed 6 ft and 3ft wide fit into the narrow section of the bedroom shown below the bathroom on the blueprint? How do you know?

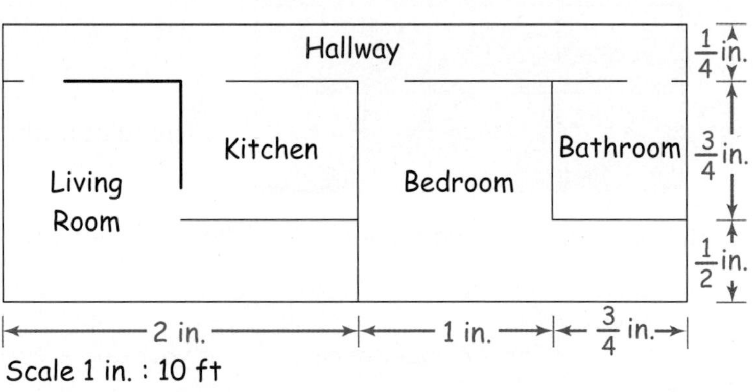

Solution

On the blueprint the narrow part of the bedroom is $\frac{1}{2}$ in. wide and $\frac{3}{4}$ in. long. Use the scale 1 in. : 10 ft to find the actual length and width of the narrow part of the bedroom.

Step 1 Write the scale as $\frac{10 \text{ ft}}{1 \text{ in.}}$.

continued on next page >

Part 2

Solution continued

Step 2 Find the actual length and width of the narrow part of the bedroom.

Multiply the length and width on the drawing by the scale.

Length:

$\frac{10 \text{ ft}}{1 \cancel{\text{in.}}} \cdot \frac{3}{4} \cancel{\text{in.}} = \frac{30}{4} \text{ ft}$

$= 7\frac{1}{2} \text{ ft}$

Width:

$\frac{10 \text{ ft}}{1 \cancel{\text{in.}}} \cdot \frac{1}{2} \cancel{\text{in.}} = \frac{10}{2} \text{ ft}$

$= 5 \text{ ft}$

Step 3 Compare the actual length and width with the size of the bed. The bed is 6 ft long and 3 ft wide. The narrow part of the bedroom is $7\frac{1}{2}$ ft long and 5 ft wide.

Yes, the bed will fit.

Part 3

Example Comparing Proportional Relationships

Before a trip to China, you want to exchange 1,500 U.S. dollars to Chinese yuan. Which bank has the better exchange rate? How many more yuan will you get if you exchange all of your money at the better exchange rate?

Bank A

U.S. Dollars ($)	Chinese Yuan (¥)
60	384
100	640
150	960
250	1,600

Bank B

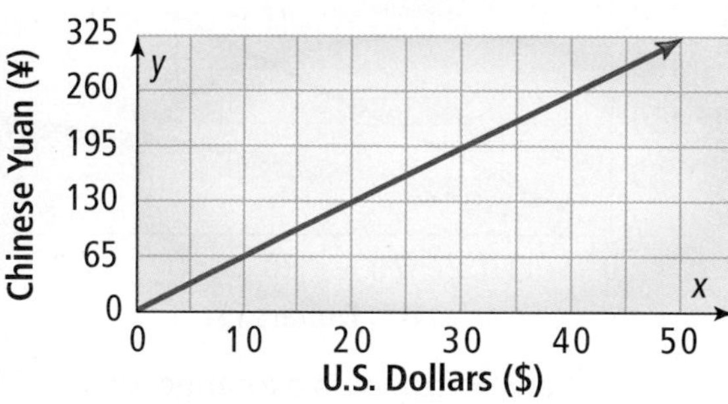

Solution

The exchange rate is equal to the **constant of proportionality**.

continued on next page >

Part 3

Solution continued

Step 1 Find the exchange rate for Bank A.

Bank A

U.S. Dollars ($)	Chinese Yuan (¥)	Chinese Yuan / U.S. Dollars
0	384	$\frac{384}{60} = 6.4$
100	640	$\frac{640}{100} = 6.4$
150	960	$\frac{960}{150} = 6.4$
250	1,600	$\frac{1,600}{250} = 6.4$

The constant of proportionality for Bank A is 6.4 yuan per U.S. dollar.

Bank A shows an exchange rate of 6.4 Chinese yuan per U.S. dollar.

$$\frac{6.4 \text{ Chinese yuan}}{1 \text{ U.S. dollar}} \cdot 1{,}500 \text{ U.S. dollars} = 9{,}600 \text{ Chinese yuan}$$

You will receive 9,600 Chinese yuan if you exchange your money at Bank A.

Step 2 Find the exchange rate for Bank B.

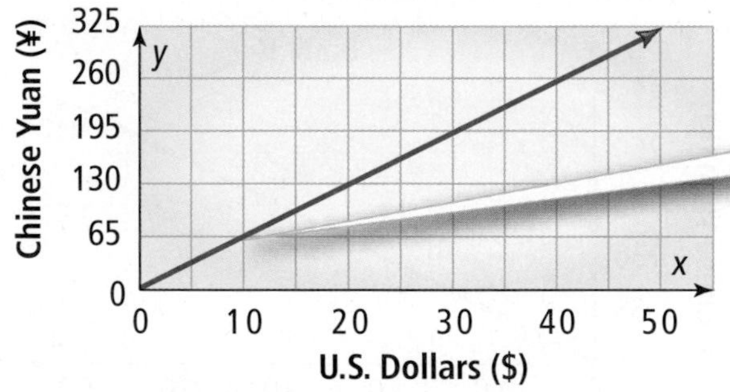

The point (10, 65) represents 65 Chinese yuan per 10 U.S. dollars. So, the constant of proportionality for Bank B is 6.5 yuan per U.S.dollar.

Bank B shows an exchange rate of 6.5 Chinese yuan per U.S. dollar.

$$\frac{6.5 \text{ Chinese yuan}}{1 \text{ U.S. dollar}} \cdot 1{,}500 \text{ U.S. dollars} = 9{,}750 \text{ Chinese yuan}$$

You will receive 9,750 Chinese yuan if you exchange your money at Bank B.

Step 3 Compare Bank A and Bank B

Bank B has a better exchange rate. You will receive 9,600 Chinese yuan from Bank A and 9,750 Chinese yuan from Bank B.

$$9{,}750 - 9{,}600 = 150 \text{ yuan}$$

If you exchange all of your money at Bank B, you will receive 150 more yuan.

Digital Resources   

1. You and your friend are each drawing a map of your neighborhood. The graph represents the scale you used for your map. The equation $y = \frac{1}{12}x$ represents your friend's scale, where x is the actual distance in feet and y is the distance on the map in inches. On whose map will a 150-foot driveway be longer?

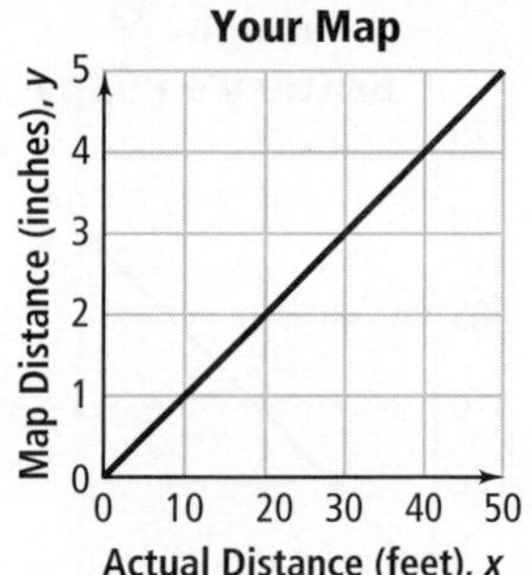

2. At a cookout, Mrs. Crawford makes $\frac{8}{9}$ lb of chicken, plus 1 lb for each guest. Express the relationship between the number of guests x and the number of pounds of chicken y with an equation. Is the relationship between x and y proportional? Explain.

3. A map of a city uses the scale 1 cm = 50 m. On the map, Second Avenue is 29 cm long. If there is a traffic cone at the start of Second Avenue and a cone every 5 m along the road, how many traffic cones are there in all?

4. Leah is planning a trip between two cities that are 24 cm apart on a map. After studying the table, she says that the map's scale is represented by the equation $y = 4x$, where x is the distance on the map in centimeters and y is the actual distance in kilometers. Then she uses that equation and claims the distance between the two cities is 6 km. This is not the correct distance.

Distances

Map Distance in Centimeters (x)	Actual Distance in Kilometers (y)
4	16
5	20
7	28
8	32

a. What is the correct distance?

b. What is Leah's likely error?

A. She found an incorrect constant of proportionality and she substituted the distance between the two cities on the map for y instead of x.

B. She substituted the distance between the two cities on the map for y instead of x.

C. She found an incorrect constant of proportionality.

5. A recipe calls for 15 oz of flour for every 8 oz of milk. Let x be the amount of milk used. Let y be the amount of flour used.

a. Express the relationship with an equation.

b. Is the relationship between x and y proportional?

c. If you use 15 oz of milk, how much flour should you use?

6. The blueprint in **Figure 1** is a scale drawing of an apartment. The scale is 1 in. = 10 ft. Would a painting $5\frac{1}{2}$ ft wide fit on the narrowest wall of the living room? Explain.

7. Challenge The value of a baseball player's rookie card began to increase once the player retired. When he retired in 1996 his card was worth \$7.46. The value has increased by \$2.52 each year since then.

a. Express the relationship relating the value of the card y in dollars and the number of years x the player has been in retirement with an equation.

b. Is the relationship between x and y proportional?

c. What was the value of the card in 2002?

8. The blueprint in **Figure 1** is a scale drawing of an apartment. The scale is 1 in. = 8 ft. The walls are 8 ft high. You want to paint the narrowest wall of the living room. Each can of paint covers 150 ft^2 and you can buy only a whole number of cans. At least how many cans should you buy?

9. **Think About the Process** The temperature 100 ft below sea level is 38°F. The temperature at sea level is 58°F. The temperature drops 5°F every 1,000 ft above sea level. Let x be the distance above sea level in thousands of feet. Let y be the temperature.
   - **a.** Express the relationship with an equation.
   - **b.** Is the relationship between x and y proportional?
   - **c.** What is the temperature 5,000 ft above sea level in degrees Fahrenheit?
   - **d.** What given information did you not use to solve this problem?
     - **A.** The temperature 100 ft below sea level
     - **B.** The rate of change of the temperature
     - **C.** The temperature at sea level

10. **Think About the Process** The weight of Michael's new puppy is represented by the table. The weight of Brittney's new puppy is represented by the graph.

Weight of Michael's Puppy

Age (months)	1	2	3
Weight (pounds)	8.6	17.2	25.8

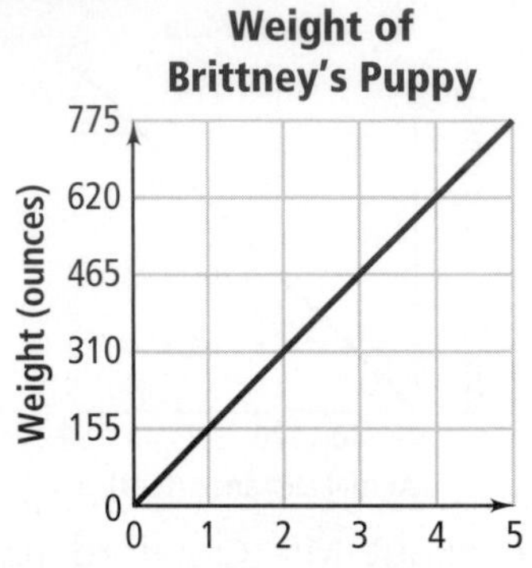

   - **a.** How can you convert pounds to ounces?
     - **A.** Multiply the number of ounces by 16.
     - **B.** Divide the number of pounds by 16.
     - **C.** Multiply the number of pounds by 16.
     - **D.** Divide the number of ounces by 16.
   - **b.** Whose dog gains weight faster?

(Figure 1)

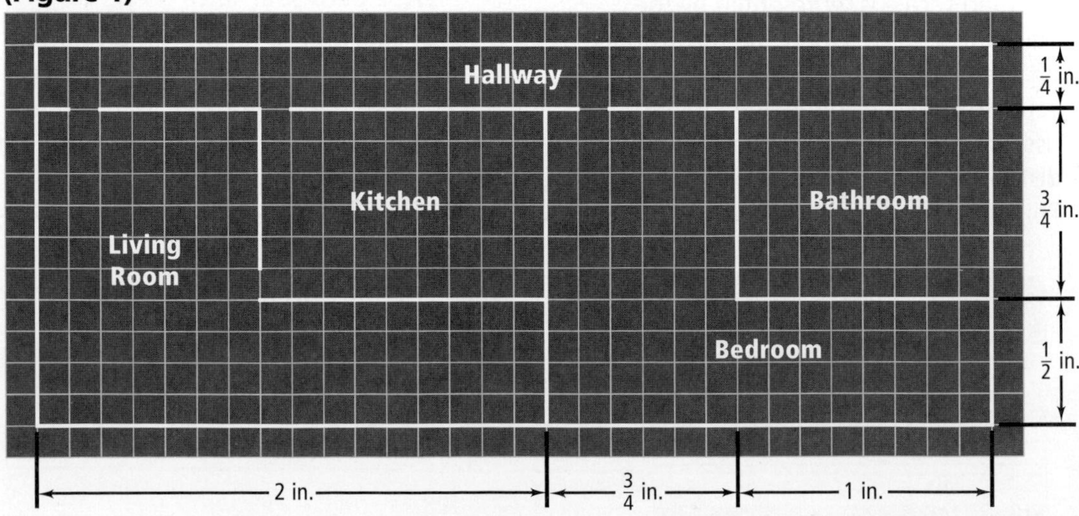

3-1 The Percent Equation

Vocabulary
percent equation

CCSS: 7.RP.A.2b, 7.RP.A.2c, Also 7.RP.A.2

Key Concept

You can use the **percent equation** to solve percent problems.

part = percent · whole

Relating $y = mx$ The percent equation is related to the equation $y = mx$. It describes the relationship between the part y and the whole x.

part = percent · whole

y
dependent variable

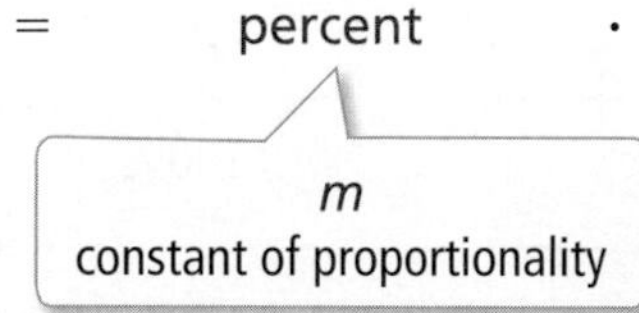

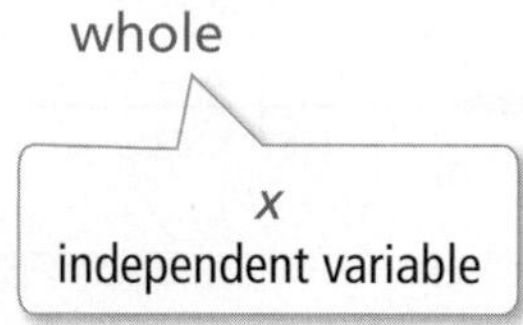

Finding the Part The part is dependent on the value of the whole and on the percent. You can see this relationship using a percent bar.

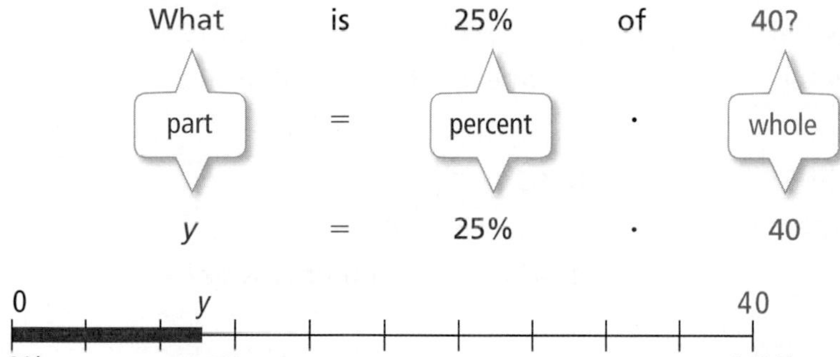

0 y 40

0% 25% 100%

Finding the Whole The whole represents 100%.

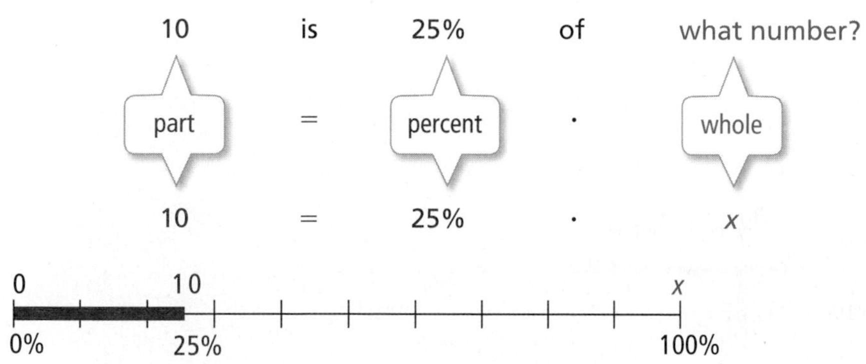

continued on next page >

Key Concept

continued

Finding the Percent The percent is the ratio that describes the proportional relationship between the part and the whole.

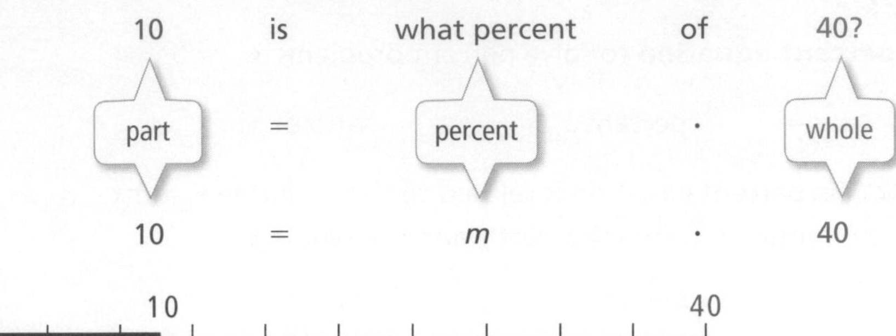

Part 1

Example Understanding Part, Percents, and Wholes

Write whether each question or equation is looking for the *part*, the *percent*, or the *whole*. Determine the portion of each statement that led you to the answer.

a. 4 is what percent of 6?

b. $65 = \frac{30}{100} \cdot x$

c. What is 79% of 126?

d. $11 = m \cdot 50$

e. $y = 0.48 \cdot 21$

f. 4% of what number is 12?

Solution

The portion of each statement leading to the answer is circled.

a. 4 is (what percent) of 6? — Percent

4 is the part. 6 is the whole.

b. $65 = \frac{30}{100} \cdot (x)$ — Whole

65 is the part. $\frac{30}{100}$ is the percent.

c. (What) is 79% of 126? — Part

79% is the percent. 126 is the whole.

d. $11 = (m) \cdot 50$ — Percent

11 is the part. 50 is the whole.

continued on next page >

Part 1

Solution continued

e. $y = 0.48 \cdot 21$ — Part

0.48 is the percent. 21 is the whole.

f. 4% of what number is 12? — Whole

4% is the percent. 12 is the part.

Part 2

Example Solving Percent Problems

Solve each percent problem.

a. 11 is what percent of 50?
b. 25 is 4% of what number?
c. What is 40% of 60?

Solution

a. **11 is what percent of 50?**

Use the percent equation.	part =	percent	· whole
Substitute.	11 =	m	· 50
Solve for m.	$\frac{11}{50}$ =	m	

To find the percent, find an equivalent ratio with a denominator of 100.

Multiply the numerator and denominator by 2.

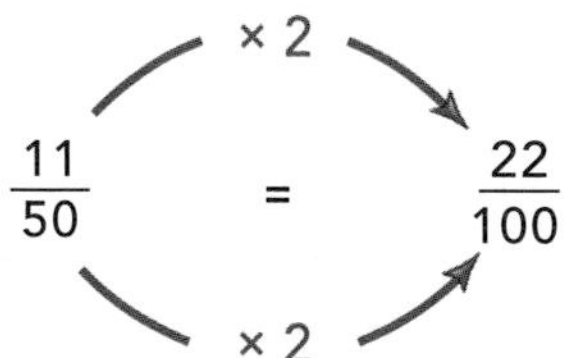

So, 11 is 22% of 50.

continued on next page >

Part 2

Solution continued

b.

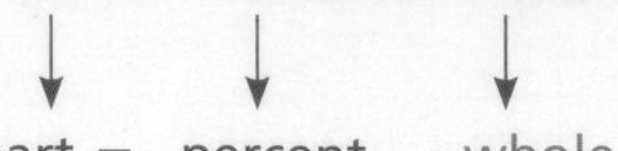

Use the percent equation.	part = percent · whole
Substitute.	$25 = 4\% \cdot x$
Convert the percent into a fraction.	$25 = \frac{4}{100} \cdot x$
Multiply each side of the equation by $\frac{100}{4}$.	$25 \cdot \frac{100}{4} = \frac{4}{100} \cdot \frac{100}{4} \cdot x$
Simplify and solve for *x*.	$\frac{2{,}500}{4} = x$
	$625 = x$

So, 25 is 4% of 625.

c.

Use the percent equation.	part = percent · whole
Substitute.	$y = 40\% \cdot 60$
Convert the percent into a fraction.	$y = \frac{40}{100} \cdot 60$
Multiply.	$y = \frac{2{,}400}{100}$
Simplify.	$y = 24$

So, 24 is 40% of 60.

Part 3

Example Calculating Percents

A hairdresser is paid \$7.50 per hour. After a year, he is to receive an 8% raise. Is the information in the letter correct? Explain.

CUTTING EDGE salon & spa

Congratulations! You have earned a raise!

Current wage: \$7.50 per hour
Percent raise: 8%
Raise amount: \$0.55 per hour

Signed,
Bobby Barber
Bobby Barber

Solution

Use the percent equation.	part =	percent	·	whole
	raise =	percentage of raise	·	original wage
Substitute.	raise =	8%	·	7.50
Solve.		$= \frac{8}{100} \cdot 7.50$		
		$= \frac{60}{100}$		
		$= 0.60$		

The "raise amount" in the letter is incorrect because the hairdresser should get a \$.60-per-hour raise rather than the \$.55-per-hour raise the letter stated.

1. Decide whether the following question is looking for the part, the percent, or the whole: 6 is what percent of 17?

2. Decide whether the following situation is looking for the part, the percent, or the whole: 6 of 18 pears are yellow.

3. 4 is what percent of 16?

4. The football team has a total of 20 jerseys. There are 4 medium-sized jerseys. What percent of the jerseys are medium-sized jerseys?

5. A local little league has a total of 60 players, of whom 80% are right-handed. How many right-handed players are there?

6. The local newspaper has letters to the editor from 40 people. If this number represents 5% of all of the newspaper's readers, how many readers does the newspaper have?

7. A student answers 90% of the questions on a math exam correctly. If he answers 27 questions correctly, how many questions are on the exam?

8. Kevin went to see his favorite sports team play. His car can go 300 miles on one tank of gas. If he used 40% of a full tank of gas, how many miles did he travel?

9. Dan is watching the birds in his backyard. He figures out that 9, or 33%, of the birds are sparrows. Does Dan need to find the part, the whole, or the percent?

10. a. Writing What is 50% of 36?

b. Write a percent problem that asks you to solve for the whole.

c. Write a problem that asks you to solve for the percent.

11. Error Analysis Tom's math teacher asks, "7 is 50% of what number?" Tom incorrectly says, "350."

a. What is the correct answer?

b. What error did Tom likely make?

A. He did not divide by 100.

B. He wrote the percent equation as percent = whole ÷ part.

C. He wrote the percent equation as whole = percent · part and did not divide by 100.

12. Car Survey In a survey of 2,000 people who owned a certain type of car, 1,100 said they would buy that type of car again. What percent of the people surveyed were satisfied with the car?

13. Think About the Process There are 4,000 books in the town's library. Of these, 2,600 are fiction.

a. To find the percent of the books that are fiction, first set up the percent equation.

A. $2,600 = m \div 4,000$

B. $2,600 = m \cdot 4,000$

C. $4,000 = m \div 2,600$

D. $4,000 = m \cdot 2,600$

b. What percent of the books are fiction?

14. a. Reasoning If 50% of the registered votes cast 228,000 votes in an election, how many registered voters are there?

b. In another election 60% of the registered voters cast 273,600 votes. How do the number of registered voters compare in the two elections?

15. Meg is a veterinarian. She found that 50% of the 16 dogs she saw this week were boxers. Steve is also a veterinarian. He found that 7 of the 35 dogs he saw this week were boxers.

a. Does Meg need to find the part, the whole, or the percent?

b. Does Steve need to find the part, the whole, or the percent?

16. Investors buy a studio apartment for \$240,000. Of this amount, they have a down payment of \$60,000.

   a. Their down payment is what percent of the purchase price?

   b. What percent of the purchase price would a \$12,000 down payment be?

17. **Think About the Process** The local movie theater decided to raise the ticket prices 25%. The original ticket prices were \$12.

   a. Set up the percent equation to find the amount by which the ticket prices rose.

   A. $y = 12 \div 25\%$

   B. $y = 25\% \cdot 12$

   C. $y = 25\% \div 12$

   D. $y = 12 + 25\%$

   b. How much did the price of tickets increase?

18. **Think About the Process** There are 5,000 books in the town's library. Of these, 4,600 are fiction.

   a. To find the percent of the books that are fiction, first set up the percent equation.

   A. $4{,}600 = m \div 5{,}000$

   B. $5{,}000 = m \div 4{,}600$

   C. $5{,}000 = m \cdot 4{,}600$

   D. $4{,}600 = m \cdot 5{,}000$

   b. What percent of the books are fiction?

19. **Challenge** A large university accepts 70% of the students who apply. Of the students the university accepts, 25% actually enroll. If 20,000 students apply, how many actually enroll?

20. **Challenge** In a company, 70% of the workers are men.

   a. If 1,380 women work for the company, how many workers are there in all?

   b. Show two different ways that you can solve this problem.

3-2 Using the Percent Equation

CCSS: 7.RP.A.2, 7.RP.A.3

Key Concept

Using Addition To find a total given a percent, use the percent equation to find the part. Then add the part to the whole.

Sales tax on an item is a percent of the item's price. Find the total price by adding the sales tax to the item's price.

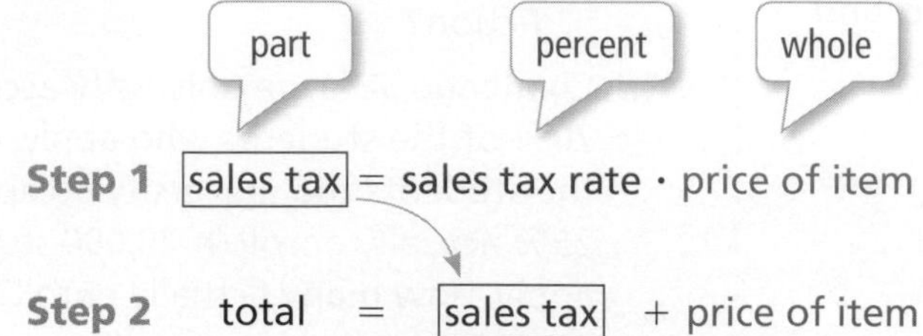

Using Subtraction To find a remainder given a percent, use the percent equation to find the part. Then subtract the part from the whole.

Some companies give salespeople a commission, or a percentage of the selling price of each item they sell. Find the amount of money the company earns on the item by subtracting the commission from the selling price.

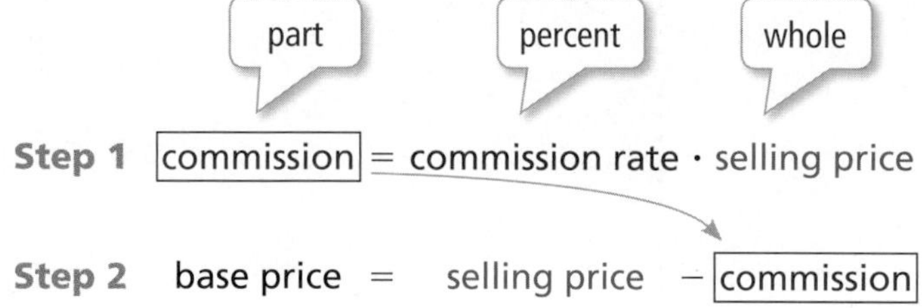

Part 1

Example Calculating Tax

A soccer team is having dinner at a restaurant to celebrate their winning season. The frazzled waiter gives them an incomplete bill. Help the team fill in the missing amounts.

The Diner

Hamburger (5)	$35.00
Spaghetti (5)	$40.00
Fries (5)	$16.00
Caesar Salad (4)	$18.00
Milkshake (11)	$33.00
Subtotal	$142.00
Meals Tax (5%)	
TOTAL	

Thank You! Please Come Again 00310

Solution

part — percent — whole

Use the percent equation.	meals tax = tax rate · price of item
Substitute.	$= 5\% \cdot 142.00$
Write 5% as a fraction.	$= \frac{5}{100} \cdot 142.00$
Multiply.	$= \frac{710}{100}$
Divide.	$= 7.10$
Find the total.	total = price of service + meals tax
Substitute.	$= 142.00 + 7.10$
Solve.	$= 149.10$

The total is $149.10.

The Diner

Hamburger (5)	$35.00
Spaghetti (5)	$40.00
Fries (5)	$16.00
Caesar Salad (4)	$18.00
Milkshake (11)	$33.00
Subtotal	$142.00
Meals Tax (5%)	$7.10
TOTAL	$149.10

Thank You! Please Come Again 00310

The meals tax is $7.10.

Part 2

Example Calculating Commissions

At a car dealership, a car salesman is trying to sell a car to his client.

His commission rate is 6%.

a. How much would the car salesman earn on each car?
b. How much would the car dealership make on each car?

Solution

a. The commission is what the car salesman will earn on the sale.

commission = commission rate · selling price

CAR 1:	CAR 2:	CAR 3:
= 0.06 · 16,800	= 0.06 · 25,400	= 0.06 · 33,000
= 1,008	= 1,524	= 1,980
The car salesman would earn $1,008.	The car salesman would earn $1,524.	The car salesman would earn $1,980.

b. The base price is what the car dealership will make on the sale.

base price = selling price − commission

CAR 1:	CAR 2:	CAR 3:
= 16,800 − 1,008	= 25,400 − 1,542	= 33,000 − 1,980
= 15,792	= 23,858	= 31,020
The car dealership would make $15,792.	The car dealership would make $23,858.	The car dealership would make $31,020.

Part 3

Example Comparing Commissions and Hourly Wages

Taylor has a new sales job at a clothing store. She is given two options for how to be paid.

Option A: Hourly wage of $7.15

Option B: 18% commission on total sales

She plans to work 4 hours per day, 5 days a week. She also estimates that she can sell about $200 worth of clothing per day. Which option would give Taylor more earnings per week? Explain.

Solution

Option A In one week, she would work:

$$\frac{4 \text{ hours}}{1 \text{ day}} \cdot \frac{5 \text{ days}}{1 \text{ week}} \cdot \frac{20 \text{ hours}}{1 \text{ week}}$$

So, with an hourly wage she would earn:

$$\frac{20 \text{ hours}}{1 \text{ week}} \cdot \frac{7.15 \text{ dollars}}{1 \text{ hour}} = \frac{143 \text{ dollars}}{1 \text{ week}}$$

With Option A, Taylor would earn $143 per week.

Option B In one week, she would sell about:

$$\frac{200 \text{ dollars}}{1 \text{ day}} \cdot \frac{5 \text{ days}}{1 \text{ week}} = \frac{1{,}000 \text{ dollars}}{1 \text{ week}}$$

So her commission would be:

$$\begin{aligned} \text{commission} &= \text{commission rate} \cdot \text{sales amount} \\ &= 18\% \cdot \$1{,}000 \\ &= 0.18 \cdot \$1{,}000 \\ &= \$180 \end{aligned}$$

With Option B Taylor would earn $180 per week.

Option B would give Taylor more earnings per week than Option A.

3-2 | Homework

1. a. Find the sales tax to complete the table.

Sales Tax

Selling Price	Rate of Sales Tax	Sales Tax
$40.00	4%	■

b. Find the total cost of the item.

2. Find the commission to complete the table.

Earning Commission

Sales	Commission Rate	Commission
$750	5%	■

3. Last month, a salesperson at a car dealership sold $205,000 worth of cars. The commission rate is 5%. How much did the salesperson earn last month in commission?

4. A salesperson at a jewelry store earns 3% commission each week. Last week, Heidi sold $720 worth of jewelry.
   - a. How much did she make in commission?
   - b. How much did the jewelry store make from her sales?

5. A salesperson works 40 hours per week at a job where he has two options for being paid. Option A is an hourly wage of $19. Option B is a commission rate of 8% on weekly sales. How much does he need to sell this week to earn the same amount with the two options?

6. The sales tax rate in a city is 9%.
   - a. Find the sales tax charged on a purchase of $600.
   - b. Then find the total cost.

7. **Mental Math** A typical tip in a restaurant is 15% of the total bill. If the bill is $140, what would the typical tip be?

8. **Reasoning** A salesperson's commission rate is 4%.
   - a. What is the commission from the sale of $33,000 worth of furnaces?
   - b. Suppose sales would double. What would be true about the commission? Explain without using any calculations.

9. **The Stock Market** Nadia is a stockbroker. She earns 4% commission each week. Last week, she sold $7,200 worth of stocks.
   - a. How much did she make last week in commission?
   - b. If she averages that same amount each week, how much did she make in commission in 2011?

10. **Error Analysis** Andrew and Cori start a new sales job. They have two options for being paid. Option A is an hourly wage of $7.50, working 40 hours a week. Option B is a commission of 6% on the weekly sales, estimating $3,600 in sales per week for an entry-level salesman. Andrew says he'll take the commission, thinking he'll make $2,160.
    - a. What was Andrew's likely error in computing the commission rate?
      - **A.** He incorrectly converted the percent to a decimal.
      - **B.** He used the equation, commission rate = commission · sales amount.
      - **C.** He used the equation, sales amount = commission rate · commission.
      - **D.** He used the equation, commission $= \frac{\text{commission rate}}{\text{sales amount}}$.
    - b. Which option gives Cori more earnings per week?
      - **A.** Option A
      - **B.** Option B
      - **C.** Both options generate the same amount of earnings.

11. Think About the Process Claudia sells insurance policies. She earns 6% commission for every policy sold. Claudia worked 5 days a week for 4 weeks and sold 38 policies. Each policy costs $337.

a. Which expression represents how much money Claudia earned on average each workday?

A. $\frac{337 \cdot 38 \cdot 0.06}{5}$

B. $\frac{337 \cdot 38 \cdot 0.06}{4}$

C. $\frac{337 \cdot 38 \cdot 6}{5 \cdot 4}$

D. $\frac{337 \cdot 38 \cdot 0.06}{5 \cdot 4}$

b. How much did Claudia earn on average each workday?

12. Writing A car salesperson works 40 hours per week at a job where she has two options for being paid. Option A is an hourly wage of $14. Option B is a commission rate on weekly sales, and she averages $7,000 in sales each week.

a. What commission rate does she need to have to earn the same amount with the two options?

b. Would you prefer a job that pays hourly or is based on commission? Explain.

13. At a real estate agency, an agent sold a house for $382,000. The commission rate is 5.5% for the real estate agency and the commission for the agent is 30% of the amount the real estate agency gets.

a. How much did the agency make on the house?

b. How much did the agent earn in commission?

14. An auctioneer works 40 hours per week at a job where she has two options for being paid. Option A is an hourly wage. Option B is a commission rate of 5% on all items sold weekly, and she averages $16,800 in weekly sales.

a. What hourly wage does she need to have to earn the same amount with the two options?

b. If the hourly wage increases by $2 and the commission rate increases by 1%, which option would earn more money for the auctioneer?

A. Option A **B.** Option B

C. Both options would generate the same amount of earnings.

15. Think About the Process A restaurant customer left $1.30 as a tip. The tax was 7% and the tip was 10% of the after tax cost.

a. Which information is not needed to compute the bill after tax and tip?

A. The tax was 7%.

B. The customer left a 10% tip.

C. The customer left $1.30 as a tip.

D. All of this information is needed to solve the problem.

b. What was the total bill?

16. Challenge Restaurants frequently add an 18% tip on the pre-tax bill when the party is 8 people or more. Last night, 10 friends went out to dinner and decided to split the bill evenly. If the bill without tax or tip was $105.58 and the tax was 5%, how much did each person owe? Round to the nearest cent as needed.

3-3 Simple Interest

Vocabulary
balance, interest, interest rate, principal, simple interest

CCSS: 7.RP.A.2, 7.RP.A.3

Key Concept

When you deposit money in a bank account, the bank pays you **interest** for the right to use your money for a period of time.

Simple Interest Formula: $I = p \cdot r \cdot t$

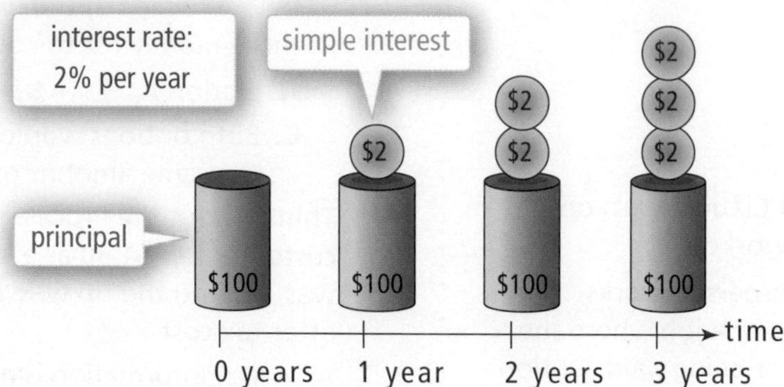

Principal (p) is the original amount of money deposited.

Interest is calculated based on a percent of the principal. That percent is called the **interest rate** (r).

Time (t) is the number of years money is deposited.

Simple interest (I) is interest calculated only on the principal.

Part 1

Example Understanding the Simple Interest Formula

Suppose you deposit $400 in a savings account and keep it in the bank for 6 years. The annual interest rate is 5%. Identify each value in the simple interest formula.

continued on next page >

Part 1

Example continued

Words Interest is principal times rate times time

to

Equation

Solution

Words Interest is principal times rate times time

Equation

$I = p \cdot r \cdot t$

$120 = 400 \cdot 0.05 \cdot 6$

Substitute $p = 400$, $r = 0.05$, and $t = 6$, then multiply, $I = 120$.

Part 2

Intro

The principal in an account plus the accumulated interest is the **balance**.

balance = principal + interest

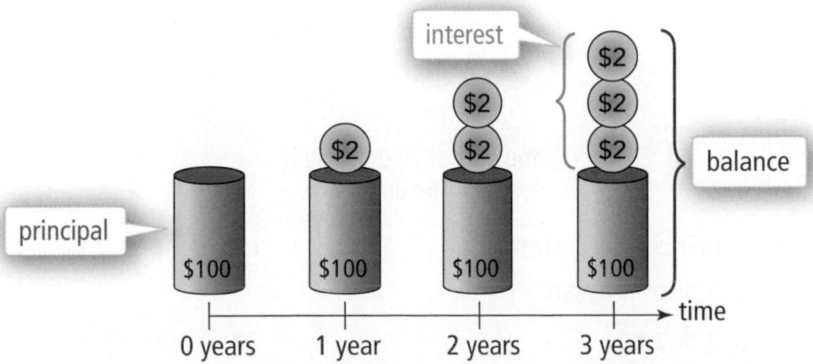

Part 2

Example Calculating Simple Interest

A bank manager wants to encourage customers to open a certificate of deposit (CD) account. He decides to make a poster to show how much interest a CD earns over time. Help the manager complete the table.

If you deposit \$2,500 at 3.5% annual interest...		
Time (years)	**Simple Interest Earned**	**New Account Balance**
0	■	■
1	■	■
2	■	■
3	■	■
4	■	■

Solution

Time: 0 years

$$I = p \cdot r \cdot t$$
$$= 2{,}500 \cdot 3.5\% \cdot 0$$
$$= 2{,}500 \cdot 0.035 \cdot 0$$
$$= 0$$

$3.5\% = \frac{3.5}{100} = 0.035$

Balance = principal + interest
= 2,500 + 0
= 2,500

Time: 1 year

$$I = p \cdot r \cdot t$$
$$= 2{,}500 \cdot 0.035 \cdot 1$$
$$= 87.50$$

You earn \$87.50 in simple interest after one year.

Balance = principal + interest
= 2,500 + 87.50
= 2,587.50

continued on next page >

Part 2

Solution continued

Time: 2 years

$$I = p \cdot r \cdot t$$
$$= 2{,}500 \cdot 0.035 \cdot 2$$
$$= 175$$

You earn $175 in simple interest after two years.

Balance = principal + interest
= 2,500 + 175
= 2,675

Time: 3 years

$$I = p \cdot r \cdot t$$
$$= 2{,}500 \cdot 0.035 \cdot 3$$
$$= 262.50$$

You earn $262.50 in simple interest after three years.

Balance = principal + interest
= 2,500 + 262.50
= 2,762.50

Time: 4 years

$$I = p \cdot r \cdot t$$
$$= 2{,}500 \cdot 0.035 \cdot 4$$
$$= 350$$

You earn $350 in simple interest after four years.

Balance = principal + interest
= 2,500 + 350

If you deposit $2,500 at 3.5% annual interest...

Time (years)	Simple Interest Earned	New Account Balance
0	$0.00	$2500.00
1	$87.50	$2,587.50
2	$175.00	$2,675.00
3	$262.50	$2,762.50
4	$350.00	$2,850.00

Part 3

Intro

In some situations, interest is accumulated on a monthly basis.

When r is an annual interest rate in the formula $I = p \cdot r \cdot t$, time t is in years.

To find how much interest you have after 3 months, you need to convert months to years.

$$t = \frac{3}{12}$$
$$= \frac{1}{4}$$

3 months' time

12 months in a year

Example Calculating Simple Interest for Partial Years

After 8 months, does Mia still have the higher balance? Explain.

Name on Account: Alex

Principal: $2,950

Annual interest rate: 4%

Name on Account: Mia

Principal: $3,000

Annual interest rate: 2.5%

Solution

Time: 8 months

or $\frac{8}{12}$ years

$$I = p \cdot r \cdot t$$
$$= 2{,}950 \cdot 4\% \cdot \frac{8}{12}$$
$$= 2{,}950 \cdot 0.04 \cdot \frac{2}{3}$$
$$= 118 \cdot \frac{2}{3}$$
$$\approx 78.67$$

After 8 months Alex has earned about $78.67 in interest.

$$I = p \cdot r \cdot t$$
$$= 3{,}000 \cdot 2.5\% \cdot \frac{8}{12}$$
$$= 3{,}000 \cdot 0.025 \cdot \frac{2}{3}$$
$$= 75 \cdot \frac{2}{3}$$
$$= 50$$

After 8 months Mia has earned $50 in interest.

Balance = principal + interest
= 2,950 + 78.67
= 3,028.67

After 8 months Alex has $3,028.67.

Balance = principal + interest
= 3,000 + 50
= 3,050

After 8 months Mia has $3,050.

Yes, Mia still has the higher balance after 8 months.

Digital Resources   

1. To find simple interest, you multiply the principal (in dollars), the interest rate (as a decimal), and the time in years. The equation $24.00 = 400 \cdot 0.015 \cdot 4$ shows how to find the simple interest for a certain account after 4 years.
   a. What is the interest rate (as a percent)?
   A. 0.015% **B.** 400%
   C. 1.5% **D.** 24.00%
   b. How much is the simple interest?
   A. \$4 **B.** \$1.50
   C. \$24.00 **D.** \$400
   c. What is the principal?
   A. \$4 **B.** \$24.00
   C. \$400 **D.** \$1.50

2. Suppose you deposited \$100 in a savings account 4 years ago. The simple interest rate is 2.2%. The interest that you earned in those 4 years is \$8.80.

   Which of the following is/are true? Select all that apply.

   A. $r = 2.2\%$ **B.** $p = 100$
   C. $I = 4$ **D.** $t = 8.80$

3. An account has a principal of \$500 and a simple interest rate of 3.3%. **Figure 1** below shows the simple interest earned and the new account balance for 1, 2, and 3 years. Complete the table in **Figure 1** for the fourth year.

4. If the simple interest on \$2,000 for 2 years is \$320, then what is the interest rate?

5. Edward deposited \$6,000 into a savings account 4 years ago. The simple interest rate is 3%.
   a. How much money did Edward earn in interest?
   b. What would be his new account balance?

6. **Think About the Process** You deposit \$2,900 into a bank account with a simple interest rate of 10%.
   a. How do you find your account balance after 5 years?
   A. First use $I = prt$ to find the simple interest earned after 5 years. Then add that to the rate.
   B. First use $I = prt$ to find the simple interest earned after 5 years. Then add that to the time.
   C. First use $I = prt$ to find the simple interest earned after 5 years. Then subtract that from the principal.
   D. First use $I = prt$ to find the simple interest earned after 5 years. Then add that to the principal.
   b. What will your account balance be after 5 years?

(Figure 1)

Interest Earned

Time (years)	Simple Interest Earned (\$)	New Account Balance (\$)
1	16.50	516.50
2	33.00	533.00
3	49.50	549.50
4	■	■

7. **Reasoning** Tommy earned $76.00 in interest after 5 years on a principal of $400. His simple interest rate is 3.8%. Jane earned $82.00 in interest after 2 years on a principal of $1,000. Her simple interest rate is 4.1%. Which bank would you rather use, Tommy's or Jane's?

   A. Tommy's because his bank paid more interest.

   B. Jane's because her bank offers a better interest rate.

   C. Tommy's because his investment took less time.

   D. Jane's because her bank accepted a smaller principal.

8. **Writing** After 21 months, Louis earned $25.90 in simple interest at a rate of 3.7%. Mia earned $16.63 in simple interest at a rate of 1.9%.

   a. Whose account has the greater principal?

   b. Which has a greater affect on the amount of simple interest earned, doubling the interest rate on the principal amount, or doubling the principal amount for a given interest rate? Explain.

9. **Advertising** A bank manager wants to encourage new customers to open accounts with principals of at least $3,000. He decides to make a poster advertising a simple interest rate of 4.8%.

   a. What must the principal be if the bank manager also wants to advertise that one can earn $10 the first month?

   b. Can the poster correctly say, "Open an account of $3,000 and earn at least $10 interest in 1 month!"?

10. Suppose you deposit $600 in a bank account with a simple interest rate of 3.3%. You want to keep your deposit in the bank long enough to earn at least $100 in interest. For how many years should you keep your deposit in the bank?

11. Suppose you have two savings accounts earning simple interest. For each account, the bank will calculate the amount of the interest each month. Account A has a principal of $700 with an interest rate of 3.0%. Account B has a principal of $1,400 with an interest rate of 1.5%. Which account will earn $150 in simple interest first?

    a. Account B

    b. Both accounts will earn $150 at the same time.

    c. Account A

12. **Think About the Process** You deposit $800 into a savings account that earns simple interest. After 5 years your balance is $960.

    a. Which step do you need to do first to find the interest rate?

    A. Add the principal to the account balance to find the simple interest earned.

    B. Subtract the principal from the account balance to find the simple interest earned.

    C. Divide the account balance by the principal to get the interest rate.

    D. Use the formula $I = prt$ to substitute and solve for the interest rate.

    b. What is the simple interest rate of your savings account?

13. **Challenge** Johnny and Carolyn have three savings plans, each earning simple interest. The passbook savings account has a principal of $840 and an interest rate of 4.68%. The CD (Certificate of Deposit) has a principal of $600 and an interest rate of 6.26%. The money-market certificate has a principal of $700 and an interest rate of 5.60%. Which of the savings plans earns the most simple interest in 21 months?

    A. passbook savings

    B. CD

    C. money-market

3-4 Compound Interest

CCSS: 7.NS.A.3

Part 1

Intro

Simple interest is calculated on the principal. **Compound interest** is calculated on the balance.

After 0 years When you first make the deposit, no interest is earned. The balance is equal to the principal.

balance = principal

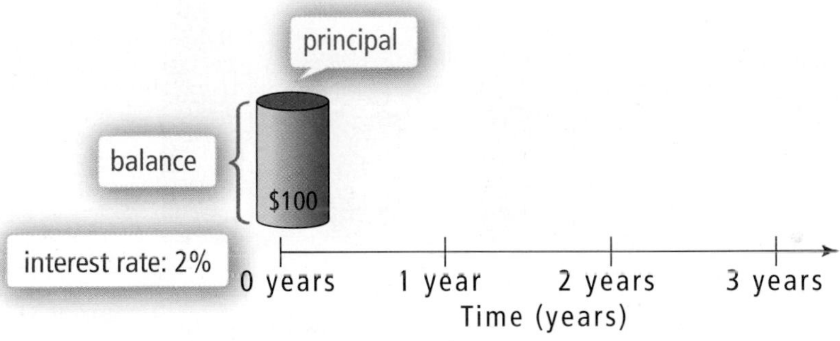

After 1 year After 1 year, compound interest and simple interest are equal.

$$\begin{aligned} \text{first year compound interest} &= \text{simple interest} \\ &= p \cdot r \cdot t \\ &= 100 \cdot 2\% \cdot 1 \\ &= 2 \end{aligned}$$

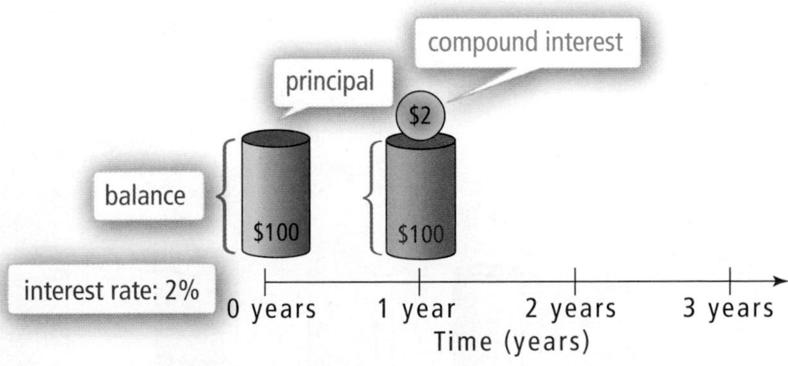

continued on next page >

Part 1

Intro continued

After 2 years After the second year, compound interest is calculated on the balance in the account, which is the principal plus the first year's interest.

compound interest = rate · balance

= 2% · (100 + 2)

= 2% · (102)

= 2.04

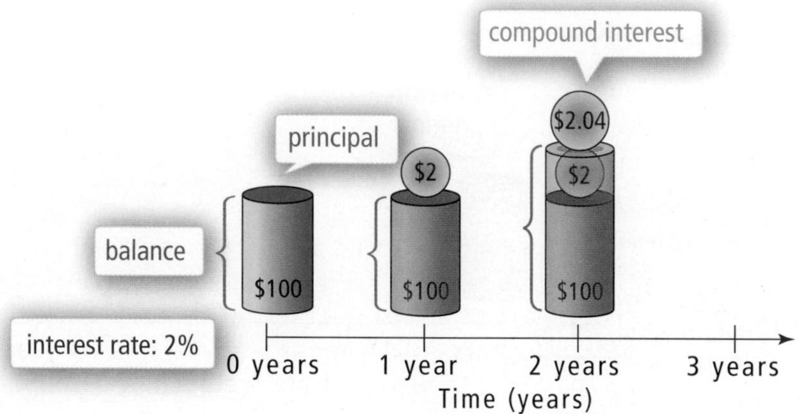

After 3 years After the third year, compound interest is calculated on the balance in the account, which is the principal plus the first and second year's interest.

compound interest = rate · balance

= 2% · (100 + 2 + 2.04)

= 2% · (104.04)

≈ 2.08

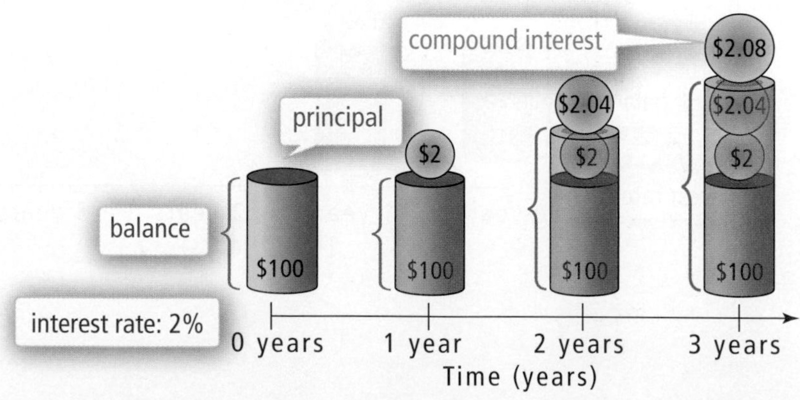

Part 1

Example Calculating Compound Interest Using a Chart

Suppose you deposit \$200 in a savings account that earns an annual interest rate of 1%, compounded annually (once per year). What is the final balance in your account after 4 years? Round to the nearest cent.

Solution

The principal is \$200.

The annual interest rate is 1%, or 0.01, compounded annually.

Compound Interest = Balance · interest rate

Final Balance = Previous Final Balance + Compound Interest

Time (years)	Compound Interest (\$)	Final Balance (\$)
0	none	200.00
1	$200.00 \cdot 0.01 = 2.00$	$200.00 + 2.00 = 202.00$
2	$202.00 \cdot 0.01 = 2.02$	$202.00 + 2.02 = 204.02$
3	$204.02 \cdot 0.01 \approx 2.04$	$204.02 + 2.04 = 206.06$
4	$206.06 \cdot 0.01 \approx 2.06$	$206.06 + 2.06 = 208.12$

So, the final balance in your account after 4 years is \$208.12.

Part 2

Intro

You can find the final balance of an account that earns compound interest by using the compound interest formula. The formula is shown here for the case of an annual interest rate compounded once per year. For this case, n is the number of years the account earns interest.

Compound Interest Formula, for annual interest compounded once a year:

$$B = p(1 + r)^n$$

final balance (B); principal (p); annual interest rate (r); number of years (n)

Part 2

Example Using the Compound Interest Formula

When Ed was born, Aunt Edna opened a money market account for him. The principal is $1,000 and will earn 5% interest, compounded annually.

Use the compound interest formula to find how much Ed would have after 10 years, 20 years, and 30 years. Round to the nearest dollar.

Solution

The principal is $1,000 and the rate is 5% so $p = 1000$ and $r = 5\%$.

After 10 years:

$$\begin{aligned} B &= p(1 + r)^n \\ &= 1{,}000(1 + 5\%)^{10} \\ &= 1{,}000(1 + 0.05)^{10} \\ &= 1{,}000(1.05)^{10} \\ &\approx 1{,}000(1.629) \\ &= 1{,}629 \end{aligned}$$

The balance after 10 years is $1,629.

After 20 years:

$$\begin{aligned} B &= p(1 + r)^n \\ &= 1{,}000(1 + 5\%)^{20} \\ &= 1{,}000(1 + 0.05)^{20} \\ &= 1{,}000(1.05)^{20} \\ &\approx 1{,}000(2.653) \\ &= 2{,}653 \end{aligned}$$

The balance after 20 years is $2,653.

After 30 years:

$$\begin{aligned} B &= p(1 + r)^n \\ &= 1{,}000(1 + 5\%)^{30} \\ &= 1{,}000(1 + 0.05)^{30} \\ &= 1{,}000(1.05)^{30} \\ &\approx 1{,}000(4.322) \\ &= 4{,}322 \end{aligned}$$

The balance after 30 years is $4,322.

Key Concept

You can also use the compound interest formula when interest is compounded more than once a year.

Compound Interest formula:

$$B = p(1 + r)^n$$

final balance (B), principal (p), interest rate for interest period (r), number of interest periods (n)

The principal amount is represented by the variable p.

The **interest period** is the length of time on which compound interest is based. The total number of interest periods that you keep the money in the account is represented by the variable n.

Interest rates are usually given as annual rates. The interest rate, r, for an interest period of less than a year is the annual interest rate divided by the number of interest periods per year.

$$r = \frac{\text{annual interest rate}}{\text{number of interest periods per year}}$$

The final balance, B, is equal to the principal plus the interest compounded over n interest periods.

Part 3

Example Finding the Total Balance of a Loan

Find the total balance owed on a 5-year, $1,000 loan that charges a 6% annual interest rate compounded every 4 months. Round to the nearest dollar.

continued on next page >

Part 3

Example continued

Solution

Know	Need	Plan
• \$1,000 principal • 6% annual interest • compounded every 4 months for 5 years	The final balance owed	• Find interest rate, r, for the interest period. • Find the total number of interest periods, n. • Calculate balance owed using the compound interest formula.

Step 1 To find r, find the number of interest periods in one year.

$$\text{Number of interest periods per year} = \frac{12}{4} = 3$$

12 months per year

interest period is 4 months

$$r = \frac{\text{annual interest rate}}{\text{number of interest periods per year}}$$

$$= \frac{6\%}{3}$$

$$= \frac{0.06}{3}$$

$$= 0.02$$

Step 2 Find the total number of interest periods.

$$n = \text{number of interest periods per year} \cdot \text{number of years invested}$$

$$= 3 \cdot 5$$

$$= 15$$

Step 3 Find the balance.

Use the compound interest formula.	$B = p(1 + r)^n$
Substitute: p = 1,000, r = 0.02, n = 15.	$= 1{,}000(1 + 0.02)^{15}$
Add.	$= 1{,}000(1.02)^{15}$
Simplify $(1.02)^{15}$.	$\approx 1{,}000(1.346)$
Multiply.	$= 1{,}346$

The total balance owed after 5 years is about \$1,346.

3-4 | Homework

Digital Resources   

1. Robert deposits \$300.00 in a savings account that earns 5% interest compounded annually. **Figure 1** shows the compound interest and the final balance for 3 years. Find the compound interest and account balance for year 4 to complete the table.

2. Randall deposits \$400 in an account that earns 5% interest compounded annually. Teresa deposits the same amount into an account that earns 5% simple interest. Which account will have a greater balance after 2 years?

A. Teresa's account balance is greater.

B. Randall's account balance is greater.

C. After 2 years, Randall's and Teresa's account balances are equal.

3. Suppose that \$9,000 is invested in an account at 6% interest. Find the account balance after 7 years if the interest is compounded annually.

4. A company will need \$50,000 in 6 years for a new addition. To meet this goal, the company deposits money in an account today that pays 5% interest compounded annually. Find the amount to the nearest hundred dollars that should be invested to total \$50,000 in 6 years.

5. a. What is the value of a \$5,000 investment after 6 years at 4% interest compounded quarterly?

b. How much interest does the investment earn?

6. Reasoning Two bank accounts open on the same day with original deposits of \$725. The first account earns 2% interest compounded annually. The second account earns 2% simple interest.

a. What is the balance of the first account after 1 year?

b. What is the balance of the second account after 1 year?

c. Which account will have a greater balance after 1 year?

A. The first account.

B. The second account.

C. They will have the same balance.

7. Think About the Process Use the information in the table to find the account balance after 7 years.

Principal	Rate	Compounded	Time
\$27,000	5%	annually	7 years

a. What is a good first step in finding the account balance?

A. Divide the annual interest rate by 100.

B. Divide the principal by the number of years.

C. Divide the annual interest rate by 12.

D. Multiply the annual interest rate by the number of years.

b. What is the account balance after 7 years?

(Figure 1)

Account Balance

Time (years)	Compound Interest	Final Balance (dollars)
0	(none)	300.00
1	$300.00 \cdot 0.05 = 15.00$	$300.00 + 15.00 = 315.00$
2	$315.00 \cdot 0.05 = 15.75$	$315.00 + 15.75 = 330.75$
3	$300.75 \cdot 0.05 = 16.54$	$330.75 + 16.54 = 347.29$
4	■	■

8. **Open-Ended** A bank account earns 4% interest compounded annually on an original deposit of $600. Find the account balance after 30 years. Round to the nearest dollar as needed.

9. **Savings Account** Kelly opened a savings account 13 years ago. She has not made any deposits or withdrawals since. The account earned 4% interest compounded annually. The account balance is now $1,166. Find Kelly's original deposit. Round to the nearest dollar as needed.

10. **Error Analysis** Isamu deposits $175 in an account that pays 3% interest compounded monthly. Isamu incorrectly claims that the account balance will be $250 after 1 year.

    a. What will be the account balance after 1 year? Round to the nearest dollar as needed.

    b. What error did Isamu likely make?

    A. Isamu computed the balance for interest compounded annually, not monthly.

    B. Isamu found the balance for simple interest, not for compound interest.

    C. Isamu used the annual interest, not the interest per period, to find the balance.

    D. Isamu used the percent interest, not the decimal interest, to find the balance.

11. **Writing** An investor considers two investment bonds. One $8,000 bond offers 9% interest compounded annually for 10 years. Another $8,000 bond offers 9% interest compounded quarterly for 10 years.

    a. How much more interest would the investor earn from the bond with quarterly compounding? Round to the nearest dollar as needed.

    b. Explain how to find the interest rate the bond with annual compounding would have to offer so the interest earned would be the same for both bonds.

12. After 30 years earning 5% interest compounded annually, the balance of a savings account is $45,880. What was the original deposit in the account to the nearest hundred dollars?

    A. $10,500 **B.** $10,400

    C. $10,700 **D.** $10,600

13. **Think About the Process** An account balance is $18,000 after 17 years with 7% interest compounded annually.

    a. You want to find the original deposit. Which formula will help you solve this problem?

    A. $p = \dfrac{B}{(1 + r)^n}$ **B.** $p = \dfrac{B}{r^n}$

    C. $p = B(1 + r)^n$ **D.** $p = \dfrac{r^n}{B}$

    b. About how much was the original deposit?

14. **Challenge** When Sam started working at age 20, he began saving $100 per month. He did this for 10 years. At the end of 10 years, this money had earned an additional $7,000 in interest. Sam then invested the savings and interest at 6% interest compounded annually, until age 60. How much money did he have at age 60? Round to the nearest hundred dollars as needed.

15. **Challenge** A $20,000 deposit earns 3.6% interest for 3 years.

    a. What is the final account balance if the interest is compounded semiannually? Round to the nearest dollar as needed.

    b. What is the final account balance if the interest is compounded quarterly?

    c. What is the final account balance if the interest is compounded monthly?

3-5 Percent Increase and Decrease

Vocabulary
percent decrease, percent increase, percent of change

CCSS: 7.RP.A.2, 7.RP.A.3

Key Concept

You can use a percent to describe how much something has increased or decreased.

A **percent of change** describes how much a quantity has changed, expressed as a percent of the original quantity.

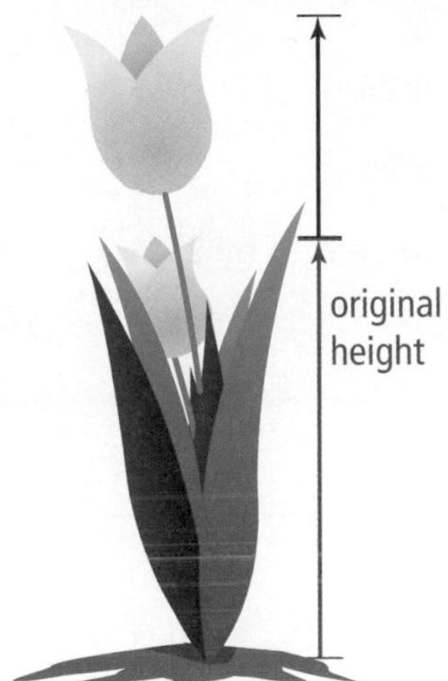

$$\text{part} = \text{percent} \cdot \text{whole}$$

$$\text{amount of change} = \text{percent of change} \cdot \text{original quantity}$$

$$\text{percent of change} = \frac{\text{amount of change}}{\text{original quantity}}$$

When a quantity increases, the percent of change is called a **percent increase**.

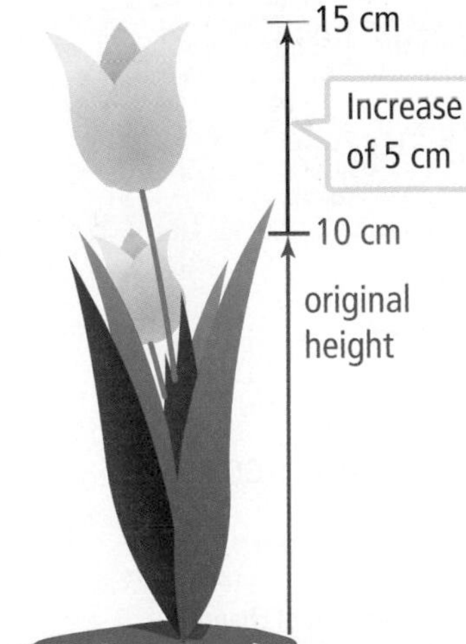

$$\text{percent of change} = \frac{\text{amount of change}}{\text{original quantity}}$$

$$\begin{aligned}\text{percent increase} &= \frac{5}{10}\\ &= \frac{1}{2}\\ &= 0.5\\ &= 50\%\end{aligned}$$

The height of the flower increased by 50%.

continued on next page >

Key Concept

continued

When a quantity decreases, the percent of change is called a **percent decrease**.

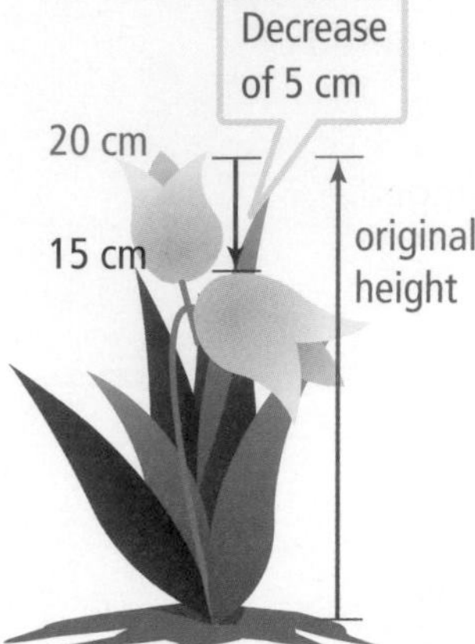

$$\text{percent of change} = \frac{\text{amount of change}}{\text{original quantity}}$$

$$\begin{aligned}\text{percent decrease} &= \frac{5}{20} \\ &= \frac{1}{4} \\ &= 0.25 \\ &= 25\%\end{aligned}$$

The height of the flower decreased by 25%.

Part 1

Example Finding Percent Increase

Identify the percent increase in each situation.

Month 1 record:	15 push-ups	100 crunches
Month 2 record:	30 push-ups	114 crunches
	■ % increase	■ % increase

Solution

Push-Ups

$$\begin{aligned}\text{amount of change} &= 30 - 15 \\ &= 15\end{aligned}$$

$$\begin{aligned}\text{percent increase} &= \frac{\text{amount of change}}{\text{original quantity}} \\ &= \frac{15}{15} = 1 \\ &= 100\%\end{aligned}$$

Crunches

$$\begin{aligned}\text{amount of change} &= 114 - 100 \\ &= 14\end{aligned}$$

$$\begin{aligned}\text{percent increase} &= \frac{\text{amount of change}}{\text{original quantity}} \\ &= \frac{14}{100} \\ &= 14\%\end{aligned}$$

Part 2

Example Finding Percent Decrease

The force of gravity on the Moon is different from the force of gravity on Earth. This means that an object has a different weight on the Moon than it does on Earth. By what percent does an astronaut's weight decrease on the Moon?

Astronaut Weight (lb)

On Earth	On the Moon
154	25.5

Solution

The astronaut's weight decreased from **154 lb** on the Earth to **25.5 lb** on the Moon.

$$\text{amount of change} = 154 - 25.5$$
$$= 128.5$$

decrease of 128.5 lb

$$\text{percent decrease} = \frac{\text{amount of change}}{\text{original quantity}}$$
$$= \frac{128.5}{154}$$
$$\approx 0.8344$$
$$= 83.44\%$$

The astronaut's weight decreased by about 83.4% on the Moon.

Part 3

Example Estimating Percent of Change

Estimate the percent of change for each Round.

a.

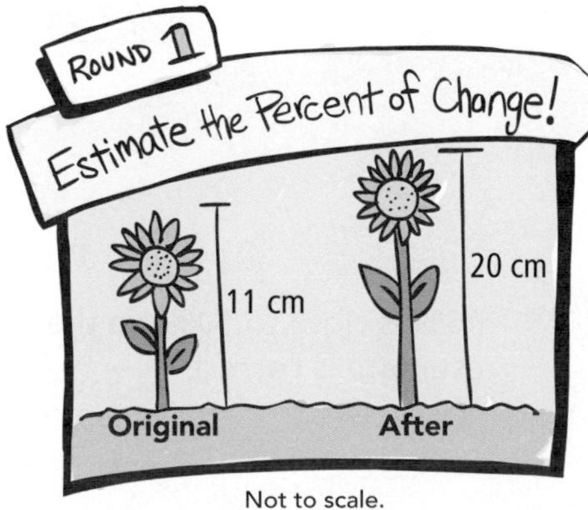

Not to scale.

b.

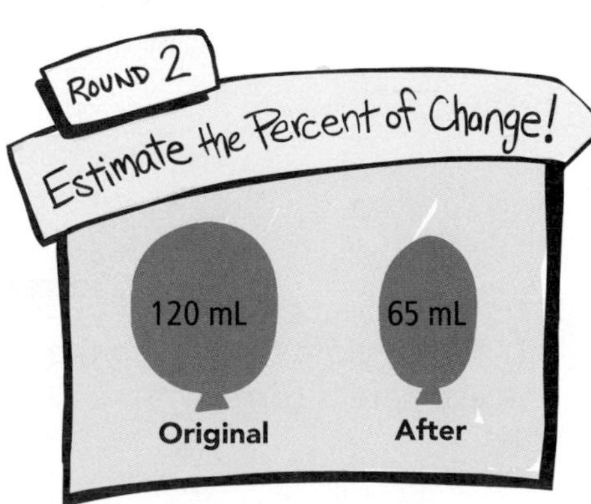

continued on next page >

Part 3

Example continued

Solution

a.

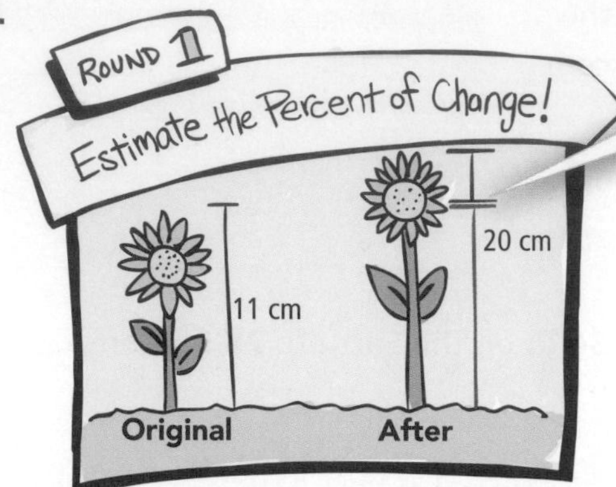

The sunflower grew by adding about three-fourths of its original size, so the percent of change is about a 75% increase.

b.

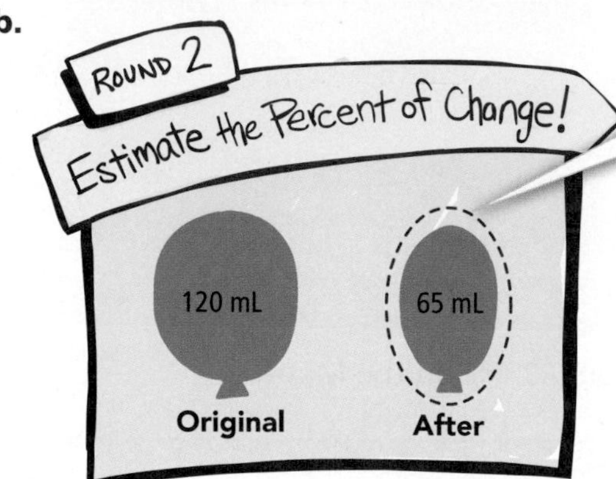

The balloon shrank by losing about half of its original size, so the percent of change is about a 50% decrease.

Check

a. $\text{percent of change} = \frac{\text{amount of change}}{\text{original quantity}}$

$= \frac{20 - 11}{11}$

$= \frac{9}{11}$

≈ 0.82

$= 82\%$ increase ✓

82% is close to 75%, so the estimate is correct.

b. $\text{percent of change} = \frac{\text{amount of change}}{\text{original quantity}}$

$= \frac{120 - 65}{120}$

$= \frac{55}{120}$

≈ 0.46

$= 46\%$ decrease ✓

46% is close to 50%, so the estimate is correct.

1. If the original quantity is 10 and the new quantity is 13, what is the percent increase?
2. Craig likes to collect records. Last year he had 10 records in his collection. Now he has 12 records. What is the percent increase of his collection?
3. If the original quantity is 5 and the new quantity is 3, what is the percent decrease?
4. At noon, a tank contained 10 cm of water. After several hours, it contained 7 cm of water. What is the percent decrease of water in the tank?
5. **Estimation** Suppose the original quantity is 13 and the new quantity is 1.
   a. Which of these is the best estimate for the percent change?
   A. 50% **B.** 25%
   C. 100% **D.** 75%
   b. Is this an example of a percent increase or a percent decrease?
6. If the original quantity is 15 and the new quantity is 19, which of these is the best estimate for the percent change?
   A. 50% increase
   B. 100% decrease
   C. 75% increase
   D. 25% increase
7. Last year, the Debate Club had 7 members. This year there are 12 members in the club. Which of these is the best estimate for the percent change in the number of club members?
   A. 25% increase
   B. 100% decrease
   C. 75% increase
   D. 50% decrease
8. Jake ordered 23 large pizzas for a party. When the party was over he had 6 large pizzas remaining. Estimate the percent change in the number of large pizzas.
   A. 100% decrease
   B. 25% increase
   C. 50% increase
   D. 75% decrease
9. **a. Writing** If the original quantity is 25 and the new quantity is 50, what is the percent increase?
   b. Explain what operation is equivalent to finding this new quantity. Write the explanation as an expression.
10. **Money** A savings account increases from \$250 to \$270. What is the percent increase of the savings account?
11. **Think About the Process** Suppose the original quantity is 175 and the new quantity is 126.
   a. What expression represents the percent decrease?
   A. $\frac{126 - 175}{175}$
   B. $\frac{175 - 126}{175}$
   C. $\frac{126 - 175}{126}$
   D. $\frac{175 - 126}{126}$
   b. What is the percent decrease?

12. **Error Analysis** The original quantity is 24 and the new quantity is 6. Karen incorrectly says the percent decrease is about 60.00%.

   a. What is the correct percent decrease?

   b. What error did Karen likely make?

   A. She divided the difference of the two quantities by the product of the two quantities.

   B. She divided the difference of the two quantities by the sum of the two quantities.

   C. She divided the difference of the two quantities by the new quantity.

   D. She divided the new quantity by the original quantity.

13. **Reasoning** This week, 973 people went to the beach. Last week, 1,189 people went to the beach.

   a. The number of people who went to the beach fell by what percent? Round to the nearest tenth of a percent as needed.

   b. Explain how you know whether the answer is greater than or less than 25%.

14. **Think About the Process** Suppose the original quantity is 75 and the new quantity is 105.

   a. What should be the first step in solving for the percent increase?

   A. Find the difference between the new quantity and the original quantity.

   B. Find the sum of the original quantity and the new quantity.

   C. Find what percent the original quantity is of the new quantity.

   D. Divide the new quantity by the original quantity.

   b. What is the percent increase?

15. **a. Mental Math** If the original quantity is 14 and the new quantity is 22, which of these is the best estimate for the percent change?

   A. 100% increase

   B. 50% increase

   C. 75% decrease

   D. 25% increase

   b. Explain how you can use mental math to find an estimate for the percent change.

16. Cari is searching online for airline tickets. Two weeks ago, the cost to fly from Boston to Denver was $300. Now the cost is $375.

   a. What is the percent increase? Round to the nearest percent as needed.

   b. What would be the percent increase if the airline charges an additional $50 baggage fee with the new ticket price?

17. On Monday, a museum had 150 visitors. On Tuesday, it had 260 visitors.

   a. Estimate the percent change in the number of visitors to the museum.

   b. Estimate how many people would have to visit the museum on Wednesday to have the same estimated percent change between Tuesday and Wednesday as between Monday and Tuesday. Explain your answer.

18. **Challenge** The seventh-grade class is raising money to have a class trip at the end of the year. They began the year with $1,500. Now they have $1,650 in the account.

   a. What is the percent increase for the money the class has raised?

   b. The class figured out that if there is a percent increase of 99% from the beginning of the year, they will have enough to pay for every student. How much money will they need to pay for every student?

3-6 Markups and Markdowns

Vocabulary
markdown,
markup

CCSS: 7.RP.A.3

Part 1

Intro

Markup is the amount of increase from the cost to the selling price.

$$\text{markup} = \text{selling price} - \text{cost}$$
$$= 28 - 16$$
$$= 12$$

The markup is $12. You can represent the amount of markup as a percent increase.

$$\text{markup} = 12$$

$$\text{percent increase} = \frac{\text{amount of change}}{\text{original quantity}}$$

$$\text{percent markup} = \frac{\text{markup}}{\text{cost}}$$
$$= \frac{12}{16}$$
$$= \frac{3}{4}, \text{ or } 75\%$$

There is a 75% markup on the shirt.

Example Calculating Percent Markup

What is the percent markup for each item? Round to the nearest percent.

Cost and Selling Prices

	Notebook	Bicycle	Car
Cost	$0.25	$180	$8,000
Selling price	$1.50	$300	$12,000

Solution

Step 1 Find the markup.

mark up = selling price − cost

$= 1.50 - 0.25$ | $= 300 - 180$ | $= 12{,}000 - 8{,}000$

$= 1.25$ | $= 120$ | $= 4{,}000$

continued on next page >

Part 1

Solution continued

Step 2 Find the percent markup.

$$\text{percent markup} = \frac{\text{markup}}{\text{cost}}$$

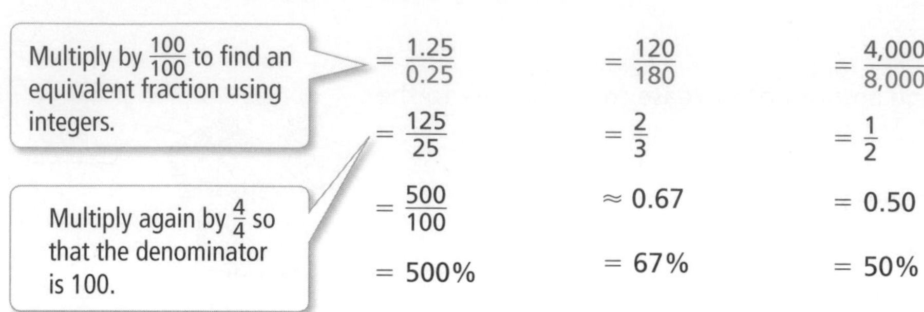

Multiply by $\frac{100}{100}$ to find an equivalent fraction using integers.

Multiply again by $\frac{4}{4}$ so that the denominator is 100.

$$= \frac{1.25}{0.25} \qquad = \frac{120}{180} \qquad = \frac{4{,}000}{8{,}000}$$

$$= \frac{125}{25} \qquad = \frac{2}{3} \qquad = \frac{1}{2}$$

$$= \frac{500}{100} \qquad \approx 0.67 \qquad = 0.50$$

$$= 500\% \qquad = 67\% \qquad = 50\%$$

The percent markups are 500% for the notebook, about 67% for the bicycle, and 50% for the car.

Part 2

Intro

Markdown is the amount of decrease from the selling price to the sale price.

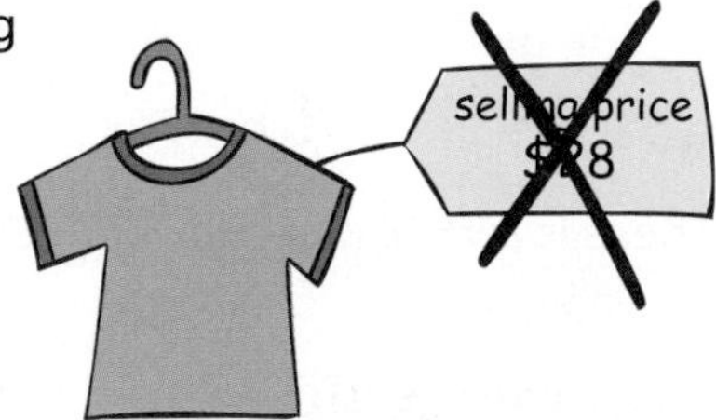

$$\text{markup} = \text{selling price} - \text{sale price}$$
$$= 28 - 21$$
$$= 7$$

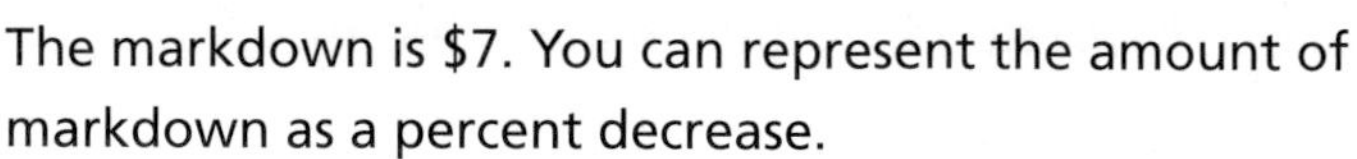

The markdown is $7. You can represent the amount of markdown as a percent decrease.

$$\text{markdown} = 7$$

$$\text{percent decrease} = \frac{\text{amount of change}}{\text{original quantity}}$$

$$\text{percent markdown} = \frac{\text{markdown}}{\text{selling price}}$$

$$= \frac{7}{28}$$

$$= \frac{1}{4}, \text{ or } 25\%$$

There is a 25% markdown on the shirt.

Part 2

Example Calculating Percent Markdown

Five years ago, a furniture store bought sofas for $835 each. What is the greatest whole percent that the manager can decrease the price of the sofa without losing money?

Solution

Know
- original cost = $835
- selling price = $1,599

Need
Greatest percent markdown without losing money

Plan
- Find the greatest markdown possible.
- Then find the greatest percent markdown possible.

Step 1 Find the greatest markdown possible without losing money.

The sale price of the sofa cannot be lower than the cost that the store bought it for. So the greatest markdown is the number that brings the price down to the original cost.

greatest markdown = selling price − cost

$= 1{,}559 - 835$

$= 764$

A markdown of more than $764 would lose the store money on the sale of the sofa.

continued on next page >

Part 2

Solution continued

Step 2 Find the greatest percent markdown possible.

$$\text{greatest percent markdown} = \frac{\text{greatest markdown}}{\text{selling price}}$$
$$= \frac{764}{1,599}$$
$$\approx 0.478$$
$$= 47.8\%$$

A markdown of more than **47.8%** would lose the store money on the sale of the sofa.

The greatest whole percent markdown that the manager can discount the sofa is 47% because 48% is greater than 0.478.

Key Concept

markup = selling price − cost

$$\text{percent markup} = \frac{\text{markup}}{\text{cost}}$$

markup = selling price − sale price

$$\text{percent markup} = \frac{\text{markdown}}{\text{selling price}}$$

Part 3

Example Calculating Profit After Percent Markdowns

Relax Yoga Store buys yoga mats for $15 each. The store has a sale the following week. Does the store still make a profit on each mat during the sale? If so, how much of a profit?

Solution

Know
- cost = $15
- selling price = $38.99
- percent markdown = 20%

Need

To find whether Relax Yoga Store profits from selling each yoga mat during the sale

Plan
- Find the sale price.
- Then find the markup from the cost to the sale price.

Step 1 Find the markdown.

$$\text{percent markdown} = \frac{\text{markdown}}{\text{selling price}}, \text{ or}$$

$$\begin{aligned}\text{markdown} &= \text{percent markdown} \cdot \text{selling price}\\ &= 20\% \cdot 38.99\\ &= 0.20 \cdot 38.99\\ &\approx 7.80\end{aligned}$$

Rewrite the formula for percent markdown, to solve for markdown.

The yoga mat is marked down by $7.80 during the sale.

continued on next page >

Part 3

Solution continued

Step 2 Find the sale price.

sale price = selling price − markdown

= 38.99 − 7.80

= 31.19

The sale price is \$31.19. This is still greater than the cost of \$15.

Step 3 Find the markup from cost to the sale price.

This is the store's profit on each yoga mat sold.

markup = sale price − cost

= 31.19 − 15.00

= 16.19

Yes, Relax Yoga Store still makes a profit of \$16.19 on each mat during the 20% off sale.

Digital Resources   

1. A computer store bought a program at a cost of $10 and sold it at a selling price of $13. Find the percent markup. Round to the nearest whole number.
2. A music store bought a CD set at a cost of $20. When the store sold the CD set, the percent markup was 40%. Find the selling price.
3. A store bought 500 toys at a cost of $20 each. The store sold all the toys at a percent markup of 40%. Find the total selling price.
4. During a sale, a dress is marked down from a selling price of $60 to a sale price of $57. What is the percent markdown?
5. A $300 suit is marked down by 20%. Find the sale price. Round to the nearest dollar as needed.
6. An exercise machine with an original selling price of $830 is marked down by 24%. What is the sale price of the exercise machine?
7. The selling price of an item is $650. It is marked down by 10%, but this sale price is still marked up from the cost of $450. Find the markup from cost to sale price.
8. The selling price of an item is $600. After 6 months of not selling, it is marked down by 30%. After another 6 months of not selling, it is further marked down by 20%. Find the sale price after both markdowns.
9. **Error Analysis** A store is instructed by corporate headquarters to put a markup of 11% on all items. An item costing $27 is displayed by the store manager at a selling price of $3. As an employee, you notice that this selling price is incorrect.
   - **a.** Find the correct selling price. Round to the nearest dollar as needed.
   - **b.** What was the manager's likely error?
     - **A.** The manager set the selling price at the cost.
     - **B.** The manager added to markup to the cost instead of subtracting it.
     - **C.** The manger subtracted the markup from the cost instead of adding it.
     - **D.** The manger set the selling price at the markup.
10. **Computer Sale** A computer store buys a computer system at a cost of $465.60. The selling price was set at $776, but after a year the computer did not sell. The store then advertises a 40% markdown on the $776 computer system. Find the sale price. Round to the nearest cent.
11. **Multiple Representations** A store advertises a 20% markdown on a dishwasher with a selling price of $952.
    - **a.** Find the sale price. Round to the nearest cent.
    - **b.** The markdown is the greatest possible without the store losing money. What does this tell you about the cost?
      - **A.** The cost is greater than the sale price.
      - **B.** The cost is less than the markdown.
      - **C.** The cost equals the markdown.
      - **D.** The cost equals the sale price.
12. **Writing** A puppy is on sale at a pet store for $324, marked down 10% from an original selling price of $360.
    - **a.** If the markup from cost to sale price was $54, what was the cost? Round to the nearest dollar.
    - **b.** How would you solve the problem if you were not given the sale price?

13. **Reasoning** Joanne cannot decide which of two washing machines to buy. The selling price of each is $650. The first is marked down by 50%. The second is marked down by 20% with an additional 30% off.

a. What is the sale price of the first washing machine? Round to the nearest dollar.

b. What is the sale price of the second washing machine?

c. Explain why Joanne should buy the first washing machine rather than the second if the machines are the same except for the selling price.

14. **Think About the Process** A store that buys and sells used video games buys a game at a cost of $29 and sells it at a selling price of $35.

a. Find the markup.

b. Find the percent markup.

15. A department store buys 300 shirts at a cost of $7,200 and sells them at a selling price of $30 each. Find the percent markup to the nearest whole number.

16. **Think About the Process** Van purchased a DVD player on sale. The original selling price was $154.30. The sale price was $132.17.

a. What is the first step in finding the percent markdown?

A. Find the cost.

B. Find the markdown.

C. Find the greatest markdown possible.

b. Find the percent markdown.

17. A diamond ring which normally sells for $1,275 is on sale for $1,020. A ruby ring which normally sells for $290 is on sale for $203.

a. What is the percent markdown for the diamond ring? Round to the nearest whole number as needed.

b. What is the percent markdown for the ruby ring?

c. Compare the percent markdown for the two rings.

18. **Challenge** Robin paid $350 for a new mountain bike to sell in her shop. She wants to price the bike so that she can offer a 30% markdown but still keep a markup of 20% of the price she paid for it. What should be the full selling price of the bike? Round to the nearest dollar as needed.

19. **Challenge** A sporting goods store bought a ski set at a cost of $255. Later, the ski set was marked down 20% from its selling price and then marked down another 30%. The total markdown is the greatest possible markdown without the store losing money. Find the original selling price. Round to the nearest dollar as needed.

3-7 Problem Solving

CCSS: 7.RP.A.3

Part 1

Example Expressing a Fee as a Percent Rate

You bought two tickets to a stock car race. Each ticket cost $17.25. You paid a total of $38.50 including an online service fee. Express the fee as a fixed charge per ticket and as a percent rate to the nearest whole percent.

Solution

Step 1 Find the fee as a fixed charge per ticket.

The cost of two tickets is:

$$17.25 \cdot 2 = 34.50$$

The fee for two tickets is:

$$38.50 - 34.50 = 4.00$$

The fee for two tickets is the total cost paid minus the cost of the two tickets.

The fee for one ticket is:

$$\frac{4.00}{2} = 2.00$$

The fee is $2.00 per ticket.

Step 2 Find the fee as a percent rate.

$$\text{fee for one ticket} = \text{fee rate} \cdot \text{cost of one ticket}$$

$$2.00 = \text{fee rate} \cdot 17.25$$

$$\text{fee rate} = \frac{2.00}{17.25}$$

Rewrite the formula to solve for fee rate.

$$\approx 0.12$$

$$= 12\%$$

The fee as a fixed charge is $2.00 per ticket. The fee as a percent rate is about 12% of the ticket cost.

Part 2

Example Using Percent Increase and Decrease

Is Kat correct? Explain.

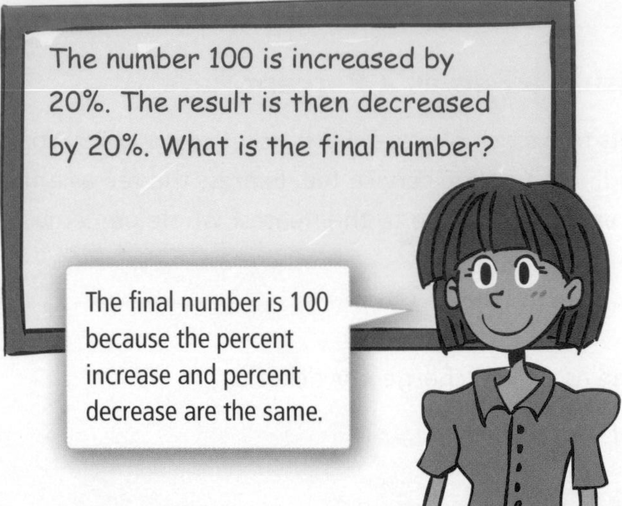

Solution

Step 1 Find the result when 100 increases by 20%.

Since percent is parts out of 100, 20% of 100 is 20.

The amount of increase is 20.

0 20 100 → 120
0% 20% 100%

$100 + 20 = 120$

The result when 100 increases by 20% is 120.

Step 2 Find the final number when 120 decreases by 20%.

Use the percent decrease formula. $\text{percent decrease} = \frac{\text{amount of decrease}}{\text{original quantity}}$

Substitute. Write 20% as a decimal. $0.20 = \frac{\text{amount of decrease}}{120}$

Multiply both sides by 120. $0.20 \cdot 120 = \frac{\text{amount of decrease}}{120} \cdot 120$

Multiply both sides by 120. Simplify. $\text{amount of decrease} = 24$

amount of decrease = 24

20% of 120 is 24.

continued on next page >

Part 2

Solution continued

This is what it looks like on a number line.

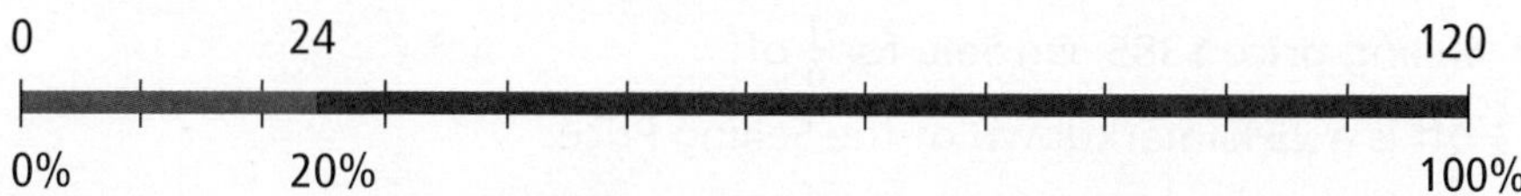

Now see what the number line looks like when 120 is decreased by 24.

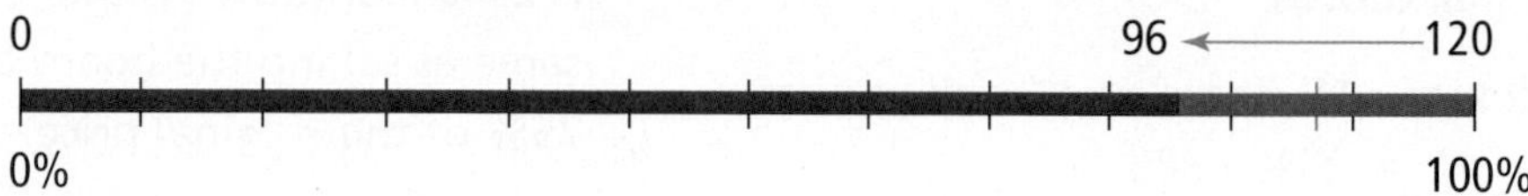

$120 - 24 = 96.$

The result when 120 decreases by 20% is 96.

Kat is not correct. The final number is not 100.

Part 3

Example Calculating Sales Tax

Suppose you are shopping for a surfboard to replace your old board. You live in a state with 6.25% sales tax. Which surfboard(s) can you afford to buy if the most you can spend is $300?

continued on next page >

Part 3

Example continued

Solution

Board 1 Selling price \$385; On Sale for $\frac{1}{4}$ off

$\frac{1}{4}$ off is a 25% markdown of the Selling Price.

Method 1

Find the markdown.

$$\begin{aligned} \text{markdown} &= \text{\% markdown} \cdot \text{selling price} \\ &= 25\% \cdot 385 \\ &= 0.25 \cdot 385 \\ &= 96.25 \end{aligned}$$

Then find the sale price.

$$\begin{aligned} \text{sale price} &= \text{selling price} - \text{markdown} \\ &= 385 - 96.25 \\ &= 288.75, \text{ or } \$288.75 \end{aligned}$$

Method 2

A 25% markdown is the same as selling the board at 75% of the original price.

$$\begin{aligned} \text{Sale price} &= 75\% \cdot \text{selling price} \\ &= 0.75 \cdot 385 \\ &= 288.75 \end{aligned}$$

The sale price is \$288.75.

Find the sales tax.

$$\begin{aligned} \text{sales tax} &= 6.25\% \cdot \text{sales tax} \\ &= 0.0625 \cdot 288.75 \approx 18.05, \text{ or } \$18.05 \end{aligned}$$

So the total cost of Board 1 is given below.

$$\begin{aligned} \text{total cost} &= \text{sale price} + \text{sales tax} \\ &= 288.75 + 18.05 = 306.80 \end{aligned}$$

The total cost of Board 1 is \$306.80.

The total cost of Board 1 is \$306.80. With \$300 to spend, you *cannot* afford to buy it.

Board 2 Selling price \$450; Our price 40% off

Method 1

Find the markdown.

$$\begin{aligned} \text{markdown} &= \text{\% markdown} \cdot \text{selling price} \\ &= 40\% \cdot 450 \\ &= 0.40 \cdot 400 \\ &= 180 \end{aligned}$$

Then find the sale price.

$$\begin{aligned} \text{sale price} &= \text{selling price} - \text{markdown} \\ &= 450 - 180 \\ &= 270, \text{ or } \$270 \end{aligned}$$

Method 2

A 40% decrease is the same as selling the board at 60% of the original price.

$$\begin{aligned} \text{Sale price} &= 60\% \cdot \text{selling price} \\ &= 0.60 \cdot 450 \\ &= 270 \end{aligned}$$

The sale price is \$270.

Find the sales tax.

$$\begin{aligned} \text{sales tax} &= 6.25\% \cdot \text{sales price} \\ &= 0.0625 \cdot 270 \approx 16.88, \text{ or } \$16.88 \end{aligned}$$

continued on next page >

Part 3

Solution continued

So the total cost of Board 2 is given below.

$$\begin{aligned}\text{total cost} &= \text{sale price} + \text{sales tax}\\ &= 270 + 16.88\\ &= 286.88\end{aligned}$$

The total cost of Board 2 is $286.88. With $300 to spend, you *can* afford to buy it.

Board 3 Selling price $390; Today $295, plus $20 off with a trade-in for your old board.

If you don't trade your old board in, the sale price is $295.

Find the sales tax.

$$\begin{aligned}\text{sales tax} &= 0.625 \cdot 295\\ &\approx 18.44, \text{ or } \$18.44\end{aligned}$$

So the total cost of Board 3, if you don't trade in your old board, is given below.

$$\begin{aligned}\text{total cost} &= \text{sale price} + \text{sales tax}\\ &= 295 + 18.44\\ &= 313.44\end{aligned}$$

The total cost of Board 3 is $313.44. With $300 to spend, you *cannot* afford to buy it.

If you do trade your old board in, the sale price of the board is $20 less.

$$\begin{aligned}\text{sale price} &= 295 - 20\\ &= 275, \text{ or } \$275\end{aligned}$$

Find the sales tax on the new price.

$$\begin{aligned}\text{sale price} &= 0.0625 \cdot 275\\ &\approx 17.19, \text{ or } \$17.19\end{aligned}$$

So the total cost for Board 3 if you do trade in your old board is given below.

$$\begin{aligned}\text{total cost} &= \text{sale price} + \text{sales tax}\\ &= 275 + 17.19\\ &= 292.19\end{aligned}$$

The total cost of Board 3 with a trade-in is $292.19.

The total cost of Board 3 with the trade-in is $292.19. In this case, you *can* afford to buy it.

3-7 | Homework

Digital Resources    

1. Emily and a friend bought two tickets to see a soccer game. Each ticket cost $8.25. The friends paid a total of $24.50, which included a fee per ticket for parking near the stadium.
   a. How much did each friend pay for the parking fee?
   b. What is the parking fee as a percent increase in the cost of a ticket?
2. The number 360 is increased by 25%. The result is then decreased by 50%. What is the final number?
3. Justin has $24 to buy a gift for his cousin, Julianne. He found a gift for $22. With 5% sales tax added on, will Justin have enough money to buy the gift for Julianne? If so, how much will he pay?
4. Two friends, Horacio and Jenna, bought two tickets to see a play at the local theater. Each ticket cost $17.25. Each friend donated $1.00 to the theater's youth program. The friends paid a total of $40.50, which also included a convenience fee.
   a. How much did each friend pay for the convenience fee?
   b. What is the convenience fee as a percent increase in the cost of a ticket?
   c. Find two more percents that you can describe as percent increases in a ticket's cost.
5. A band expects to put 16 songs on their next CD. The band writes and records 62.5% more songs than they expect to put on the CD. During the editing process, 50% of the songs are removed. How many songs will there be on the final CD?
6. Brett hoped to get 100 pumpkins from his garden this year. Since the weather was favorable, 20% more pumpkins grew than he expected. Unfortunately, animals ate 30% of all the pumpkins that grew.
   a. How many pumpkins were left?
   b. Is the final number of pumpkins more than or less than he hoped?
7. Emma saves 10% of her weekly earnings for living expenses. She usually makes $560 each week. This week she made 10% more. Emma incorrectly claims that she has $560 left for spending money this week.
   a. Calculate the amount of spending money Emma has left for the week.
   b. What error did Emma likely make?
      A. Emma used the percent saved for living expenses only to calculate the final amount.
      B. Emma used the percent increase in salary only to calculate the final amount.
      C. Emma assumed that if the percent increase in salary and the percent saved for living expenses are the same, the final amount does not change.
      D. Emma assumed that if the percent increase in salary and the percent saved for living expenses are the same, the final amount doubles.
8. Ron wants to buy a video game with a selling price of $48, on sale for 50% off. The sales tax in his state is 4.5%.
   a. How much will Ron have to pay in all?
   b. If he has $25, can he afford to purchase the game?
9. Kyrsten and Samantha are roommates who split the cost of rent and utilities (electricity, water, heat, etc.) evenly every month. Each roommate pays $357.75 for rent. The roommates pay $849.50 per month for combined rent and utilities. Kyrsten wants cable TV. She will pay the $52.00 cable bill fully each month. What is the cost of the cable as a percent increase of Kyrsten's utilities cost?

See your complete lesson at MyMathUniverse.com

10. Think About the Process Victoria bought four airplane tickets. Each ticket cost $106. She paid $453.68 in all, including a processing fee.

a. What was the processing fee per ticket?

b. What was the fee as a percent increase in the cost of a ticket?

c. If she had bought three tickets at the same rate, what would she have paid in all?

11. Chester wants to buy a new car. He finds an ad for a car that costs $27,200. Suppose that the local sales tax is 7%.

a. How much tax would Chester have to pay?

b. What is the cost of the car including tax?

c. If Chester has $29,864 saved, can he pay cash to buy the car?

12. Think About the Process You have 20 quarters. You find 40% more quarters in your room. Then you go shopping and spend 50% of the total number of quarters.

a. What expression represents the total number of quarters you take with you shopping?

A. $20 + (20 \div 0.50)$

B. $20 + (20 \div 40)$

C. $20 + (20 \times 0.40)$

D. $20 + (20 \times 40)$

b. How much money do you have left?

13. Challenge In a pile of red clay bricks, each brick weighs 2 pounds. Workers add bricks to the pile and the weight increases by 15%. Then workers remove bricks from the pile and the weight decreases by 20%. The final pile of bricks weighs 552 pounds.

a. How many bricks were in the original pile?

b. Describe two methods for finding the original number of bricks.

14. Challenge Michele wants to buy a pair of sandals, sunglasses, and a shirt. The pair of sandals costs $5. The sunglasses cost twice as much as the pair of sandals. The shirt costs twice as much as the sunglasses. The tax in Michele's city is 4%.

a. What is the total sales tax?

b. What is the total of the purchases?

c. If Michele has $38 saved, can she afford all the items?

4-1 Rational Numbers, Opposites, and Absolute Value

Vocabulary
absolute value, opposites, rational numbers

CCSS: 7.NS.A.1, 7.NS.A.1a

Part 1

Intro

A **rational number** is a number that can be written in the form $\frac{a}{b}$ or $-\frac{a}{b}$, where *a* and *b* are whole numbers and $b \neq 0$.

You can also think of rational numbers as the whole numbers, fractions, and decimals you already know, and their opposites.

Here are some examples of rational numbers.

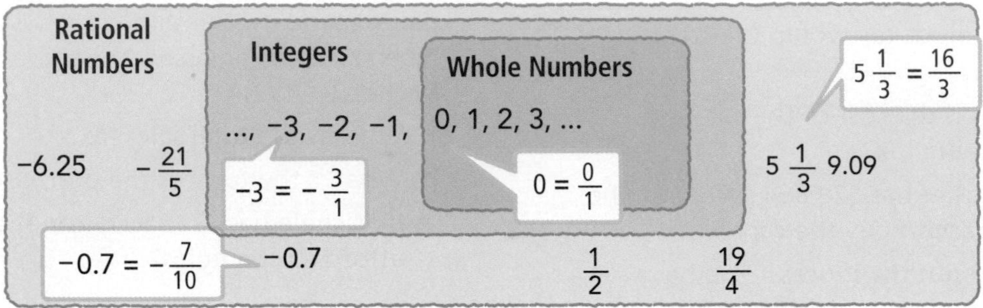

Example Classifying Numbers

Decide if each number is a rational number, a whole number, or an integer.

$1\frac{1}{6}$	$\frac{2}{3}$	−0.1	0	−125
−7	$-\frac{3}{4}$	$-2\frac{1}{4}$	1.9	13

Solution

Whole numbers are zero and the counting numbers.

0, 13

Integers include whole numbers and their opposites.

0, −7, −125, 13

Rational numbers can be written in the form $\frac{a}{b}$ or $-\frac{a}{b}$.

$1\frac{1}{6}$, $\frac{2}{3}$, −0.1, 0, −125, −7, $-\frac{3}{4}$, $-2\frac{1}{4}$, 1.9, 13.

Part 2

Intro

The **absolute value** of a number is its distance from 0 on the number line. The symbol for the absolute value of a number n is $|n|$.

The absolute value of a positive number is the number itself.

$$|2| = 2$$

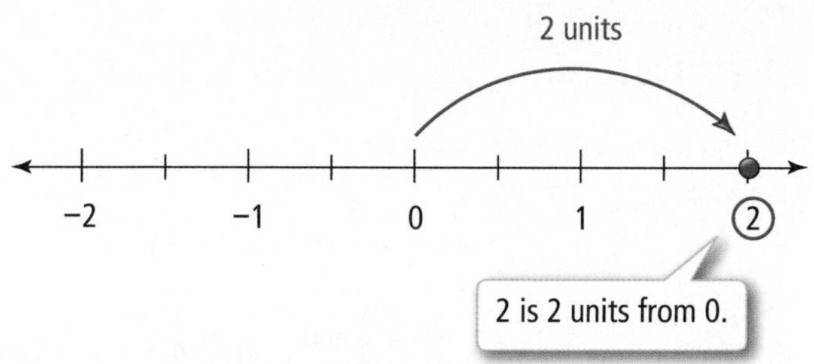

The absolute value of a negative number is the opposite of the number.

$$|-1.4| = 1.4$$

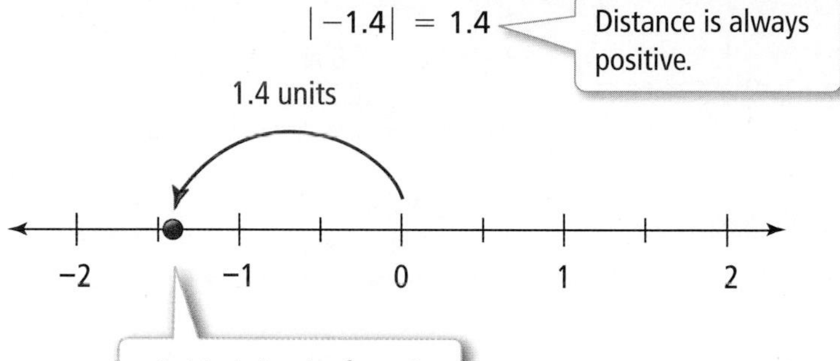

Two numbers that are opposites have the same absolute value.

$$\left|\frac{3}{2}\right| = \left|\frac{3}{2}\right| \text{ and } \left|-\frac{3}{2}\right| = \frac{3}{2}$$

$\frac{3}{2}$ units $\quad$ $\frac{3}{2}$ units

−2 −1 0 1 2

Both $\frac{3}{2}$ and $-\frac{3}{2}$ are $\frac{3}{2}$ units from 0.

Part 2

Example Comparing Absolute Values

Complete each statement with the symbol <, =, or > to correctly compare the absolute values.

a. $|-5| \blacksquare |3|$ **b.** $\left|-\frac{1}{2}\right| \blacksquare -\frac{1}{4}$

c. $|-7.6| \blacksquare |6|$ **d.** $|3.1| \blacksquare |-3.1|$

e. $|-1| \blacksquare |-3|$ **f.** $\left|4\frac{1}{2}\right| \blacksquare \left|-\frac{9}{2}\right|$

Solution

a. $|-5| > |3|$

$|-5| = 5$ and $|3| = 3$
$5 > 3$

b. $\left|-\frac{1}{2}\right| > \left|-\frac{1}{4}\right|$

$\left|-\frac{1}{2}\right| = \frac{1}{2}$ and $\left|-\frac{1}{4}\right| = \frac{1}{4}$
$\frac{1}{2} > \frac{1}{4}$

c. $|-7.6| > |6|$

$|-7.6| = 7.6$ and $|6| = 6$
$7.6 > 6$

d. $|3.1| = |-3.1|$

$|3.1| = 3.1$ and $|-3.1| = 3.1$
$3.1 = 3.1$

e. $|-1| < |-3|$

$|-1| = 1$ and $|-3| = 3$
$1 < 3$

f. $\left|4\frac{1}{2}\right| = \left|-\frac{9}{2}\right|$

$\left|4\frac{1}{2}\right| = 4\frac{1}{2}$ and $\left|-\frac{9}{2}\right| = \frac{9}{2}$

$4\frac{1}{2} = \frac{9}{2}$

Part 3

Intro

You can use positive and negative rational numbers to represent changes in real-world quantities. Two changes represented by opposites result in no change.

Here are some examples:

A woman gets her hair cut. Thirty minutes later, her hair is $-1\frac{3}{4}$ inches shorter. One month later, her hair is $1\frac{3}{4}$ inches longer.

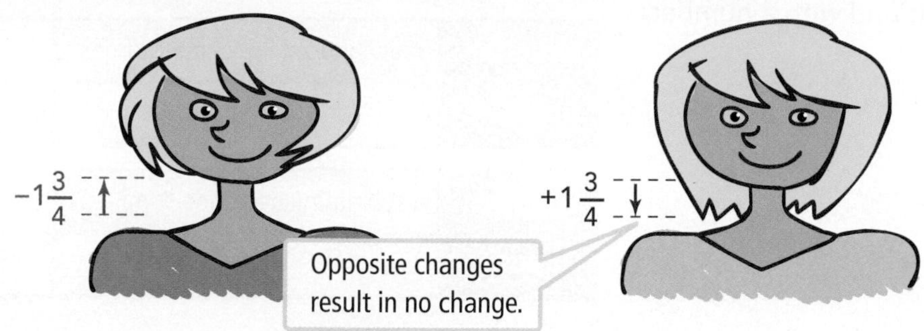

The temperature increases by 20 degrees. Four hours later, the temperature decreases by 20 degrees.

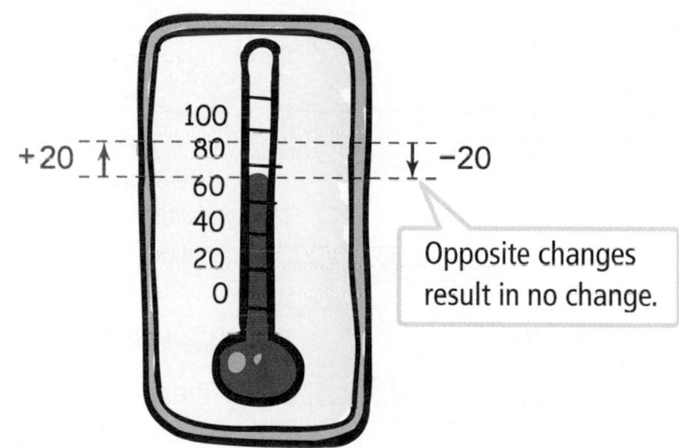

A girl puts $10 in the bank. Four hours later, she takes out $10.

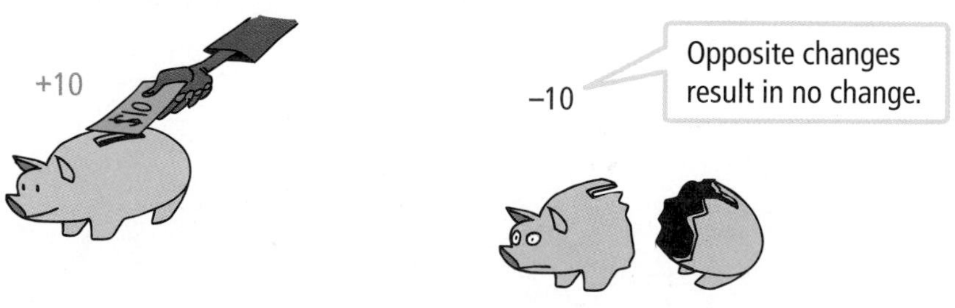

Part 3

Example Representing Situations and Their Opposites

Write a positive or negative number to represent the change described in each situation.

Describe the opposite change in words and with a number.

Situations and Their Opposites

	Words	Number
Situation	You climbed up 7 stairs.	
Opposite		

Situation	Your car used 9.2 gallons of gas.	
Opposite		

Situation	A submarine descends $\frac{3}{8}$ mi.	
Opposite		

Solution

Situations and Their Opposites

	Words	Number
Situation	You climbed up 7 stairs.	+7
Opposite	You walked down 7 stairs.	−7

The opposite of climbing up 7 stairs is walking down 7 stairs, which can be represented by −7.

Situation	Your car used 9.2 gallons of gas.	−9.2
Opposite	You put 9.2 gallons of gas in your car's gas tank.	+9.2

The opposite of your car using 9.2 gallons of gas is your putting 9.2 gallons of gas into your car, which can be represented by +9.2.

Situation	A submarine descends $\frac{3}{8}$ mi.	$-\frac{3}{8}$
Opposite	A submarine rises $\frac{3}{8}$ mi.	$+\frac{3}{8}$

The opposite of a submarine descending $\frac{3}{8}$ mile is a submarine rising $\frac{3}{8}$ mile, which can be represented by $+\frac{3}{8}$.

Key Concept

Rational Numbers A rational number is a number that can be written in the form $\frac{a}{b}$ or $-\frac{a}{b}$, where a and b are whole numbers and $b \neq 0$.

These are examples of rational numbers.

$-2.1 = -2\frac{1}{10} = -\frac{21}{10}$

$3 = \frac{3}{1}$

$-3 \quad -2.1 \quad -1 \quad \frac{3}{4} \quad 2 \quad 3$

$-4 \quad -3 \quad -2 \quad -1 \quad 0 \quad 1 \quad 2 \quad 3 \quad 4$

Absolute Value The absolute value of a number is its distance from 0 on the number line.

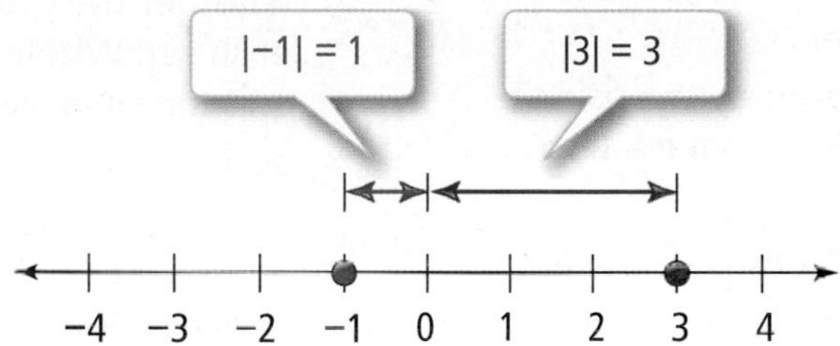

Opposites Opposites are two numbers that are the same distance from 0 and in opposite directions.

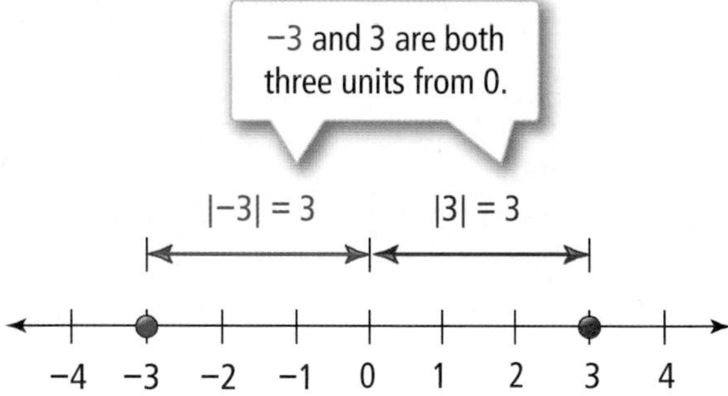

4-1 | Homework

Digital Resources    

1. Use the Venn diagram to determine the smallest region in which to place A when $A = 0.127$.

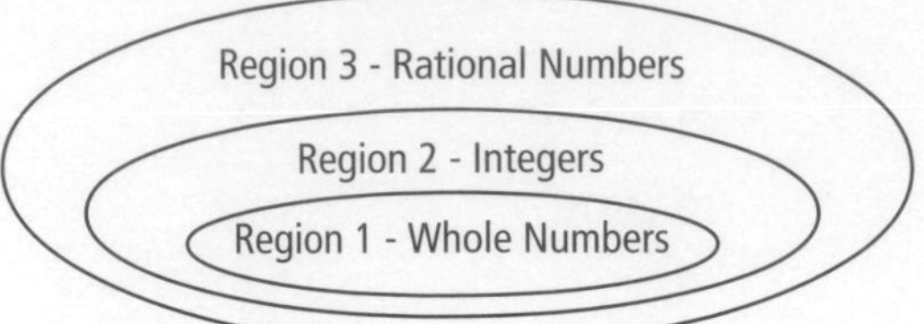

A. Integers

B. Rational numbers

C. Whole numbers

2. Determine whether -34 belongs to each set: Whole Numbers, Integers, and Rational Numbers.

3. Insert $<$, $>$, or $=$ between the pair of numbers $|-13|$ ■ $|19|$ to make a true statement.

4. Which list shows the values in order from least to greatest?

A. $|-32|, |0.74|, |-10|$

B. $|-10|, |0.74|, |-32|$

C. $|-32|, |-10|, |0.74|$

D. $|0.74|, |-32|, |-10|$

E. $|0.74|, |-10|, |-32|$

F. $|-10|, |-32|, |0.74|$

5. A worker in a silver mine descends 57 feet. Use an integer to represent the change in the worker's position.

6. In a recent year, the number of DVDs shipped to an online retailer was 70,000 less than the previous year. Use an integer to describe the change in the number of DVDs shipped.

7. Which of these situations can be represented by the opposite of -9?

A. You walk down 9 flights of stairs.

B. You climb up 9 flights of stairs.

C. The temperature drops 9° F.

D. You spend $9 on a book.

8. a. Writing Use the Venn diagram to determine the smallest region in which to place A in when $A = 45 + 10$.

Region 3 - Rational Numbers

Region 2 - Integers

Region 1 - Whole Numbers

b. Explain why all integers are rational numbers, but not all rational numbers are integers.

9. Think About the Process Determine whether the given number belongs to each set: Whole Numbers, Integers, and Rational Numbers.

a. $3 + 8$

b. Explain how you can determine whether a sum of two numbers is a rational number without doing any calculations.

10. Error Analysis Your friend classified $-25 - 20$ as an integer only.

a. Determine whether $-25 - 20$ belongs to each set: Whole Numbers, Integers, and Rational Numbers.

b. What error did your friend make?

A. Your friend did not classify $-25 - 20$ as a rational number.

B. Your friend incorrectly classified $-25 - 20$ as an integer.

C. Your friend did not classify $-25 - 20$ as a whole number.

11. a. Reasoning Insert $<$, $>$, or $=$ between the pair of numbers $|3.22|$ ■ $|-3.22|$ to make a true statement.

b. What must be true about two numbers that have the same absolute value?

12. **Submarine Depth** Two submarines are underwater. The number $-4{,}456$ represents Submarine A's position (in feet) relative to the surface. The number $-3{,}429$ represents Submarine B's position (in feet) relative to the surface. Which submarine is closer to the surface?

   A. Submarine B is closer to the surface.

   B. Submarine A is closer to the surface.

   C. Both submarines are at an equal distance away from the surface.

13. **a. Open-Ended** Which of these situations can be represented by the opposite of -53? Select all that apply.

   A. Max saved $53.

   B. A book was 53 pages longer than you expected.

   C. Julia drove for 53 minutes.

   D. The temperature was -53°F.

   b. Describe two more situations that can be represented by the opposite of -53.

14. Insert $<$, $>$, or $=$ between the pair of numbers $|-3|$ ■ $|6\frac{3}{5}|$ to make a true statement.

15. Which of these situations can be represented by the opposite of 80? Select all that apply.

   A. An airplane descends 80 m.

   B. An elevator ascends 80 m.

   C. The cost of a train ticket is $80 less than expected.

   D. You remove 80 songs from an MP3 player.

16. Which of these situations can be represented by the opposite of 8.6? Select all that apply.

   A. The temperature went up 8.6° C.

   B. The cost of theater tickets increased by $8.60.

   C. A giraffe gained 8.6 kg.

   D. An elephant lost 8.6 kg.

   E. Your car used 8.6 gallons of gas.

   F. The water level in a lake dropped 8.6 cm.

17. **Think About the Process**

   I $|-3|, |2|, |0|$ **II** $|-2|, |3|, |0|$

   a. What is the first step in ordering each list of numbers from least to greatest?

   A. Evaluate each absolute value.

   B. Order absolute values from greatest to least.

   C. Multiply each number by -1.

   D. Order absolute values from least to greatest.

   b. Which list of numbers is in order from least to greatest?

   A. I **B.** II

   C. Neither **D.** Both I and II

18. **Challenge** Order the values $|19.01|$, $|\frac{6}{5}|$, $|7\frac{5}{6}|$, $|-129|$, and $|-118|$ from greatest to least.

19. **Challenge** Two divers are exploring a coral reef in the Pacific Ocean. Sean is $91\frac{1}{5}$ feet below the surface of the ocean and Liz is $105\frac{5}{8}$ feet below the surface.

   a. Use a rational number to represent Sean's depth.

   b. Use a rational number to represent Liz's depth.

   c. Who is deeper in the water?

4-2 Adding Integers

CCSS: 7.NS.A.1b, Also 7.NS.A.1

Key Concept

You can use a number line model to compare adding positive and negative numbers to 3. Imagine that you are walking along the number line, facing the positive direction.

Three Plus Five Move in the positive direction if n is positive.

$3 + n$ when $n = 5$

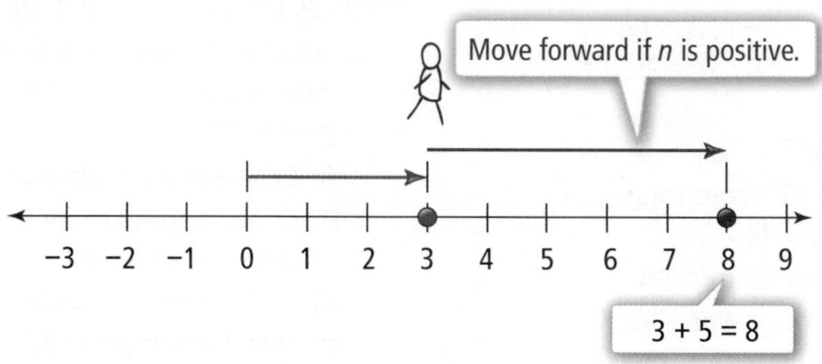

Three Plus Negative Five Move in the negative direction if n is negative.

$3 + n$ when $n = -5$

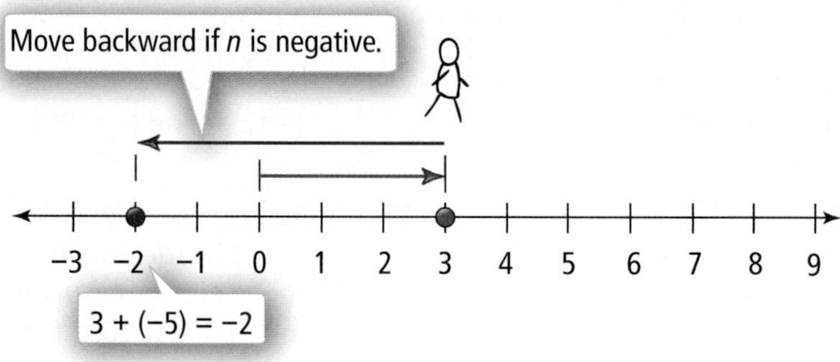

Distance from 3 Find the distance.

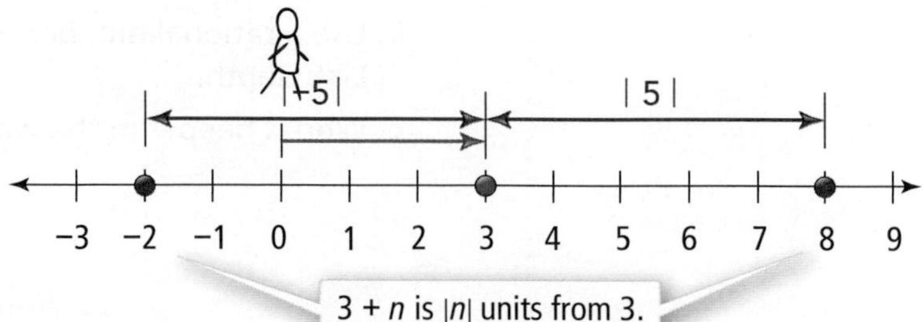

Part 1

Example Describing Sums of Numbers Using Number Lines

Find the sum of 2 + (−8). Then complete the statement.

2 + (−8) is ■ units from 2, in the ■ direction.

Solution

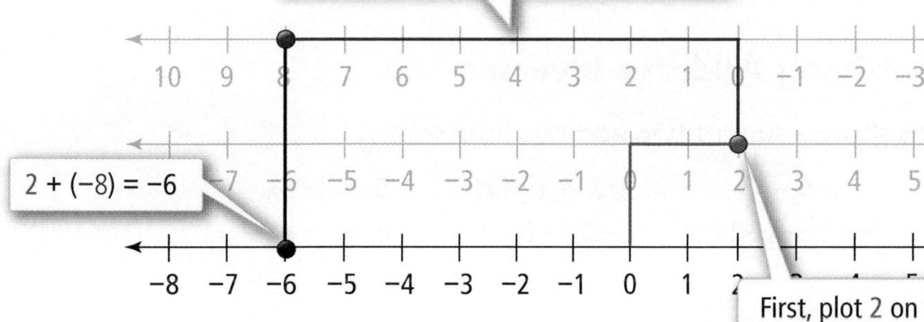

2 + (−8) is 8 units from 2, in the negative direction.

Part 2

Intro

The sum of a number and its opposite is 0.

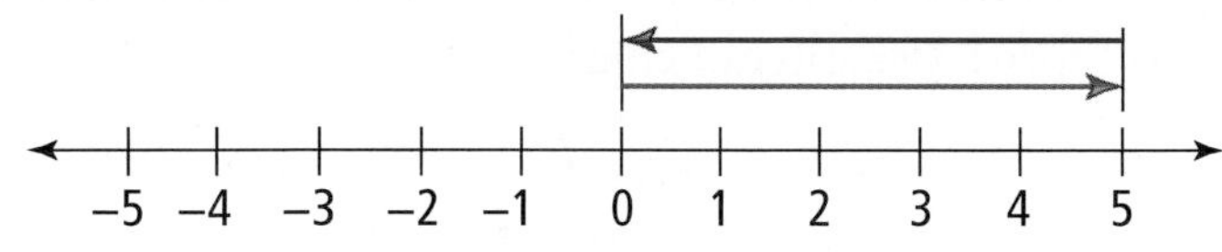

5 + (−5) = 0

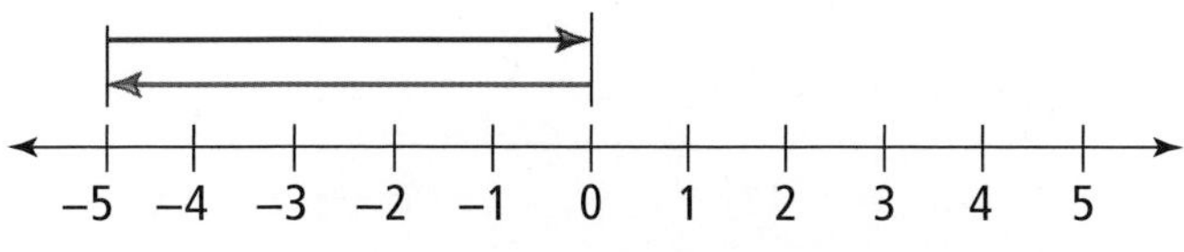

(−5) + 5 = 0

continued on next page >

Part 2

Intro continued

Two numbers that have a sum of 0 are **additive inverses.**

Inverse Property of Addition Every number has an additive inverse. The sum of a number and its additive inverse is zero.	
Arithmetic	**Algebra**
$5 + (-5) = 0$ $(-5) + 5 = 0$	For any number a: $a + (-a) = 0$ $-a + a = 0$

Example Identifying Additive Inverses

Which expressions show a sum of two additive inverses?

$8 + 8$	$-5 + 5$	$12 + (-12)$	$5 + (-5)$
$-8 + 8$	$-12 + (-12)$	$-5 + (-5)$	$8 + (-8)$

Solution

Yes: $-5 + 5$, $12 + (-12)$, $5 + (-5)$, $-8 + 8$, $8 + (-8)$

No: $8 + 8$, $-12 + (-12)$, $-5 + (-5)$

Part 3

Example Modeling Integer Addition

In some card games, players can get both positive and negative points. Find each player's score after 2 turns. Use integer chips.

Points Earned

Player	Turn 1	Turn 2	Total
Asa	−12	5	■
Dan	−15	−9	■
Joy	13	−21	■
Kim	−16	25	■

continued on next page >

Part 3

Example continued

Solution

Asa: $-12 + 5 = -7$

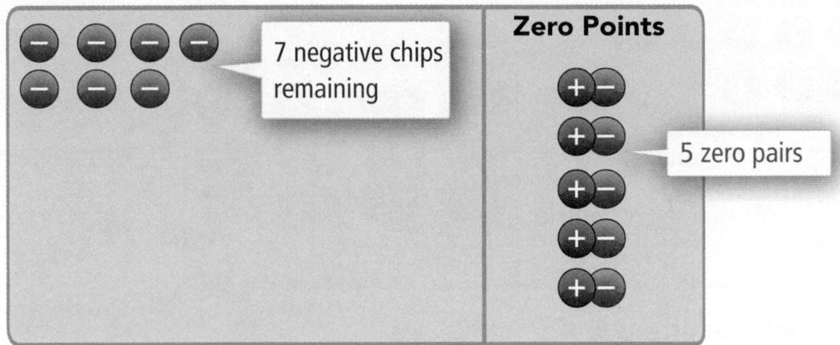

Asa's score after two turns is -7.

Dan: $-15 + -9 = -24$

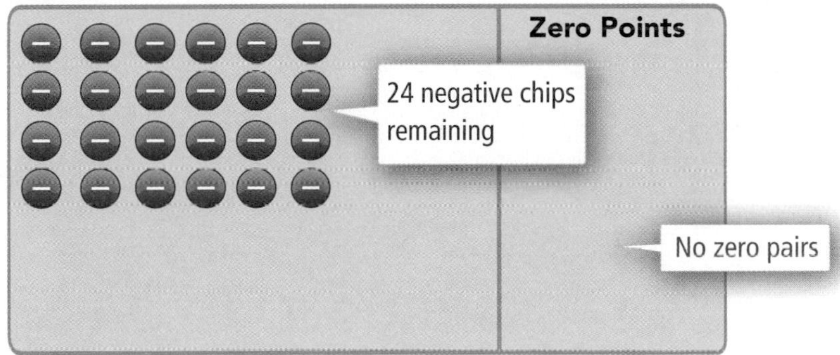

Dan's score after two turns is -24.

Joy: $13 + -21 = -8$

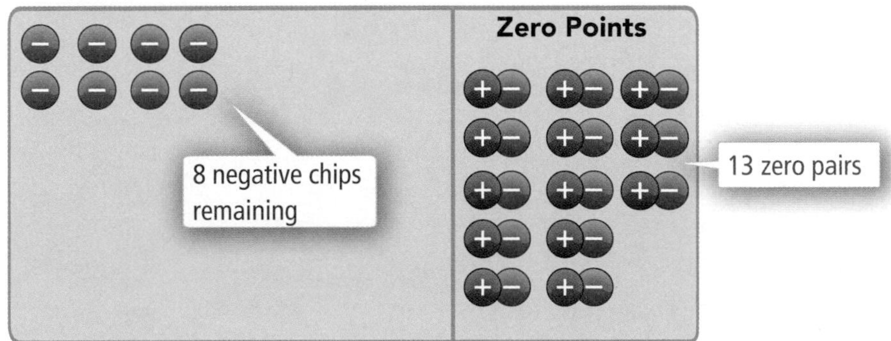

Joy's score after two turns is -8.

continued on next page >

Part 3

Solution continued

Kim: $-16 + 25 = 9$

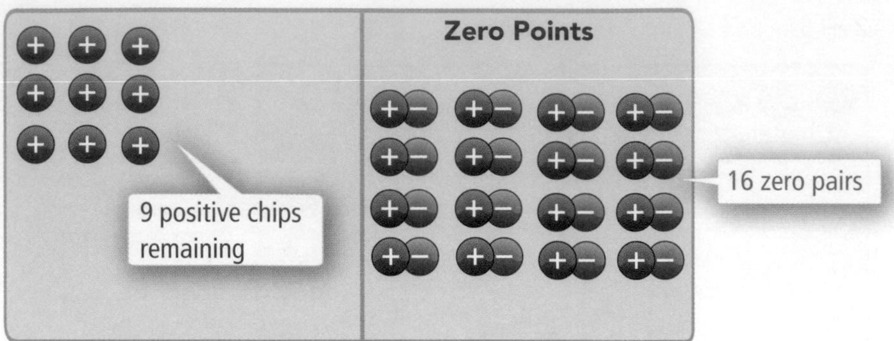

Kim's score after two turns is 9.

Digital Resources    

1. a. Complete the statement, "5 + (−3) is ■ units from 5, in the ■ direction."
   b. Use a number line to find the sum 5 + (−3).

2. a. Complete the statement, "−1 + (−3) is ■ units from −1 in the ■ direction."
   b. Use a number line to find the sum −1 + (−3).

3. Which pairs of integers are additive inverses? Select all that apply.
   A. 4, −4 **B.** 4, 4
   C. 5, −5 **D.** 5, −4

4. Which of the following are sums of additive inverses? Select all that apply.
   A. 2 + 2 **B.** 3 + (−2)
   C. 2 + (−2) **D.** −3 + 3

5. Which pairs of integers are additive inverses? Select all that apply.
   A. −79, −(−79)
   B. −79, 79
   C. 79, −(−79)
   D. −(−79), −(−79)

6. Use the model to find the sum −6 + (−2).

7. Use the model to find the sum 2 + (−1).

8. Suppose a deep sea diver dives from the surface to 81 feet below the surface. He then dives down 14 more feet. The diver's depth is represented by the sum −81 + (−14).
   a. Find the sum.
   b. What is the diver's present depth?
      A. 67 feet below the surface
      B. −95 feet below the surface
      C. 95 feet below the surface
      D. −67 feet below the surface

9. a. **Writing** Find the sum 6 + (−2) using a number line.
   b. Show the sum (−2) + 6 using a number line.
   c. How is your diagram for the sum (−2) + 6 similar to your diagram for the sum 6 + (−2)?
   d. How is it different?

10. **Walking** Mario walks 7 blocks east from his home and arrives at his favorite restaurant. When he arrives, he discovers that he dropped his wallet along the way. He retraces his steps for 5 blocks until he finds his wallet. An expression for how many blocks east Mario is from his home after finding his wallet is the sum 7 + (−5). How many blocks east is Mario from his home after finding his wallet?

11. **Error Analysis** From the following list, Meghan has to select all pairs that are additive inverses. Meghan selects 6, −6 and −7, 7.
    a. Which pairs are additive inverses? Select all that apply.
       A. 6, − (−6) **B.** −7, 7
       C. −7, −7 **D.** 7, 7
       E. 6, −6
    b. What error did Meghan make?
       A. Although the pairs 6, −6 and −7, 7 are additive inverses, Meghan did not select all pairs of additive inverses.
       B. The pair −7, 7 are not additive inverses.
       C. The pair 6, −6 are not additive inverses.
       D. None of the pairs Meghan selected are additive inverses.
    c. Give two reasons why Meghan might have made the error she made.

See your complete lesson at MyMathUniverse.com

12. a. Reasoning Which of the following are sums of additive inverses? Select all that apply.

A. $-9 + (-9)$ **B.** $-9 + 9$

C. $9 + 9$ **D.** $9 + (-9)$

b. For any number, describe a simple process you can use to name its inverse. Give examples to show the process for a positive number, a negative number, and a number that is neither positive nor negative.

13. Multiple Representations A car backs up 23 feet, followed by 9 more feet. The car's position can be represented by the sum $-23 + (-9)$.

a. Find the sum.

b. Represent the situation with a drawing. Superimpose a number line in the drawing to represent the situation in a third way.

14. a. Find the sum $-3 + (-8)$ using a number line.

b. Find the sum $-8 + (-3)$.

c. Compare the results. What property of addition do they illustrate?

15. a. Which of the following are sums of additive inverses? Select all that apply.

A. $-(-41) + 41$

B. $-(-41) + (-41)$

C. $-41 + (-41)$

D. $41 + (-41)$

b. Explain how you know how each sum compares to zero without doing any computing.

16. Think About the Process To find the sum $-4 + (-2)$ using a number line, first plot -4.

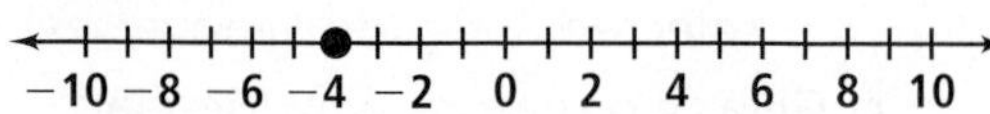

a. What is the next step?

b. Find the sum.

17. Think About the Process In a game show, a player gains 500 points in the first round. In the second round, the player loses 200 points. The final score is represented by the sum $500 + (-200)$.

a. How do you know if the sum $500 + (-200)$ is negative or positive?

b. What is the final score?

A. -700 points

B. 300 points

C. -300 points

D. 700 points

18. a. Challenge Use the models to find the sums $1 + (-2)$ and $-2 + 4$.

b. Find the sum of the sums.

c. Sketch models of the sums (zero pairs removed) and then sketch how they go together to form the final sum.

19. Challenge In City A, the temperature rises 9°F from 8 A.M. to 9 A.M. Then the temperature drops 8°F from 9 A.M. to 10 A.M. In City B, the temperature drops 2°F from 8 A.M. to 9 A.M. Then the temperature drops 3°F from 9 A.M. to 10 A.M.

a. Which expression represents the change in temperature for City A?

A. $9 + (-8)$ **B.** $-9 + 8$

C. $9 + 8$ **D.** $-9 + (-8)$

b. What is the change in temperature for City A?

c. Which expression represents the change in temperature for City B?

A. $2 + 3$ **B.** $-2 + 3$

C. $2 + (-3)$ **D.** $-2 + (-3)$

d. What is the change in temperature for City B?

e. Which city has the greater change in temperature?

4-3 Adding Rational Numbers

CCSS: 7.NS.A.1b, 7.NS.A.1d

Part 1

Intro

You can use properties of addition to simplify a sum of rational numbers with different signs.

For example, simplify $-7 + 4$.

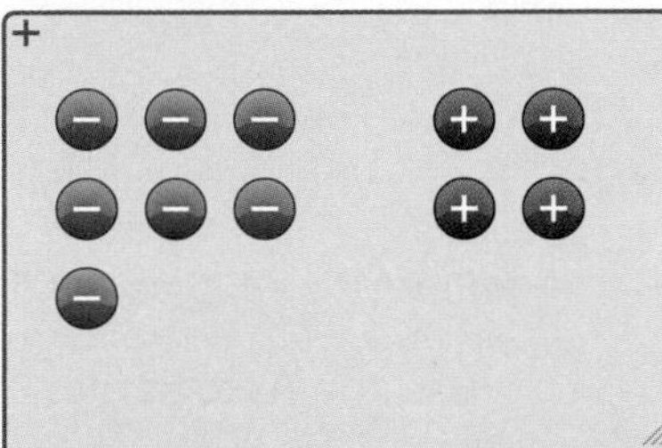

Rewrite -7 as $-3 + (-4)$. $-7 + 4 = [-3 + (-4)] + 4$

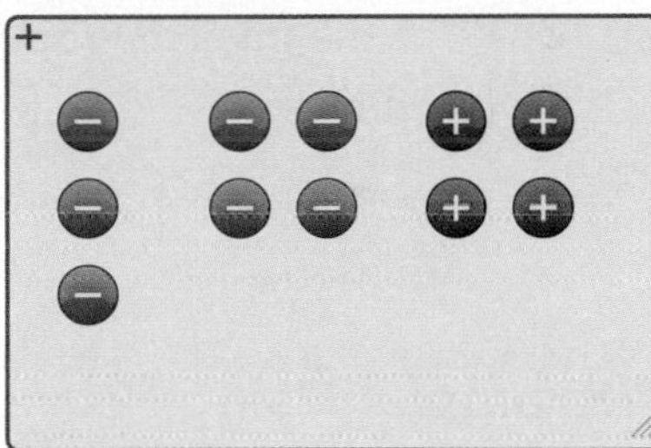

Use the Associative Property of Addition. $= -3 + (-4) + 4)$

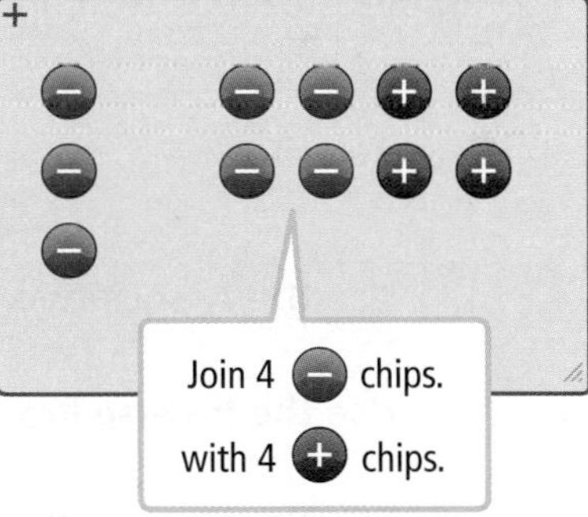

Use the Inverse Property of Addition. $= -3 + 0$

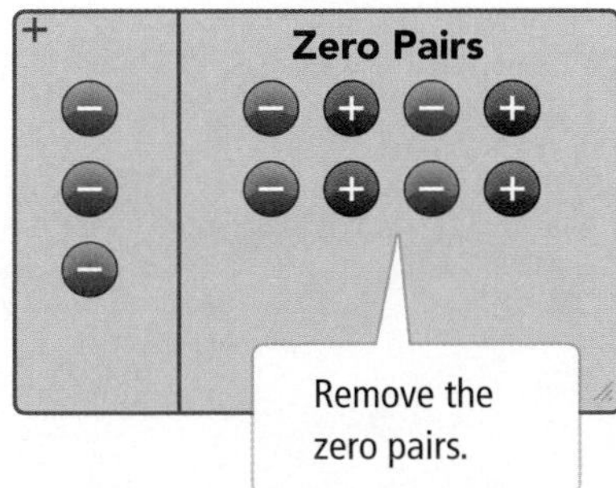

Part 1

Intro continued

Use the Identity Property of Addition. $= -3$

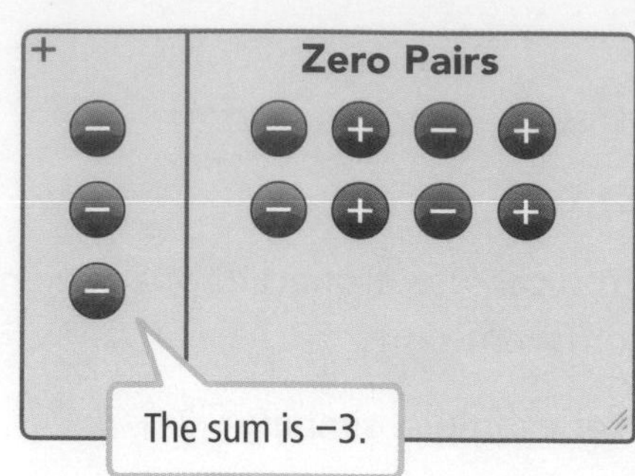

Now try it with decimals. Simplify $3.5 + (-5.5)$.

Rewrite -5.5 as $-3.5 + (-2)$. $3.5 + (-5.5) = 3.5 + [-3.5 + (-2)]$

Use the Associative Property of Addition. $= [3.5 + (-3.5)] + (-2)$

Use the Inverse Property of Addition. $= 0 + (-2)$

Use the Identity Property of Addition. $= -2$

Example Using Properties to Add Rationals

Complete the steps to simplify $\frac{3}{5} + \left(-\frac{1}{5}\right)$.

Rewrite $\frac{3}{5}$. $\frac{3}{5} + \left(-\frac{1}{5}\right) = (■ + ■) + \left(-\frac{1}{5}\right)$

Use the Associative Property of Addition. $= ■ + (■ + ■)$

Use the Inverse Property of Addition. $= ■ + ■$

Use the Identity Property of Addition. $= ■$

continued on next page >

Part 1

Example continued

Solution

Rewrite $\frac{3}{5}$.	$\frac{3}{5} + \left(-\frac{1}{5}\right) = \left(\frac{2}{5} + \frac{1}{5}\right) + \left(-\frac{1}{5}\right)$
Use the Associative Property of Addition.	$= \left(\frac{2}{5}\right) + \left[\frac{1}{5} + \left(-\frac{1}{5}\right)\right]$
Use the Inverse Property of Addition.	$= \frac{2}{5} + 0$
Use the Identity Property of Addition.	$= \frac{2}{5}$

Group $\frac{1}{5}$ with $\left(-\frac{1}{5}\right)$ instead of with $\left(\frac{2}{5}\right)$.

So $\frac{3}{5} + \left(-\frac{1}{5}\right) = \frac{2}{5}$.

Key Concept

While using number line models, integer chips, and properties of addition, you may have found methods for adding numbers with the same sign and numbers with different signs.

To add two numbers with the same sign:

- Add the absolute values of the numbers.
- Use the sign of the numbers as the sign of the sum.

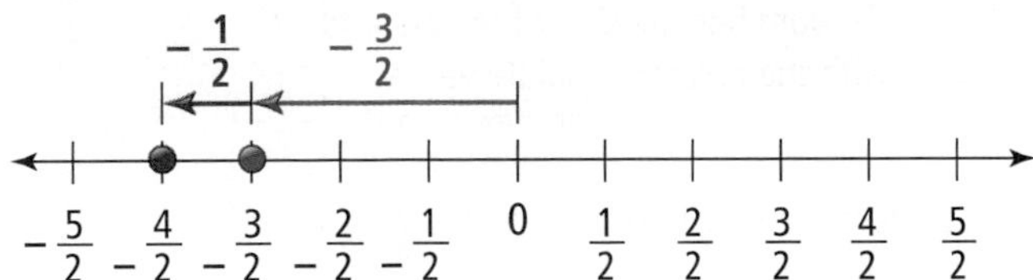

To add two numbers with different signs:

- Find the absolute values of the numbers.
- Subtract the lesser absolute value from the greater absolute value.
- Use the sign of the number with the greater absolute value as the sign of the sum.

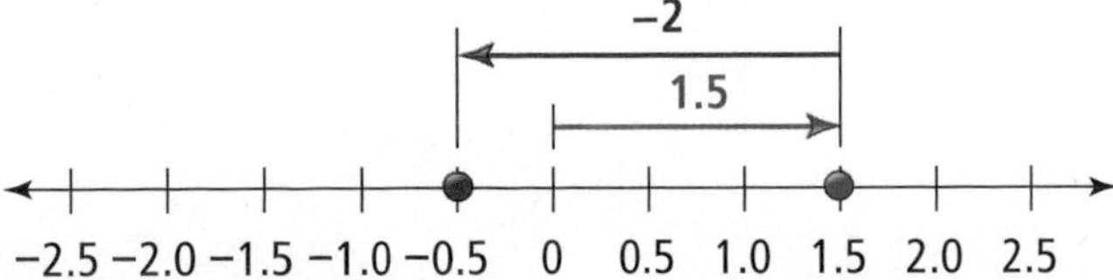

Part 2

Example Adding Rational Numbers

Find each sum.

a. $-\frac{3}{4} + \left(-\frac{9}{4}\right)$

b. $5.1 + (-8.3)$

Solution

a. $-\frac{3}{4} + \left(-\frac{9}{4}\right) = -?$

$-\frac{3}{4}$ and $-\frac{9}{4}$ are both negative. The sum will be negative.

$\left|-\frac{3}{4}\right| + \left|-\frac{9}{4}\right|$

The signs are the same, so add the absolute values.

$\frac{3}{4} + \frac{9}{4}$

$\left|-\frac{3}{4}\right| = \frac{3}{4}$ and $\left|-\frac{9}{4}\right| = \frac{9}{4}$.

$\frac{3+9}{4}$

$\frac{12}{4}$, or 3

So, $-\frac{3}{4} + \left(-\frac{9}{4}\right) = -3$.

b. $5.1 + (-8.3) = ?$

The signs are different.

$5.1 + (-8.3) = -?$

The sum has the sign of the addend with the greater absolute value.

$|-8.3| - |5.1|$

Subtract the lesser absolute value from the greater.

$8.3 - 5.1 = 3.2$

So, $5.1 + (-8.3) = -3.2$.

Part 3

Example Finding Sums of Rational Numbers

You plant a seed $3\frac{1}{2}$ in. below the ground.

Find the sum $-3\frac{1}{2}$ in. + $15\frac{3}{4}$ in. What does the sum represent?

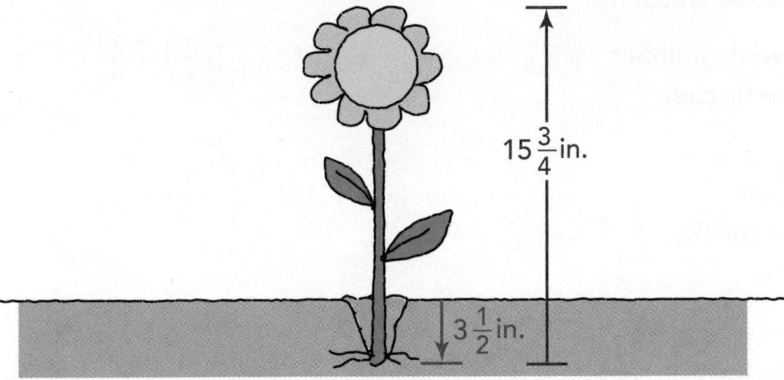

Solution

Method 1

Write each mixed number as an improper fraction. $-3\frac{1}{2} + 15\frac{3}{4} = -\frac{7}{2} + \frac{63}{4}$

Find a common denominator. For 2 and 4, use 4. $= -\frac{14}{4} + \frac{63}{4}$

Add the fractions. $= \frac{49}{4}$

Rewrite the improper fraction as a mixed number. $= 12\frac{1}{4}$

The sum $-3\frac{1}{2} + 15\frac{3}{4}$ represents the height of the flower above the ground. The flower is $12\frac{1}{4}$ in. above the ground.

Part 3

Solution continued

Method 2

Separate the whole numbers and the fractions. $-3\frac{1}{2} + 15\frac{3}{4} = -3 + \left(-\frac{1}{2}\right) + 15 + \frac{3}{4}$

Group the whole number parts and the fraction parts. $= [-3 + 15] + \left[\left(-\frac{1}{2}\right) + \frac{3}{4}\right]$

Find a common denominator for the fraction parts. $= [-3 + 15] + \left[\left(-\frac{2}{4}\right) + \frac{3}{4}\right]$

Add the whole number parts and the fraction parts separately. $= 12 + \frac{1}{4}$

Combine to create a mixed number. $= 12\frac{1}{4}$

The flower is $12\frac{1}{4}$ in. above the ground.

1. Find the sum of $\frac{12}{13} + \left(-\frac{1}{13}\right)$.
2. Find the value of the expression $(-8.6) + 7.2$.
3. Find the sum of $-7.5 + (-7.6)$.
4. Find the sum of $\frac{2}{3} + \left(-\frac{1}{3}\right)$.
5. In her garden Pam plants the tomato seed $2\frac{3}{4}$ in. below the ground. After one month the tomato plant has grown a total of $12\frac{1}{2}$ in. How many inches is the plant above the ground?
6. Greg is at his house. He gets in the car and drives north 9.6 miles and stops at the store. Then he turns around and drives south 8.4 miles to go to his friend's house. How far is the friend's house from Greg's house?
7. Simplify the expression. $\left(-\frac{11}{21}\right) + \frac{9}{21}$.
8. a. **Writing** Simplify the expression $\left(-\frac{8}{15}\right) + \left(\frac{1}{15}\right)$.

   b. Show how to simplify in steps, using a property of operations for each step. Explain the property you use in each step.
9. a. **Reasoning** Simplify the expression $(-13.2) + 8.1$.

   b. How are $(-13.2) + 8.1$ and $13.2 + (-8.1)$ related? Explain without computing.

   c. Using a property of operations, what can you say about their sum?
10. a. **Error Analysis** Simplify the expression $-2.6 + (-5.4)$.

    b. On the test, when Tom simplified the expression he got -2.8. What mistake did Tom likely make when he simplified the expression?

    A. He found the absolute value of just the second number.

    B. He found the absolute value of just the first number.

    C. He found the absolute value of both numbers, but then used the wrong sign.

    D. He did not find the absolute value of either number.
11. **Think About the Process**

    a. Which absolute value expression would you use to find the absolute value of $3.1 + (-6.3)$?

    A. $|3.1| - |-6.3|$

    B. $|-6.3| - |3.1|$

    C. $|-6.3| + |3.1|$

    D. $|3.1| + |-6.3|$

    b. Find $3.1 + (-6.3)$.
12. a. **Mental Math** Simplify the expression $-5\frac{3}{4} + \left(\frac{-1}{4}\right)$.

    b. Describe the steps you use to simplify this expression using mental math. Tell why this expression allows you to use mental math.
13. **Stock Market** At the beginning of the day the stock market goes up $30\frac{1}{2}$ points and stays at this level for most of the day. At the end of the day the stock market goes down $120\frac{1}{4}$ points from the high at the beginning of the day. What is the total change in the stock market from the beginning of the day to the end of the day?
14. a. Simplify the expression $100.9 + (-70.5)$.

    b. Show how, using the properties of operations, you can begin with the expression $100.9 + (-70.5)$ and write an equivalent sum that has the form $125.9 + (a)$.
15. **Estimation** A group of students go out on a boat to go scuba diving. The instructor takes the group 54.96 feet below the surface to start. Then they go up 22.38 feet and stop to see some fish. Which of the following is the best estimate for the total change in distance from the group of students' original position at the surface?

    A. −20 feet   B. −50 feet

    C. −30 feet   D. −70 feet

16. Estimation The seventh-grade class is going hiking in the mountains. At the beginning of the day the class hikes $500\frac{1}{4}$ yards up the mountain and stops for lunch. After lunch the class goes $175\frac{1}{2}$ yards down the mountain and stops for a break.

a. Estimate the change in elevation from the beginning of the day to when the class stops for a break.

A. 500 yards　　**B.** 325 yards

C. −325 yards　　**D.** −175 yard

b. Find the exact change in elevation.

17. a. Challenge Simplify the expression $7\frac{3}{34} + \left(-17\frac{1}{7}\right)$.

b. Write another expression that has the same value as this expression.

18. Think About the Process The science class wants to see how far a paper airplane will travel on a windy day. The teacher throws the paper airplane and it goes forward 8.5 feet. Then the paper airplane returns 6.1 feet before it hits the ground.

a. What should be the first step in calculating the distance the paper airplane is from the teacher?

A. Subtract the lesser absolute value from the greater absolute value.

B. Use the sign of the number with the greater absolute value as the sign of the sum.

C. Find the absolute values of the numbers.

D. Decide whether each number is positive or negative.

b. What is the distance from the teacher to where the paper airplane hit the ground?

19. Challenge Some friends are going on a coaster ride at an amusement park. They board their car on a platform that is $15\frac{3}{4}$ feet above the ground. The car starts by going down $80\frac{3}{4}$ feet. Then the car goes up $30\frac{1}{2}$ feet and comes to a stop. What is the change in height above ground from where the friends started on the platform to where they are when their car stops?

4-4 Subtracting Integers

CCSS: 7.NS.A.1, 7.NS.A.1c

Part 1

Intro

You have $15 before you spend $8. How much money do you have left?

Subtract 8 from 15. $15 - 8 = 7$ You have $7 left.

You can show subtraction on a number line. Imagine that you are walking on the number line. Begin at 0, face in the positive direction, and walk forward 15 units.

The subtraction sign tells you to turn around. The positive number 8 tells you to move forward 8 units.

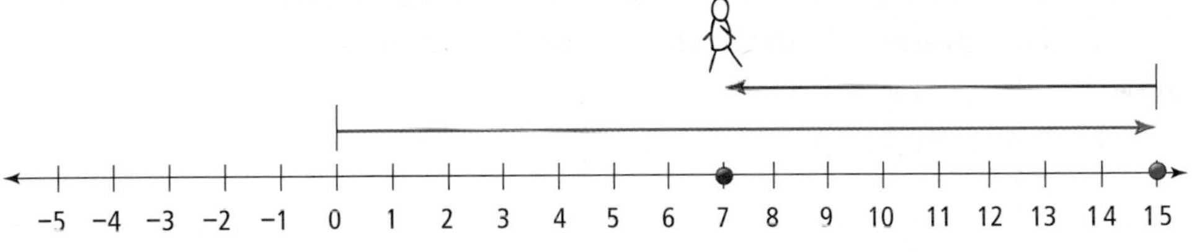

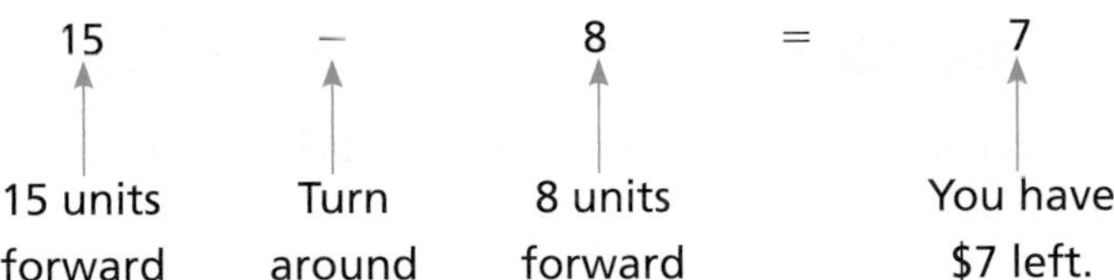

Turning around and moving forward is the same as moving backward. This number line model represents both $15 - 8$ and $15 + (-8)$.

$15 - 8 = 7$ $\quad\quad$ $15 + (-8) = 7$

Subtracting 8 is the same as adding the opposite of 8.

You have $7. You borrow money from your friend to buy a $20 sweater. How much are you in debt?

$7 - 20 = ?$

How do you subtract 20 from 7?

continued on next page >

Part 1

Intro continued

You can show subtraction on a number line. Begin at 0, face in the positive direction, and move forward 7 units.

The subtraction sign tells you to turn around. The positive number 20 tells you to move forward 20 units. You are 13 dollars in debt.

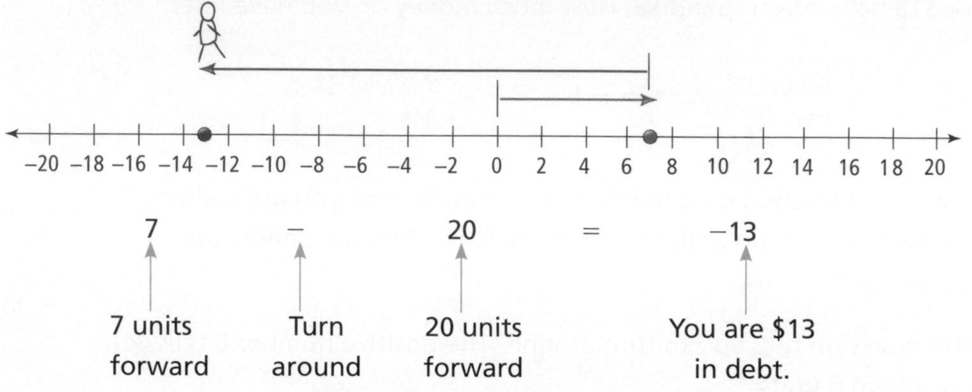

Turning around and moving forward is the same as moving backward. This number line model represents both the difference $7 - 20$ and the sum $7 + (-20)$.

$7 - 20 = -13$ $\qquad$ $7 + (-20) = -13$

Subtracting 20 is the same as adding the opposite of 20.

Example Using Number Lines to Add and Subtract Integers

Write equivalent subtraction and addition expressions for each number line model.

a.

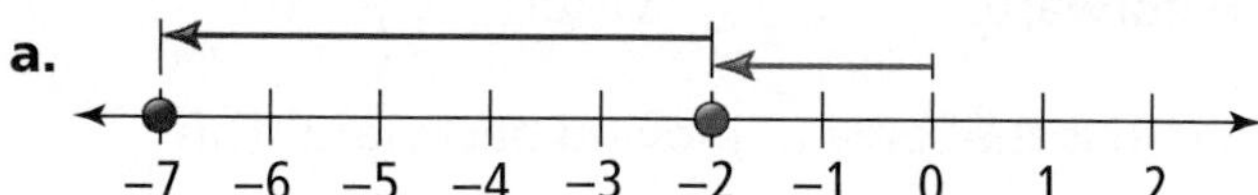

b.

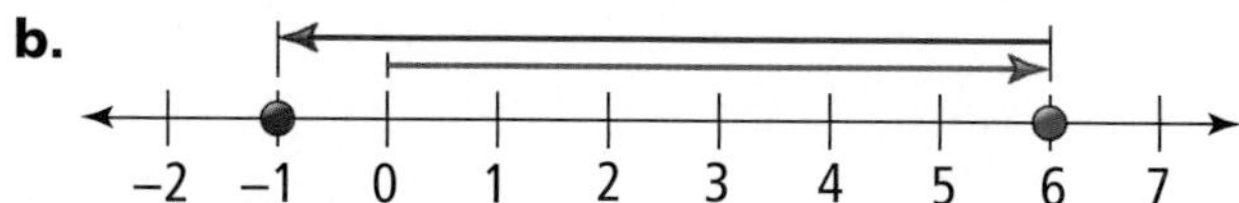

Solution

a.

−5 or + (−5)

−2

−7 −6 −5 −4 −3 −2 −1 0 1 2

The diagram represents $-2 - 5$, or $-2 + (-5)$.

Subtracting 5 is the same as adding the opposite of 5.

continued on next page >

Part 1

Solution continued

b.

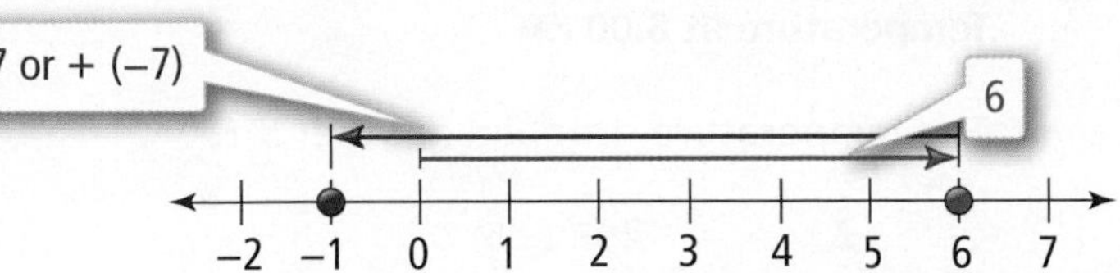

The diagram represents 6 − 7, or 6 + (−7).

Subtracting 7 is the same as adding the opposite of 7.

Part 2

Example Representing Situations with Integer Subtraction

Between 6:00 A.M. and noon, the temperature rose from 0°F to 8°F. By 5:00 P.M., the temperature had dropped by 10°F. By 8:00 P.M., the temperature dropped another 5°F.

Write and simplify a subtraction expression for the temperature at 5:00 P.M. and at 8:00 P.M. Model each expression on a thermometer.

Solution

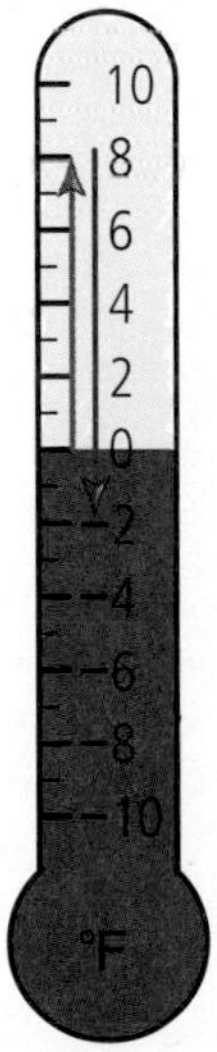

Temperature at 5:00 P.M.

The temperature rose from 0°F to 8°F.

The temperature dropped by 10°F.

$$8 - 10 = 8 + (-10)$$
$$= -2$$

The temperature at 5:00 P.M. is −2°F.

continued on next page >

Part 2

Solution continued

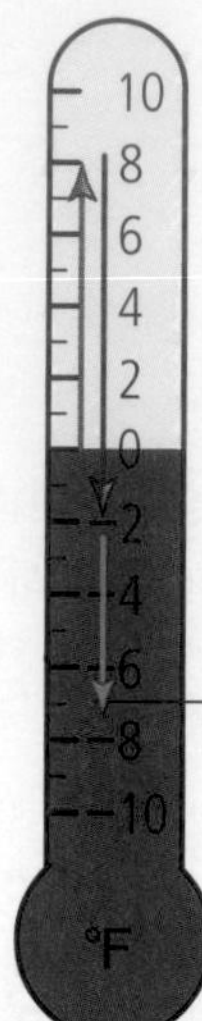

Temperature at 8:00 P.M.

The temperature dropped another 5°F.

$$-2 - 5 = -2 + (-5)$$
$$= -7$$

The temperature at 8:00 P.M. is −7°F.

Part 3

Intro

Subtracting is the process of "taking away" a quantity. How can you "take away" a negative quantity?

You borrow $13 from your friend so you can buy a sweater. You have a debt of $13. −13 represents your debt.

You can "take away" your debt by paying back $13.

$-13 - (-13) = 0 \qquad -13 + 13 = 0$

Subtracting −13 is the same as adding the opposite of −13.

Example Subtracting Integers

What is the value of each expression?

a. $-4 - (-3) = ■$ **b.** $6 - (-1) = ■$ **c.** $1 - (-6) = ■$

d. $-3 - (-4) = ■$ **e.** $-5 - (-2) = ■$ **f.** $-2 - (-5) = ■$

Part 3

Example continued

Solution

a. To subtract −3, add its opposite, 3.

$$-4 - (-3) = -4 + 3$$
$$= -1$$

b. To subtract −1, add its opposite, 1

$$6 - (-1) = 6 + 1$$
$$= 7$$

c. To subtract −6, add its opposite, 6.

$$1 - (-6) = 1 + 6$$
$$= 7$$

d. To subtract −4, add its opposite, 4

$$-3 - (-4) = -3 + 4$$
$$= 1$$

e. To subtract −2, add its opposite, 2.

$$-5 - (-2) = -5 + 2$$
$$= -3$$

f. To subtract −5, add its opposite, 5.

$$-2 - (-5) = -2 + 5$$
$$= 3$$

Key Concept

To subtract an integer, add its opposite.

Arithmetic	Algebra
$5 - 7 = 5 + (-7)$	$a - b = a + (-b)$
$5 - (-7) = 5 + 7$	$a - (-b) = a + b$

4-4 | Homework

Digital Resources

1. Which subtraction expression does the number line in **Figure 1** show?

   A. −3 − 6 **C.** 6 − 3

   B. 3 − 6 **D.** −6 − 3

2. Which number line model shows the subtraction 2 − 5?

   A.

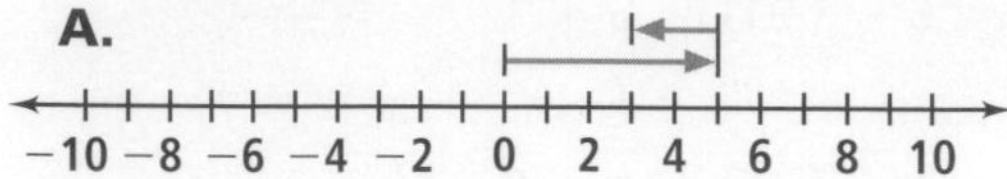

   B.

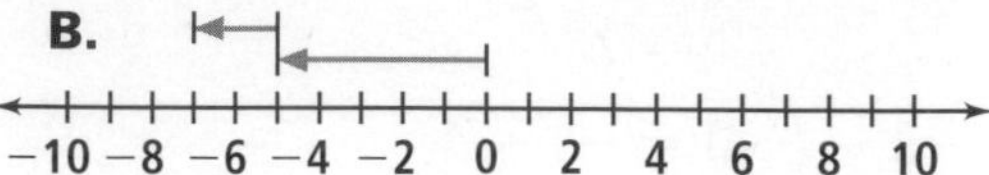

   C.

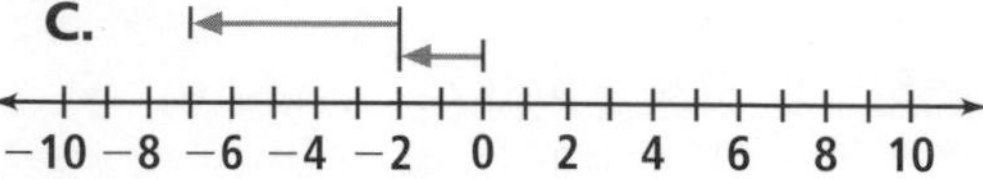

   D.

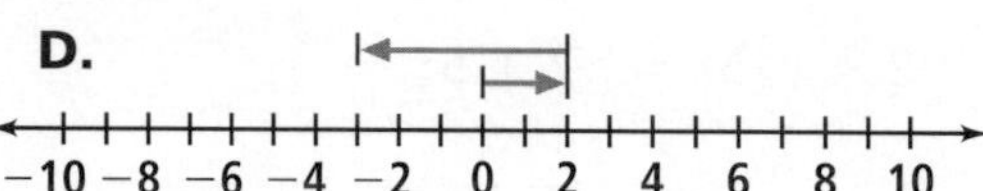

3. The temperature at the beginning of the day was 6°F. The temperature dropped 9°F by the end of the day. What was the temperature at the end of the day? Use the number line model to find 6 − 9.

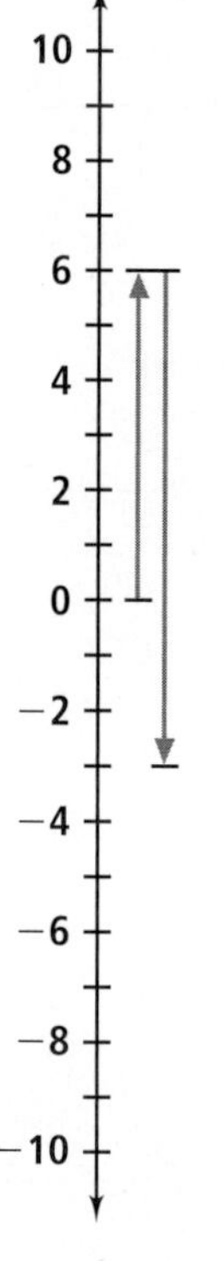

4. Youssef and his sister are fixing a bicycle. Youssef puts 2 tools back in his tool bag. His sister takes 7 tools out of the bag. The difference 2 − 7 represents the change in the number of tools in the bag. Use a number line model to find 2 − 7.

   A.

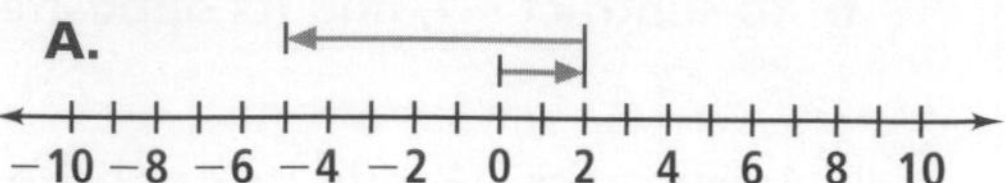

   B.

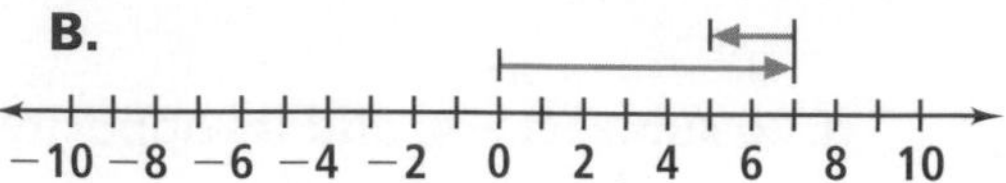

   C.

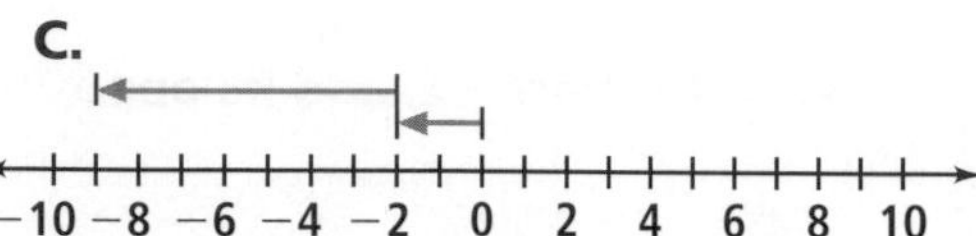

   D.

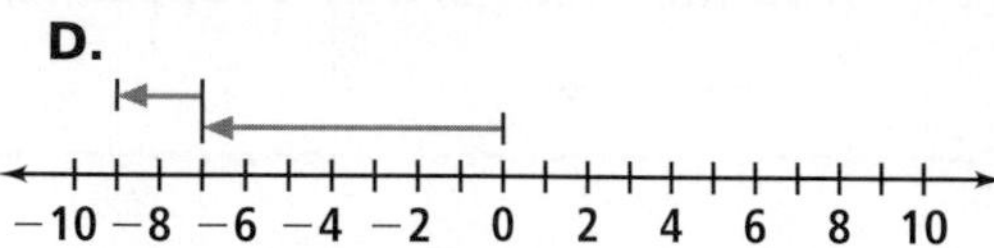

5. Find the value of the expression 2 − (−5).

6. Find the value of the expression −9 − (−5).

7. **a. Open Ended** Write a subtraction expression for the number line in **Figure 2**.

   b. Draw a number line model for a subtraction expression that is different from but has the same value as the one in part (a).

(Figure 1)

−10 −8 −6 −4 −2 0 2 4 6 8 10

8. **a. Reasoning** Use the number line model to find $-4 - 5$.

b. What can you say about the sign of a positive integer subtracted from a negative integer?

9. **Think About the Process** A man goes to a gym to lift weights. One day, when he starts his workout, he adds 4 lb to the bar. Later, for a different exercise, he removes 13 lb from the bar. The number line models the changes to the weight on the bar.

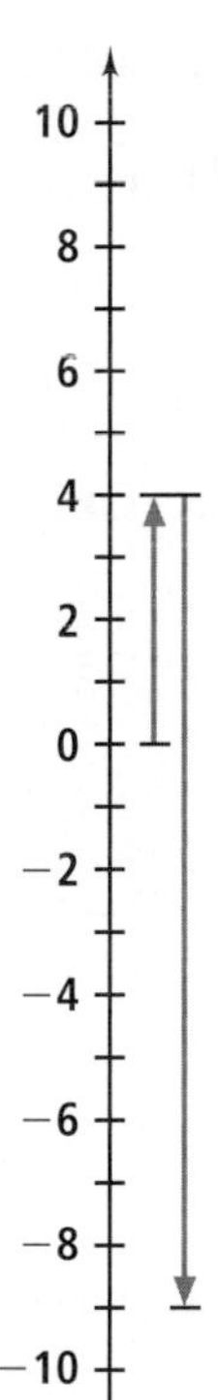

a. Why do the arrows point in the directions they do?

A. to show that the man removes weight, then adds weight to the bar

B. to show that the man adds weight, then removes weight from the bar

C. to show that the man removes weight, then removes more weight from the bar

D. to show that the man adds weight, then adds more weight to the bar

b. What is the change in the weight on the bar for the second exercise relative to the weight on the bar before the man started his workout?

10. Use a number line model to subtract 5 from -13.

11. Subtract -20 from 17.

12. **a.** Subtract -6 from -3.

b. What is the difference between the difference of -3 and -6 and the difference of -6 and -3? Show how you found your answer.

13. **Think About the Process**

a. Which addition expression is equivalent to $7 - (-3)$?

A. $-3 + 7$ **B.** $-7 + 3$

C. $7 + 3$ **D.** $3 + (-7)$

b. Find $7 - (-3)$.

14. **Challenge** What number do you have to subtract from -4 to get -2?

(Figure 2)

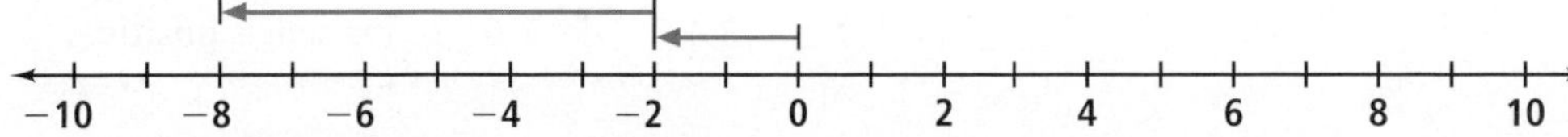

See your complete lesson at MyMathUniverse.com

4-5 Subtracting Rational Numbers

CCSS: 7.NS.A.1, 7.NS.A.1b

Key Concept

You subtract a fraction or a decimal the same way you subtract an integer.

For any rational numbers a and b:

$$a - b = a + (-b)$$

$$a - (-b) = a + b$$

Write subtraction as adding the opposite. $-\frac{3}{5} - \frac{4}{5} = -\frac{3}{5} + \left(-\frac{4}{5}\right)$

Add numbers with the same sign. $= -\frac{7}{5}$

Write subtraction as adding the opposite. $-9.1 - (-7.6) = -9.1 + 7.6$

Add numbers with different signs. $= -1.5$

Part 1

Example Predicting The Sign of Differences of Rational Numbers

Determine if each difference is negative, zero, or positive.

a. $\frac{1}{2} - \left(-\frac{1}{4}\right)$ **b.** $-5 - \left(-3\frac{3}{4}\right)$ **c.** $-4.7 - (-4.7)$ **d.** $5.7 - 8\frac{1}{2}$

e. $-2.6 - (-3.1)$ **f.** $-3\frac{1}{2} - \left(-3\frac{1}{2}\right)$ **g.** $-\frac{4}{3} - \left(-\frac{2}{3}\right)$ **h.** $-0.8 - 0.8$

Solution

Rewrite the subtraction as adding the opposite. Then think about the relationship of the addends.

a. $\frac{1}{2} - \left(-\frac{1}{4}\right) = \frac{1}{2} + \frac{1}{4}$ — The sum of two positives is **positive**.

b. $-5 - 3\frac{3}{4} = -5 + \left(-3\frac{3}{4}\right)$ — The sum of two negatives is **negative**.

c. $-4.7 - (-4.7) = -4.7 + 4.7$ — The sum of two additive inverses is **zero**.

d. $5.7 - 8\frac{1}{2} = 5.7 + \left(-8\frac{1}{2}\right)$ — $\left|-8\frac{1}{2}\right| > |5.7|$, so the sum is **negative**.

e. $-2.6 - (-3.1) = -2.6 + 3.1$ — $|3.1| > |-2.6|$, so the sum is **positive**.

continued on next page >

Part 1

Solution continued

f. $-3\frac{1}{2} - \left(-3\frac{1}{2}\right) = -3\frac{1}{2} + 3\frac{1}{2}$

The sum of two additive inverses is **zero**.

g. $-\frac{4}{3} - \left(-\frac{2}{3}\right) = -\frac{4}{3} + \frac{2}{3}$

$\left|-\frac{4}{3}\right| > \left|\frac{2}{3}\right|$, so the sum is **negative**.

h. $-0.8 - 0.8 = -0.8 + (-0.8)$

The sum of two negatives is **negative**.

Part 2

Example Subtracting Rational Numbers on Number Lines

Model each subtraction expression on a number line. Find the value of the expression.

a. $-\frac{1}{2} - \frac{5}{6} = \blacksquare$

b. $-2\frac{1}{4} - \left(-3\frac{1}{2}\right) = \blacksquare$

Solution

a.

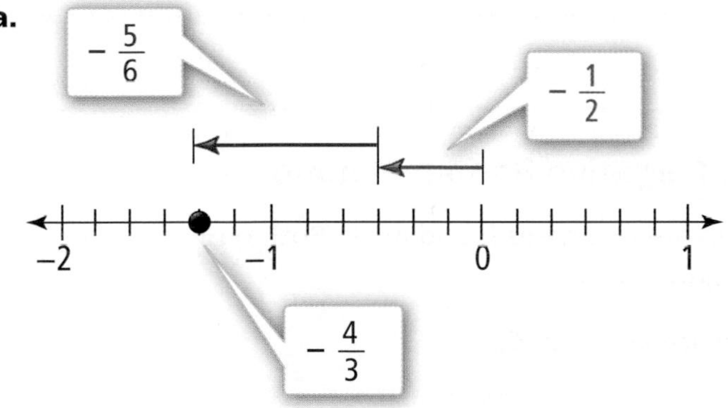

Write the subtraction as adding the opposite. $-\frac{1}{2} - \frac{5}{6} = -\frac{1}{2} + \left(-\frac{5}{6}\right)$

Find a common denominator. $= -\frac{3}{6} + \left(-\frac{5}{6}\right)$

Add the fractions. $= -\frac{8}{6}$

Simplify. $= -\frac{4}{3}$

So, $-\frac{1}{2} - \frac{5}{6} = -\frac{4}{3}$.

continued on next page >

Part 2

Solution continued

b.

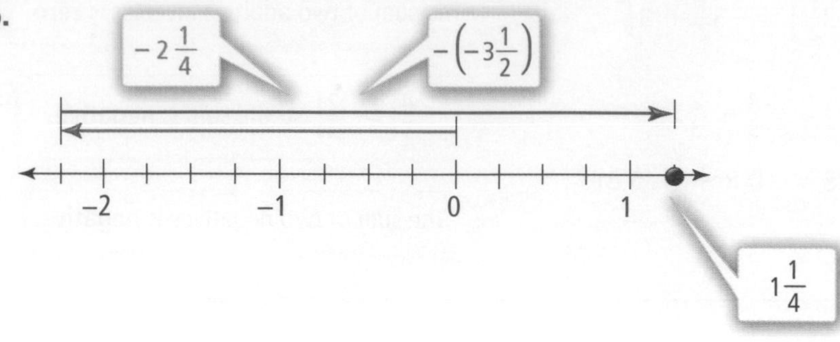

Write the subtraction as adding the opposite.	$-2\frac{1}{4} - \left(-3\frac{1}{2}\right) = -2\frac{1}{4} + 3\frac{1}{2}$
Find a common denominator.	$= -2\frac{1}{4} + 3\frac{2}{4}$
Add the mixed numbers.	$= 1\frac{1}{4}$

So, $-2\frac{1}{4} - \left(-3\frac{1}{2}\right) = 1\frac{1}{4}$.

Part 3

Example Comparing Negative Rational Numbers

Carbon dioxide and nitrogen are two gases found in air. Both gases can be used as coolants in solid or liquid form.

Carbon dioxide becomes dry ice at −78.5°C.

Nitrogen becomes liquid nitrogen at −195.79°C.

Which of these temperatures is higher? How much higher?

Solution

Know
Two negative temperatures

Need
How much higher one temperature is than the other

Plan
Use the temperatures' positions on a number line to identify which temperature is higher than the other. Subtract the lesser number from the greater number.

continued on next page >

Part 3

Solution continued

Step 1 Identify which temperature is higher than the other.

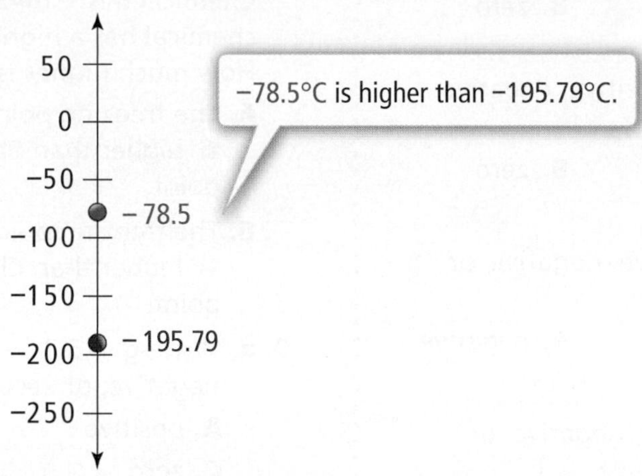

Step 2 Subtract the lesser number from the greater number.

Write the subtraction as adding the opposite.	$-78.5 - (-195.79) = -78.5 + 195.79$
Find the absolute value of each number.	$\lvert -78.5 \rvert = 78.5$ $\lvert -195.79 \rvert = 195.79$
Subtract the lesser absolute value from the greater.	$195.79 - 78.5 = 117.29$
Use the sign of the number with the greater absolute value.	$-78.5 + 195.79 = 117.29$

So, −78.5°C is 117.29°C higher than −195.79°C.

4-5 | Homework

Digital Resources

1. a. Is $3.2 - 5.7$ positive, negative, or zero?

   A. negative B. zero
   C. positive

   b. Is $3.2 - (-5.7)$ positive, negative, or zero?

   A. negative B. zero
   C. positive

2. a. Is $\frac{2}{5} - \left(-\frac{5}{6}\right)$ positive, negative, or zero?

   A. positive B. negative
   C. zero

   b. Is $\frac{2}{5} - \left(\frac{5}{6}\right)$ positive, negative, or zero?

   A. zero B. positive
   C. negative

3. Decide if each expression describes a difference that is positive, negative, or zero.

   a. Is $-4.5 - (-6.1)$ positive, negative, or zero?

   A. negative B. positive
   C. zero

   b. Is $-4.5 - 6.1$ positive, negative, or zero?

   A. positive B. zero
   C. negative

4. Draw a point on a number line to indicate the difference $1\frac{1}{3} - 4\frac{5}{6}$.

5. Which number line in **Figure 1** models $\frac{1}{4} - \left(-\frac{5}{8}\right)$ correctly?

6. Find the value of the expression $11.0 - (-2.1)$.

7. The temperature in a town is 36.6°F during the day and −12.6°F at night. Find the difference in the temperatures.

8. The freezing point of Chemical A is −70.2°C. The freezing point of Chemical B is −164.21°C. Which chemical has a higher freezing point? How much higher is it?

   A. The freezing point of Chemical B is ■° higher than Chemical A's freezing point.

   B. The freezing point of Chemical A is ■° higher than Chemical B's freezing point.

9. a. **Writing** Is $5.3 - 5.3$ positive, negative, or zero?

   A. positive B. negative
   C. zero

   b. Is $5.3 - (-5.3)$ positive, negative, or zero?

   A. negative B. positive
   C. zero

   c. How can you use the answer for the first part to help you answer the second part?

10. a. **Reasoning** Is $-\frac{1}{3} - \frac{4}{5}$ positive, negative, or zero?

    A. negative B. positive
    C. zero

    b. What can you say about the sign of the difference when you subtract $-m - n$, for any positive rational numbers m and n?

    A. The difference is always zero.
    B. The difference is always negative.
    C. The difference is always positive.
    D. The difference is negative if $|n| > |m|$ and positive if $|n| < |m|$.

(Figure 1)

A.

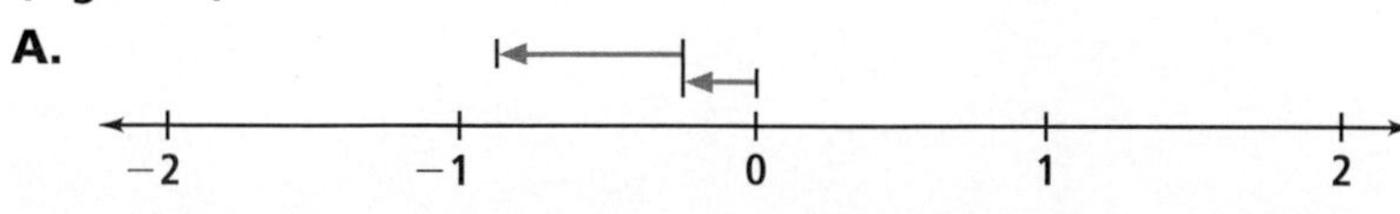

B.

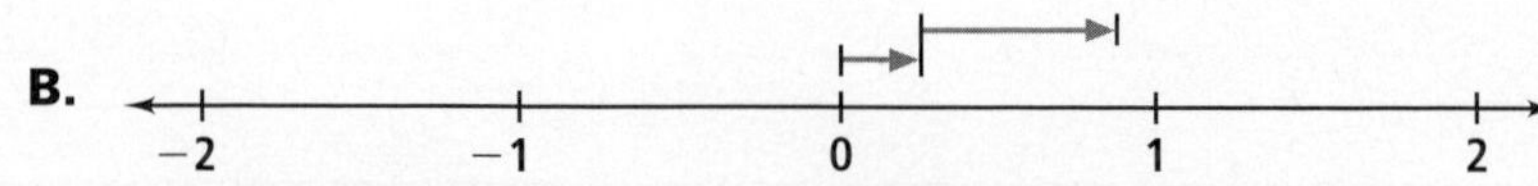

11. a. Multiple Representations Which addition expression is equivalent to $-\frac{1}{3} - \left(-\frac{5}{12}\right)$?

A. $\frac{1}{3} + \frac{5}{12}$ **B.** $-\frac{1}{3} + \frac{5}{12}$

C. $\frac{1}{3} + \left(-\frac{5}{12}\right)$ **D.** $-\frac{1}{3} + \left(-\frac{5}{12}\right)$

b. Draw the point on a number line that represents $-\frac{1}{3} - \left(-\frac{5}{12}\right)$.

c. Find the value of the expression $-\frac{1}{3} - \left(-\frac{5}{12}\right)$.

12. a. Error Analysis Your friend says that the value of the expression 27.08 − (−18.04) is 9.04. What is the correct value?

b. What mistake did your friend likely make?

A. Your friend used the wrong sign in their answer.

B. Your friend added 27.08 and −18.04.

C. Your friend made an error when subtracting.

13. Flying Home A bird flies from the bottom of a canyon that is $89\frac{3}{5}$ feet below sea level to a nest that is $528\frac{1}{5}$ feet above sea level. What is the difference in elevation between the bottom of the canyon and the bird's nest?

14. Is $1\frac{9}{14} - \left(-\frac{2}{13}\right) - 1\frac{9}{14}$ positive, negative, or zero?

A. positive **B.** negative

C. zero

15. Decrease −8.19 by −11.08.

16. Think About the Process

a. What is the first step when finding $2\frac{3}{4} - 5\frac{1}{2}$?

A. Plot $2\frac{3}{4}$ on the number line.

B. Plot $-5\frac{1}{2}$ on the number line.

C. Plot $-2\frac{3}{4}$ on the number line.

D. Plot $5\frac{1}{2}$ on the number line.

b. Which number line in **Figure 2** models the subtraction correctly?

c. What is the value of $2\frac{3}{4} - 5\frac{1}{2}$?

17. Think About the Process Subtract −14.7 − (−7.1).

a. What is the first step when finding the value of this expression?

A. Find the opposite of −7.1.

B. Find the opposite of −14.7.

b. What is the value of −14.7 − (−7.1)?

18. Challenge The temperatures at sunrise and sunset are shown in the table.

Daily Temperatures

	Temperature at Sunrise (°C)	Temperature at Sunset (°C)
Day 1	−11.31	13.49
Day 2	−7.69	25.25

a. What was the temperature change on Day 1?

b. What was the temperature change on Day 2?

c. On which day did the temperature change the most?

(Figure 2)

A.

−6 −5 −4 −3 −2 −1 0 1 2 3 4 5 6

B.

−6 −5 −4 −3 −2 −1 0 1 2 3 4 5 6

4-6 Distance on a Number Line

CCSS: 7.NS.A.1c

Part 1

Intro

Different types of clouds occur at different levels of the atmosphere. Stratus clouds occur about 2 km above the ground. Cirrus clouds occur about 10 km above the ground. Nimbostratus clouds appear about 1.3 km above the ground. Altostratus clouds occur about 4.1 km above the ground. Cumulonimbus clouds occur from 2.8 km to 6.6 km above the ground.

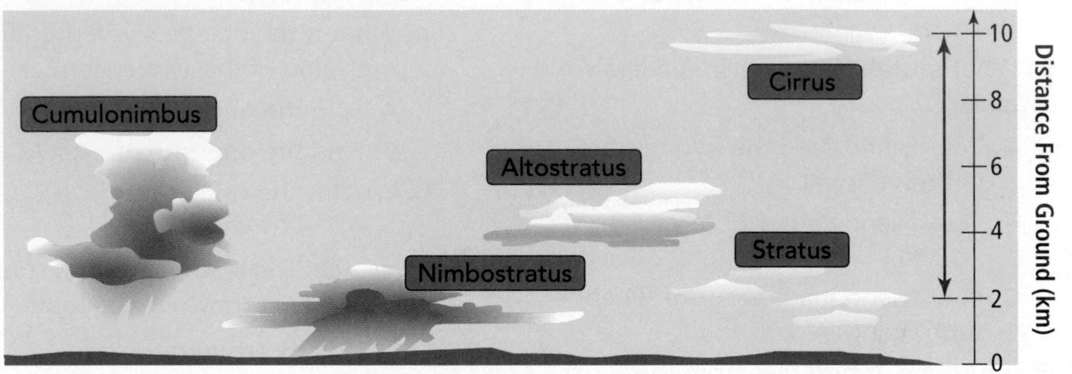

If you subtract the height of the stratus cloud from the height of the cirrus cloud, you find out how much higher the cirrus cloud is than the stratus cloud.

If you subtract the height of the cirrus cloud from the height of the stratus cloud, you find out how much higher the stratus cloud is than the cirrus cloud.

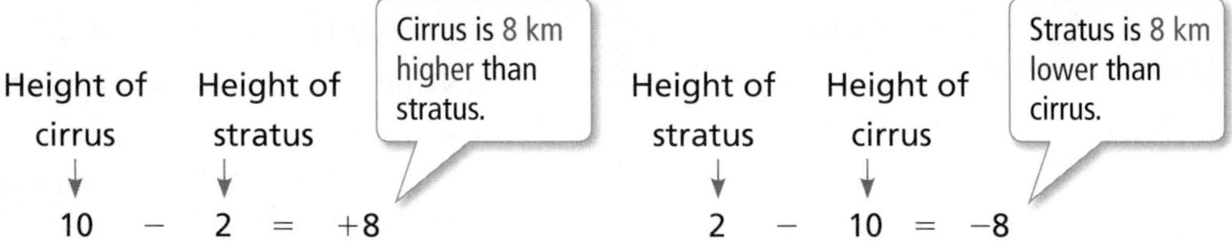

Reversing the order of the subtraction changes the sign of the difference but not the absolute value of the difference.

Distance between the clouds

$$|10 - 2| = |2 - 10| = 8$$

The absolute value of the difference of the cloud heights is the distance between the clouds, without the information about which cloud is higher or lower.

continued on next page >

Part 1

Example Finding Distances Between Positive Coordinates

Write two different absolute value expressions for the distance in kilometers between the nimbostratus cloud and the altostratus cloud. How far apart are the clouds?

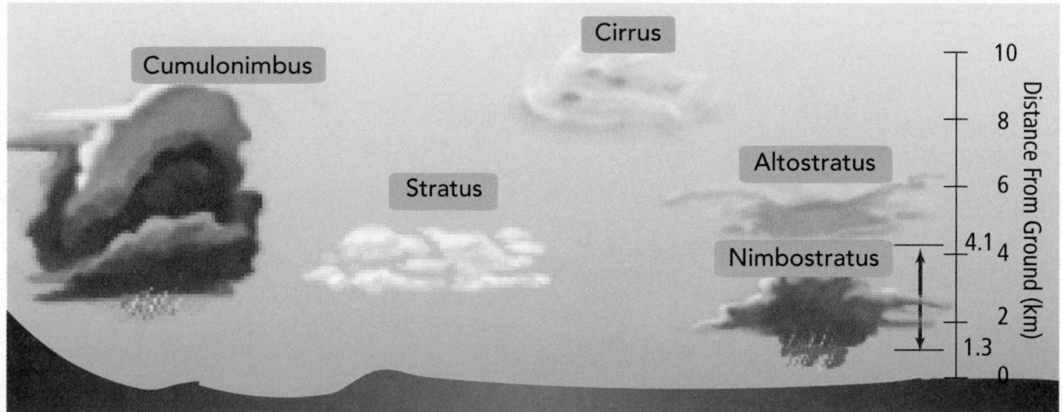

Solution

The distance between the clouds is the absolute value of the difference in their heights.

The nimbostratus cloud is at a height of 1.3 km.
The altostratus cloud is at a height of 4.1 km.

You can write the difference in either order.

$$|4.1 - 1.3| = |2.8| = 2.8 \qquad |1.3 - 4.1| = |-2.8| = 2.8$$

The nimbostratus cloud and the altostratus cloud are 2.8 km apart.

Part 2

Example Finding Distances Between Negative Coordinates

You can also use absolute value to find the distance between points on a number line when one or both coordinates are negative.

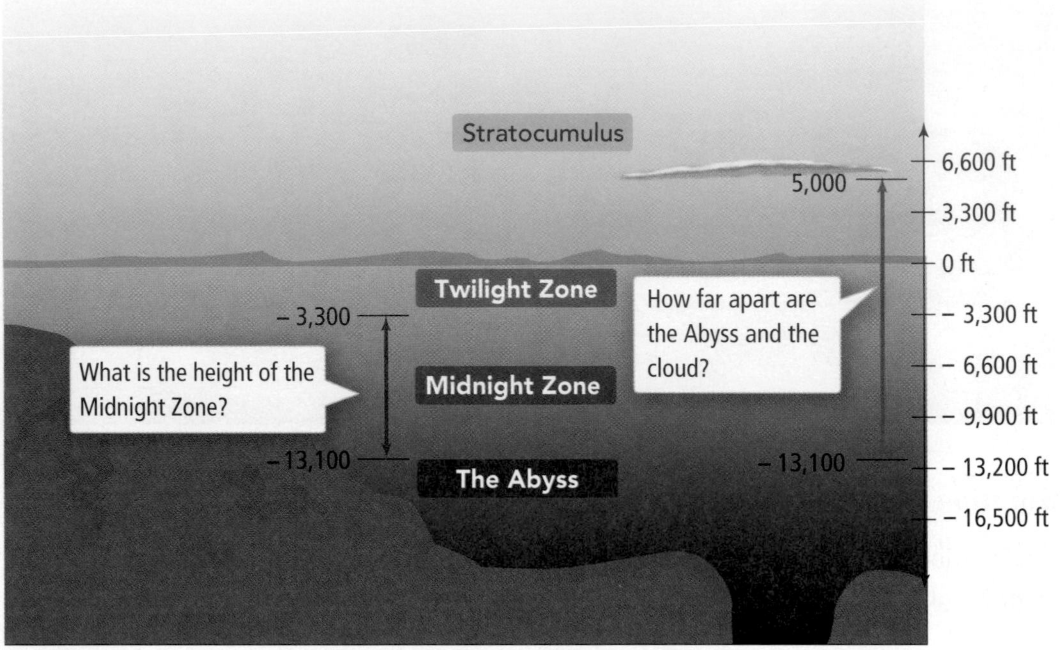

Solution

To find the height of the Midnight Zone, find the distance between −3,300 and −13,100.

The distance is equal to the absolute value of the difference.

Write the subtraction as adding the opposite.

$$\begin{aligned} |-3{,}300 - (-13{,}100)| &= |-3{,}300 + 13{,}100| \\ &= |9{,}800| \\ &= 9{,}800 \end{aligned}$$

The height of the Midnight Zone is 9,800 ft.

continued on next page >

Part 2

Solution continued

To find how far apart the Abyss and the cloud are, find the distance between −13,100 and 5,000.

The distance is equal to the absolute value of the difference.

Write the subtraction as adding the opposite.

$$\begin{aligned} |5{,}000 - (-13{,}100)| &= |5{,}000 + 13{,}100| \\ &= |18{,}100| \\ &= 18{,}100 \end{aligned}$$

The Abyss and the cloud are 18,100 ft apart.

Key Concept

The distance between any two rational numbers a and b on the number line is the absolute value of their difference.

distance between a and b $= |a - b| = |b - a|$

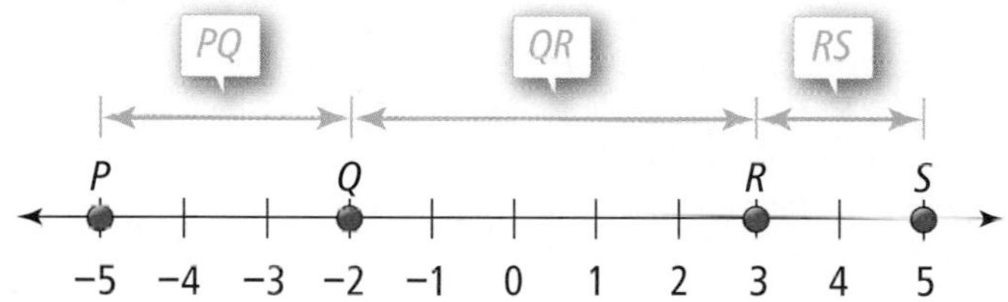

Distance Between P and Q

$$\begin{aligned} PQ &= |-2 - (-5)| \\ &= |-2 + 5| \\ &= |3| \\ &= 3 \end{aligned}$$

Distance Between Q and R

$$\begin{aligned} QR &= |3 - (-2)| \\ &= |3 + 2| \\ &= |5| \\ &= 5 \end{aligned}$$

Distance Between R and S

$$\begin{aligned} RS &= |5 - 3| \\ &= |2| \\ &= 2 \end{aligned}$$

Part 3

Example Writing Absolute Value Expressions to Find Distance

Which expression represents each of the following?

$|-5 - (-1)|$ $\quad |5 - 1|$ $\quad |5 - (-1)|$ $\quad |-5 - 1|$

a. Distance between 5 and -1

b. Distance between -5 and -1

c. Distance between 5 and 1

Solution

The distance between a and b is $|a - b|$.

a. Distance between 5 and $-1 = |5 - (-1)|$

b. Distance between -5 and $-1 = |-5 - (-1)|$

c. Distance between 5 and $1 = |5 - 1|$

Digital Resources   

1. Find the distance between the numbers 3.9 and 8.3.
2. Suppose an airplane is flying 11,000 feet above the ground. Another airplane is directly above at 35,000 feet above the ground. How far apart are the airplanes?
3. Suppose City A is 44.4 km east of City B. City C is 127.5 km east of City B. How far apart are City A and City C?
4. Find the distance between -422 and 166.
5. Mischa dives from a platform that is 5 meters above water. Her dive takes her 2.1 meters below the surface of the water. How far does Mischa's dive take her?
6. Which of the expressions represent the distance between -8 and 7 on a number line? Select all that apply.

   A. $|-8 + 7|$ **B.** $|7 + 8|$
   C. $|-7 + 8|$ **D.** $|8 - 7|$
   E. $|7 - 8|$ **F.** $|-8 - 7|$

7. Which of the pairs of numbers are 13.7 units apart on a number line? Select all that apply.
   A. -26.3 and -12.6
   B. -26.3 and 12.6
   C. -3.2 and -10.5
   D. 3.2 and 10.5
   E. -3.2 and 10.5
   F. 26.3 and -12.6
8. **Mental Math** Find the distance between the numbers 420 and 450 on a number line.
9. **Reasoning** A group of friends are rock climbing. Travis is 30.7 feet above the ground. Shayla is directly below Travis at 17.7 feet above the ground.
   a. How far apart are they?
   b. Kiera and Alfonso are climbing another wall. Kiera is 17.7 feet above the ground. Alfonso is directly above Kiera at 30.7 feet above the ground. How far apart are they?
   c. Write two different equations for finding the two distances. Explain why the answers are alike or different.
10. **Writing** Suppose a diver is swimming 13.2 feet below sea level. A whale is swimming 851 feet below sea level.
    a. How much lower is the whale than the diver?
    b. How would this distance change if the diver was at 13.2 feet above sea level? Explain your answer.
11. Suppose two friends are standing next to each other. One friend runs 29.5 yards in one direction. The other friend runs 19.6 yards in the opposite direction, stops, and then continues in the same direction for 12.6 more yards. How far apart are the friends?
12. **Marine Biology** A group of marine biologists are scuba diving. For safety, they dive in pairs. The two divers in a pair must be, at most, 35 feet away from each other at all times. One diver is 122 feet below sea level. The other diver is directly below at 159 feet below sea level.
    a. How far apart are the divers?
    b. Are they within the maximum distance allowed?

13. Error Analysis A student incorrectly writes the distance between -57 and -34 on the number line as $|-57 - 34|$.

a. Which expression represents the distance between -57 and -34 on the number line?

A. $|34 + 57|$ **B.** $|57 + 34|$
C. $|-57 + 34|$ **D.** $|-34 - 57|$

b. What was the student's likely error?

A. The student wrote the terms in the wrong order.

B. The student subtracted the numbers instead of adding.

C. The student did not first write the absolute value of each number.

D. The student added the numbers instead of subtracting.

14. a. Find the distance between 148.1 and 65.45 on the number line.

b. Find the distance between 1,159.2 and 1,192.5 on the number line.

c. Which distance is greater?

A. The distance on the number line between 148.1 and 65.45 is greater.

B. The distance on the number line between 1,159.2 and 1,192.5 is greater.

C. The distances are the same.

15. a. How far apart are $-20{,}593$ and -814.18 on the number line?

b. How far apart are $-20{,}593$ and 814.18 on the number line?

c. Which pair of numbers is farther apart, $-20{,}593$ and -814.18 or $-20{,}593$ and 814.18?

A. $-20{,}593$ and 814.18

B. $-20{,}593$ and -814.18

C. They are the same distance apart.

d. Explain how to find which pair of numbers is farther apart without actually finding the distances.

16. Think About the Process

a. How can you find the distance between the numbers $3\frac{1}{4}$ and $6\frac{5}{8}$ on the number line? Select all that apply.

A. Find the quotient of $6\frac{5}{8}$ divided by $3\frac{1}{4}$.

B. Find the absolute value of $6\frac{5}{8} - 3\frac{1}{4}$.

C. Find the product of $3\frac{1}{4}$ and $6\frac{5}{8}$.

D. Find the sum of $3\frac{1}{4}$ and $6\frac{5}{8}$.

E. Find the absolute value of $3\frac{1}{4} - 6\frac{5}{8}$.

b. What is the distance between $3\frac{1}{4}$ and $6\frac{5}{8}$ on the number line?

17. Think About the Process

a. Without finding the distance, decide if the distance between $-7{,}981$ and $-13{,}540$ on the number line is positive or negative.

b. Find the distance between $-7{,}981$ and $-13{,}450$ on the number line.

18. Challenge The ceiling of the first floor in a house is 10 ft above the ground. The ceiling of the second floor in the house is 21.9 ft above the ground. A shelf on the second floor is 181.356 cm above the ceiling of the first floor. (Use the conversion factors $\frac{1 \text{ in.}}{2.54 \text{ cm}}$ and $\frac{1 \text{ ft}}{12 \text{ in.}}$.)

a. How far apart are the shelf and the ground?

b. How far apart are the shelf and the second floor's ceiling?

19. Challenge Sari and Ramon are playing catch. Sari throws a baseball 28 ft to Ramon. Ramon catches the ball, turns around, and runs 18 ft farther away from Sari. He throws the ball back to Sari, but overthrows by 24 in. How far is Ramon from the ball? (Use the conversion factor $\frac{1 \text{ ft}}{12 \text{ in.}}$ as necessary.)

4-7 Problem Solving

CCSS: 7.EE.B.3, Also 7.NS.A.1b, 7.NS.A.1c

Part 1

Example Modeling with Rational Numbers on Number Lines

Three friends all live on the same street that runs west to east. Juan lives $2\frac{1}{2}$ blocks from Amy. Michele lives $3\frac{3}{4}$ blocks from Juan.

Find all possible locations for Juan's house and Michele's house on the diagram. Name the coordinates of each location.

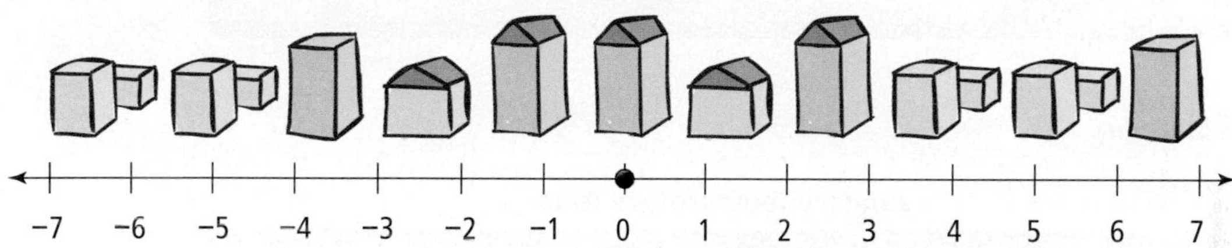

Solution

Juan could live $2\frac{1}{2}$ blocks east of Amy, or $2\frac{1}{2}$ blocks west.

Michele could live $3\frac{3}{4}$ blocks east of Juan, or $3\frac{3}{4}$ blocks west.

So, there are two possible locations for Juan's house and four possible locations for Michele's house.

Juan could live at $2\frac{1}{2}$ and then Michele can live at $6\frac{1}{4}$ or $-1\frac{1}{4}$.

Or, Juan can live at $-2\frac{1}{2}$ and then Michele can live at $1\frac{1}{4}$ or $-6\frac{1}{4}$.

Part 2

Example Solving Subtraction Equations with Rational Numbers

Write an equation that expresses "Variation From Normal" in terms of "Recorded Temperature" and "Normal Temperature." Use your equation to complete the table.

January Temperature Data

	Recorded Temperature (°F)	Normal Temperature (°F)	Variation From Normal (°F)
High	41	15	26
Low	−35	−4	■
Average Low	■	−4.4	4.2

Solution

January Temperature Data

	Recorded Temperature (°F)	Normal Temperature (°F)	Variation From Normal (°F)
High	41	15	26
Low	−35	−4	−31
Average Low	−0.2	−4.4	4.2

Variation From Normal = Recorded Temperature − Normal Temperature

$$V = R - N$$

To find the variation from normal for the low temperature, let $R = -35$ and $N = -4$.

Substitute for R and N. $V = -35 - (-4)$

Write subtraction as adding the opposite. $V = -35 + 4$

Add two numbers with different signs. $V = -31$

The variation from normal for the low temperature is −31°F.

continued on next page >

Part 2

Solution continued

To find the recorded temperature for the average low temperature, let $N = -4.4$ and $V = 4.2$.

Substitute for *N* and *V*. $4.2 = R - (-4.4)$

Write subtraction as adding the opposite. $4.2 = R + 4.4$

$4.4 - 4.4 = 0$

Subtract 4.4 from each side of the equation. $4.2 - 4.4 = R + 4.4 - 4.4$

Write subtraction as adding the opposite. $4.2 + (-4.4) = R$

Add two numbers with different signs. $-0.2 = R$

The recorded temperature for the average low temperature is -0.2°F.

Part 3

Example Finding Range by Subtracting Integers

What is the range of the data represented by the box plot? What is the interquartile range of the data?

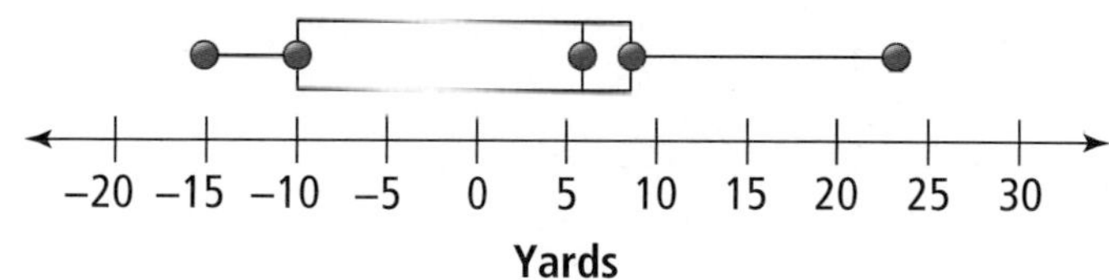

Solution

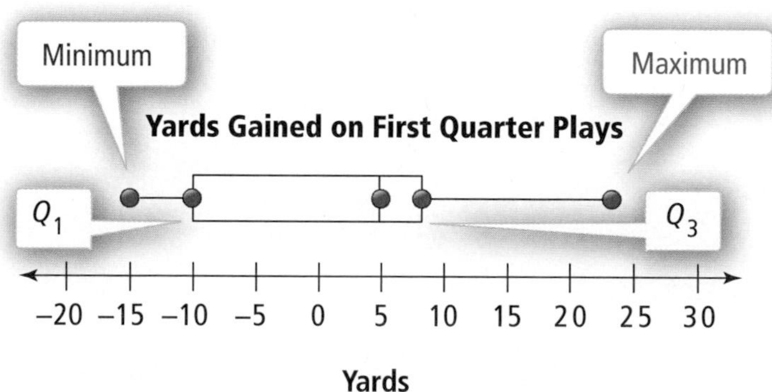

continued on next page >

Part 3

Solution continued

The range is the difference between the maximum and the minimum.

$$\text{range} = \text{maximum} - \text{minimum}$$

Substitute for the maximum and the minimum. $= 23 - (-15)$

Write the subtraction as adding the opposite. $= 23 + 15$

Add two numbers with the same sign. $= 38$

The range of the data is 38 yards.

The interquartile range (*IQR*) is the difference between the third quartile (Q_3) and the first quartile (Q_1).

$$IQR = Q_3 - Q_1$$

Substitute for Q_1 and Q_3. $= 8 - (-10)$

Write the subtraction as adding the opposite. $= 8 + 10$

Add two numbers with the same sign. $= 18$

The interquartile range of the data is 18 yards.

Digital Resources   

1. Three roads, A, B, and C, all run south to north. They each meet a highway that runs west to east. Road B is 4.2 km east of Road A. Road C is 2.4 km west of Road B. Describe the location of Road C with respect to Road A.

2. The formula $V = R - N$ describes the variation V of the recorded temperature R from the normal temperature N. If the recorded temperature is -3.6°F and the normal temperature is 9.5°F, what is the variation from the normal temperature?

3. There are ten bird baths in a park. On the first day of spring, the bird baths are filled. Several weeks later, the overall change in the water level is found. The results are shown in the table in **Figure 1.** What is the range of the data?

4. **Figure 2** shows the daily high temperatures for a city during eleven days last February.

a. What is the range of the temperatures?

b. What is the interquartile range (IQR) of the temperatures?

5. Three friends all live on the same street that runs west to east. Beth lives 5 blocks from Ann. Carl lives 2 blocks from Beth. If the street is represented by a number line and Ann's house is located at 0, what are the possible locations for Carl's house?

6. Chase lives $2\frac{3}{5}$ blocks west of Ellie. They draw a number line to model this situation. Because Ellie lives $3\frac{1}{2}$ blocks east of school, they give her house the coordinates $3\frac{1}{2}$. Chase incorrectly claims that the coordinate of his house is $6\frac{1}{10}$.

a. What is the correct coordinate of Chase's house?

b. What is Chase's likely error?

A. He subtracted $3\frac{1}{2}$ from the coordinate for Ellie's house.

B. He added $3\frac{1}{2}$ to the coordinate for Ellie's house.

C. He subtracted $2\frac{3}{5}$ from the coordinate for Ellie's house.

D. He added $2\frac{3}{5}$ to the coordinate for Ellie's house.

7. At a fair last weekend, Rebecca sold homemade jewelry. If she sold the jewelry for R dollars and it cost her C dollars to make the jewelry, the formula $P = R - C$ describes her profit P in dollars. If her profit was \$30.54 and she sold the jewelry for \$72.12, how much did it cost her to make the jewelry?

8. Julia is hanging birdhouses on her fence, which includes one red post. The first birdhouse is 21.2 in. to the right of the red post. The second birdhouse is 29.1 in. to the left of the first birdhouse. Describe the location of the second birdhouse with respect to the red post. Use integers to estimate the distance.

(Figure 1)

Changes in Amount of Water (gallons)									
2.4	1.4	−2.3	2.9	2.3	−1.2	−1.4	−1.8	2.5	0.9

(Figure 2)

Daily High Temperatures (°F)										
1.6	2.4	−1.4	12.1	11.7	7.7	12.5	8.4	4.2	3.9	0.9

9. The formulas for converting temperatures between degrees Celsius (C) and degrees Fahrenheit $C = \frac{5}{9}(F - 32)$ and $F = \frac{9}{5}C + 32$.

   a. Express 14°F in degrees Celsius.

   b. Express −15°C in degrees Fahrenheit.

   c. Which temperature is colder?

10. In a certain city, Third Avenue, which runs west to east, meets Main Street, which runs south to north. A library, city hall, and a school are all on Third Avenue. The library is 400 yds west of Main St. City Hall is 300 yds west of the library. The school is 200 yds east of city hall. Describe the location of the school with respect to Main Street.

11. **Think About the Process** In a certain area, speeding fines are computed with the formula $D = 10(x - 50) + 55$, where D is the cost in dollars of the fine if a person is caught driving x miles per hour. Last night, Cody got a $125 speeding fine.

   a. How could you rewrite the formula to make it easier to find how fast he was driving?

      A. $x = \frac{1}{10}(D + 445)$

      B. $x = \frac{1}{10}(D - 445)$

      C. $x = \frac{1}{10}D - 445$

      D. $x = \frac{1}{10}D + 445$

   b. How fast was Cody driving?

12. **Challenge** The formula $\frac{W}{2} - 3H = 53$ models the recommended weight W, in pounds, of a man, where H represents the man's height, in inches, over 5 feet. Brian is 5 feet $8\frac{3}{4}$ inches tall. Jonah is 5 feet $11\frac{3}{4}$ inches tall.

   a. What is the recommended weight for Brian?

   b. What is the recommended weight for Jonah?

   c. How much greater is Jonah's recommended weight than Brian's recommended weight?

13. **Think About the Process** The box plot represents the daily low temperatures in degrees Celsius of a certain city last winter. Suppose you want to find the range of the data represented by the box plot.

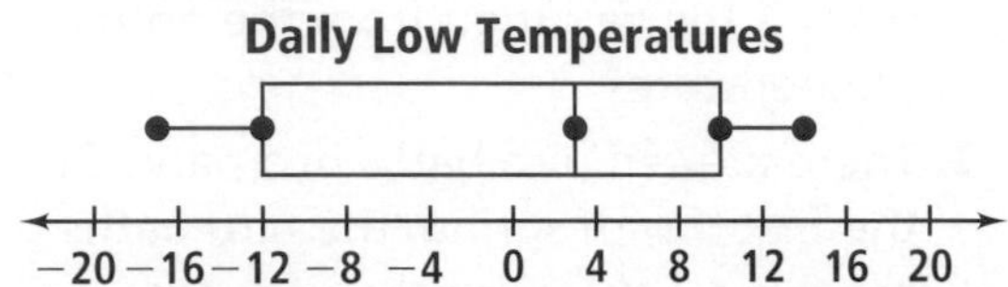

   a. Which of these expressions should you use?

      A. $10 - (-12)$

      B. $14 - 3$

      C. $14 - 10$

      D. $14 - (-17)$

      E. $10 - 3$

   b. What is the range?

14. **Challenge** Julia and George perform the same experiment. The box plot in **Figure 3** represents Julia's data. The table in **Figure 3** shows George's data.

   a. What is the range of Julia's data?

   b. What is the range of George's data?

   c. Whose data have the greater range?

   d. What is the interquartile range (IQR) of Julia's data?

   e. What is the interquartile range (IQR) of George's data?

   f. Whose data have the greater IQR?

(Figure 3)

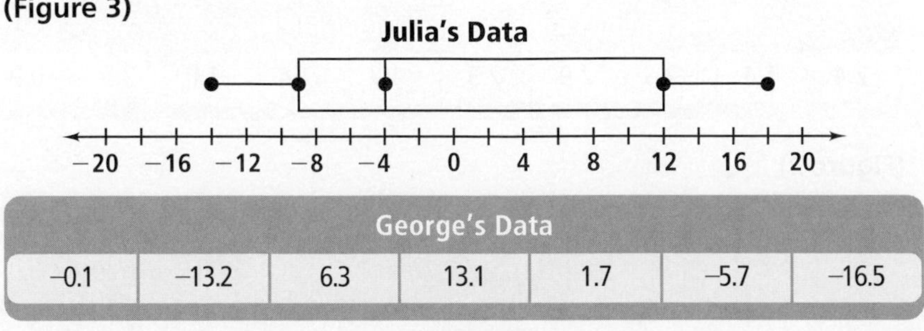

George's Data						
−0.1	−13.2	6.3	13.1	1.7	−5.7	−16.5

5-1 Multiplying Integers

CCSS: 7.NS.A.2a, Also 7.NS.A.2, 7.NS.A.2c

Part 1

Intro

You know that multiplication is repeated addition.

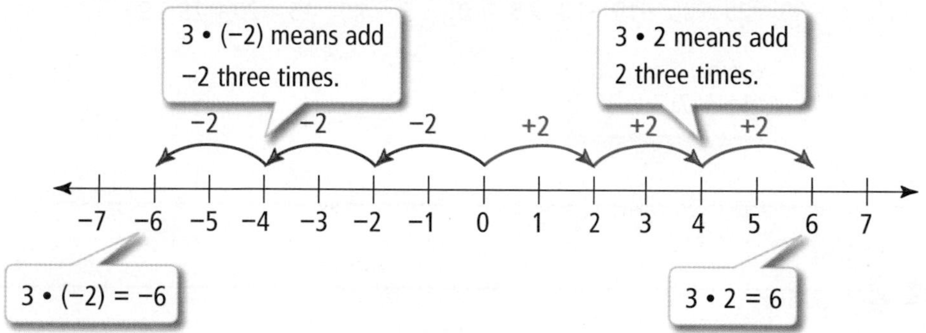

Because multiplication is commutative, you can also find the value of $-2 \cdot 3$:

$$\begin{aligned} -2 \cdot 3 &= 3 \cdot (-2) \\ &= -6 \end{aligned}$$

Example Multiplying Positive and Negative Integers

If a glacier is retreating at a rate of 7 feet per year, then the product $4(-7)$ represents the retreat, in feet, of the glacier over 4 years.

Complete a number line model to find the product $4(-7)$.

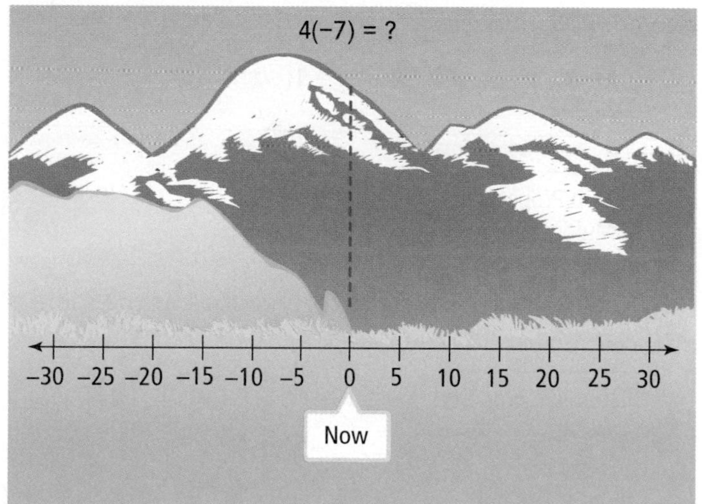

continued on next page >

Part 1

Example continued

Solution

Multiplication is repeated addition, so you can add -7 four times.

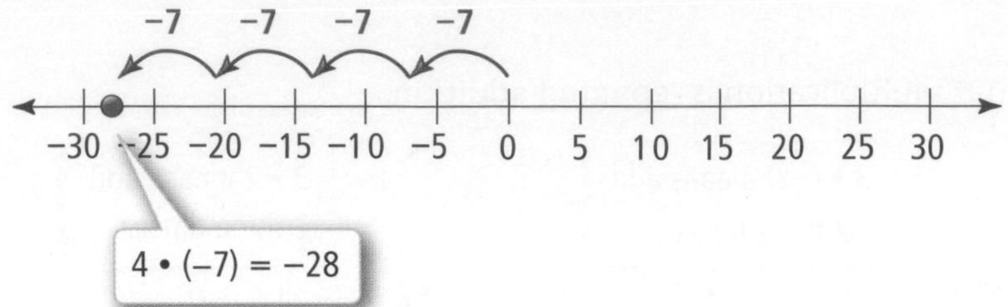

Part 2

Intro

What does it mean to multiply two negative integers?

You know that 1 and -1 are additive inverses.

$$0 = 1 + (-1)$$

You can use properties of operations to show that $-1(-1)$ and -1 are also additive inverses.

Inverse Property of Addition

Zero Property of Multiplication

$$-1(-1 + 1)$$
$$-1(0)$$
$$0$$

Now use the distributive property to look at the same problem a different way.

Distributive Property

$$-1(-1 + 1) = -1(-1) + (-1)(1)$$
$$-1(0)$$
$$0 = -1(-1) + (-1)$$
$$0 = 1 + (-1)$$
$$-1(-1) = 1$$

Identity Property of Multiplication

continued on next page >

Part 2

Intro continued

You can use the fact that $-1(-1) = 1$ to find the product of any two negative integers.

$$-3(-2) = -3(-2)$$
$$= (-1 \cdot 3)(-1 \cdot 2)$$
$$= -1(-1) \cdot 3(2)$$
$$= 1 \cdot 6$$
$$= 6$$

Commutative and Associative Properties

$-1(-1) = 1$

Example Multiplying Two Negative Integers

You can use the product $-4(-7)$ to represent where the glacier's position was 4 years ago.

Use the fact that $-1(-1) = 1$ to show that the product $-4(-7)$ is 28.

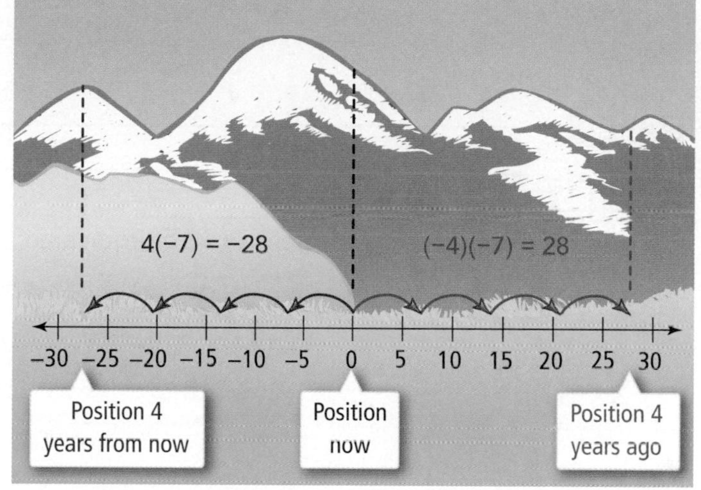

Solution

$$-4(-7) = [-1 \times 4] \times [-1 \times 7]$$
$$= [-1 \times (-1)] \times [4 \times 7]$$
$$= 1 \times 28$$
$$= 28$$

Use $-1(-1) = 1$.

Commutative and Associative Properties

Key Concept

You can use the signs of the factors to determine the sign of a product of integers.

Different Signs = Negative	Same Signs = Positive
positive × negative = negative	positive × positive = positive
+ · − = −	+ · + = +
6 · −5 = −30	6 · 5 = 30
negative × positive = negative	negative × negative = positive
− · + = −	− · − = +
−6 · 5 = −30	−6 · −5 = 30

Part 3

Example Multiplying Three Integers

Classify each product as equivalent to 12 or equivalent to −12.

$-1 \times (-2) \times 6$	$3 \times (-4)$	$-3 \times (-4) \times (-1)$
$2 \times (-2) \times 3$	$12(-1)$	$-4 \times (-3)$
$-1 \times (-12)$	$-2(6)$	$3(-2)(-2)$

continued on next page >

Part 3

Example continued

Solution

Equivalent to 12

Same sign = positive product

$-1 \times (-12) = 12$

$-4 \cdot (-3) = 12$

Same sign = positive product

$-1 \times (-2) \times 6 = 2 \times 6$
$= 12$

Same sign = positive product

Same sign = positive product

$3(-2)(-2) = -6(-2)$
$= 12$

Different signs = negative product

Equivalent to -12

Different signs = negative product

$3 \cdot (-4) = -12$

$-2(6) = -12$

$12(-1) = -12$

Different signs = negative product

Different signs = negative product

$2 \times (-2) \times 3 = -4 \times 3$
$= -12$

Same sign = positive product

$-3(-4)(-1) = 12(-1)$
$= -12$

Different signs = negative product

Digital Resources   

1. Multiply $7 \cdot (-5)$.
2. A beach towel loses 3 mg with each wash-and-dry cycle. The product $7(-3)$ represents change in the mass after 7 wash-and-dry cycles. Use a number line to find the product.
3. Find the product $-1(-24)$.
4. Find $(-6)(-2)$.
5. Multiply $-5(2)$.
6. Multiply $(5) \cdot (-9) \cdot (-2)$.
7. a. **Writing** Find the product $-41(-1)$.
   b. Describe how you use the properties of multiplication to find the product.
8. a. Multiply $-13 \cdot 4$.
   b. Explain why you can find $-13 \cdot (4)$ by finding $4 \cdot (-13)$.
9. **Reasoning** Anya withdraws \$12 from her bank account once each day for four days.
   a. What integer represents the change in the amount in the account?
   b. Find the integer that would represent the change in the amount in the account if Anya deposits \$12 into her bank account once each day for four days.
   c. Explain the difference between the integer for the withdrawals and the integer for the deposits.
10. a. **Error Analysis** Find $(5)(-8)(2)$.
    b. Describe an error you could make that results in the opposite of the correct product.
11. **Football** A football team loses 6 yards on each of 4 consecutive plays. Find the total change in yards from where the team started.
12. Some friends played a board game. During the game, one unlucky player had to move back 6 spaces 9 turns in a row. Find a number to represent that player's movements for those 9 turns.
13. a. **Multiple Representations** Use a number line to find $-35(2)$.
    b. Which of these products has the same value? Select all that apply.
    A. $14(-5)$
    B. $14(-10)$
    C. $5(-14)$
    D. $7(-10)$
    E. $10(-14)$
    F. $2(-35)$
    G. $10(-7)$
14. a. Find the product $(-4)(-6)$.
    b. Find the product $(-7)(-8)$.
    c. Which product is greater?
15. **Think About the Process**
    a. To use the fact that $(-1)(-1) = 1$ to find $-4 \cdot (-9)$, what do you do first?
    A. Write each factor as the product of -1 and a positive number.
    B. Write each factor as the product of 1 and a negative number.
    C. Write each factor as the product of 1 and a positive number.
    D. Write each factor as the product of -1 and a negative number.
    b. Find the product $-4 \cdot (-9)$.
16. Hot air balloons generally descend at a rate of 200 to 400 feet per minute. Four balloons descend 295 feet per minute for 7 minutes. Find the total change in altitude for all 4 balloons.

See your complete lesson at MyMathUniverse.com

17. Challenge A gold mine has two elevators, one for equipment and another for the miners. The equipment elevator descends 4 feet per second. The elevator for the miners descends 14 feet per second. One day, the equipment elevator begins to descend. After 26 seconds, the elevator for the miners begins to descend.

a. What is the position of the equipment elevator relative to the surface after another 19 seconds?

b. What is the position of the miners' elevator relative to the surface after another 19 seconds?

c. At that time, which elevator is deeper?

18. Think About the Process Before multiplying, determine if the product $-4(-4)(6)$ is positive or negative.

a. Is the product positive or negative?

b. Multiply $-4(-4)(6)$ to find the product.

c. Explain how you can tell the sign of a product without actually multiplying.

19. Challenge The product $(\pm2)(\pm4)(\pm9)$ is positive.

a. Find the product $(\pm2)(\pm4)(\pm9)$.

b. Find different ways to write the signs of the factors. Tell how many different ways there are in all.

5-2 Multiplying Rational Numbers

CCSS: 7.NS.A.2, 7.NS.A.2a

Key Concept

The sign rules for multiplying integers work for all rational numbers.

Different Signs = Negative	Same Signs = Positive
positive × negative = negative	positive × positive = positive
$+ \cdot - = -$	$+ \cdot + = +$
$\frac{2}{3} \cdot -\frac{5}{7} = -\frac{10}{21}$	$4 \cdot 1.8 = 7.2$
negative × positive = negative	negative × negative = positive
$- \cdot + = -$	$- \cdot - = +$
$-\frac{3}{5} \cdot \frac{1}{2} = -\frac{3}{10}$	$-5.2 \cdot -0.3 = 1.56$

Part 1

Example Predicting Signs for Products of Rational Numbers

Is each product *positive* or *negative*? Explain.

a. $-13 \times (-3) \times (-3)$

b. $-\frac{1}{2} \cdot 12 \cdot \left(-\frac{1}{4}\right)$

c. $-0.06 \times (-1.3)$

d. $\frac{2}{3}(-7)$

e. $5.1 \cdot (-4.7)$

f. $-3\frac{1}{2} \times 5\frac{6}{7}$

g. $-0.5.(1.5)(-0.6)(-2)$

h. $-\frac{1}{8}\left(-\frac{7}{8}\right)(10)$

Solution

Sample explanations:

a. An odd number of negative factors give a negative product.

$-13 \times (-3) \times (-3)$

$(-)(-)(-)$

$(+)(-)$

$-$

b. An even number of negative factors give a positive product.

$-\frac{1}{2} \cdot 12 \cdot \left(-\frac{1}{4}\right)$

$(-)(+)(-)$

$(-)(-)$

$+$

continued on next page >

Part 1

Solution continued

Negative

a. $-13 \times (-3) \times (-3)$

d. $\frac{2}{3}(-7)$

e. $5.1 \cdot (-4.7)$

f. $-3\frac{1}{2} \times 5\frac{6}{7}$

g. $-0.5.(1.5)(-0.6)(-2)$

Positive

b. $-\frac{1}{2} \cdot 12 \cdot \left(-\frac{1}{4}\right)$

c. $-0.06 \times (-1.3)$

h. $\left(-\frac{1}{8}\right)\left(-\frac{7}{8}\right)(10)$

Part 2

Intro

A number line model can help you understand the meaning of a product of rational numbers, such as $\frac{2}{3} \cdot \left(-\frac{1}{2}\right)$.

To show the factor $-\frac{1}{2}$, divide the number line from -1 to 0 into two halves.

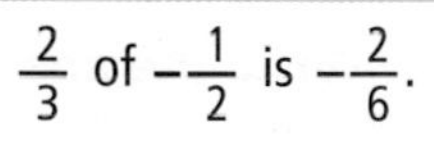

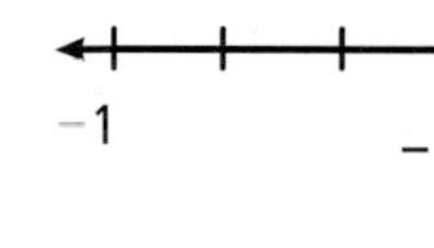

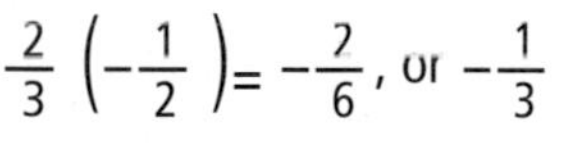

To find $\frac{2}{3}$ of $\frac{1}{2}$, divide each half into thirds. Now the number line is divided into sixths. Count two of these.

Example Multiplying Rational Numbers

Find each product.

a. $\frac{8}{9} \cdot \left(-\frac{3}{4}\right)$

b. $-1\frac{3}{7} \cdot (-2)$

continued on next page >

Part 2

Example continued

Solution

a.

The signs are different, so the product is negative. $\frac{8}{9} \cdot \left(-\frac{3}{4}\right) = -\left(\frac{8}{9} \cdot \frac{3}{4}\right)$

Multiply numerators. Multiply denominators. $= -\frac{8 \cdot 3}{9 \cdot 4}$

Divide by the common factors, 3 and 4. $= -\frac{{}^{2}\cancel{8} \cdot \cancel{3}^{1}}{{}_{3}\cancel{9} \cdot \cancel{4}_{1}}$

$= -\frac{2}{3}$

b.

The signs are the same, so the product is positive. $-1\frac{3}{7}(-2) = 1\frac{3}{7}(2)$

Write each number as a fraction. $= \frac{10}{7} \cdot \frac{2}{1}$

Multiply numerators. Multiply denominators. $= \frac{20}{7}$

Write the answer as a mixed number. $= 2\frac{6}{7}$

Part 3

Example Multiplying Rational Numbers in Real-World Situations

An investor owns 203.72 shares of Glacial Futures stock. The value of a share of stock drops \$.15. Find the total change in the value of the investor's stocks.

Solution

Words	total change in value	equals	number of shares	times	change per share
Equation	T	=	203. 72	×	− 0.15

Use a negative number to represent the drop in value.

Write the equation.	$T = 203.72 \cdot (-0.15)$
The signs are different, so the product is negative.	$= -(203.72 \cdot 0.15)$
Multiply.	$= -30.558$
Round to the nearest cent.	≈ -30.56

The total change in the value of the stocks is −\$30.56. The value of the shares dropped \$30.56.

1. Is the product $-8 \cdot (-3)$ positive or negative?
2. Is the product $(-0.39)(-0.06)(0.29)$ positive or negative?
3. Find the product $-\frac{5}{6} \cdot \frac{1}{8}$.
4. Multiply $-2\frac{1}{2} \cdot -1\frac{2}{3}$.
5. Multiply $-7\frac{1}{2} \cdot 2\frac{3}{4}$.
6. Multiply $(-0.6)(-0.62)$.
7. Multiply $(-2.271)(16.47)$.
8. A farmer has 140 bushels of wheat to sell at his roadside stand. He sells an average of $15\frac{3}{5}$ bushels each day. Represent the total change in the number of bushels he has for sale after 6 days.
9. **a. Writing** What is the sign of a^2b when $a = 5$ and $b = 8$?
   b. Does the sign of the product depend on the sign of *a*, the sign of *b*, or the signs of both *a* and *b*? Explain.
10. **Think About the Process**
    a. What is the first step in finding the product $-4\frac{7}{8} \cdot \left(-2\frac{1}{2}\right)$?
    A. Multiply the integers.
    B. Find the sign of the product.
    C. Multiply the fractions.
    D. Change the sign of the second factor.
    b. Find the product $-4\frac{7}{8} \cdot \left(-2\frac{1}{2}\right)$.
11. **Reasoning** What is the sign of the product $(-2)\left(\frac{1}{6}\right)(-7)$? Explain your reasoning.
12. **Error Analysis** Kyle incorrectly says that the product $-\left(-\frac{6}{7}\right)\cdot\left(-\frac{1}{11}\right)$ is $\frac{6}{77}$.
    a. What is the correct product?
    b. What was Kyle's likely error?
    A. He found the product of two negative numbers and ignored the first negative sign.
    B. He multiplied the numerator and denominator wrong.
    C. He multiplied the numerators wrong.
    D. He multiplied the denominators wrong.
13. **Temperature** Suppose there is a 1.1°F drop in temperature for every thousand feet that an airplane climbs into the sky. If the temperature on the ground is 59.7°F, what will be the temperature when the plane reaches an altitude of 11,000 ft?
14. **a. Estimation** Estimate the product (14.93) (−12.66) by rounding each factor to the nearest integer and multiplying.
    b. Find the exact product.
15. Multiply $-\frac{6}{11}\cdot\left(-\frac{1}{13}\right)$.
16. A container holds 80,000 ounces of water. There is a small leak in the container. Every 96 minutes, 1.9 ounces of water leak out. Represent the total change in the amount of water in the container after 8 hours.
17. **Think About the Process** A ticket to see your favorite baseball team costs \$49.64. That price decreases by \$0.41 for every game lost during the regular season.
    a. Which equation would be used to find the cost *C* of a ticket after *L* losses?
    A. $C = 49.64 - 0.41L$
    B. $C = 49.64 + 0.41L$
    C. $C = \frac{49.64}{0.41L}$
    D. $C = 49.64(0.41L)$
    b. Represent the total change in the cost of a ticket after the team loses 31 games.
    c. What is the price of a ticket after the team loses 31 games?

18. A farmer has 220 bushels of apples to sell at his roadside stand. He sells an average of $16\frac{3}{5}$ bushels each day. Represent the total change in the number of bushels he has for sale after 6 days.

19. Temperature Suppose there is a 1.2°F drop in temperature for every thousand feet that an airplane climbs into the sky. If the temperature on the ground is 63.2°F, what will be the temperature when the plane reaches an altitude of 5,000 ft?

20. Think About the Process A ticket to see your favorite baseball team costs \$37.49. That price decreases by \$0.28 for every game lost during the regular season.

a. Which equation would be used to find the cost C of a ticket after L losses?

A. $C = 37.49 - 0.28L$

B. $C = \frac{37.49}{0.28L}$

C. $C = 37.49(0.28L)$

D. $C = 37.49 + 0.28L$

b. Represent the total change in the cost of a ticket after the team loses 29 games.

c. What is the price of a ticket after the team loses 29 games?

21. Challenge Place the products $4\frac{4}{7} \cdot 4\frac{4}{7}$, $5\frac{5}{6} \cdot \left(-6\frac{6}{7}\right)$, and $-5\frac{1}{8} \cdot \left(-2\frac{1}{4}\right)$ in order from least to greatest.

22. Challenge A company's stock began the day at \$38.12 per share. That price drops by \$1.45 each hour.

a. What is the price per share after 5 hours?

b. What would it be after 28 hours if this rate continues?

c. Explain what the signs of the answers mean in this context.

5-3 Dividing Integers

CCSS: 7.NS.A.2b, Also 7.NS.A.2

Key Concept

Every multiplication statement has two related division statements.

$-6 \cdot 3 = -18$					$-6 \times -3 = 18$			
$-18 \div 3 = -6$					$\frac{18}{-3} = -6$			
and					and			
$-18 \div -6 = 3$					$\frac{18}{-6} = -3$			

You can use the inverse relationship between multiplication and division to check an answer to a division question.

a. Is $\frac{15}{-5} = -3$? Yes!

b. Is $-16 \div (-4) = -4$? No!

c. What is 0 divided by 6?
Is $\frac{0}{6} = 0$? Yes!

d. What is 6 divided by 0?
Is $\frac{6}{0} = 6$? No!

Check

a. $-3 \times (-5) = 15$ ✓

b. $-4 \times (-4) \neq -16$ ✗

c. $0 \times 6 = 0$ ✓
For any nonzero number a, $\frac{0}{a} = 0$.

d. $6 \times 0 \neq 6$ ✗
Division by zero is undefined.

You can use these rules to determine the sign of a quotient.

Different Signs = Negative				
positive ÷ negative = negative				
+	÷	−	=	−
18	÷	−3	=	−6
negative ÷ positive = negative				
−	÷	+	=	−
−18	÷	3	=	−6

Same Signs = Positive				
positive ÷ positive = positive				
+	÷	+	=	+
		$\frac{18}{3}$	=	6
negative ÷ negative = positive				
−	÷	−	=	+
		$\frac{-18}{-3}$	=	6

See your complete lesson at MyMathUniverse.com

Part 1

Intro

What is $6 \div 0$?

In other words, "How many 0's make 6?" You can't make 6 from groups of 0.

This quotient is undefined.

Example Locating Quotients on Number Lines

Plot each quotient at its value on a number line. Do not include it if it is an undefined expression.

$$0 \div (-3) \qquad \frac{-27}{-9} \qquad -22 \div 11 \qquad \frac{48}{-12}$$

$$-10 \div 2 \qquad \frac{18}{0} \qquad -20 \div (-4) \qquad \frac{8}{4} \qquad -10 \div 0$$

Solution

different signs = negative quotient $\quad \frac{0}{a} = 0 \quad$ same sign = positive quotient

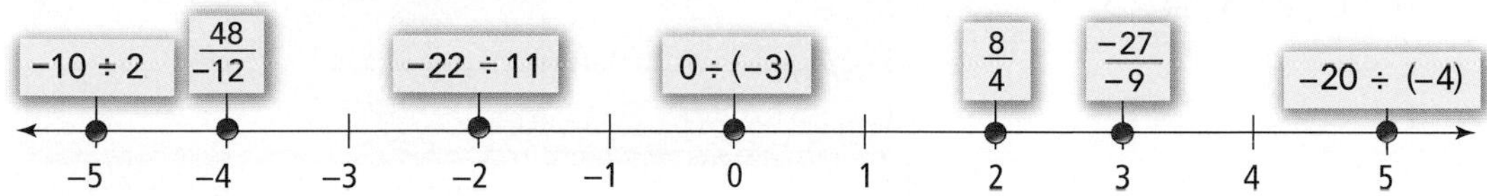

Two expressions are undefined.

$-10 \div 0$

$\frac{18}{0}$

You cannot divide by 0.

Part 2

Intro

You can rewrite any negative number as the product of -1 and a positive number. This allows you to rewrite any rational number as the quotient of two integers.

$$-\frac{3}{4} = -1 \cdot \frac{3}{4} = \frac{-1}{1} \cdot \frac{3}{4} = \frac{-3}{4} \qquad -\frac{3}{4} = -1 \cdot \frac{3}{4} = \frac{1}{-1} \cdot \frac{3}{4} = \frac{3}{-4}$$

For all integers p and q, where $q \neq 0$:

$$-\frac{p}{q} = \frac{-p}{q} = \frac{p}{-q}$$

Example Writing Equivalent Quotients of Integers

Use these integers to write at least three different quotients $\frac{p}{q}$ equivalent to each rational number.

−6 −4 −3 −2 −1

0 1 2 3 4 5 6

Rational Number	Quotients of integers, $\frac{p}{q}$
−3	■
2	■
0	■
$-\frac{2}{3}$	■
1.5	■

Solution

Sample:

Rational Number	Quotients of integers, $\frac{p}{q}$
−3	$\frac{-6}{2}, \frac{3}{-1}, \frac{-3}{1}$
2	$\frac{-4}{-2}, \frac{6}{3}, \frac{-2}{-1}$
0	$\frac{0}{4}, \frac{0}{-2}, \frac{0}{-1}$
$-\frac{2}{3}$	$\frac{-2}{3}, \frac{4}{-6}, \frac{2}{-3}$
1.5	$\frac{6}{4}, \frac{-3}{-2}, \frac{-6}{-4}$

Part 3

Example Dividing Integers to Find Unit Rates

A glacier retreated 21 feet over 6 years. Express the movement of the glacier as a unit rate. Use estimation to check the reasonableness of your answer.

Solution

Use a negative number to represent the retreat of the glacier.

The rate is $\frac{-21 \text{ feet}}{6 \text{ years}}$.

To find the unit rate, divide the numerator and the denominator of the rate by 6.

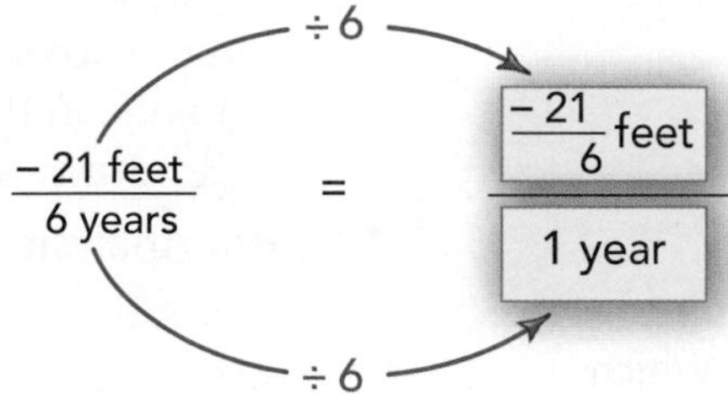

The quotient is negative. $= -\frac{21}{6}$ feet per year

Divide out the common factor, 3. $= -\frac{7}{2}$ per year

The unit rate is $-\frac{7}{2}$, or $-3\frac{1}{2}$ feet per year.

Check

You know the rate is negative because the quotient of numbers with different signs is negative. To check that $3\frac{1}{2}$ is reasonable for the absolute value of the rate, use an estimate of $21 \div 7 = 3$. Since 6 is less than 7, dividing 21 by 6 should give an answer greater than 3. So $-3\frac{1}{2}$ feet per year is a reasonable answer.

Digital Resources 

1. Classify the quotient $-50 \div 5$ as positive, negative, zero, or undefined.

2. Is the expression $\frac{-42}{7}$ undefined? If not, divide.

3. Which of the quotients are equivalent to $-\frac{5}{8}$? Select all that apply.

   A. $\frac{-5}{8}$ B. $\frac{5}{-8}$
   C. $\frac{-5}{-8}$ D. $\frac{5}{8}$
   E. $-\frac{5}{-8}$ F. $-\frac{-5}{8}$

4. Which of the quotients are equivalent to -5? Select all that apply.

   A. $\frac{5}{-1}$ B. $\frac{-5}{-1}$
   C. $\frac{-15}{-3}$ D. $\frac{-1}{-5}$
   E. $\frac{-15}{3}$ F. $\frac{-5}{1}$

5. A cave diver descends 110 feet in 10 minutes at a constant rate. Which of the expressions shows the rate of the cave diver's change in depth?

   A. $\frac{-110 \text{ feet}}{-10 \text{ minutes}}$ B. $\frac{10 \text{ feet}}{-110 \text{ minutes}}$
   C. $\frac{110 \text{ feet}}{10 \text{ minutes}}$ D. $\frac{-110 \text{ feet}}{10 \text{ minutes}}$

6. A parachutist descends 24 feet in 2 seconds. Express the rate of the parachutist's change in height as a unit rate.

7. The population of a certain city decreased by 9,126 in 30 years. Express the change in population per year as a unit rate.

8. a. **Writing** Find the quotient $\frac{-16}{0}$.

   b. How would the answer be different for the quotient $\frac{0}{-16}$?

   c. What are the rules for divisions involving 0?

9. a. **Reasoning** Which of the quotients are equivalent to $-\frac{48}{17}$? Select all that apply.

   A. $\frac{-17}{-48}$ B. $\frac{48}{-17}$
   C. $\frac{-48}{17}$ D. $\frac{48}{17}$
   E. $\frac{-48}{-17}$ F. $\frac{17}{48}$

   b. Explain how using the product of -1 and a positive number allows you to do this.

10. Carla is looking at her bank statement from last month. She writes the expression $-\frac{791}{543}$ to compare the change in the account from deposits and withdrawals.

   a. Which two of the following quotients are equivalent to $-\frac{791}{543}$?

   A. $\frac{791}{-543}$ B. $\frac{543}{791}$
   C. $\frac{-791}{-543}$ D. $\frac{-791}{543}$
   E. $\frac{-543}{-791}$ F. $\frac{-543}{791}$

   b. Which quotient of integers best represents the ratio of the change in the account from deposits to the change in the account from withdrawals? Explain.

11. **Error Analysis** Eva incorrectly classifies the quotient $-\frac{-81}{-9}$ as positive.

   a. Which of the following is the correct classification of the quotient?

   A. The quotient is zero.
   B. The quotient is undefined.
   C. The quotient is negative.

   b. Which of the following could cause Eva's error? Select all that apply.

   A. She did not see the negative sign in front of the fraction.
   B. She used the idea that $-(-81)$ is a positive number.
   C. She used the rule that an expression of this form with a negative numerator and negative denominator simplifies to a positive number.
   D. She used the rule that an expression of this form with three negative signs simplifies to a negative number.

12. **Business Loss** A company loses \$78 as a result of a shipping delay. The 6 owners of the company must share the loss equally.

   a. Write an expression for the earnings per person.

   b. Evaluate the expression.

See your complete lesson at MyMathUniverse.com

13. Multiple Representations Which of the quotients are equivalent to 2.5? Select all that apply.

A. $\frac{10}{-4}$ **B.** $\frac{-10}{-4}$

C. $\frac{-5}{2}$ **D.** $\frac{10}{4}$

E. $\frac{-5}{-2}$ **F.** $\frac{5}{2}$

14. A team has 5 members. Their combined score in a game is −5. Two team members scored above zero. Their combined score is 4. These team members all have the same score. Three team members scored below zero. Their combined score is −9. These team members all have the same score.

a. Which expression shows the score of a team member who scored above zero?

A. $-2 \div 4$ **B.** $4 \div (-2)$

C. $4 \div 2$ **D.** $4 \div (-3)$

b. Evaluate the quotient.

c. Which expression shows the score of a team member who scored below zero?

A. $-9 \div (-2)$ **B.** $-9 \div (-3)$

C. $-3 \div (-9)$ **D.** $-9 \div 3$

d. Evaluate the quotient.

15. Think About the Process

a. How can you find the sign of the quotient $\frac{-152}{-8}$ before performing the division?

A. Use the rule for two numbers with the same sign. In this case, the quotient is positive.

B. Use the rule for two numbers with different signs. In this case, the quotient is positive.

C. Use the rule for two numbers with different signs. In this case, the quotient is negative.

D. Use the rule for two numbers with the same sign. In this case, the quotient is negative.

b. Find the quotient $\frac{-152}{-8}$.

16. Think About the Process The price of a stock steadily decreased by a total of $127 over the past 15 months.

a. What is the first step in expressing the change in price as a rate in the form of a quotient of integers?

A. Write the ratio as a unit rate.

B. Simplify the quotient.

C. Divide the number of months by the change in price.

D. Find the sign of each number.

b. Write the change in price as a rate.

A. $\frac{\$15}{-127 \text{ months}}$ **B.** $\frac{-\$127}{-15 \text{ months}}$

C. $\frac{-\$127}{15 \text{ months}}$ **D.** $\frac{\$127}{15 \text{ months}}$

17. The temperature in a town increased 16°F in 5 hours. The temperature decreased 31°F in the next 8 hours. Which of the expressions shows the rate of the total change in temperature?

A. $\frac{-15°\text{F}}{13 \text{ hours}}$ **B.** $\frac{47°\text{F}}{13 \text{ hours}}$

C. $\frac{15°\text{F}}{13 \text{ hours}}$ **D.** $\frac{47°\text{F}}{-13 \text{ hours}}$

18. a. Challenge If the ratio $\frac{-396}{x + 10}$ is equivalent to 22, find the value of x.

b. Write another pair of equivalent ratios like these.

c. Show how to find the value of x.

19. Challenge A hiker is walking down a mountain. She walked 7,656 feet in 24 minutes. In that time, she descended 1,914 feet from the top of the mountain. She then walked 8,450 feet in 26 minutes. In that time, she descended 4,225 more feet. Express the average rate of change in altitude of the hiker from her starting point to her ending point as a unit rate. Simplify your answer.

5-4 Dividing Rational Numbers

Vocabulary
reciprocals

CCSS: 7.NS.A.2, 7.NS.A.2b

Part 1

Intro

Two numbers whose product is 1 are reciprocals.

Reciprocals: $\frac{1}{2} \cdot 2 = 1$ Reciprocals: $-\frac{2}{3} \cdot -\frac{3}{2} = 1$

Write the reciprocal of a nonzero rational number by switching its numerator and denominator.

$\frac{p}{q}$ Reciprocals $\frac{q}{p}$ $-\frac{p}{q}$ Reciprocals $-\frac{q}{p}$

Example Finding Reciprocals

Find the choice that is the reciprocal of the number.

	Number	Reciprocal		
a.	$-\frac{7}{4}$	$\frac{7}{4}$	$\frac{4}{7}$	$-\frac{4}{7}$
b.	$\frac{5}{2}$	2	$\frac{2}{5}$	$-\frac{2}{5}$
c.	$\frac{1}{8}$	8	$-\frac{1}{8}$	-8
d.	-6	$\frac{1}{6}$	$-\frac{1}{6}$	6
e.	$-1\frac{2}{3}$	$-1\frac{3}{2}$	-3	$-\frac{3}{5}$

continued on next page >

Part 1

Example continued

Solution

Find each reciprocal by switching the numerator and denominator of the number. Check that the product is 1.

	Number	Reciprocal	Check
a.	$-\frac{7}{4}$	$-\frac{4}{7}$	$-\frac{7}{4} \cdot \left(-\frac{4}{7}\right) = \frac{28}{28} = 1$
b.	$\frac{5}{2}$	$\frac{2}{5}$	$\frac{5}{2} \cdot \left(\frac{2}{5}\right) = \frac{10}{10} = 1$
c.	$\frac{1}{8}$	8	$\frac{1}{8} \cdot (8) = \frac{8}{8} = 1$
d.	$-6 = -\frac{6}{1}$	$-\frac{1}{6}$	$-\frac{6}{1} \cdot \left(-\frac{1}{6}\right) = \frac{6}{6} = 1$
e.	$-1\frac{2}{3} = -\frac{5}{3}$	$-\frac{3}{5}$	$\left(-1\frac{2}{3}\right) \cdot \left(-\frac{3}{5}\right) = \left(-\frac{5}{3}\right) \cdot \left(-\frac{3}{5}\right) = \frac{15}{15} = 1$

Part 2

Intro

Dividing a number by 3 and multiplying a number by $\frac{1}{3}$ give the same result.

Divide by 3.

$15 \div 3 = 5$

Multiply by the reciprocal of 3.

$15 \times \frac{1}{3} = 5$

Dividing a number by -3 and multiplying a number by $-\frac{1}{3}$ give the same result.

Divide by -3.

$15 \div (-3) = -5$

Multiply by the reciprocal of -3.

$15 \times \left(-\frac{1}{3}\right) = -5$

To divide by a nonzero rational number, multiply by its reciprocal.

Divide by $\frac{p}{q}$.

$-\frac{1}{3} \div \frac{2}{3}$ ⟶

Multiply by $\frac{q}{p}$.

$-\frac{1}{3} \times \frac{3}{2} = -\frac{1}{2}$

Divide by $-\frac{p}{q}$.

$-5 \div \left(-\frac{1}{10}\right)$ ⟶

Multiply by $-\frac{q}{p}$.

$-5 \times \left(-\frac{10}{1} = 50\right)$

Part 2

Example Dividing with Equivalent Multiplication Expressions

Find the equivalent multiplication expression for each division expression.

	Division Expression	Multiplication Expression		
a.	$-\frac{1}{9} \div \frac{7}{18}$	$-\frac{1}{9} \times \left(-\frac{7}{18}\right)$	$-9 \times \frac{7}{18}$	$-\frac{1}{9} \times \frac{18}{7}$
b.	$\frac{6}{5} \div (-2)$	$\frac{6}{5} \cdot \left(-\frac{1}{2}\right)$	$\frac{5}{6} \cdot (-2)$	$\frac{5}{6} \cdot 2$
c.	$-4 \div \frac{1}{3}$	$-\frac{1}{4}(3)$	$-4\left(-\frac{1}{3}\right)$	$-4(3)$
d.	$-\frac{5}{8} \div \left(-\frac{3}{8}\right)$	$-\frac{8}{5} \cdot \left(-\frac{3}{8}\right)$	$-\frac{5}{8} \cdot \frac{3}{8}$	$-\frac{5}{8} \cdot \left(-\frac{8}{3}\right)$

Solution

To divide by a rational number, multiply by its reciprocal.

a. $-\frac{1}{9} \div \frac{7}{18} = -\frac{1}{9} \times \frac{18}{7}$

b. $\frac{6}{5} \div (-2) = \frac{6}{9} \cdot \left(-\frac{1}{2}\right)$

c. $-4 \div \frac{1}{3} = -4(3)$

d. $-\frac{5}{8} \div \left(-\frac{3}{8}\right) = -\frac{5}{8} \cdot \left(-\frac{8}{3}\right)$

Part 3

Example Solving Equations Using Division on Rational Numbers

On a research expedition, three oceanographers in a small submarine descend $\frac{4}{5}$ mi per hour.

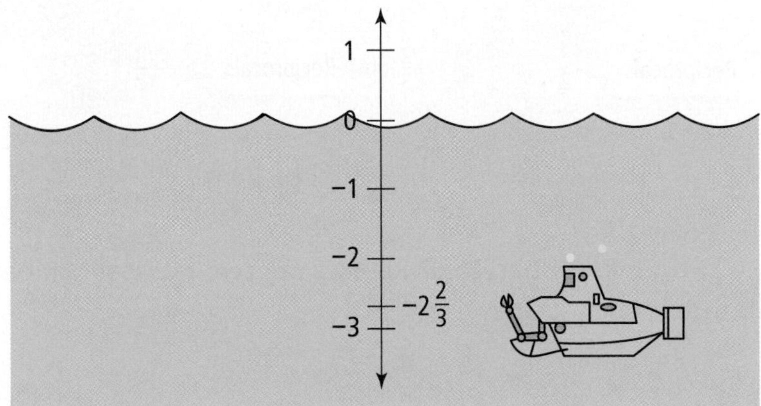

The equation $d = -\frac{4}{5}t$ gives the depth d, in miles, of a submarine at t hours.

How long does it take the submarine to reach $2\frac{2}{3}$ miles below sea level?

Solution

To find the value of t, substitute for d and solve.

$$d = -\frac{4}{5}t$$

Substitute $-2\frac{2}{3}$ for d.

$$-2\frac{2}{3} = -\frac{4}{5}t$$

Divide each side by $-\frac{4}{5}$.

$$-2\frac{2}{3} \div \left(-\frac{4}{5}\right) = -\frac{4}{5}t \div \left(-\frac{4}{5}\right)$$

Rewrite division as multiplication.

$$-2\frac{2}{3} \cdot \left(-\frac{5}{4}\right) = -\frac{4}{5}t \cdot \left(-\frac{5}{4}\right)$$

Write $-2\frac{2}{3}$ as an improper fraction.
Use the Commutative Property.
negative × negative = positive

$$-\frac{8}{3} \cdot \left(-\frac{5}{4}\right) = -\frac{4}{5} \cdot \left(-\frac{5}{4}\right)t$$

A product of reciprocals is 1.

$$\frac{8 \cdot 5}{3 \cdot 4} = 1 \cdot t$$

Write the improper fraction as a mixed number.

$$\frac{10}{3} = t, \text{ or } t = 3\frac{1}{3}$$

It takes the submarine $3\frac{1}{3}$ hours, or 3 hours 20 minutes, to reach $2\frac{2}{3}$ miles below sea level.

Key Concept

Reciprocals of rational numbers Two numbers whose product is 1 are reciprocals.

$\frac{p}{q}$ — Reciprocals — $\frac{q}{p}$ $\qquad$ $-\frac{p}{q}$ — Reciprocals — $-\frac{q}{p}$

$\frac{2}{3}$ — Reciprocals — $\frac{3}{2}$ $\qquad$ $-\frac{2}{3}$ — Reciprocals — $-\frac{3}{2}$

$\frac{2}{3} \cdot \frac{3}{2} = 1$ $\qquad$ $-\frac{2}{3} \cdot \left(\frac{3}{2}\right) = 1$

Dividing by a rational number To divide by a nonzero rational number, multiply by its reciprocal.

Divide by $\frac{p}{q}$. $\qquad$ Multiply by $\frac{q}{p}$.

$-\frac{1}{3} \div \frac{2}{3} \longrightarrow -\frac{1}{3} \times \frac{3}{2} = -\frac{1}{2}$

Divide by $-\frac{p}{q}$. $\qquad$ Multiply by $-\frac{q}{p}$.

$-5 \div \left(-\frac{1}{10}\right) \longrightarrow -5 \times \left(-\frac{10}{1} = 50\right)$

Digital Resources

1. Which of these is the reciprocal of $-\frac{14}{5}$?

   A. $\frac{5}{14}$ B. $-\frac{5}{14}$

   C. $-\frac{14}{5}$ D. $\frac{14}{5}$

2. Find the reciprocal of $\frac{4}{7}$. Simplify your answer.

3. Which multiplication expression is equivalent to the division expression $-\frac{7}{17} \div \frac{13}{34}$?

   A. $-\frac{17}{7} \times \frac{13}{34}$ B. $-\frac{17}{7} \times \frac{34}{13}$

   C. $-\frac{7}{17} \times \frac{13}{34}$ D. $-\frac{7}{17} \times \frac{34}{13}$

4. Divide $\frac{5}{7} \div \left(-\frac{11}{5}\right)$ and simplify.

5. Solve $-\frac{9}{2}y = \frac{27}{2}$ for y.

6. The equation $d = \frac{2}{5}t$ describes the distance d, in yards, an object travels in t minutes. How long does it take the object to travel $1\frac{4}{5}$ yards?

7. Find the reciprocal of $-4\frac{7}{8}$.

8. a. **Writing** Which of the numbers $-\frac{7}{13}$, $1\frac{6}{7}$, $-1\frac{6}{7}$, and $\frac{7}{13}$ is the reciprocal of $1\frac{6}{7}$?

   b. Which is the reciprocal of $\frac{7}{13}$?

   c. What do you notice about the reciprocals of $1\frac{6}{7}$ and $\frac{7}{13}$? Explain.

9. a. **Reasoning** Find the reciprocal of $1\frac{1}{17}$.

   b. Find the reciprocal of $\frac{17}{18}$.

   c. Explain how finding the first reciprocal simplifies finding the second reciprocal.

10. a. **Error Analysis** Your friend says the quotient $\frac{3}{4} \div \frac{1}{4}$ is $\frac{1}{3}$. What is the correct quotient?

    b. What mistake did your friend likely make?

    A. Your friend multiplied with the reciprocal of the first fraction, not the second fraction.

    B. Your friend multiplied $\frac{4}{3} \times 4$.

    C. Your friend added the fractions instead of dividing.

    D. Your friend multiplied $\frac{3}{4} \times \frac{1}{4}$.

11. **Think About the Process** You want to write a multiplication expression equivalent to $-2\frac{1}{8} \div 6\frac{4}{5}$.

    a. What is the first step?

    A. Find the reciprocal of the divisor.

    B. Find the reciprocal of the dividend.

    C. Multiply the numerators of the fractions.

    D. Write the mixed numbers as improper fractions.

    b. Which multiplication expression is equivalent to $-2\frac{1}{8} \div 6\frac{4}{5}$?

    A. $-\frac{17}{8} \times \frac{34}{5}$ B. $\frac{8}{17} \times \frac{5}{34}$

    C. $-\frac{17}{8} \times \frac{5}{34}$ D. $-\frac{8}{17} \times \frac{34}{5}$

12. **Gardening** A certain plant grows $1\frac{2}{5}$ inches every week. How long will it take the plant to grow $4\frac{4}{5}$ inches?

    A. 3 weeks, 3 days

    B. 2 weeks, 3 days

    C. 3 weeks, 2 days

    D. 3 weeks, 3 days

13. **Open-Ended** Which multiplication expression is equivalent to $\frac{5}{8} \div \frac{1}{16}$?

    A. $\frac{8}{5} \times \frac{1}{16}$ B. $\frac{5}{8} \times \frac{1}{16}$

    C. $\frac{5}{8} \times 16$ D. $\frac{8}{5} \times 16$

14. Perform the indicated operation.

$3\frac{1}{6} \div \left(-1\frac{4}{9}\right)$

15. Find the quotient $\frac{7}{15} \div 6.2$.

16. A weather balloon rises at a speed of $\frac{3}{7}$ mile per hour.

a. Which equation correctly models the height b of the balloon in miles after t hours?

A. $t = \frac{3}{7}b$ **B.** $b = \frac{3}{7} + t$

C. $b = \left(1\frac{5}{9}\right)t$ **D.** $b = \frac{3}{7}t$

b. Suppose the balloon stops rising at a height of $1\frac{5}{9}$ miles. How long did it take the balloon to reach that height?

A. $\frac{27}{98}$ hour **B.** $\frac{17}{27}$ hour

C. $4\frac{17}{27}$ hours **D.** $3\frac{17}{27}$ hours

17. Think About the Process To solve the equation $\frac{9}{5}m = \frac{3}{7}$ for m, the first step is to divide each side of the equation by $\frac{9}{5}$.

a. What is the next step?

A. Find the reciprocal of $\frac{9}{5}$.

B. Write $\frac{9}{5}$ as a mixed number.

C. Multiply $\frac{9}{5} \times \frac{3}{7}$.

D. Find the common denominator for $\frac{9}{5}$ and $\frac{3}{7}$.

b. What is the solution?

18. Challenge Solve the equation $1.8c = 7.5$ for c. Give an exact answer.

19. Challenge Between 11 P.M. and 8:36 A.M., the water level in a swimming pool decreased by $\frac{8}{25}$ in. Assuming that the water level decreased at a constant rate, how much did the water level drop each hour? Simplify your answer.

5-5 Operations With Rational Numbers

Vocabulary
complex fraction

CCSS: 7.NS.A.2c, 7.NS.A.3, Also 7.NS.A.2

Key Concept

Simplify: $-5(3 + 2) + (-4)$

Order of Operations Use the order of operations to simplify.

1. Evaluate expressions inside grouping symbols.
2. Multiply and divide from left to right.
3. Add and subtract from left to right.

Write the expression.	$-5(3 + 2) + (-4)$
Work inside parentheses.	$-5(5) + (-4)$
Multiply.	$-25 + (-4)$
Add.	-29

Distributive Property For any numbers *a*, *b*, and *c*:

$$a(b + c) = ab + ac$$

$$a(b - c) = ab - ac$$

You can use the Distributive Property to multiply before you add the numbers inside the parentheses.

Distribute −5.	$-5(3 + 2) + (-4) = (-5)(3) + (-5)(2) + (-4)$
Multiply from left to right.	$= -15 + (-10) + (-4)$
Add from left to right.	$= -25 + (-4)$
	$= -29$

Part 1

Example Using the Distributive Property with Rational Numbers

Choose the expression that correctly shows using the Distributive Property to rewrite the expression $-6\left(-\frac{1}{2}+\frac{1}{3}\right)$. Then find the value of the expression.

$-6\left(-\frac{1}{2}\right)+\frac{1}{3}$ $\qquad$ $-6\left(-\frac{1}{2}\right)+6\left(\frac{1}{3}\right)$ $\qquad$ $-6\left(-\frac{1}{2}\right)+(-6)\left(\frac{1}{3}\right)$

Solution

The expression that shows the correct application of the Distributive Property is $-6\left(-\frac{1}{2}\right)+(-6)\left(\frac{1}{3}\right)$.

$$-6\left(-\frac{1}{2}+\frac{1}{3}\right)=-6\left(-\frac{1}{2}\right)+(-6)\left(\frac{1}{3}\right)$$
$$=3+(-2)$$
$$=1$$

Part 2

Example Using Formulas with Rational Numbers

You can use the formula $F=\frac{9}{5}C+32$ to convert a temperature given in degrees Celsius to degrees Fahrenheit.

a. −10 degrees Celsius $\qquad$ **b.** −40 degrees Celsius

Solution

a. Convert −10 degrees Celsius to degrees Fahrenheit.

Write the equation.	$F=\frac{9}{5}C+32$
Substitute −10 for C.	$F=\frac{9}{5}(-10)+32$
Write −10 as a fraction.	$=\frac{9}{5}\left(-\frac{10}{1}\right)+32$
positive × negative = negative	$=-\left(\frac{9}{5}\cdot\frac{10}{1}\right)+32$
Divide out the common factor.	$=-\left(\frac{9\cdot\cancel{10}^{2}}{_{1}\cancel{5}\cdot 1}\right)+32$
Multiply.	$=-18+32$
Add.	$=14$

Order of Operations: Multiply $\frac{9}{5}(-10)$, and then add 32.

−10 degrees Celsius is 14 degrees Fahrenheit.

continued on next page >

Part 2

Solution continued

b. Convert −40 degrees Celsius to degrees Fahrenheit.

Write the equation	$F = \frac{9}{5}C + 32$
Substitute −40 for *C*.	$F = \frac{9}{5}(-40) + 32$
Write −40 as a fraction.	$= \frac{9}{5}\left(-\frac{40}{1}\right) + 32$
positive × negative = negative	$= -\left(\frac{9}{5} \cdot \frac{40}{1}\right) + 32$
Divide out the common factor.	$= -\left(\frac{9 \cdot \cancel{40}^{8}}{\cancel{5}_{1} \cdot 1}\right) + 32$
Multiply.	$= -72 + 32$
Add.	$= -40$

−40 degrees Celsius is −40 degrees Fahrenheit.

Part 3

Intro

A **complex fraction** is a fraction $\frac{A}{B}$ where A and/or B are fractions and B is not zero.

The expression $\frac{-\frac{3}{4}}{10}$ is a complex fraction.

Main fraction bar

NOT the main fraction bar

$$\frac{-\frac{3}{4}}{10}$$

You can rewrite a complex fraction as a division expression by interpreting the main fraction bar as division.

Main fraction bar

$$\frac{-\frac{3}{4}}{10} = -\frac{3}{4} \div 10$$

Example Simplifying Complex Fractions

A lock is a chamber used to move a boat from one water level to another along a river.

After a boat enters a lock, the water inside the lock drains out, lowering the boat to the new level.

continued on next page >

Part 3

Example continued

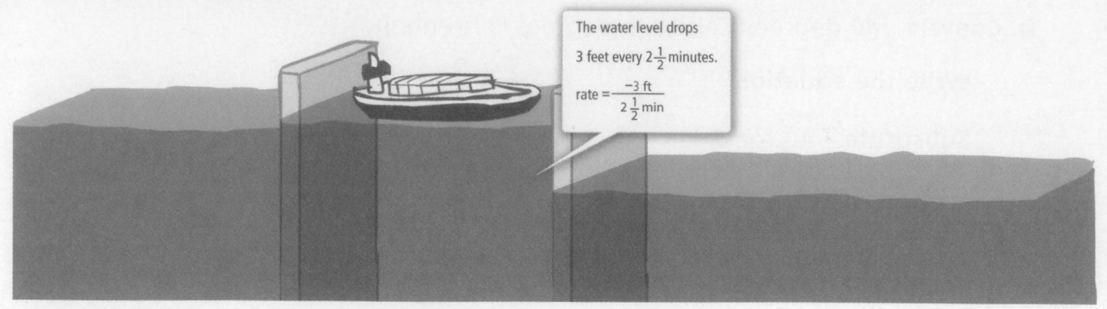

Rewrite the complex fraction $-\frac{3}{2\frac{1}{2}}$ as a division expression. Then simplify. Tell what you answer means in terms of the problem situation.

Solution

The main fraction bar represents division.	$\frac{-3}{2\frac{1}{2}} = -3 \div 2\frac{1}{2}$
Write the mixed number as a fraction.	$= -3 \div \frac{5}{2}$
To divide by $\frac{5}{2}$, multiply by its reciprocal.	$= -3 \cdot \frac{2}{5}$
The product is negative.	$= -\frac{6}{5}$
Write the improper fraction as a mixed number.	$= -1\frac{1}{5}$

The water level in the lock drops $1\frac{1}{5}$ feet per minute.

1. a. Simplify the expression $-8\left(-\frac{3}{4} + 6\right)$ by applying the Distributive Property.

   b. Evaluate the expression $-8\left(-\frac{3}{4} + 6\right)$.

2. a. Apply the Distributive Property to simplify the expression $-8(-2.5 - 7)$.

   b. Evaluate the expression $-8(-2.5 - 7)$.

3. Simplify the expression $4.5(-6) + 19$.

4. Use the formula $F = \frac{9}{5}C + 32$ to convert $-20°C$ to degrees Fahrenheit.

5. Simplify the complex fraction $\frac{-\frac{1}{4}}{-12}$.

6. The water level of a lake fell by $1\frac{1}{2}$ in. during a $1\frac{2}{3}$-week-long dry spell. Simplify the complex fraction $\frac{-1\frac{1}{2}}{1\frac{2}{3}}$ to find the average rate at which the water level changed every week.

7. a. **Writing** Simplify the complex fraction $\frac{\frac{3}{4}}{2\frac{1}{4}}$.

   b. Explain why, when dividing fractions with the same denominator, you can find the quotient by dividing the numerators. Use the complex fraction as an example.

8. **Reasoning**

   I. $-4\left(-1\frac{1}{2} - 9\right)$

   II. $-4\left(\left(-1 - \frac{1}{2}\right) - 9\right)$

   a. Use the Distributive Property to rewrite expression I. Which expression is correct?

   A. $-4\left(-1\frac{1}{2}\right) - (-4)(9)$

   B. $-4\left(-1\frac{1}{2}\right) - 4(9)$

   C. $-4\left(-1\frac{1}{2}\right) - 9$

   b. Evaluate expression I.

   c. Use the Distributive Property to rewrite expression II. Which expression is correct?

   A. $-4(-1) - (-4)\left(\frac{1}{2}\right) - (-4)(9)$

   B. $-4(-1) - (-4)\left(-\frac{1}{2}\right) - (-4)(-9)$

   C. $-4(-1) + (-4)\left(\frac{1}{2}\right) - (-4)(9)$

   d. Evaluate expression II.

   e. Copy expressions I and II. Circle the parts in the two expressions that are different. How do the expressions inside your circles compare? Explain your reasoning.

9. **Error Analysis** In evaluating the expression $\frac{9}{4}(-20) + 18$, Jenny found the value to be 63. She thinks that the number is too great, but is not sure what she did wrong.

   a. Evaluate the expression.

   b. What was Jenny's likely error?

   A. She multiplied $\frac{9}{4}$ by 20 instead of -20.

   B. She multiplied -20 by $\frac{4}{9}$ instead of $\frac{9}{4}$.

   C. She subtracted 18 instead of adding.

   D. She divided $\frac{9}{4}$ by -20 instead of multiplying.

10. **Home Heating Repair** Stewart's home is heated by hot water circulating in pipes. Recently, the system developed a small leak. It loses $1\frac{3}{5}$ milliliters every 10 minutes. Use the complex fraction $\frac{-1\frac{3}{5}\text{ milliliters}}{10\text{ minutes}}$ to find the change of the amount of water in the system per minute.

11. a. Open-Ended Use the Distributive Property to simplify the expression $-8\left(-2\frac{1}{2} + 3\right)$. Which expression is correct?

A. $-8\left(-2\frac{1}{2}\right) + 3$

B. $-8\left(-2\frac{1}{2}\right) + (-8)(3)$

C. $-8\left(-2\frac{1}{2}\right) + 8(3)$

b. Evaluate the expression.

c. Give an example of how to use the Distributive Property $a(b - c) = ab - ac$ to simplify an expression with $a < 0$ and $b < 0$. Choose values for *a, b,* and *c*.

12. a. Mental Math Simplify the expression $\frac{5}{4}(-8) + 1$.

b. Explain how you can use mental math to find the answer.

13. Mental Math

a. Evaluate $-2\left(-\frac{1}{2} - 1\right)$ by applying the Distributive Property.

b. Explain how you can use mental math to find the value.

14. A landscaper is working on a plot of land that is 409 feet above sea level on its western border. The land slopes upward from west to east on both sides of the border with a $\frac{\text{vertical change}}{\text{horizontal change}}$ ratio of $\frac{19}{17}$. The expression $\frac{19}{17}x + 728$ models the elevation of the land on both sides of the border, with *x* representing distance east from the border. A neighbor directly to the west asks the landscaper to calculate the elevation of a point exactly 34 feet west of the border, at $x = -34$. Find the elevation of that point.

15. What is the value of $-\frac{1}{6}x + 21$ when $x = -60$?

16. Think About the Process Robin works as a customer service representative. She knows that the amount in dollars of her yearly bonus is represented by the expression $-3.5x + 172$, where *x* is the number of complaints customers had about her during the year. To find her bonus if she gets 12 complaints, she substitutes 12 for *x*.

a. What should be her next step?

A. Multiply -3.5 by 12.

B. Add 12 and 172.

C. Use the Distributive Property.

b. What would her bonus be?

17. a. Challenge Simplify $\frac{\frac{\frac{3}{5}}{\frac{1}{3}}}{-\frac{\frac{2}{2}}{5}}$.

b. Are $\frac{\frac{\frac{a}{b}}{\frac{c}{d}}}{\frac{e}{f}}$ and $\frac{\frac{a}{b}}{\frac{\frac{c}{d}}{\frac{e}{f}}}$ equal? Explain.

18. Challenge After a heavy rain, a river reached the edge of its banks. Any more rain and there would be a flood. After a few hours, the river went down $\frac{1}{5}$ inch. Then another rainstorm hit and dropped $\frac{1}{4}$ inch of rain. The river rises by $\frac{1}{20}$ of the amount of rain that falls.

a. Use the expression $-\frac{1}{5} + \frac{\frac{1}{4}}{20}$ to find how the new water level compares to the riverbank.

b. Did the new rain cause a flood?

5-6 Problem Solving

CCSS: 7.NS.A.3, 7.EE.B.3

Part 1

Example Finding Means of Data Sets

Find the mean daily high temperature in Montreal during the first two weeks of February.

Montreal, Daily High Temperatures: February 1–14

Temperature	−10°C	−9°C	−5°C	−1°C	2°C	4°C
Frequency	3	1	3	2	3	2

Solution

To find the mean of a data set, you find the sum of the data values and divide by the number of data values.

$$\text{mean} = \frac{3(-10) + 1(-9) + 3(-5) + 2(-1) + 3(2) + 2(4)}{3 + 1 + 3 + 2 + 3 + 2}$$

$$= \frac{-30 + (-9) + (-15) + (-2) + 6 + 8}{14}$$

$$= \frac{-42}{14}$$

$$= \frac{-6}{2}$$

$$= -3$$

The sum of the data values is the sum of the products *frequency* × *temperature*.

The number of data values is the sum of the frequencies.

The mean daily high temperature in Montreal during the first two weeks of February was −3°C.

Part 2

Example Performing Operations with Rational Numbers

Find the error in each student's work and describe the error. Then find the value of the expression $-2 - 4(5-1)$.

Paula's Work

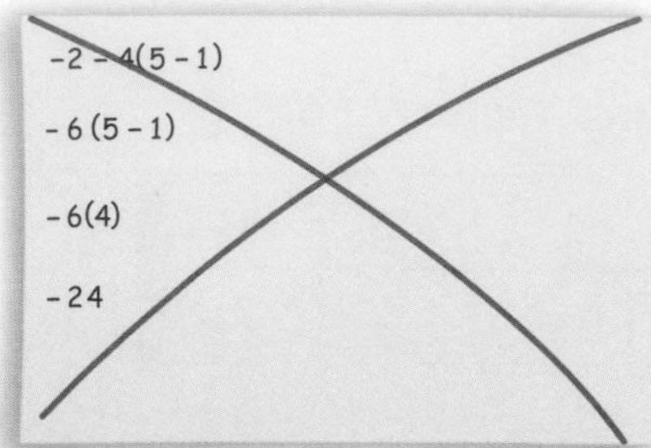

Aaron's Work

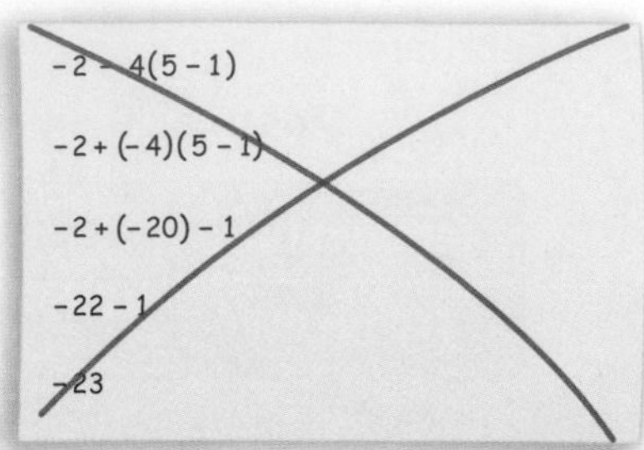

Solution

Paula did operations in the wrong order. She subtracted before working inside parentheses and multiplying by 4.

Aaron used the Distributive Property incorrectly. He did not multiply 1 by 4.

Sample correct work:

Work inside parentheses first.

$-2 - 4(5 - 1)$

$-2 - 4(4)$

$-2 - 16$

-18

Multiply before subtracting.

Part 3

Example Finding and Using Constants of Proportionality

Some squirrels hibernate in the winter. The table shows how one squirrel's weight loss depends on the number of days of hibernation.

a. Show that the relationship between days of hibernation and change in weight is a proportional relationship. What is the constant of proportionality?

b. How much weight does the squirrel lose during 132 days of hibernation?

Mr. Squirrel's Winter

Days of hibernation	Change in weight (oz)
7	−0.42
30	−1.8
75	−4.5
120	−7.2

Solution

a. To decide if the relationship is proportional, check the ratio $\frac{\text{change in weight}}{\text{days of hibernation}}$ for each row of the table.

Mr. Squirrel's Winter

Days of hibernation	Change in weight (oz)	$\frac{\text{change in weight}}{\text{days of hibernation}}$
7	−0.42	$\frac{-0.42}{7} = -0.06$
30	−1.8	$\frac{-1.8}{30} = -0.06$
75	−4.5	$\frac{-4.5}{75} = -0.06$
120	−7.2	$\frac{-7.2}{120} = -0.06$

Since all of the ratios $\frac{\text{change in weight}}{\text{days of hibernation}}$ are equivalent, the relationship between change in weight and days of hibernation is a proportional relationship.

The constant of proportionality is −0.06 ounces per day.

b. The constant of proportionality is the unit rate of ounces per day.

$$\begin{aligned}\text{total change in weight} &= \text{number of days of hibernation} \times \text{unit rate}\\ &= 132 \times (-0.06)\\ &= -7.92\end{aligned}$$

The squirrel loses a total of 7.92 ounces.

1. A biologist studying fish in a particular stream catches six specimens. **Figure 1** below lists the lengths and weights of the fish. Find the mean length and weight of the fish.
2. Simplify the expression $-3 - 5(6 - 2)$.
3. In digging a hole, the construction crew records the depth of the hole relative to the ground level. The starting depth is zero feet. The table shows the proportional relationship between the depth of the hole and the number of hours digging.

Digging a Hole

Hours	Depth (feet)
3	−8.25
5	−13.75
7	−19.25
11	−30.25

   a. Find the constant of proportionality.
   b. How many hours of digging does it take for the depth of the hole to reach −41.25 feet?
4. The table shows the proportional relationship between a hedgehog's weight loss and the number of days of hibernation.

Weight Loss of Hedgehog

Days of Hibernation	Change in Weight (oz)
8	−0.24
28	−0.84
75	−2.25
93	−2.79

   a. How much weight does the hedgehog lose during 115 days of hibernation?
   b. Explain how you know that the relationship between the hedgehog's weight loss and the number of days of hibernation is proportional.
5. A swimming pool is draining at a constant rate. The table shows the proportional relationship between the change in the water level and the number of hours the pool is draining.

Draining Swimming Pool

Hours Draining	Change in Water Level (in.)
2	−3.5
9	?
17	−29.75
23	?

   a. Find the constant of proportionality.
   b. Find the change in the water level at 9 hours.
   c. Find the change in the water level at 23 hours.

(Figure 1)

Fish Measurements						
Length (inches)	$5\frac{1}{2}$	$11\frac{3}{4}$	$8\frac{1}{4}$	$9\frac{1}{4}$	14	$9\frac{3}{4}$
Weight (pounds)	$\frac{1}{4}$	$4\frac{3}{4}$	$1\frac{1}{2}$	3	$5\frac{3}{4}$	$1\frac{3}{4}$

6. **Figure 2** below shows the temperatures of the water in 15 different beakers. Round the temperatures to the nearest integer to estimate the mean temperature.

7. Simplify the expression $1\frac{1}{2} + 7\left(\frac{6}{7} - \frac{3}{7}\right)$.

8. A basketball team played six games. In those games, the team won by 9 points, lost by 18, won by 8, won by 11, lost by 3, and won by 5. What was the mean difference in game scores over the six games?

9. **Think About the Process** In a classroom there are 6 students who are $5\frac{1}{2}$ feet tall, 2 students who are $4\frac{3}{4}$ feet tall, 4 students who are $4\frac{1}{4}$ feet tall, and 2 students who are 6 feet tall.

   a. Which expression represents the mean height of the students in the classroom?

   A. $\dfrac{6\left(5\frac{1}{2}\right) + 2\left(4\frac{3}{4}\right) + 4\left(4\frac{1}{4}\right) + 2(6)}{6 \times 2 \times 4 \times 2}$

   B. $\dfrac{6\left(5\frac{1}{2}\right) + 2\left(4\frac{3}{4}\right) + 4\left(4\frac{1}{4}\right) + 2(6)}{6 + 2 + 4 + 2}$

   C. $\dfrac{6\left(4\frac{1}{2}\right) + 2\left(5\frac{3}{4}\right) + 4\left(6\frac{1}{4}\right) + 2(6)}{6 + 2 + 4 + 2}$

   b. What is the mean height of the students in the classroom?

   c. Explain what you can do with the answer to make it more useful.

10. **Think About the Process** Recently traffic has been declining on a certain freeway. The table shows the proportional relationship between the change in the number of cars over time.

Decline of Traffic

Time (Weeks)	Change in Number of Cars Per Hour
1	−2.25
6	−13.5
10	−22.5
12	−27

   a. How would you find the rate at which the traffic is declining?

   A. Divide the number of weeks by the change in the number of cars per hour.

   B. Multiply the change in the number of cars per hour times the number of weeks.

   C. Divide the change in the number of cars per hour by the number of weeks.

   D. Multiply the number of cars per hour times the number of weeks.

   b. What is the change in the number of cars per hour at 19 weeks?

11. **Challenge** The quiz scores for a math class are in the table.

Class Quiz Scores						
Score	3	4.5	6.5	8	8.5	10
Frequency	1	4	4	5	2	2

   a. What is the mean quiz score?

   b. What is the median quiz score?

(Figure 2)

Temperatures in Beakers					
Temperature	4.5°C	3.7°C	4.3°C	4.1°C	2.9°C
Frequency	3	4	2	3	2

6-1 Repeating Decimals

Vocabulary
repeating decimal

CCSS: 7.NS.A.2b, 7.NS.A.2d

Part 1

Intro

When you want to convert a fraction to a decimal, you can use long division to find the decimal expansion.

A **repeating decimal** has a decimal expansion that repeats the same non-zero digit, or block of digits, without end. Some repeating decimals repeat the same digit. You can show that a decimal continues by using three dots. You can also use a bar to show that a single digit repeats.

Fraction	Decimal Expansion
$\frac{2}{9}$	$9\overline{)2.000\ldots}$ = 0.222... ; − 18, 20, − 18, 20, − 18, 2, ⋮
$\frac{2}{9} = 0.\overline{2}$	$= 0.\overline{2}$

Dots mean digits continue without end.

A bar means that "2" repeats without end.

continued on next page >

Part 1

Intro continued

Some decimals repeat the same block of digits. You can represent the repeating block of digits with a bar over the digits that repeat.

Fraction: $\frac{2}{11}$

Decimal Expansion:

$$\begin{array}{r} 0.1818\ldots \\ 11\overline{)2.0000\ldots} \\ -11 \\ \hline 90 \\ -88 \\ \hline 20 \\ -11 \\ \hline 90 \\ -88 \\ \hline 2 \\ \vdots \end{array}$$

$\frac{2}{11} = 0.\overline{18}$

$= 0.\overline{18}$

A bar means that "18" repeats without end.

Example Identifying Repeating Decimals

Which of the following are repeating decimals?

$-8.4\overline{6}$	-0.0088	0.555	$0.\overline{125}$
18.35	0.2	$0.\overline{36}$	$-4.199\overline{9}$

Solution

Repeating: $-8.4\overline{6}$, $0.\overline{125}$, $0.\overline{36}$, $-4.199\overline{9}$

Not repeating: -0.0088, 0.555, 18.35, 0.2

Key Concept

A **repeating decimal** has a decimal expansion that repeats the same non-zero digit, or block of digits, without end. A repeating decimal is a rational number.

Repeating decimals: $0.\overline{2}$, $0.\overline{18}$, $3.\overline{54}$

Not repeating decimals: 0.2, 0.18, 3.54

Part 2

Intro

A quotient is a repeating decimal if the remainders in each long division step repeat in a pattern.

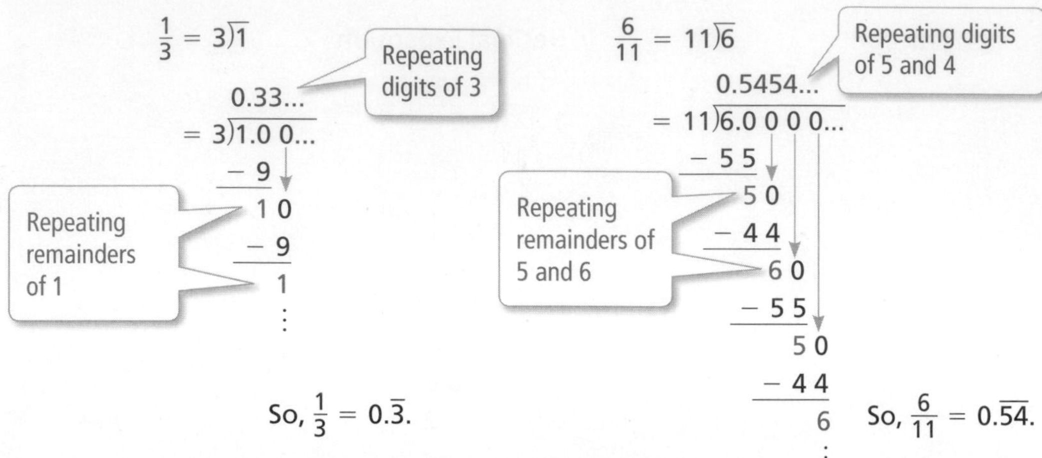

So, $\frac{1}{3} = 0.\overline{3}$.

So, $\frac{6}{11} = 0.\overline{54}$.

Example Converting Fractions to Repeating Decimals

Use long division to complete the table of decimal expansions. What do you notice about the expansions of ninths and elevenths?

Ninths		Elevenths	
$\frac{1}{9} =$		$\frac{1}{11} =$	
$\frac{2}{9} =$		$\frac{2}{11} =$	
$\frac{3}{9} =$		$\frac{3}{11} =$	
$\frac{4}{9} =$		$\frac{4}{11} =$	
$\frac{5}{9} =$		$\frac{5}{11} =$	

continued on next page >

Part 2

Example continued

Solution

Ninths:

```
   0.11...
9)1.0 0...
 - 9
    1 0
  - 9
      1
      ⋮
```

$\frac{1}{9} = 0.\overline{1}$

Repeating decimal

```
   0.22...
9)2.0 0...
 - 1 8
    2 0
  - 1 8
      2
      ⋮
```

$\frac{2}{9} = 0.\overline{2}$

```
   0.33...
9)3.0 0...
 - 2 7
    3 0
  - 2 7
      3
      ⋮
```

$\frac{3}{9} = 0.\overline{3}$

```
   0.44...
9)4.0 0...
 - 3 6
    4 0
  - 3 6
      4
      ⋮
```

$\frac{4}{9} = 0.\overline{4}$

```
   0.55...
9)5.0 0...
 - 4 5
    5 0
  - 4 5
      5
      ⋮
```

$\frac{5}{9} = 0.\overline{5}$

continued on next page >

Part 2

Solution continued

Elevenths:

```
     0.0909...
11)1.0 0 0 0...
   - 0
     100
    - 99
       10
      - 0
       100
      - 99
          1
          ⋮
```

$\frac{1}{11} = 0.\overline{09}$

```
     0.1818...
11)2.0 0 0 0...
 - 1 1
     90
   - 88
     20
   - 11
       90
     - 88
        2
        ⋮
```

$\frac{2}{11} = 0.\overline{18}$

```
     0.2727...
11)3.0 0 0 0...
 - 2 2
     80
   - 77
     30
   - 22
       80
     - 77
        3
        ⋮
```

$\frac{3}{11} = 0.\overline{27}$

```
     0.3636...
11)4.0 0 0 0...
 - 3 3
     70
   - 66
     40
   - 33
       70
     - 66
        4
        ⋮
```

$\frac{4}{11} = 0.\overline{36}$

```
     0.4545...
11)5.0 0 0 0...
 - 4 4
     60
   - 55
     50
   - 44
       60
     - 55
        5
        ⋮
```

$\frac{5}{11} = 0.\overline{45}$

Ninths	Elevenths
$\frac{1}{9} = 0.\overline{1}$	$\frac{1}{11} = 0.\overline{09}$
$\frac{2}{9} = 0.\overline{2}$	$\frac{2}{11} = 0.\overline{18}$
$\frac{3}{9} = 0.\overline{3}$	$\frac{3}{11} = 0.\overline{27}$
$\frac{4}{9} = 0.\overline{4}$	$\frac{4}{11} = 0.\overline{36}$
$\frac{5}{9} = 0.\overline{5}$	$\frac{5}{11} = 0.\overline{45}$

The repeating blocks of digits are multiples of 11.

The repeating blocks of digits are multiples of 9.

Part 3

Intro

Mixed numbers can also be represented with a decimal expansion. $2\frac{1}{3}$ represents 2 wholes and a third of a whole. To change it to a decimal representation, keep the whole-number part of the mixed number and convert the fraction part of the mixed number to a decimal.

Mixed Number	Decimal
$2\frac{1}{3}$	2.3333...

Example Comparing Numbers in Multiple Forms

A special effects artist uses miniatures to shoot a scene in which a jet flies through a tunnel. Will the plane fit through the tunnel?

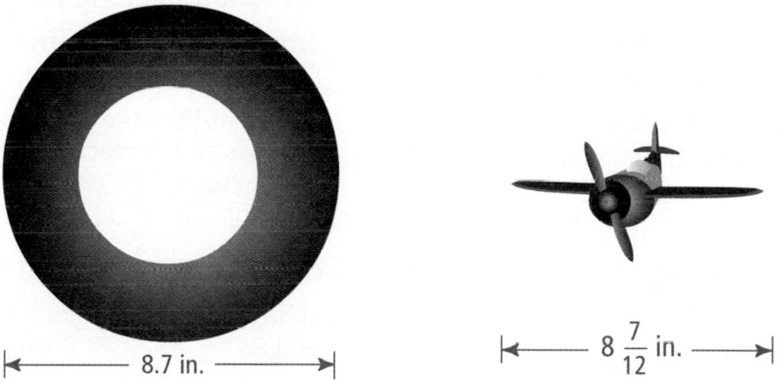

Solution

To compare $8\frac{7}{12}$ with 8.7, write $8\frac{7}{12}$ as a decimal. The whole-number part stays the same. Convert the fractional part to a decimal.

```
     0.5833...
12)7.0 0 0 0...
  - 6 0
     1 00
    - 96
       40
     - 36
       40
        ⋮
```

$$\frac{7}{12} = 0.58\overline{3}$$

Since $8.58\overline{3}$ is less than 8.7, the jet plane will fit through the tunnel.

Digital Resources

1. a. Is $4.\overline{333}$ a repeating decimal?
   b. Is 7.561 a repeating decimal?
2. Write the repeating decimal 0.966666666... using a bar over the repeated digit(s).
3. Write the decimal expansion for $\frac{2}{3}$.
4. Write the decimal expansion for $\frac{3}{11}$.
5. Write the decimal equivalent for $8\frac{4}{9}$.
6. You have a pizza with diameter $6\frac{1}{3}$ in., and a square box that is 6.38 in. across.
   a. What is the decimal expansion for $6\frac{1}{3}$?
      A. $6.\overline{38}$ B. 6.3
      C. $6.\overline{3}$ D. 6.33
   b. Is the box big enough to fit the pizza inside?
7. a. **Reasoning** Is $9.\overline{373}$ a repeating decimal? Why or why not?
      A. No, the decimal does not have a decimal expansion that repeats without end.
      B. Yes, the decimal does not have a decimal expansion that repeats without end.
      C. Yes, the decimal has a decimal expansion that repeats without end.
      D. No, the decimal has a decimal expansion that repeats without end.
   b. Is 9.373 a repeating decimal? Why or why not?
      A. No, the decimal has a decimal expansion that repeats without end.
      B. No, the decimal does not have a decimal expansion that repeats without end.
      C. Yes, the decimal has a decimal expansion that repeats without end.
      D. Yes, the decimal does not have a decimal expansion that repeats without end.
   c. Which is greater, $9.\overline{373}$ or 9.373? Explain.
8. a. **Open-Ended** Write the repeating decimal 0.429429429... using a bar over the repeating digits.
   b. Show two other ways to represent this number using a bar over the repeating digits.
9. a. **Writing** Find the decimal equivalent for $\frac{1}{3}$.
      A. $\frac{1}{3} = 0.333333$ B. $\frac{1}{3} = 0.\overline{3}$
      C. $\frac{1}{3} = 0.\overline{4}$ D. $\frac{1}{3} = 0.3$
   b. Can you think of a shortcut to find the decimal expansion for $\frac{2}{3}$ without using long division?
10. a. **Error Analysis** Your friend used long division and concluded that the decimal expansion for $\frac{1}{6}$ is 6. What is the correct decimal expansion?
      A. 0.16 B. 0.161616
      C. $0.1\overline{6}$ D. $0.\overline{7}$
   b. What mistake did your friend likely make?
      A. Your friend divided 6 by 1, not 1 by 6.
      B. Your friend rounded the decimal to the nearest hundredth.
      C. Your friend rounded the repeated digits.
      D. Your friend did not write the decimal using overbar notation.
11. **Stacking Boxes** You have one box that is $3\frac{3}{11}$ feet tall and a second box that is 3.27 feet tall.
   a. What is the correct decimal expansion for $3\frac{3}{11}$?
      A. 3.27 B. 3.61
      C. $3.\overline{27}$ D. $3.\overline{33}$
   b. If you stack the boxes, about how tall will the stack be?

See your complete lesson at MyMathUniverse.com

12. a. Which decimals are repeating?
$3.\overline{647}$, 3.611, $3.\overline{641}$

b. Order the decimals from least to greatest.

A. $3.\overline{647}$, $3.\overline{641}$, 3.611

B. $3.\overline{647}$, 3.611, $3.\overline{641}$

C. 3.611, $3.\overline{641}$, $3.\overline{647}$

D. $3.\overline{641}$, $3.\overline{647}$, 3.611

13. Write the repeating decimal 0.9359535953... using a bar over the repeated digits.

14. a. Write the decimal expansion for $\frac{12}{13}$.

A. 0.923076 **B.** $0.\overline{92307}$

C. 0.92307 **D.** $0.\overline{923076}$

b. Explain how you determine if the digits repeat and what the pattern is when you use a calculator to divide.

15. Write the decimal expansion for $9\frac{11}{27}$.

A. $9.\overline{4}$ **B.** $9.4\overline{70}$

C. $9.\overline{407}$ **D.** $9.4\overline{07}$

16. Think About the Process

a. How would you set up the long division to find the decimal expansion for $\frac{3}{11}$?

A. $11\overline{)3}$ **B.** $8\overline{)3}$

C. $3\overline{)11}$ **D.** $8\overline{)11}$

b. What is the decimal expansion for $\frac{3}{11}$?

A. $0.\overline{27}$ **B.** 0.27

C. $0.2\overline{7}$ **D.** 0.273

17. Think About the Process

a. What can you do before dividing to help you find the decimal expansion for $19\frac{4}{12}$?

A. Write the mixed number as an improper fraction.

B. Divide the whole number part by the denominator.

C. Divide the whole number part by the numerator.

D. Write the fraction in simplest form.

b. What is the correct decimal expansion?

A. $19\frac{4}{12} = 19.333333$

B. $19\frac{4}{12} = 19.3$

C. $19\frac{4}{12} = 19.\overline{34}$

D. $19\frac{4}{12} = 19.\overline{3}$

18. a. Challenge What is the decimal expansion for $\frac{4}{13}$?

A. $0.\overline{307}$ **B.** $0.\overline{307692}$

C. 0.307692 **D.** 0.307

b. What is the decimal expansion for $\frac{9}{13}$?

A. 0.692307 **B.** $0.\overline{692}$

C. $0.\overline{692307}$ **D.** 0.692

c. What do you notice about the two decimals?

19. Challenge Gary brings $3\frac{1}{9}$ pounds of hamburger to cook at Bobby's cookout.

a. If Bobby already bought $5\frac{4}{11}$ pounds of hamburger, how many pounds of meat do they have in total?

b. What is the decimal expansion for $3\frac{1}{9}$?

A. 3.4 **B.** 3.11

C. $3.\overline{1}$ **D.** $3.\overline{36}$

c. What is the decimal expansion for $5\frac{4}{11}$?

A. $5.\overline{1}$ **B.** 5.36

C. $5.\overline{36}$ **D.** 5.11

d. If they are making hamburgers that are each $\frac{1}{3}$ pound, how many hamburgers can they make?

6-2 Terminating Decimals

Vocabulary
terminating decimal

CCSS: 7.NS.A.2d, Also 7.NS.A.2b

Key Concept

A **terminating decimal** has a decimal expansion that ends in zeros.

$$\frac{3}{4} = 4\overline{)3}$$

$$\begin{array}{r} 0.75 \\ 4\overline{)3.00} \\ -\,28 \\ \hline 20 \\ -\,20 \\ \hline 0 \end{array}$$

$$\begin{array}{r} 0.75000... \\ 4\overline{)3.00000...} \end{array}$$

Remove the trailing zeros of a terminating decimal.

$$\frac{3}{4} = 0.75$$

Part 1

Intro

Here are some common fractions and their decimal expansions.

$\frac{1}{2} = 0.5$	$\frac{1}{3} = 0.\overline{3}$
$\frac{1}{4} = 0.25$	$\frac{1}{5} = 0.2$
$\frac{1}{6} = 0.1\overline{6}$	$\frac{1}{8} = 0.125$
$\frac{1}{9} = 0.\overline{1}$	$\frac{1}{10} = 0.1$

Example Identifying Terminating Decimals

Decide if each decimal or fraction terminates or does not terminate.

0.3	0.001	$\frac{1}{3}$	41.75	
0.84...	$\frac{1}{6}$	−9.875	$1.7\overline{2}$	$\frac{1}{8}$

continued on next page >

Part 1

Example continued

Solution

Terminates: 0.3, 0.001, 41.75, −9.875, $\frac{1}{8}$ = 0.125

Does not terminate: $\frac{1}{3}$, 0.84..., $\frac{1}{6}$, $1.7\overline{2}$

$= 0.\overline{3}$ $= 0.1\overline{6}$

Part 2

Example **Converting Fractions to Terminating Decimals**

A recipe for a six-foot sub calls for $1\frac{3}{4}$ pounds of cheese. You want to get the exact amount from the deli counter. If the cheese is placed on a digital scale, what decimal number should the digital scale show?

Solution

The whole number stays the same, 1.

Convert $\frac{3}{4}$ to a decimal.

$$\begin{array}{r} 0.75 \\ 4\overline{)3.00} \\ -\,2\,8 \\ \hline 20 \\ -\,20 \\ \hline 0 \end{array} = 0.75$$

The digital scale should show 1.75 pounds.

Part 3

Example Writing Mixed Numbers as Terminating Decimals

Write each mixed number as its decimal equivalent.

a. $7\frac{1}{8}$ **b.** $7\frac{1}{2}$ **c.** $7\frac{21}{75}$ **d.** $7\frac{3}{5}$ **e.** $7\frac{12}{25}$

Solution

a. Write $7\frac{1}{8}$ as a decimal. The whole, 7, stays the same.
Convert the fraction part, $\frac{1}{8}$, to a decimal.

$$\begin{array}{r} 0.125 \\ 8\overline{)1.000} \\ -\ 8\ \ \ \\ \hline 20\ \ \\ -\ 16\ \ \\ \hline 40\ \\ -\ 40\ \\ \hline 0 \end{array}$$

$\frac{1}{8} = 0.125$

$7\frac{1}{8}$ as a decimal is 7.125.

Now follow the steps for the other mixed numbers.

b. $7\frac{1}{2}$

$$\begin{array}{r} 0.5 \\ 2\overline{)1.0} \\ -\ 10 \\ \hline 0 \end{array}$$

$7\frac{1}{2} = 7.5$

c. $7\frac{21}{75}$

$$\begin{array}{r} 0.28 \\ 75\overline{)21.00} \\ -\ 150\ \\ \hline 600 \\ -\ 600 \\ \hline 0 \end{array}$$

$7\frac{21}{75} = 7.28$

d. $7\frac{3}{5}$

$$\begin{array}{r} 0.6 \\ 5\overline{)3.0} \\ -\ 30 \\ \hline 0 \end{array}$$

$7\frac{3}{5} = 7.6$

e. $7\frac{12}{25}$

$$\begin{array}{r} 0.48 \\ 25\overline{)12.00} \\ -\ 100\ \\ \hline 200 \\ -\ 200 \\ \hline 0 \end{array}$$

$7\frac{12}{25} = 7.48$

Digital Resources   

1. Is the fraction $\frac{1}{3}$ equivalent to a decimal that terminates or a decimal that does not terminate? Use the table of fractions and their decimal expansions to find your answer.

Fractions and Their Decimal Expansions	
$\frac{1}{2} = 0.5$	$\frac{1}{3} = 0.\overline{3}$
$\frac{1}{4} = 0.25$	$\frac{1}{5} = 0.2$
$\frac{1}{6} = 0.1\overline{6}$	$\frac{1}{7} = 0.\overline{142857}$
$\frac{1}{8} = 0.125$	$\frac{1}{9} = 0.\overline{1}$
$\frac{1}{10} = 0.1$	$\frac{1}{11} = 0.\overline{09}$
$\frac{1}{12} = 0.08\overline{3}$	$\frac{1}{13} = 0.\overline{076923}$

2. Is $1.08\overline{3}$ a terminating, repeating, or non-repeating decimal? Can you tell?

3. Convert $\frac{19}{25}$ to a decimal.

4. A recipe calls for $\frac{1}{2}$ c of milk. Express this as a decimal.

5. Convert $1\frac{16}{25}$ to a decimal.

6. At a grocery store, you want to buy $3\frac{1}{5}$ lb of ham. What decimal should the digital scale show?

7. a. Reasoning Is the fraction $\frac{1}{100}$ equivalent to a decimal that terminates or a decimal that does not terminate?

Fractions and their Decimal Expansions	
$\frac{1}{10} = 0.1$	$\frac{1}{20} = 0.05$
$\frac{1}{30} = 0.0\overline{3}$	$\frac{1}{40} = 0.025$
$\frac{1}{50} = 0.02$	$\frac{1}{60} = 0.01\overline{6}$
$\frac{1}{70} = 0.0\overline{142857}$	$\frac{1}{80} = 0.0125$
$\frac{1}{90} = 0.0\overline{1}$	$\frac{1}{100} = 0.01$
$\frac{1}{110} = 0.0\overline{09}$	$\frac{1}{120} = 0.008\overline{3}$

b. What must be true about the denominator of a fraction in order for the fraction to correspond to a terminating decimal? Explain.

8. a. Is 37.5 a terminating, repeating, or non-repeating decimal?

b. What is the difference between 37.5 and $37.4\overline{9}$?

9. a. Writing Is 212.1234... a terminating, repeating, or non-repeating decimal?

b. Show how slight changes to the decimal give you decimals of each of the other two types.

10. Error Analysis Ariel incorrectly says that $2\frac{5}{8}$ is the same as 2.58.

a. Convert $2\frac{5}{8}$ to a decimal correctly.

b. What was Ariel's likely error?

A. She divided 8 by 5 instead of dividing 5 by 8.

B. She wrote the decimal to two places instead of three places.

C. She used the fraction digits as the decimal digits.

D. She switched the digits 5 and 8 and should have written 2.85.

11. Air Pressure You are adding air to a tire. The air pressure in the tire should be $32\frac{27}{200}$ pounds per square inch. What decimal should you watch for on the digital pressure gauge?

12. A bowl weighs $\frac{11}{40}$ lb.

a. Express this as a decimal.

b. Explain how you can find the decimal by thinking of the denominator as a 4 and then using mental math.

13. a. Convert $\frac{35}{80}$ to a decimal.

b. Describe any clues that $\frac{35}{80}$ provides as to whether its decimal will be terminating or repeating.

c. If it terminates, does $\frac{35}{80}$ provide any clues as to how many decimal places to expect? Explain.

14. a. Convert $117\frac{151}{200}$ to a decimal.

b. Describe a situation in which a mixed number would be easier to use than a decimal.

c. Describe a situation in which a decimal would be easier to use than a mixed number.

15. At a butcher shop, Hilda bought $8\frac{17}{20}$ lb of beef and some pork. She left with $18\frac{8}{25}$ lb of meat. Express the number of pounds of pork she bought using a decimal.

16. Think About the Process

a. Which procedure would you use to convert a fraction to a decimal?

A. $\text{numerator}\overline{)\text{denominator}}$

B. $\frac{\text{denominator}}{\text{numerator}} \cdot 100$

C. $\text{denominator}\overline{)\text{numerator}}$

D. $\frac{\text{numerator}}{\text{denominator}} \cdot 100$

b. Convert $\frac{4}{5}$ to a decimal.

17. Think About the Process

a. What is the first step in converting a mixed number to a decimal?

A. Multiply by -1.

B. Convert the mixed number to an improper fraction.

C. Divide the numerator by the denominator.

D. Express the mixed number as the sum of an integer and a fraction.

b. $-11\frac{3}{20} = ■$

18. Challenge A recipe for lasagna calls for $\frac{58}{125}$ lb of beef per person.

a. Express this as a decimal.

b. You want to use this recipe to make enough lasagna for 25 people. If beef at your grocery store costs $2 per pound, how much would you spend of the beef?

19. Challenge The maximum weight a delivery truck can carry is 3,300 lb worth of packages. If the weight of the packages exceeds maximum weight, the truck will not be sent out for deliveries. The truck has 10 packages that weigh $154\frac{11}{20}$ lb each and 3 packages the weigh 300.5 lb each.

a. Express the total weight of the packages in the truck as a decimal.

b. Will the truck be sent out?

6-3 Percents Greater Than 100

CCSS: 7.NS.A.3

Part 1

Intro

You can use percents greater than 100 to describe amounts that are greater than the whole.

To estimate an amount that is greater than 100 percent of a whole, think about how the percent relates to 100%. 100% of a whole is the whole.

100% of Year 1 population

200% of a whole is twice the whole.

200% of Year 1 population

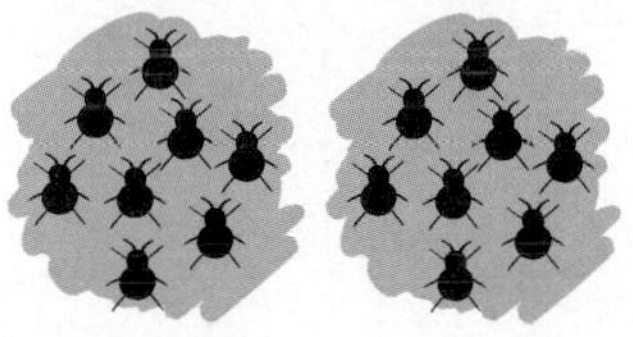

300% of a whole is three times the whole.

300% of Year 1 population

400% of a whole is four times the whole.

400% of Year 1 population

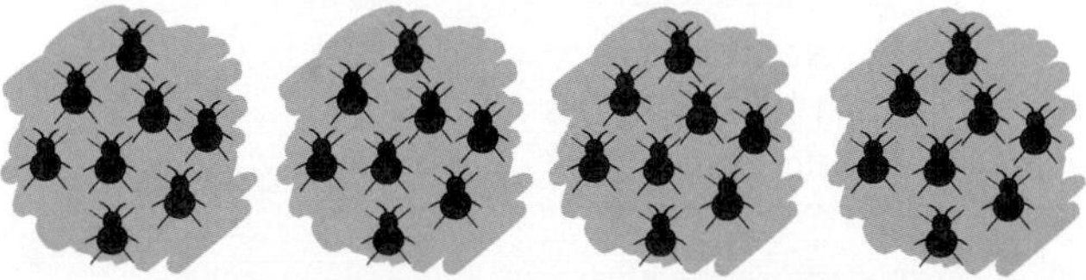

475% of a whole is more than 400%, but less than 500%, of the whole.

475% of Year 1 population

Part 1

Example Understanding Percents Greater Than 100

Classify each as being less than 10, greater than 10 but less than 100, or greater than 100.

200% of 1	125% of 25	125% of 100	300% of 2
200% of 75	1,000% of 15	400% of 26	700% of 5

Solution

Less than 10

200% of 1 — Two times 1 is 2.

300% of 2 — Three times 2 is 6.

Greater than 10 but less than 100

125% of 25 — 200% of 25 is two times 25, or 50. So 125% is less than 50.

700% of 5 — Seven times 5 is 35.

Greater than 100

200% of 75 — Two times 75 is greater than 100.

400% of 26 — 400% of 25 is 100. So 400% of 26 is greater than 100.

125% of 100 — A percent greater than 100% of 100 is greater than 100.

1,000% of 15 — Ten times 15 is 150.

Key Concept

Calculate percents greater than 100 the same way you calculate other percents.

What is 130% of 800?

$$\begin{aligned} \text{part} &= \text{percent} \cdot \text{whole} \\ &= 130\% \cdot 800 \\ &= \frac{130}{100} \cdot 800 \\ &= 130 \cdot 8 \\ &= 1{,}040 \end{aligned}$$

Use the percent equation.

130% of 800 is 1,040

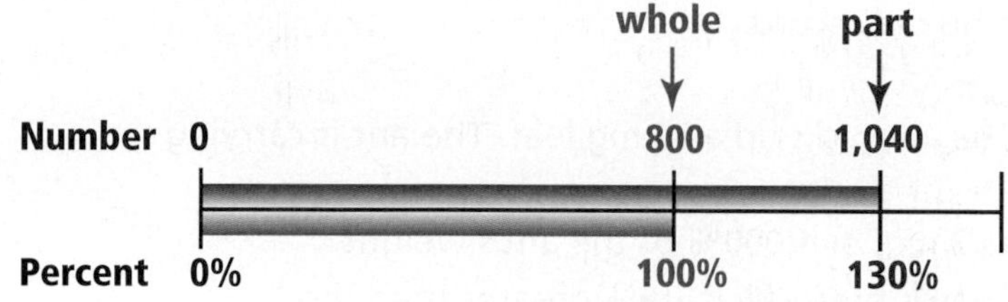

Part 2

Example Calculating Percents Greater Than 100

A study found that the alligator population this year is 120% of last year's population. If last year's population was 60, how many alligators are there this year?

Solution

This year's population — Last year's population

Write the percent equation.	part = percent · whole
Substitute the percent and the whole.	$= 120\% \cdot 60$
Write the percent as a fraction.	$= \left(\frac{120}{100}\right) \cdot 60$
Divide the numerator and denominator by 20.	$= \left(\frac{6}{5}\right) \cdot 60$
Use the Commutative and Associative Properties.	$= 6 \cdot \left(\frac{60}{5}\right)$
Divide 60 by 5.	$= 6 \cdot 12$
Multiply.	$= 72$

There are 72 alligators this year.

Part 3

Example Using Percents Greater Than 100

Classify each as *true* or *false*. Then correct any false statements.

a. A pet grasshopper jumped 6% higher than his old jump record. His new record is 106% of his old record.

b. An ant weighs 3 mg. The ant picks up a 30 mg leaf. The ant is carrying 110% of its weight.

c. The wingspan of a Monarch butterfly is 2.5% greater than the wingspan of a Queen butterfly. The Monarch's wingspan is 125% of the Queen's wingspan.

Solution

a. A pet grasshopper jumped 6% higher than his old jump record. His new record is 106% of his old record.

True.

b. An ant weighs 3 mg. The ant picks up a 30 mg leaf. The ant is carrying 110% of its weight.

False. 30 mg is 10 times 3 mg, or 1,000% of the ant's weight.

c. The wingspan of a Monarch butterfly is 2.5% greater than the wingspan of a Queen butterfly. The Monarch's wingspan is 125% of the Queen's wingspan.

False. A wingspan that is 2.5% greater than the Queen's wingspan is 100% + 2.5%, or 102.5% of the Queen's wingspan.

Digital Resources   

1. Is 700% of 5 less than 10, greater than 10 but less than 100, or greater than 100?
2. Is 250% of 44 less than 100, greater than 100 but less than 150, or greater than 150?
3. A new health drink has 130% of the recommended daily allowance (RDA) for a certain vitamin. The RDA for this vitamin is 30 mg. How many milligrams of the vitamin are in the drink?
4. On Saturday, Breanne drove 10 miles. On Sunday, she drove 70 miles. The number of miles Breanne drove on Sunday is what percent of the number of miles she drove on Saturday?
5. Suppose a bunny's second hop is 8% higher than her first hop. Is the statement below true or false? If the statement is false, correct it.

   "The bunny's second hop is 108% of her first hop."
6. Suppose the wingspan of a certain adult bird is 7.5% greater than the wingspan of its baby. Classify the statement as true or false. If the statement is false, correct it.

   The wingspan of the adult bird is 175% of the wingspan of the baby bird.

   A. The statement is false. The wingspan of the adult bird is ■% of the wingspan of the baby bird.

   B. The statement is true.
7. Emma went on a shopping trip. She bought a pair of shoes and a sweater. Emma spent 2% more on the sweater than on the shoes. The cost of the sweater is what percent of the cost of the shoes?
8. **Mental Math** When a bush was first planted in a garden, it was 10 cm tall. After two months, it was 400% as tall as when it was first planted. Use mental math to find how tall the bush was after the two months.
9. a. **Reasoning** Which of these is the best estimate for 380% of 60?

   A. greater than 0 but less than $1 \cdot 60$

   B. greater than $1 \cdot 60$ but less than $2 \cdot 60$

   C. greater than $2 \cdot 60$ but less than $3 \cdot 60$

   D. greater than $3 \cdot 60$

   b. Explain the reasoning behind your choice.
10. **Rabbit Population** The rabbit population in a certain area is 200% of last year's population. There are 1,100 rabbits this year. How many were there last year?
11. a. Your friend estimated that it would take 5 hours to finish an art project. It actually took him 16 hours to finish the project. The amount of time it took to finish the project was what percent of the estimated time?

   b. What does it mean to have more than 100% of something? Give at least two examples.
12. **Estimation** Garden A has area 25 square meters. Garden B has area 61.2 square meters.

   a. Round the area of garden B to the nearest 10 square meters. The area of garden B is about ■% of the area of garden A.

   b. Now use the exact area of garden B. The area of garden B is exactly ■% of the area of garden A.

13. Error Analysis Your teacher asks you and your friend to classify the following statement as true or false. If it is false, you must correct it.

"Last week Alisha ran 4 miles. This week Alisha ran 9 miles. She ran 102% of last week's distance."

Your friend says that the statement is false and that Alisha ran 2.25% of last week's distance.

a. What is the correct response to your teacher?

b. What error did your friend likely make?

A. Your friend said the given statement is false, but the given statement is true.

B. Your friend used the percent equation but did not divide by 100.

C. Your friend used the percent equation but did not multiply by 100.

D. Your friend used the percent equation and switched values for the whole and the part.

14. In football, a touchdown is worth 6 points. During a football game, Team A scores 12 points. Team B scores 5 touchdowns. Team B scores what percent of the points Team A scores? Round to the nearest percent as needed.

15. Think About the Process Last month you spent $50 on clothing. This month you spent 190% of what you spent last month.

a. Set up a percent equation to model this situation.

A. 190% = percent · 50

B. 50 = 190% · whole

C. part = 190% · 50

b. You spent $■ this month.

16. Think About the Process Juanita and Heather go to a restaurant for lunch. The cost of the meal is $29.00. They decide to leave $34.80 to include a tip for the waiter.

a. Set up a percent equation to model this situation.

A. $34.80 = 29.00 \cdot m$

B. $29.00 = m \cdot 34.80$

C. part = $34.80 \cdot 29.00$

D. $34.80 = m \cdot 29.00$

b. The total amount they spend is ■% of the cost of the meal.

17. Challenge Your friend sells you a bicycle for $63 and a helmet for $20. The total cost is 150% of what your friend spent originally.

a. How much did your friend spend originally? Round to the nearest dollar.

b. How much money did your friend earn by selling his bicycle and helmet to you? Round to the nearest dollar.

6-4 Percents Less Than 1

CCSS: 7.NS.A.3

Part 1

Intro

A percent less than 1 describes a very small amount of something.

$1000 is 100% of $1000

$100 is 10% of $1000

$10 is 1% of $1000

$1 is 0.1% of $1000

Example Understanding Percents Less Than 1

Decide whether or not each expression is equivalent to $\frac{1}{2}\%$.

$\frac{1}{2}$ 0.05 $\frac{1}{5}$ 0.005 0.05 50%

$\frac{1}{200}$ $\frac{1}{50}$ 0.5%

Solution

1% is equivalent to $\frac{1}{100}$. $\frac{1}{2}\%$ is half of 1%.

Equivalent to $\frac{1}{2}\%$:

0.5%

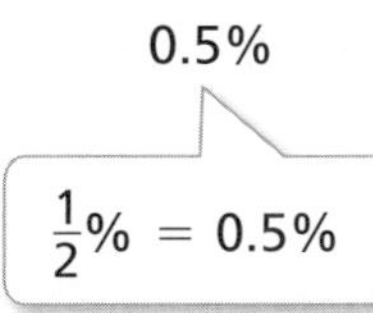

$\frac{1}{2}\% = 0.5\%$

0.005

$0.5\% = 0.005$

$\frac{1}{200}$

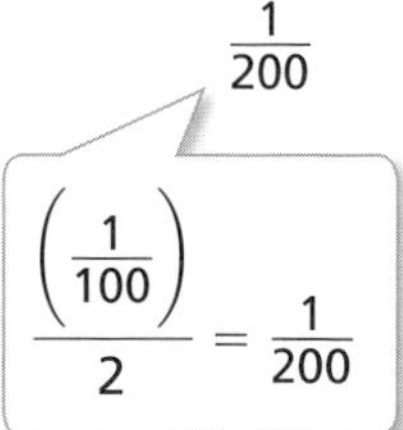

$$\frac{\left(\frac{1}{100}\right)}{2} = \frac{1}{200}$$

Not Equivalent to $\frac{1}{2}\%$:

50% $\frac{1}{2}$ 0.5 0.05 $\frac{1}{5}$ $\frac{1}{50}$

Key Concept

Calculate percents less than 1 the same way you calculate other percents.

What is 0.75% of 200?

$$\begin{aligned} \text{part} &= \text{percent} \cdot \text{whole} \\ &= 0.75\% \cdot 200 \\ &= 0.0075 \cdot 200 \\ &= 1.5 \end{aligned}$$

Use the percent equation.

1.5 is 0.75% of 200.

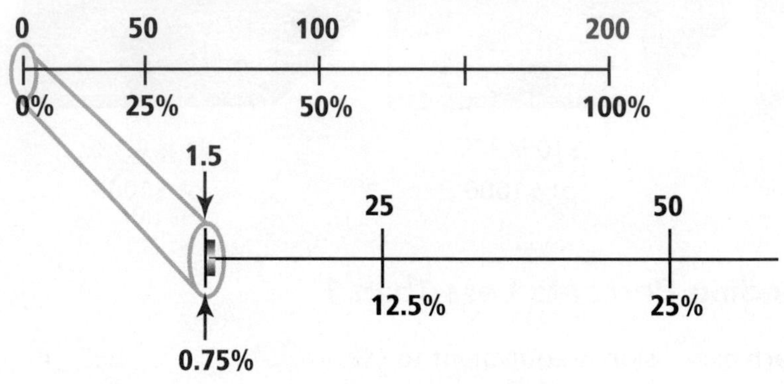

Part 2

Example Finding Missing Values for Percents Less Than 1

Choose from the numbers below to solve each problem.

800	500	1.5	200
0.025	25	15	0.5

a. ■ is $\frac{1}{4}$% of 200 **b.** 15 is ■% of 1,000 **c.** 4 is 0.5% of ■

continued on next page >

Part 2

Example continued

Solution

a. What is $\frac{1}{4}\%$ of 200?

$$\text{part} = \text{percent} \cdot \text{whole}$$
$$\text{part} = \tfrac{1}{4}\% \cdot 200$$
$$= \frac{\left(\frac{1}{4}\right)}{100} \cdot 200$$
$$= \frac{1}{4} \cdot 2$$
$$= \frac{1}{2}, \text{ or } 0.5$$

$\frac{1}{4}\%$ of 200 is 0.5.

b. 15 is what percent of 1,000?

$$\text{part} = \text{percent} \cdot \text{whole}$$
$$15 = m \cdot 1{,}000$$
$$\frac{15}{1{,}000} = m$$
$$0.015 = m$$
$$1.5\% = m$$

15 is 1.5% of 1,000.

c. 4 is 0.5% of what?

$$\text{part} = \text{percent} \cdot \text{whole}$$
$$4 = 0.5\% \cdot x$$
$$4 = \frac{0.5}{100} \cdot x$$
$$4 = \frac{5}{1{,}000} \cdot x$$
$$\frac{4{,}000}{5} = x$$
$$800 = x$$

4 is 0.5% of 800.

Part 3

Example Using Percents Less Than 1

What percent of West Virginia's total area is covered by bodies of water?

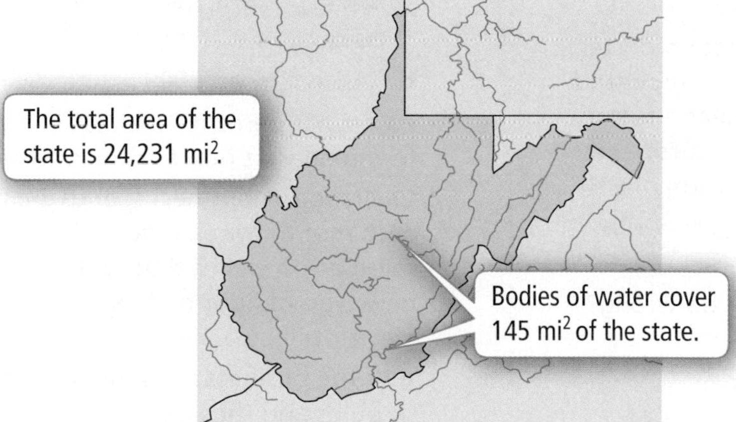

Solution

$$\text{part} = \text{percent} \cdot \text{whole}$$
$$145 = m \cdot 24{,}231$$
$$\frac{145}{24{,}231} = m$$
$$0.006 \approx m$$
$$0.6\% = m$$

Bodies of water cover about 0.6% of West Virginia's total area.

1. $\frac{7}{9}$% of a quantity is equal to what fraction of the quantity?
2. Write 0.27% as a decimal.
3. What is 0.8% of $5,700?
4. What percent of 2,000 is 4?
5. A forest covers 43,000 acres. A survey finds that 0.2% of the forest is old-growth trees. How many acres of old-growth trees are there?
6. A company that makes hair-care products had 3,000 people try a new shampoo. Of the 3,000 people, 9 had a mild allergic reaction. What percent of the people had a mild allergic reaction?
7. a. **Reasoning** Write 0.25% as a fraction.
   b. You can read 0.25% as "25-hundredths percent" or as "25-hundredths of one percent." Describe situations where you would prefer to use each form.
8. Write 0.975% as a fraction.
9. **Error Analysis** A newspaper reporter wrote an article about the amount of a toxin found in a river near a factory. In the article, the reporter incorrectly used 0.25 as the decimal form of $\frac{1}{4}$%.
   a. What is the correct way to write $\frac{1}{4}$% as a decimal?
   b. What did the reporter do wrong?
10. Find the value of n.

    0.83% of n is 18.26
11. a. **Writing** Find 0.76% of 8,500.
    b. Describe a situation in which you would need a percent less than 1 to solve a problem.
    c. Make up a problem for your situation. Give the problem to a friend or relative to solve. Compare his or her solution with your solution.
12. **Mining** A mine produces ore that is about 0.6% nickel. About how much ore from this mine would you need to get 1,800 kg of nickel?
13. a. 153 is 0.9% of what number?
    b. Would you expect the answer to be a lot less than 153, slightly less than 153, slightly greater than 153, or a lot greater than 153? Explain.
14. A spaceship on a journey between planets would have to recycle as much air and water as possible. Suppose the crew on such a spaceship used 85.61 L of water one day and recycled all but 0.68 L. About what percent of the water was lost? Round to the nearest hundredth as needed.
15. **Think About the Process**
    a. What equation should you use to find what percent 74.1 is of 7,800?
       A. $7,800 = m \cdot 74.1$
       B. $m = 74.1 \cdot 7,800$
       C. $74.1 = m \cdot 7,800$
       D. $m = 74.1 + 7,800$
    b. 74.1 is ■% of 7,800.
16. 28 is what percent of 58,230? Round to the nearest hundredth as needed.
17. **Challenge** A business spends $4,300 each month for electricity. A salesperson claims that switching to a new type of light bulb will reduce the electric bill by 0.3%.
    a. If the business buys the new light bulbs and the salesperson's claim is true, how much would the business spend each month for electricity?
    b. Describe or show two ways to solve this problem.

18. Challenge The residents of an apartment building tried to conserve water during a drought. The residents used 2,700 gallons of water each day before starting to conserve. After starting to conserve, the residents used 2,689.20 gallons per day.

a. By what percent did the resident reduce their water use?

b. Describe or show two ways to solve this problem.

19. Error Analysis A newspaper reporter wrote an article about the amount of a toxin found in a river near a factory. In the article, the reporter incorrectly used 0.2 as the decimal form of $\frac{1}{5}$%.

a. What is the correct way to write $\frac{1}{5}$% as a decimal?

b. What did the reporter do wrong?

20. a. Writing Find 0.78% of 6,000.

b. Describe a situation in which you would need a percent less than 1 to solve a problem.

c. Make up a problem for your situation. Give the problem to a friend or relative to solve. Compare his or her solution with your solution.

21. To write $\frac{3}{4}$% as a decimal, think of the percent as $\frac{3}{4} \cdot 1\%$.

a. What are the next steps to find the decimal equivalent?

First write $\frac{3}{4}$ as ■ and 1% as ■.

Then <u>subtract/add/multiply/divide</u>.

b. Find the decimal equivalent.

22. a. Think About the Process What equation should you use when you find what percent of 59.5 is of 7,000?

A. $7{,}000 = m \cdot 59.5$

B. $m = 59.5 + 7{,}000$

C. $m = 59.5 \cdot 7{,}000$

D. $59.5 = m \cdot 7{,}000$

b. Find the percent.

6-5 Fractions, Decimals, and Percents

CCSS: 7.NS.A.2d, 7.NS.A.3, Also 7.NS.A.2b

Part 1

Intro

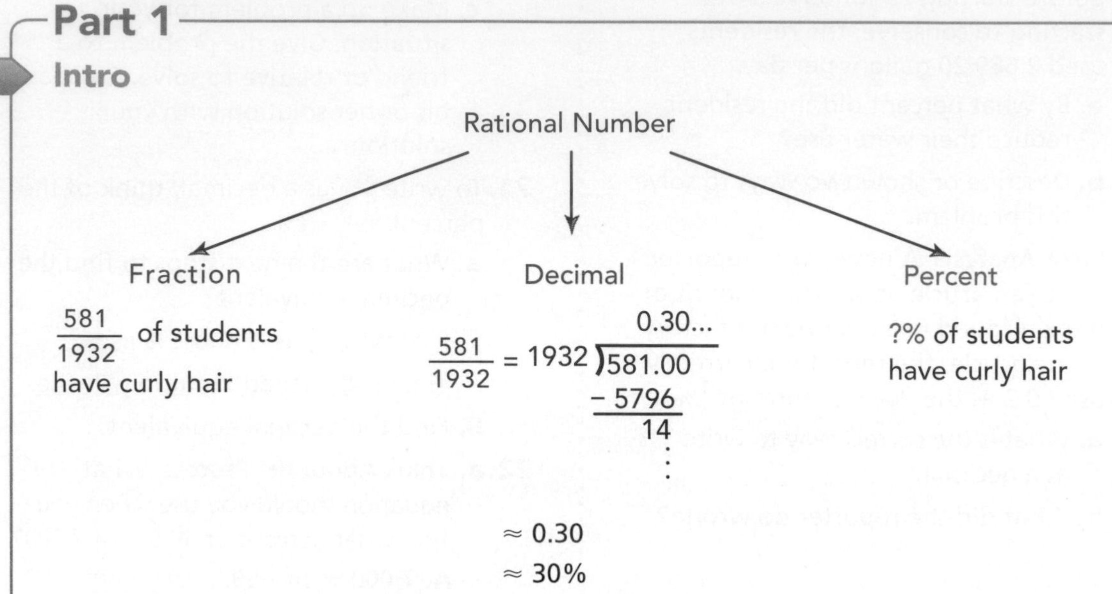

About 30% of students have curly hair.

Example Comparing Fractions and Percents

To be elected, a U.S. presidential candidate must receive more than 50% of the 538 electoral votes. In the 1976 presidential election, Gerald R. Ford received 240 electoral votes. Did he win the election? Explain.

Solution

Know	Need	Plan
Gerald R. Ford received 240 out of the 538 possible electoral votes.	Determine whether Ford won the election.	Use long division to convert Ford's results to a decimal. Convert the decimal to a percent. Then compare the percent to 50%.

Gerald R. Ford received $\frac{240}{538}$ of the votes.

Step 1 Convert the fraction to a decimal.

$$\frac{240}{538} = \frac{120}{269}$$

continued on next page >

Part 1

Solution continued

$$
\begin{array}{r}
0.446 \\
269\overline{)120.000} \\
-107\ 6 \\
\hline
1240 \\
-1076 \\
\hline
1640 \\
-1614 \\
\hline
26
\end{array}
\approx 0.446
$$

Use long division.

Step 2 Convert the decimal into a percent.

$$0.446 \approx 45\%$$

Step 3 Compare the percent to 50%.

45% is less than 50%, so Gerald R. Ford did not win the 1976 Presidential election.

Part 2

Example Writing a Percent as a Ratio

A research article claims that 64% of people in the United States can roll their tongue. Suppose your school has 250 students. Write the ratio of students who can roll their tongue to the total number of students.

Solution

Method 1 Convert the percent to a fraction with a denominator of 250.

$$
\begin{aligned}
64\% &= \frac{66}{100} \div \frac{4}{4} \\
&= \frac{16}{25} \cdot \frac{10}{10} \\
&= \frac{160}{250}
\end{aligned}
$$

The ratio of students who can roll their tongue to the total number of students is $\frac{160}{250}$, or 160 : 250.

continued on next page >

Part 2

Solution continued

Method 2 Use the percent equation.

Number of students who can roll their tongue

Total number of students

$$\text{part} = \text{percent} \cdot \text{whole}$$
$$= 64\% \cdot 250$$
$$= 0.64 \cdot 250$$
$$= 160$$

The ratio of students who can roll their tongue to the total number of students is 160 : 250.

Key Concept

Convert a Fraction

Fraction to Decimal

$\frac{1}{8} \longrightarrow 8\overline{)1.000}$ with quotient 0.125

Divide the numerator by the denominator.

Fraction to Percent

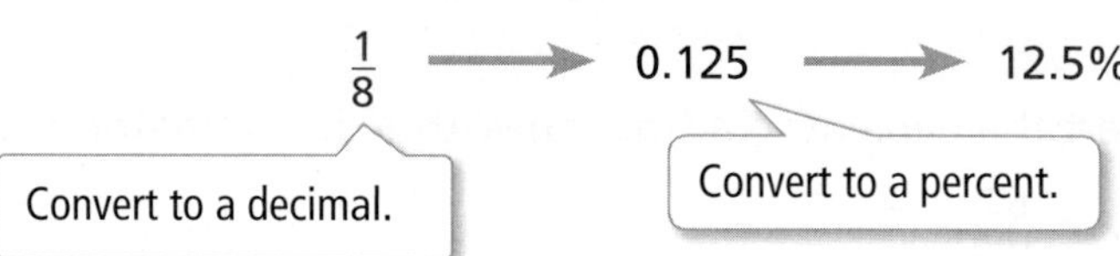

Convert a Decimal

Decimal to Fraction

$0.125 \longrightarrow \frac{125}{1000} \longrightarrow \frac{1}{8}$

Write as a fraction over a power of 10.

Simplify.

continued on next page >

Key Concept

continued

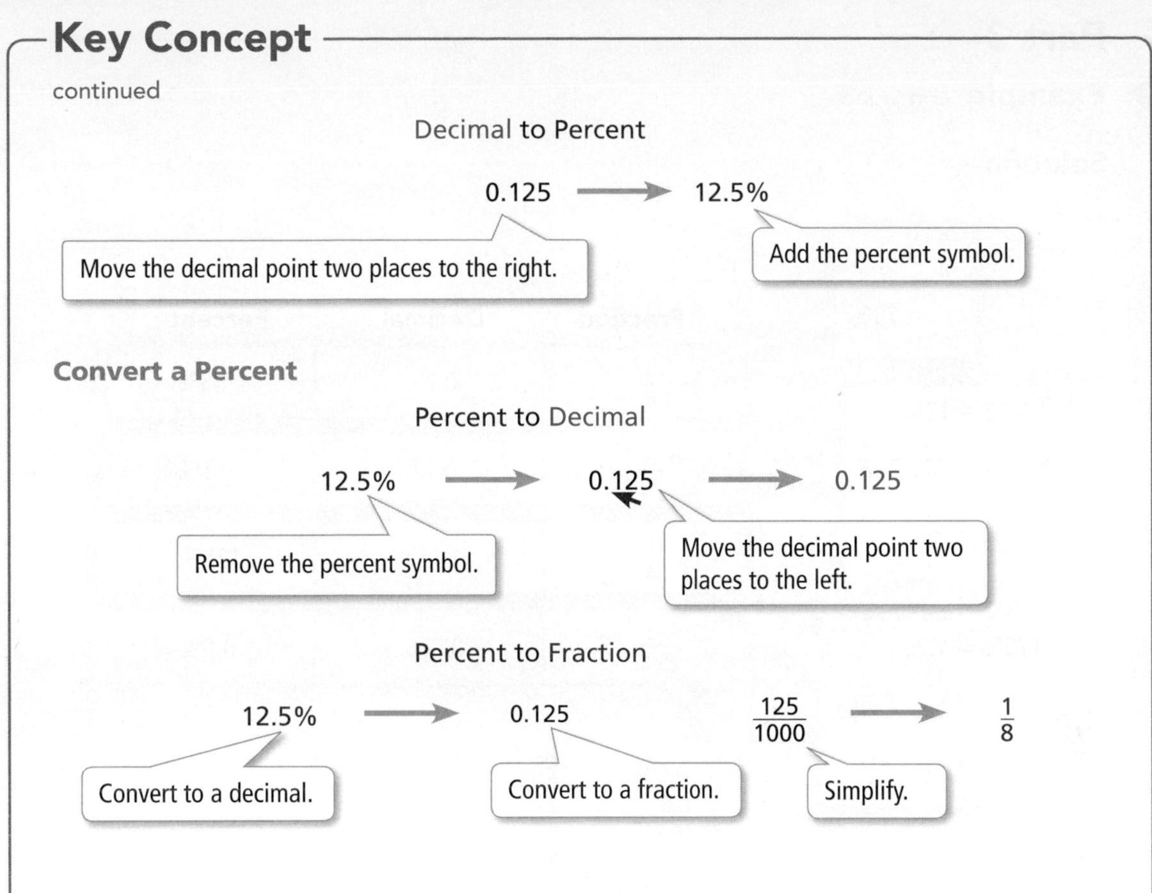

Part 3

Example Converting Between Fractions, Decimals, and Percents

Choose from the values below to rewrite each given number.

$\frac{3}{25}$	75	1.75	0.06
120	$\frac{7}{4}$	25	6
60	$\frac{3}{50}$	12	0.75
0.6	1.2	$\frac{3}{500}$	$\frac{3}{250}$

a. Write $\frac{3}{4}$ as a decimal and a percent.
b. Write 0.12 as a fraction and a percent.
c. Write 175% as a fraction and a decimal.
d. Write 0.006 as a fraction and a percent.

continued on next page >

Part 3

Example continued

Solution

$\frac{3}{4} = 0.75$
$= 75\%$

$0.12 = 12\%$
$= \frac{12}{100} \div \frac{4}{4}$
$= \frac{3}{25}$

$175\% = 1.75$
$= \frac{175}{100} \div \frac{25}{25}$
$= \frac{7}{4}$

$0.006 = 0.6\%$
$= \frac{0.6}{100} \times \frac{10}{10}$
$= \frac{6}{1{,}000} \div \frac{2}{2}$
$= \frac{3}{500}$

Fraction	Decimal	Percent
$\frac{3}{4}$	0.75	75%
$\frac{3}{25}$	0.12	12%
$\frac{7}{4}$	1.75	175%
$\frac{3}{500}$	0.006	0.6%

1. Write the ratio 69 : 75 as a fraction, a decimal, and a percent.
2. A student scores 60% on a 70 question test. What is the ratio of the actual number of questions answered correctly to the actual total number of questions?

   A. 42 : 70 **B.** 28 : 70
   C. 3 : 5 **D.** 60 : 100

3. Write the fraction $\frac{60}{200}$ as a decimal and as a percent.
4. **a.** Write 86% as a fraction. Simplify your answer.

   b. Find 86% of 50.

5. **Multiple Representations** A survey asked students in the 7th grade for their preference, water or fruit juice. The table shows the ratio of students who prefer juice to the total number of students.

7th Grade

Ratio	Fraction	Decimal	Percent
37 : 100	$\frac{37}{100}$	0.37	37%

In Mr. Greene's class, 15 students out of 30 prefer juice. Complete a similar table for the ratio of the actual number of students who prefer juice to the total number of students in Mr. Greene's class.

6. **Library Books** In the school library, there are 110 fiction books, 250 nonfiction books, and 125 magazines. The ratio of fiction books to magazines is 110 : 125. Write the ratio of fiction books to magazines as a fraction, a decimal, and a percent.
7. **Writing** A survey finds that 56% of people prefer to drink orange juice instead of cranberry juice.

   a. In a group of 275 people, what is the ratio of the actual number of people who prefer orange juice to the total number of people?

   b. Does writing the percent as a ratio in simplest form help you solve this problem? Explain your reasoning.

8. An electronics store is having a sale. One item has a price tag of $191.00 and a sign "On sale for 31% of the original price."

   a. As a decimal, 31% is ■.

   b. The sale price of the item would be $■.

   c. A closer look shows that the sign says "31% off the original price." What would be this sale price? Can you use your first answer to help you find this answer? Explain your reasoning.

9. **Error Analysis** Over the course of one year, the price of a $340 antique increases to 170% of its original price. Your friend uses the percent equation "new price = 170% × $340" and finds that the new price of the antique is $200.00.

   a. Which ratio compares the actual new price to the original price?

   A. 340 : 578 **B.** 578 : 340
   C. 170 : 100 **D.** 17 : 10

   b. What mistake did your friend likely make?

   A. Your friend divided by 170.
   B. Your friend multiplied by 0.17 instead of 1.7.
   C. Your friend divided by 1.7.
   D. Your friend multiplied by 170 instead of 1.7.

See your complete lesson at MyMathUniverse.com

10. Open-Ended Two machines produce the same type of widget. Machine A produces 85 widgets, 68 of which are damaged. Machine B produces 28 widgets, 21 of which are damaged. The fraction of damaged widgets for Machine A is $\frac{68}{85}$ of $\frac{4}{5}$. The fraction of damaged widgets for Machine B is $\frac{21}{28}$ or $\frac{3}{4}$.

a. Write each as a fraction as a decimal and a percent.

b. Select a small percent that would allow for a small number of damaged widgets. Find the number of widgets by which each machine exceeded the acceptable number of widgets.

11. A research study concluded that 32% of people prefer comedies to dramas. If a group of 550 people are asked the same question, what is the ratio of the actual number of people who prefer dramas to the total number of people?

A. 32 : 100 **B.** 176 : 550

C. 374 : 550 **D.** 176 : 374

12. Multiple Representations The first column of the table suggests two ratios. Find the ratio of girls to boys. Then write each ratio as a fraction, a decimal, and a percent.

Student Ratios

Description	Ratio
25 girls to 59 total students	25 : 59
girls to boys	■ : ■

13. Think About the Process You are to write a ratio as a fraction, a decimal, and a percent.

a. The first term of a ratio is greater than the second term. What does that tell you to expect for the fraction, the decimal, and the percent?

A. a proper fraction, a decimal between 0 and 1, a percent between 0 and 100

B. a proper fraction, a decimal greater than 1, a decimal percent

C. an improper fraction, a decimal greater than 1, a percent with a decimal place

D. an improper fraction, a decimal greater than 1, a percent greater than 100

b. The ratio 132 : 60 as a fraction is ■.

The ratio 132 : 60 as a decimal is ■.

The ratio 132 : 60 as a percent is ■%.

14. Think About the Process

a. How can you write a percent as an equivalent fraction?

A. Write the percent as a fraction with the percent as the numerator and 100 in the denominator. Then simplify your answer.

B. Write the percent as a fraction with the percent as the numerator and 10 in the denominator. Then simplify your answer.

C. Write the percent as a fraction with the percent as the denominator and 100 in the numerator. Then simplify your answer.

D. Write the percent as a fraction with the percent as the denominator and 10 in the numerator. Then simplify your answer.

b. Write 8% as a fraction.

c. Write 8% as a decimal.

15. a. Challenge Write 52% as a decimal and a simplified fraction.

b. Find 52% of 175.

c. Did you use the decimal or the fraction to find 52% of 175? Explain.

6-6 Percent Error

Vocabulary
accuracy, percent error

CCSS: 7.RP.A.3

Key Concept

Accuracy is the degree to which an estimate or measurement agrees with an accepted or actual value of that measurement. You can describe accuracy with a measure called **percent error.**

$$\text{percent error} = \frac{|\text{measured or estimated value} - \text{actual value}|}{\text{actual value}}$$

$$= \frac{|36 - 45|}{45}$$

$$= \frac{|-9|}{45}$$

$$= 0.20\text{, or } 20\%$$

So the guess "36 passengers" is off by 20%.

Part 1

Example Finding Percent Error

Find the percent error of each estimated value to the nearest whole percent.

	A	B	C
Estimated Value	40	63	125
Actual Value	45	75	99
Percent Error	■	■	■

continued on next page >

Part 1

Example continued

Solution

$$\text{percent error} = \frac{|\text{measured or estimated value} - \text{actual value}|}{\text{actual value}}$$

	A	B	C
Estimated Value	40	63	125
Actual Value	45	75	99
Percent Error	11%	16%	26%

$$\begin{aligned}\%\text{ error} &= \frac{|40 - 45|}{45} \\ &= \frac{|-5|}{45} \\ &= \frac{1}{9} \\ &= 0.\overline{1} \\ &\approx 0.11, \text{ or } 11\%\end{aligned}$$

$$\begin{aligned}\%\text{ error} &= \frac{|63 - 75|}{75} \\ &= \frac{|-12|}{75} \\ &= \frac{4}{25} \\ &= 0.16, \text{ or } 16\%\end{aligned}$$

$$\begin{aligned}\%\text{ error} &= \frac{|125 - 99|}{99} \\ &= \frac{|26|}{99} \\ &= \frac{26}{99} \\ &= 0.\overline{26} \\ &\approx 0.26, \text{ or } 26\%\end{aligned}$$

Part 2

Example Comparing Percent Error

Anyone who guesses within 5% of the actual number of jellybeans in a jar is a winner. Suppose there are 486 jellybeans in the jar. Who wins?

Jay: 450
Lisa: 475
Sarah: 388
Javier: 501

Solution

$$\text{percent error} = \frac{|\text{measured or estimated value} - \text{actual value}|}{\text{actual value}}$$

There are 486 jellybeans in the jar.

continued on next page >

Part 2

Solution continued

Jay's guess, 450:

$= \frac{|450 - 486|}{486}$

$= \frac{|-36|}{486}$

≈ 0.074, or 7.4% — Not a winner.

Lisa's guess, 475:

$= \frac{|475 - 486|}{486}$

$= \frac{|-11|}{486}$

≈ 0.023, or 2.3% — A winner!

Sara's guess, 388:

$= \frac{|388 - 486|}{486}$

$= \frac{|-98|}{486}$

≈ 0.202, or 20.2% — Not a winner.

Javier's guess, 501:

$= \frac{|501 - 486|}{486}$

$= \frac{|15|}{486}$

≈ 0.031, or 3.1% — A winner!

Lisa and Javier are the winners.

Part 3

Intro

The number 1 is a value that is 3 units away from the actual value. The measurement 1 is off by 75%.

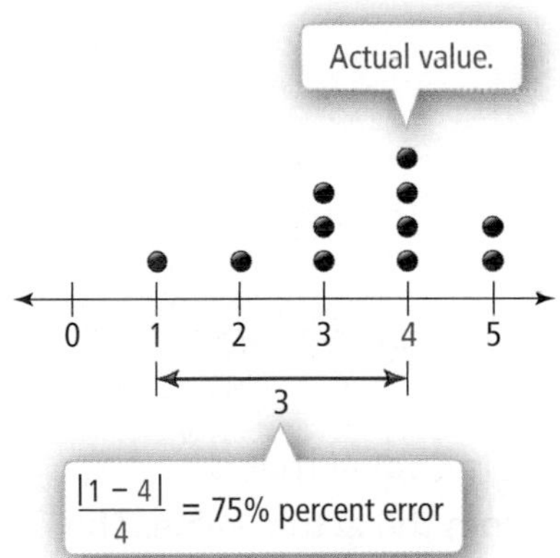

The number 2 is a value that is 2 units away from the actual value. The measurement 2 is off by 50%.

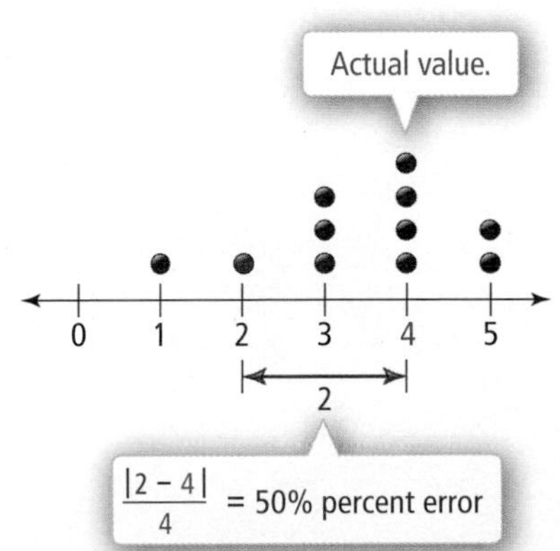

continued on next page >

Part 3

Intro continued

The number 3 is a value that is 1 unit away from the actual value. The measurement 3 is off by 25%.

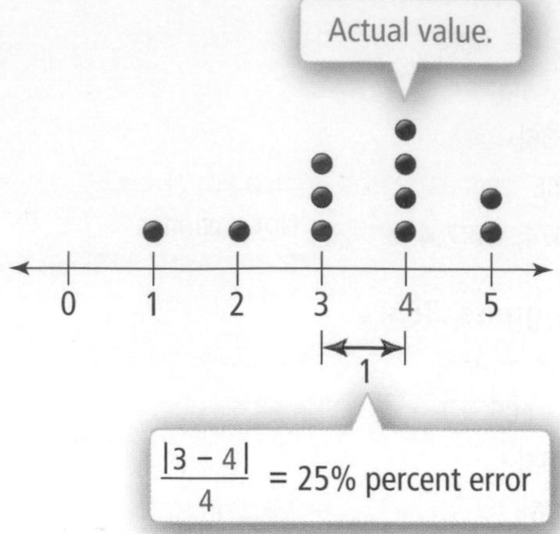

Suppose 4 is the actual value of the quantity that is being measured.

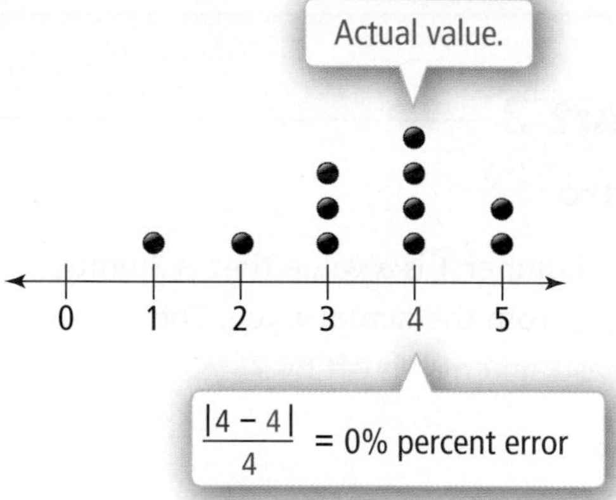

The number 5 is a value that is 1 unit away from the actual value. The measurement 5 is off by 25%.

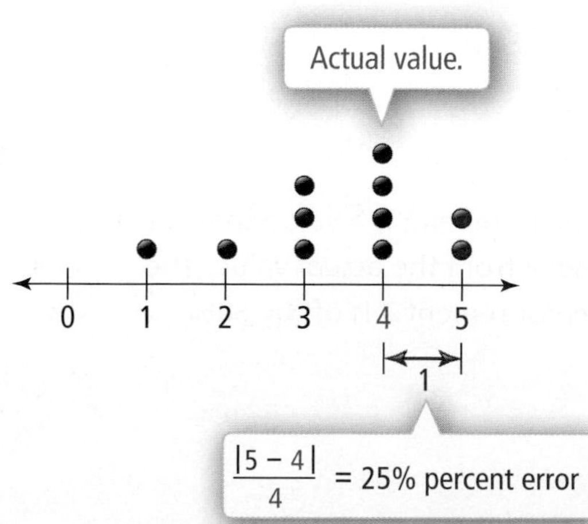

Part 3

Example Using a Dot Plot to Compare Percent Error

The dot plot shows the measurements made by a science class. If the rock's actual mass is 1.1 g, what is the greatest percent error among the measurements? Round to the nearest tenth of a percent.

Measurements of a Rock

0.8 0.9 1.0 1.1 1.2 1.3

Grams

Solution

The greatest percent error comes from the measurement that deviates the most from the actual value.

Measurements of a Rock

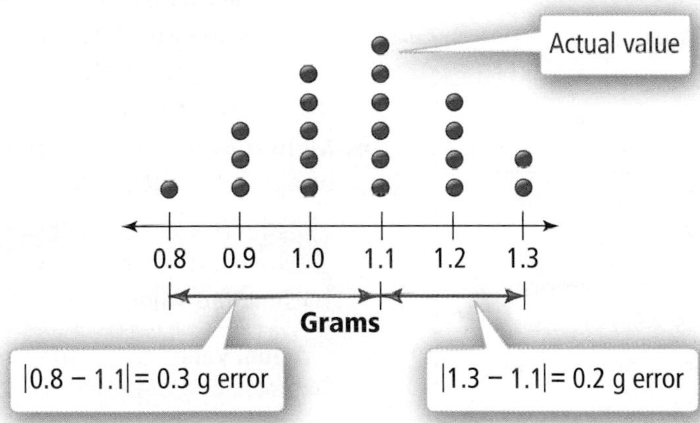

The greatest percent error comes from the measurement 0.8 g.

$$\text{percent error} = \frac{|\text{measured or estimated value} - \text{actual value}|}{\text{actual value}}$$

$$= \frac{|0.8 - 1.1|}{1.1}$$

$$= \frac{|0.3|}{1.1}$$

$$\approx 0.273, \text{ or } 27.3\%$$

The greatest percent error among the measurements is about 27.3%.

Digital Resources    

1. Carissa predicted she answered 8 questions correctly out of 10 on a test. She actually got 9 answers correct. By what percent was Carissa's prediction off?

2. a. Find the percent error for each measured value.

Percent Errors

	A	B
Measured Value	8	98
Actual Value	10	100

b. Of A and B, which has the greater percent error?

3. In a science lab, students had to measure the mass of a rock. They made this dot plot of their results. The actual mass of the rock is 3.5 grams.

Rock Measurements

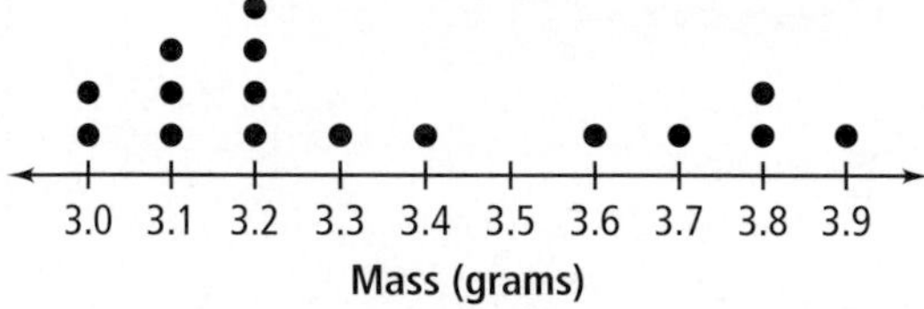

a. The greatest percent error among the measurements is ■%.

b. The least percent error among the measurements is ■%.

4. a. Find the percent error of the measured value. Measured value: 15. Actual value: 20.

b. If the percent error must be less than 20%, is the measured value acceptable?

5. a. **Error Analysis** Anya claims that the percent error of the estimated value is 30%. Find the percent error. Estimated value: 10. Actual value: 7.

b. What error did Anya likely make?

A. She divided the absolute value of the difference between the estimated value and actual value by the actual value.

B. She divided the estimated value by the absolute value of the difference between the estimated value and the actual value.

C. She divided the absolute value of the difference between the estimated value and actual value by the estimated value.

D. She divided the actual value by the absolute value of the difference between the estimated value and the actual value.

6. **Mental Math** Find the percent error of each estimated value.

Percent Errors		
Estimated Value	96	420
Actual Value	100	400

7. a. **Writing** Find the percent error for each measured value.

Percent Errors

	A	B
Measured Value	6	14
Actual Value	10	20

b. Which has the greater percent error, A or B?

c. Is it possible for a measured value to be greater than or less than the actual value? Explain why this does not matter when you find percent error.

See your complete lesson at MyMathUniverse.com

8. **Car Payments** Emily predicted her car payment to be \$250 each month. Her actual car payment is \$275 each month. Enrique predicted his car payment to be \$200 each month. His actual care payment is \$225 each month.

   a. By what percent was Emily's prediction off?

   b. By what percent was Enrique's prediction off?

   c. Which prediction had the smaller percent error?

      A. Enrique's prediction

      B. Emily's prediction

9. **Reasoning** A meteorologist predicted that there would be 10 inches of snowfall. There were 22 inches of snowfall.

   a. By how much was the meteorologist's prediction off?

   b. If the percent error for the prediction should be less than 60%, was the prediction acceptable?

   c. Explain how the percent error of a meteorologist's prediction can be greater than 100%. For this to happen, must the predicted amount be greater than or less than the actual amount, or can it be either?

10. **Think About the Process** To find the percent error of the estimated value below, first find *A*, the absolute value of the difference between the estimated value and the actual value.

   Estimated value: 40

   Actual value: 43

   a. What are the next steps?

   Divide *A* by the actual value. Then divide by 100%.

   Divide *A* by the estimated value. Then multiply by 100%.

   Divide *A* by the estimated value. Then divide by 100%.

   Divide *A* by the actual value. Then multiply by 100%.

   b. The percent error is ■%.

11. The label on a package of bolts says that each bolt has a diameter of 0.35 inch. To be in the package, the percent error of the diameter must be less than 5%. A test on the production line shows a bolt with a diameter of 0.33 inch. Should this bolt go in the package?

12. **Think About the Process** Tom and Li each have a jar of marbles. The table shows the predicted and actual numbers of marbles in each jar.

Number of Marbles

	Tom's Jar	Li's Jar
Predicted Number	205	295
Actual Number	225	275

   a. How would you find the prediction with the smaller percent error?

      A. Find the sum of the actual values and the predicted values and compare.

      B. Find the percent error for the predicted values and compare.

      C. Find the difference between the actual values and the predicted values and compare.

      D. Find the percent error for the actual values and compare.

   b. Which prediction had the smaller percent error?

13. **Challenge** A scientist uses a scale to find the mass of an object. The scale shows the mass to be 29.3 grams. The scientist knows that the scale reading is 3% greater than the actual mass. What is the actual mass of the object?

6-7 Problem Solving

CCSS: 7.NS.A.3

Part 1

Example Using Percents Greater Than 100 in Real-World Situations

A babysitter makes \$8 an hour. She does such a good job that the parents of the children she cares for give her a 25% raise. Calculate her new hourly wage using a percent greater than 100.

Solution

A 25% raise is equivalent to a new wage of 125%, or 1.25, of her original wage.

Use the percent equation.

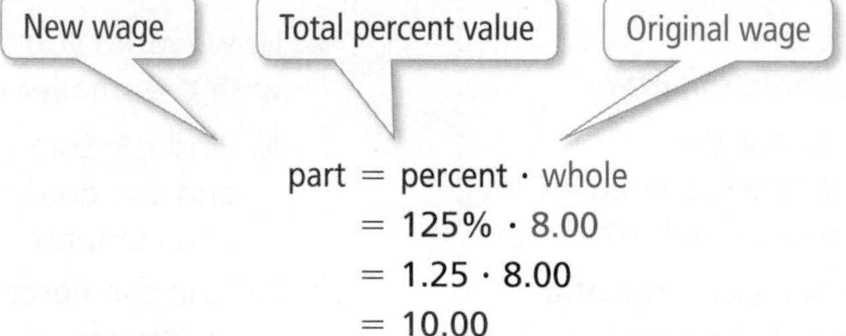

$$\begin{aligned} \text{part} &= \text{percent} \cdot \text{whole} \\ &= 125\% \cdot 8.00 \\ &= 1.25 \cdot 8.00 \\ &= 10.00 \end{aligned}$$

Her new wage is \$10.00 per hour.

Part 2

Example Using Percents Less Than 1 in Real-World Situations

An oil truck weighed $26\frac{3}{5}$ tons at the start of a cross-country trip. The driver estimates that he used fuel equivalent to 0.95% of the truck's starting weight during the trip.

Did he lose any of the cargo during the trip? If so, how much?

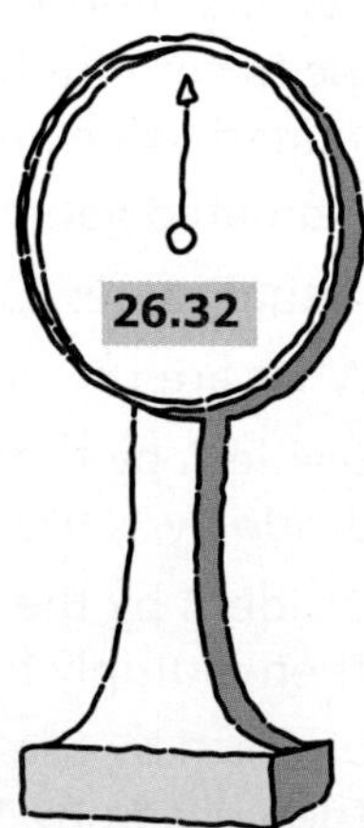

continued on next page >

Part 2

Example continued

Solution

Oil truck weight at start: $26\frac{3}{5} = 26.6$ tons.

Oil truck weight at end: 26.32 tons

Calculate the estimated weight of gas used.

Convert the percent to a decimal.

$$0.95\% \text{ of start weight} = 0.0095 \cdot 26.6$$
$$\approx 0.25 \text{ tons}$$

The oil truck weight at the start minus the gas used should equal the oil truck weight at the end.

$$26.6 - 0.25 \stackrel{?}{=} 26.32$$
$$26.35 \neq 26.32$$

They are not equal, so some cargo was lost.

The oil truck lost $26.35 - 26.32 = 0.03$ ton of cargo on the trip.

Part 3

Example Finding Percent Error in Real-World Situations

A condominium association needs to collect monthly fees that total $1,200 per month. The fee paid by the owner of each unit is based on the percent of the building that the unit occupies.

How much more does the condominium association collect than it needs each month, due to the rounding of the percents of the ownership?

What is the percent error of the fees paid? Round to the nearest tenth of a percent.

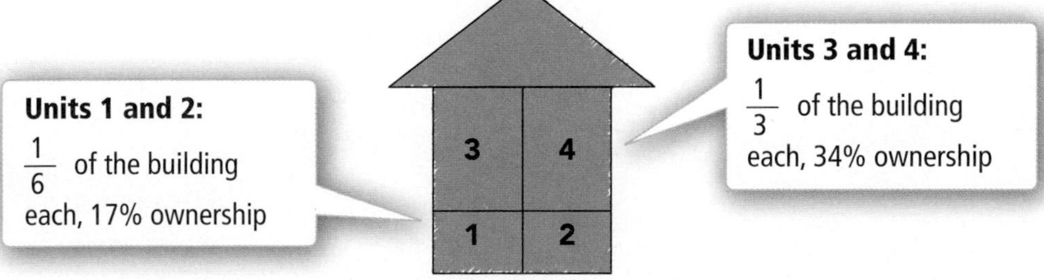

continued on next page >

Part 3

Example continued

Solution

Step 1 Find the amount that each owner pays.

According to the percents of ownership, the monthly fees are:
Unit 1: $17\% \cdot 1{,}200 = \$204$
Unit 2: $17\% \cdot 1{,}200 = \$204$
Unit 3: $34\% \cdot 1{,}200 = \$408$
Unit 4: $34\% \cdot 1{,}200 = \$408$

Step 2 Find the total amount that the association collects.

The total fees collected are: $2(204) + 2(408) = 408 + 816$
$= \$1{,}224$

Step 3 Find the difference between the amount collected and the amount needed.

The association collects \$1,224. The association needs \$1,200.
The difference is $1{,}224 - 1{,}200 = 24$.
The association collects \$24 per month more than it needs.
\$1,200 is the actual amount needed.
The total fees paid, \$1,224, is the measured amount.

The percent error on the fees paid is:

$$\frac{|\text{measured amount} - \text{actual amount}|}{\text{actual amount}}$$

$$= \frac{|1{,}224 - 1{,}200|}{1{,}200}$$

$$= \frac{24}{1{,}200}$$

$$= 0.02, \text{ or } 2\%$$

1. A person earns $16,000 one year and gets a 5% raise in salary. Calculate the new yearly salary using a percent greater than 100.
2. A jewelry salesperson earns $5\frac{1}{5}$% commission on all sales. Today he sold $4,930 in jewelry. What is his total commission earned?
3. Six roommates buy a sofa for $620. If each roommate pays 15% of the price, will their total amount be equal to the price of the sofa? If not, by what percent will their total differ from the price?
   - **a.** No, their total will be greater than the price by ■%.
   - **b.** No, their total will be less than the price by ■%.
   - **c.** Yes, their total will be equal to the price.
4. Three friends go grocery shopping and the total comes to $100. Each friend gives the cashier 34% of the total.
   - **a.** By what percent did they overpay?
   - **b.** What should be the total amount of their change?
5. Last year, a college's tuition was $44,500. This year, the tuition increased by 4%. Find this year's tuition by using a percent greater than 100.
6. You and your friend have lunch at a diner that adds a 15% tip when you pay with a credit card. Your friend says the tip on the $26 bill will be $0.39 and the total amount will be $26.39.
   - **a.** Calculate the total amount that the diner will charge to your credit card using a percent greater than 100.
   - **b.** What is your friend's possible error?
     - **A.** He calculated a 1.5% tip, not a 15% tip.
     - **B.** He divided the amount of the bill by 15.
     - **C.** He multiplied the amount of the bill by 0.15.
     - **D.** He divided the amount of the bill by 1.15.
7. A football player completed 56.8% of her passes last season. She threw 250 passes.
   - **a.** How many passes did she complete?
   - **b.** This season she has thrown 351 passes and has completed 195. By how much did her completion percent change from last season to this season?
   - **c.** How did the number of complete passes change?
8. An antique dealer has a fund of $1,160 for investments. She spends 50% of the fund on a 1911 rocking chair. She then sells the chair for $710, all of which she returns to the fund.
   - **a.** What was the percent gain on the investment?
   - **b.** What percent of the original value of the fund is the new value of the fund?
9. Three adults go out to dinner and the total comes to $34 after tax and tip. James will pay 34% of the total. Caitlin will pay 50%, and Amara will pay 17%. If each person rounds up to the nearest dollar, by what percent will they overpay?
10. Scott's phone bill was $100.80 in July. This is 20% greater than his bill from June.
    - **a.** Use a percent greater than 100 to find the amount of Scott's phone bill in June.
    - **b.** Can you find the amount of Scott's phone bill in June by finding 80% of his phone bill in July? Explain.

11. Think About the Process In October, a store had 175 customers purchase items. In November, there were 12% more customers.

a. What equation can you use to find the number of customers the store had in November?

A. whole = percent · part

B. percent = part · whole

C. whole = (percent · part) · 100

D. part = percent · whole

b. During November, the store had ■ customers.

12. Think About the Process A manufacturer of electronic components expects 1.02% of its products to be defective. In a recent production run, 277 components were found to be defective.

a. Which form of the percent equation would be most useful for finding the number of good components?

A. percent $= \frac{\text{part}}{\text{whole}}$

B. part = percent · whole

C. whole $= \frac{\text{part}}{\text{percent}}$

b. When there were 277 defective components, there likely were ■ good components.

13. Challenge A real estate agency sells a house for $354,000. The real estate agent earns a commission of $7\frac{3}{4}$%. The real estate agency keeps $11\frac{1}{8}$% of the sale. Taxes take $1\frac{1}{8}$%, and the rest goes to the seller. How much does the seller get from the sale of the house?

14. Challenge A company is having a fundraiser for a local charity. Its goal is to reach $6,500. The accounting department raised 37% of the goal. The sales department raised 69% of the amount that the accounting department raised. All other departments combined raised 37% of the goal.

a. Is the amount the company raised equal to its goal?

b. If not, by what percent (percent error) does the amount raised differ from the fundraising goal?

c. Describe or show two ways to solve this problem.

7-1 Expanding Algebraic Expressions

Vocabulary
expand an algebraic expression

CCSS: 7.EE.A.1, 7.EE.A.2

Part 1

Intro

The algebraic expression $3(x + 2)$ is a product with two factors. You can use the Distributive Property to rewrite the product as the sum of two terms.

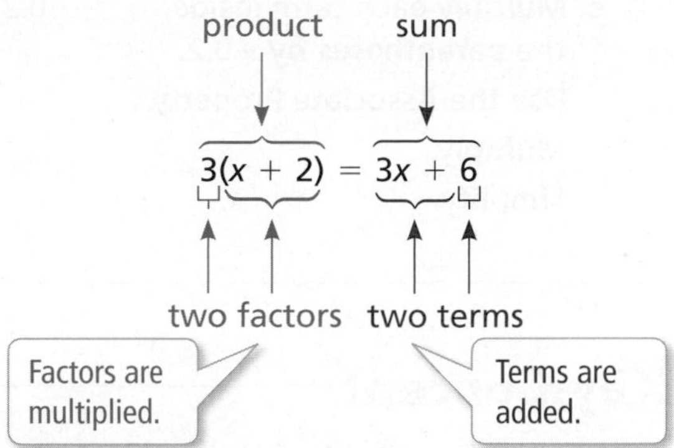

When you distribute a negative number, be careful with the signs of the numbers.

Multiply each term inside the parentheses by -2.

Use the Associative Property.

$$-2(-3y + 5) = -2(-3y) + -2(5)$$
$$= [-2(-3)]y + -2(5)$$
$$= 6y + (-10)$$
$$= 6y - 10$$

Example Rewriting Products Using the Distributive Property

Choose the equivalent sum or difference for each product from the choices.

a. $a(2 + b)$	$a(b + 2)$	$2a + b$	$2a + ab$
b. $5(1 - 4c)$	$5 - 20c$	$(1 - 4c)(5)$	$5 - 4c$
c. $-0.2(7x - 0.3)$	$-1.4x + 0.06$	$-1.4x + -0.06$	$1.4x + 0.06$

Solution

To find a sum or difference equivalent to each product, use the Distributive Property.

a. Multiply each term inside the parentheses by *a*.
Use the Commutative Property.

$$a(2 + b) = a(2) + ab$$
$$= 2a + ab$$

continued on next page >

Part 1

Solution continued

b. **Multiply each term inside the parentheses by 5.** $5(1 - 4c) = 5(1) - 5(4c)$

Use the Associate Property. $= 5(1) - (5 \cdot 4)c$

Multiply. $= 5 - 20c$

c. **Multiply each term inside the parentheses by −0.2.** $-0.2(7x - 0.3) = -0.2(7x) - (-0.2)(0.3)$

Use the Associate Property. $= (-0.2 \cdot 7)x - (-0.2)(0.3)$

Multiply. $= -1.4x - (-0.06)$

Simplify. $= -1.4x + 0.06$

Key Concept

You **expand an algebraic expression** when you use the Distributive Property to rewrite a product as a sum or difference of terms.

From the left

Distribute from the left.

$$1.5(2x + 3) = 1.5(2x) + 1.5(3)$$
$$= (1.5 \cdot 2)x + 1.5(3)$$
$$= 3x + 4.5$$

Associative Property

From the right

Distribute from the right.

$$(3a - b)5 = 3a \cdot 5 - b \cdot 5$$
$$= 3 \cdot 5 \cdot a - 5 \cdot b$$
$$= 15a - 5b$$

Commutative Property

A variable

Distribute a variable.

$$y(2x - 3) = y(2x) - (y)(3)$$
$$= (2x)y - 3y$$
$$= 2xy - 3y$$

Commutative Property

Associative Property

continued on next page >

Key Concept

continued

A negative number

Distribute a negative number.

$$
\begin{aligned}
-5(2x - 3) &= -5(2x) - (-5)(3) \\
&= (-5 \cdot 2)x - (-5)(3) \quad \text{Associative Property} \\
&= -10x - (-15) \\
&= -10x + 15
\end{aligned}
$$

Over three terms

Distribute over three terms.

$$
\begin{aligned}
\tfrac{1}{3}(3x - 9y + 2) &= \tfrac{1}{3}(3x) - \tfrac{1}{3}(9y) + \tfrac{1}{3}(2) \\
&= (\tfrac{1}{3} \cdot 3)x - (\tfrac{1}{3} \cdot 9)y + \tfrac{1}{3}(2) \quad \text{Associative Property} \\
&= x - 3y + \tfrac{2}{3}
\end{aligned}
$$

Part 2

Example Expanding Algebraic Expressions

Determine which three expressions can be expanded. Then expand.

$$7m + 7n \quad (6a - 10b)\left(\frac{1}{2}\right) \quad -4(x + 10y - 9) \quad 3x(2y) \quad 3x(2 + y)$$

Solution

The three expressions that can be expanded are the ones that are products in which one factor has at least two terms.

$$(6a - 10b)\left(\frac{1}{2}\right) \qquad -4(x + 10y - 9) \qquad 3x(2 + y)$$

$$
\begin{aligned}
(6a - 10b)\left(\frac{1}{2}\right) &= (6a)\left(\frac{1}{2}\right) - (10b)\left(\frac{1}{2}\right) \\
&= 6\left(\frac{1}{2}\right)a - (10)\left(\frac{1}{2}\right)b \quad \text{Commutative Property} \\
&= 3a - 5b \quad \text{Associative Property}
\end{aligned}
$$

continued on next page >

Part 2

Solution continued

$$\begin{aligned}-4(x + 10y - 9) &= -4x + (-4)(10y) - (-4)(9)\\ &= -4x + (-4 \cdot 10)y - (-4)(9)\\ &= -4x + (-40)y - (-36)\\ &= -4x - 40y + 36\end{aligned}$$

Associative Property

$$\begin{aligned}3x(2 + y) &= 3x(2) + 3xy\\ &= (3 \cdot 2)x + 3xy\\ &= 6x + 3xy\end{aligned}$$

Commutative Property

The expressions $3x(2y)$ and $7m + 7n$ cannot be expanded.

The expression $3x(2y)$ is a product, but neither factor has more than one term. You cannot use the Distributive Property to expand the expression $3x(2y)$, although you can use the Commutative and Associate Properties to rewrite it as $6xy$.

The expression $7m + 7n$ is a sum, not a product. A sum cannot be expanded.

Part 3

Example Using the Distributive Property for Area Problems

An architect draws plans for extending a rectangular deck. Let x represent the increase, in meters, of the deck's length. Use the expression below.

$$3.7(4.5 + x)$$

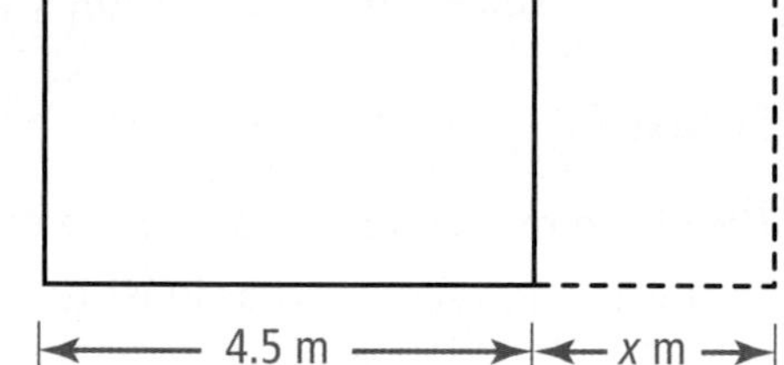

a. What does each factor of the expression represent? What does the expression represent?

b. Use the Distributive Property to expand the expression. What does each term of your new expression represent?

continued on next page >

Part 3

Example continued

Solution

a. 3.7 represents the width, in meters, of the deck.

$(4.5 + x)$ represents the length, in meters, of the extended deck.

The expression $3.7(4.5 + x)$ represents the area, in square meters, of the extended deck.

b. $3.7(4.5 + x) = (3.7 \cdot 4.5) + 3.7 \cdot x$

$= 16.65 + 3.7x$

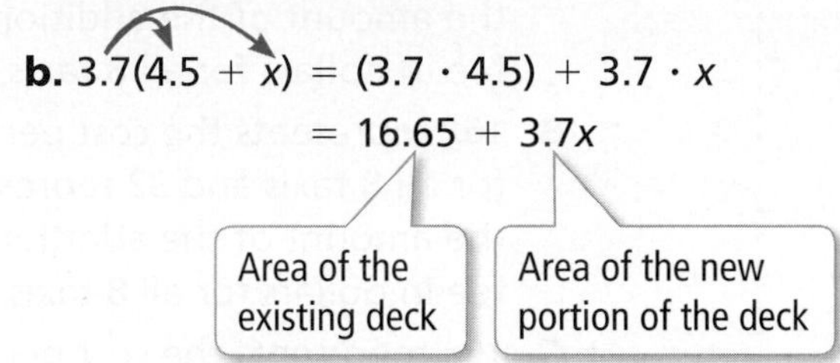

Digital Resources    

1. Find a sum equivalent to the product $6(y + x)$.
2. Find a difference equivalent to the product $11(x - y)$.
3. Expand $3(n + 7)$.
4. Use the Distributive Property to expand the expression $7(9x - 2)$.
5. **Multiple Representations** Find an equivalent expression to represent the product shown as a sum.
   a. Which expression is equivalent to $3(2x + 4)$?
   A. $6x + 4$
   B. $6x + 12$
   C. $5x + 7$
   D. $2x + 12$
   b. Draw an algebra tile model for each expression. Then demonstrate how both expressions are equal.
6. A large group of friends needs to call a taxi service to get home. The taxi cab company charges \$2 per mile plus an additional fee of \$4 for each taxi cab. The group will need 8 taxi cabs. Let x represent the number of miles. The expression $8(2x + 4)$ represents the total cost for everyone to get home.
   a. What do the factors 8 and $(2x + 4)$ represent?
   A. $(2x + 4)$ represents the number of taxis needed and 8 represents the cost of each taxi.
   B. 8 represents the number of miles traveled by taxi and $(2x + 4)$ represents the cost of each taxi.
   C. 8 represents the number of taxis needed and $(2x + 4)$ represents the cost of each taxi.
   D. $(2x + 4)$ represents the number of miles traveled by taxi and 8 represents the cost of each taxi.
   b. Which expression is equivalent to $8(2x + 4)$?
   A. $16x + 32$
   B. $2x + 32$
   C. $16x + 4$
   D. $10x + 12$
   c. What does each term of the new expression represent?
   A. $10x$ represents the cost per mile for all 8 taxis and 12 represents the amount of the additional fee in dollars for all 8 taxis.
   B. $16x$ represents the cost per mile for all 8 taxis and 32 represents the amount of the additional fee in dollars for all 8 taxis.
   C. $16x$ represents the cost per mile for all 8 taxis and 4 represents the amount of the additional fee in dollars for all 8 taxis.
   D. $2x$ represents the cost per mile for all 8 taxis and 32 represents the amount of the additional fee in dollars for all 8 taxis.
7. **Geometry** The perimeter of a square can be found using the formula $P = 4s$ where s is the side length of the square. If you were to increase the length s by 9, the expression for the perimeter would become $4(s + 9)$. Which expression represents the perimeter of the larger square?
   A. $4s + 36$
   B. $5s + 13$
   C. $s + 36$
   D. $4s + 9$
8. **a. Open-Ended** Expand the expression $\frac{1}{2}(4t - 10)$.
   b. Describe a situation in which you would want to write and then expand an algebraic expression.
9. **a. Writing** Use the Distributive Property to expand $3(4x + 2)$.
   b. How are the expressions the same? Explain.
   c. How are the expressions different? Explain.

10. Which expression is equivalent to $4(7(7x - 3y) - 6)$?

A. $49x - 12y - 24$

B. $49x - 84y - 24$

C. $196x - 3y - 6$

D. $196x - 84y - 24$

11. Think About the Process The expression shows the difference of two products.

$$3(4x + 1) - 2(y - 3)$$

a. How would you use the Distributive Property to expand the expression?

A. Add 3 to each term in $(y - 3)$. Then subtract 2 from each term in $(4x + 1)$.

B. Multiply each term in $(y - 3)$ by 3. Then multiply each term in $(4x + 1)$ by -2.

C. Add 3 to each term in $(4x + 1)$. Then subtract 2 from each term in $(y - 3)$.

D. Multiply each term in $(4x + 1)$ by 3. Then multiply each term in $(y - 3)$ by -2.

b. $3(4x + 1) - 2(y - 3) =$ ■

12. Think About the Process For a party, you plan to buy 2 cupcakes for each guest and 5 additional cupcakes to have as extras. Cupcakes cost $1.75 each. Let x represent the number of guests you invite to your party. The expression $1.75(2x + 5)$ represents the total cost of all the cupcakes.

a. How would you rewrite the expression so that you can find the total cost of the additional cupcakes?

A. Multiply each term in $(2x + 5)$ by 2.

B. Add 5 to each term in $(2x + 5)$.

C. Multiply each term in $(2x + 5)$ by 1.75.

D. Add 1.75 to each term in $(2x + 5)$.

b. What does each term in the new expression represent?

A. $1.75 + 2x$ represents the cost of the additional cupcakes. 6.75 is the cost, in dollars, of the cupcakes for the guests.

B. $1.75 + 2x$ represents the cost of the cupcakes for the guests. 6.75 is the cost, in dollars, of the additional cupcakes.

C. $3.5x$ represents the cost of the cupcakes for the guests. 8.75 is the cost, in dollars, of the additional cupcakes.

D. $3.5x$ represents the cost of the additional cupcakes. 8.75 is the cost, in dollars, of the cupcakes for the guests.

13. Challenge The bakery manager at the grocery store decides to have an 18% off sale on all bread. You decide to purchase 5 loaves of bread. Let b be the original price of a loaf of bread.

a. Which expression represents the correct expansion of the expression $5(b - 0.18b)$?

A. $5b + 0.90b$

B. $5b - 0.90$

C. $5b - 0.90b$

D. $5b + 0.90$

b. What do the terms of the expansion represent?

A. $5b$ represents the cost of 5 loaves of bread at the original price. 0.90 is subtracted from $5b$ to find the sale price.

B. $5b$ represents the cost of 5 loaves of bread at the original price. $0.90b$ is added to $5b$ to find the sale price.

C. $5b$ represents the cost of 5 loaves of bread at the original price. 0.90 is added to $5b$ to find the sale price.

D. $5b$ represents the cost of 5 loaves of bread at the original price. $0.90b$ is subtracted from $5b$ to find the sale price.

7-2 Factoring Algebraic Expressions

Vocabulary
factor an algebraic expression, like terms

CCSS: 7.EE.A.1, 7.EE.A.2

Part 1

Intro

You can use the Distributive Property to rewrite a product, expanding the product as a sum. You can also reverse this process, using the Distributive Property to write a sum of terms as a product of factors.

Expanding

Rewrite $5(2x + 9)$ as a sum.

$5(2x + 9) = 5(2x) + 5(9)$

$= 10x + 45$

Factoring

Rewrite $10x + 45$ as a product.

$10x + 45 = 5 \cdot 2x + 5 \cdot 9$

$= 5(2x + 9)$

5 is the GCF of $10x$ and 45.

Example Factoring Algebraic Expressions

Factor each algebraic expression.

a. $8a + 4 = 4(\blacksquare + \blacksquare)$

b. $3.5m - mn = (\blacksquare)(3.5 - n)$

c. $14x + 21 = (\blacksquare)(\blacksquare + \blacksquare)$

d. $y - xy = (\blacksquare)(\blacksquare - \blacksquare)$

e. $12a + 16b - 10c = (\blacksquare)(\blacksquare + \blacksquare - \blacksquare)$

Solution

a.

4 is factored out of each term.

$8a + 4 = 4(2a + 1)$

$4 \cdot 2a \quad 4 \cdot 1$

Rewrite each term using the factor 4.

The factored form of $8a + 4$ is $4(2a + 1)$.

b.

The GCF of the terms is m.

$3.5m - mn = (m)(3.5 - n)$

Factor out m.

The factored form of $3.5m - mn$ is $m(3.5 - n)$.

continued on next page >

Part 1

Solution continued

c.

Step 1 Identify the GCF. The GCF of $14x$ and 21 is 7.

$$14x + 21 = 7 \cdot 2x + 7 \cdot 3$$
$$= 7(2x + 3)$$

Step 2 Write each term using the GCF as a factor.

Step 3 Factor out the GCF.

Step 4 Insert parentheses around the remaining factors of the terms.

The factored form of $14x + 21$ is $7(2x + 3)$.

d.

The GCF of y and xy is y.

$$y - xy = 1 \cdot y - x \cdot y$$
$$= y(1 - x)$$

The factored form of $y - xy$ is $y(1 - x)$.

e.

The GCF of $12a$, $16b$, and $10c$ is 2.

$$12a + 16b - 10c = 2 \cdot 6a + 2 \cdot 8b - 2 \cdot 5c$$
$$= 2(6a + 8b - 5c)$$

The factored form of $12a + 16b - 10c$ is $2(6a + 8b - 5c)$.

Part 2

Intro

Terms that have identical variable parts are like terms.

Like Terms	Not Like Terms
$2x$ and $-3x$	$2x$ and $2y$
$2x^2$ and $-3x^2$	$2x^2$ and $-3x$
$2xy$ and $-3xy$	$2xy$ and $2x$
2 and −3	2 and $-3y$

Two numbers are like terms.

You can use factoring with the Distributive Property to add or subtract like terms.

$$9x + 7x = x(9 + 7)$$
$$= x(16)$$
$$= 16x$$

$$y + 2.5y - 3y = y(1 + 2.5 - 3)$$
$$= y(3.5 - 3)$$
$$= y(0.5)$$
$$= 0.5y$$

Example Identifying Like Terms

Determine which three expressions have like terms. Then combine the like terms.

$2y + 3x$ $\quad -5a + 8a$ $\quad 6 - 4p$

$7xy - 10x$ $\quad 12 + ab$ $\quad n + 6.25n$

Solution

Like terms have identical variable parts, so these expressions have like terms:

$-5a + 8a$ $\quad n + 6.25n$ $\quad 7xy - 10xy$

These expressions do not have like terms:

$2y + 3x$ — Different variables

$6 - 4p$ — Constant term; Variable term

$12a + ab$ — Variable terms not identical

Use the Distributive Property to combine like terms.

$$-5a + 8a = a(-5 + 8)$$ Factor out a.
$$= a(3)$$
$$= 3(a)$$

continued on next page >

Part 2

Solution continued

$$n + 6.25n = n(1 + 6.25)$$
Factor out n.
$$= n(7.25)$$
$$= 7.25n$$

$$7xy - 10xy = xy(7 - 10)$$
Factor out xy.
$$= xy(-3)$$
$$= -3xy$$

Part 3

Example Combining Like Terms

The produce manager at the grocery store increases the price per pound of all types of fruits by 3%. Let p be the original price per pound of a type of fruit. Use this expression for the new price per pound of a type of fruit.

$$p + 0.03p$$

a. Write an equivalent expression by combining like terms.

b. Use the original expression and your equivalent expression to describe two ways the produce manager can find the new price per pound for a type of fruit.

Solution

a. $p + 0.03p = p(1 + 0.03)$ Factor out p.
$$= p(1.03)$$
$$= 1.03p$$

b. $p + 0.03p$

To find the new price per pound, the produce manager finds 3% of the original price per pound and adds that amount to the original price per pound.

$1.03p$

The produce manager finds the new price per pound by multiplying the original price per pound by 1.03.

Key Concept

Expand Rewrite a product as a sum or difference.

To expand an algebraic expression, use the Distributive Property to rewrite a product as a sum or difference of terms.

Expand: $-6(3x - 4)$

Distributive Property	$-6(3x - 4) = -6(3x) - (-6)(4)$
Associative Property	$= [-6(3)]x - (-6)(4)$
	$= -18x - (-24)$
	$= -18x + 24$

Factor Rewrite an expression as a product.

To factor an algebraic expression, write the expression as a product.

Factor: $15x + 21$

Step 1 Identify the GCF of the terms and write each term with the GCF as a factor.

The GCF of 15 and 21 is 3. There is no common variable factor.

$$15x + 21 = 3 \cdot 5x + 3 \cdot 7$$

Step 2 Use the Distributive Property to factor out the GCF, inserting parentheses around the remaining factors of the terms.

$$15x + 21 = 3 \cdot 5x + 3 \cdot 7$$
$$= 3(5x + 7)$$

Combine Like Terms Like terms have identical variable parts.

You can use the Distributive Property to combine like terms.

Combine like terms: $1.8a + 0.4a$

Use the Distributive Property to factor out the variable part.	$1.8a + 0.4a = a(1.8 + 0.4)$
Add the numbers inside the parentheses.	$= a(2.2)$
Use the Commutative Property to write the number factor first.	$= 2.2a$

See your complete lesson at MyMathUniverse.com

Digital Resources

1. Complete the factored form of the algebraic expression $18a + 3 = 3(■ + ■)$.
2. Factor the algebraic expression $16a + 10$.
3. Which of the expressions have like terms? Select all that apply.
   A. $-6m + 4m$ B. $t + 6.75t$
   C. $10m + mn$ D. $6 - 6p$
   E. $9xy - 4xy$ F. $2y + 5x$
4. Combine the like terms $-6m + 4m$. Simplify your answer.
5. **Think About the Process**
   a. In the expression below, identify the like terms. Select all that apply.
   $7 + 14s + 5k - 2s - 2k - 14$
   A. $7, -14$
   B. $-2k, -2s, -14$
   C. $14s, 5k, 7$
   D $5k, -2k$
   E. $14s, -2s$
   F. $-2s, 7$
   b. Combine like terms: $7 + 14s + 5k - 2s - 2k - 14 = ■$
6. A student received a coupon for 17% off the total purchase price at a clothing store. Let b be the original price of the purchase. Use the expression $b - 0.17b$ for the new price of the purchase. Write an equivalent expression by combining like terms.
7. At a college, the cost of tuition increased by 10%. Let b be the former cost of tuition. Use the expression $b + 0.10b$ for the new cost of tuition.
   a. Write an equivalent expression by combining like terms.
   b. What does your equivalent expression tell you about how to find the new cost of tuition?
8. a. **Error Analysis** Your friend incorrectly factors the expression $15x - 20xy$ as $5x(3 - 4xy)$. Factor the expression correctly.
   b. What error did your friend likely make?
   A. Your friend did not factor the variable from the second term.
   B. Your friend did not have the correct operation inside the parentheses.
   C. Your friend did not factor the variable from the first term.
   D. Your friend did not simplify the terms inside the parentheses.
9. a. **Reasoning** Which of the expressions have like terms? Select all that apply.
   A. $14m + mn$
   B. $2y + 2x + 4$
   C. $-\frac{3}{4}m + 8m + m$
   D. $4 - 3p$
   E. $5.75t + 7.75t - t$
   F. $8xy - 6xy$
   b. Explain why the other expressions do not have like terms.
10. **Mental Math** Combine the like terms $39z + 17z + 15z + 11z + 43z + 5z$.
11. **Art** An art teacher made a copy of a small painting. To make the painting easier to see, the teacher enlarged the area of the painting by 49%. Let d represent the area of the original painting. The expression $d + 0.49d$ is one way to represent the area of the new painting. Which expressions will give the area of the new painting? Select all that apply.
    A. $149d$ B. $d + 49d$
    C. $0.49d$ D. $d(1 + 0.49)$
    E. $1.49d$
12. **Writing** A farmer recently sold a large plot of land. The sale decreased his total acreage by 8%. Let v be the original acreage.
    a. Find two equivalent expressions that will give the new acreage.
    b. Use the expressions to describe two ways to find the new acreage.

13. Estimation The manager of a store increases the price of a popular product by 7%. Let t be the original price of the product. The new price is $t + 0.07t$.

a. Find an expression equivalent to $t + 0.07t$.

A. $1.93t$ **B.** $0.93t$
C. $1.07t$ **D.** $0.07t$

b. If the original price was \$19.99, estimate the new price by first rounding the original price to the nearest dollar.

A. \$18.59 **B.** \$19.99
C. \$21.40 **D.** \$38.58

14. Combine like terms in the expression $9x + 4.88xy + 22y + 32y - 14x + 9.88$.

15. Complete the factored form of the linear expression.

$15x + 10y = (\blacksquare)(\blacksquare + \blacksquare)$

A. $15x + 10y = (5)(2x + 3y)$
B. $15x + 10y = (5y)(3x + 2)$
C. $15x + 10y = (5x)(3 + 2y)$
D. $15x + 10y = (5)(3x + 2y)$

16. Think About the Process You are given the linear expression $12x + 18y + 26$.

a. Which step is the first step in factoring the linear expression?

A. Add the numerical coefficients.
B. Use the Distributive Property to factor out the GCF.
C. Identify the GCF.
D. Write each term of the expression using the GCF as a factor.

b. Factor the linear expression.

17. Challenge A customer at a clothing store is buying a pair of pants and a shirt. The store is having a 15%-off sale on all pants. The customer has a coupon for 10% off her entire purchase. The coupon cannot be combined with any other offers, so she can choose only one option. Let n represent the original price of the pants and s represent the price of the shirt.

a. Which two expressions represent the "15%-off sale on all pants" option?

A. $0.85n + s$
B. $n - 0.15n + s$
C. $n + 0.85n - s$
D. $0.15n + s$
E. $n + 0.15n + s$
F. $0.15s + n$

b. Which two expressions represent the "10% off her entire purchase" option?

A. $(n + s) - 0.10(n + s)$
B. $n + 1.10s$
C. $0.10(n + s)$
D. $0.9(n - s)$
E. $0.9(n + s)$
F. $0.10n + 0.9s$

c. If the original cost of the pants is \$25 and the shirt is \$10, which option should the customer choose?

A. The customer should choose the "10% off her entire purchase" option.
B. The customer should choose the "15%-off sale on all pants" option.

7-3 Adding Algebraic Expressions

Vocabulary
coefficient, constant, simplify an algebraic expression

CCSS: 7.EE.A.1, 7.EE.A.2

Part 1

Intro

Terms Quantities that you add to form an algebraic expression are the terms of the expression. Each term is a number, a variable, or the product of a number and one or more variables.

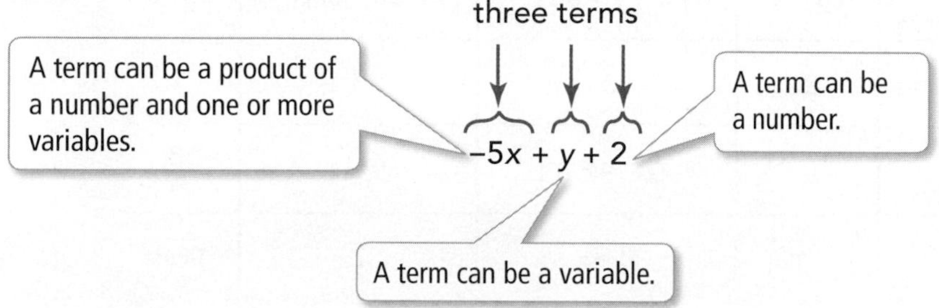

Coefficients The number factor of a term is the **coefficient** of the term. When you don't see a number factor, remember that 1 is always a factor.

Constants A term without a variable is a **constant** term.

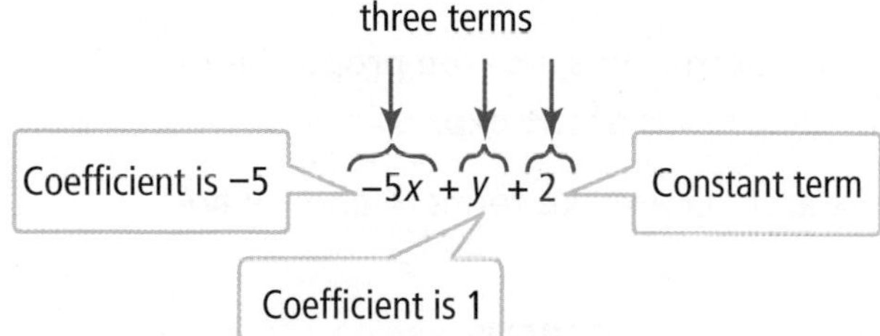

Terms of a Difference Because you can always rewrite a difference as a sum, a difference also has terms.

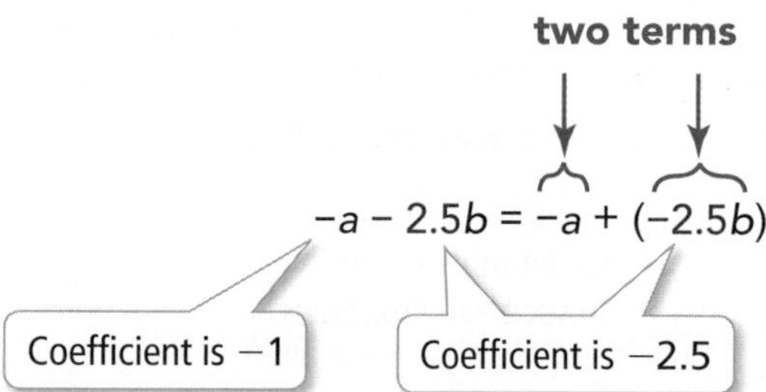

See your complete lesson at MyMathUniverse.com

Part 1

Example Identifying Parts of Algebraic Expressions

For each algebraic expression, identify the number of terms. Then list the coefficients and any constant terms.

$12a - 3$ $\quad 0.2x - y + 8.1z$ $\quad 7 + 9n - 6mn$ $\quad \frac{3}{4}s$

Solution

Expression	$12a - 3$	$0.2x - y + 8.1z$	$7 + 9n - 6mn$	$\frac{3}{4}s$
Number of Terms	2	3	3	1
Coefficient(s)	12	0.2, −1, 8.1	9, −6	$\frac{3}{4}$
Constant(s)	−3	None	7	None

Part 2

Intro

When you add two algebraic expressions, use the properties of operations to combine the like terms of the expressions.

Identify Like Terms $-5x$ and $11x$ are like terms. 4 and -9 are like terms.

like terms like terms

$$(-5x + 4) + (11x - 9)$$

Regroup Terms You can use the commutative and associative properties of addition to move the terms around and group the like terms.

Commutative and Associative Properties

$$(-5x + 4) + (11x - 9) = (-5x + 11x) + [4 + (-9)]$$

continued on next page >

Part 2

Intro continued

Combine Like Terms To combine the like variable terms, use the Distributive Property to factor out the variable part. Then simplify.

$$\begin{aligned}(-5x + 4) + (11x - 9) &= (-5x + 11x) + [4 + (-9)] \\ &= x(-5 + 11) + [4 + (-9)] \\ &= 6x + (-5) \\ &= 6x - 5\end{aligned}$$

Example Adding Two Algebraic Expressions

Complete each equation with one of the expressions. You can use an expression more than once.

$-3r + 7$ $\quad$ $2r - 7$ $\quad$ $-2r - 7$

a. $(2r + 7) + (-5r) = \square$

b. $(r + 4) + (-3r - 11) = \square$

c. $5(r + 1) + (-8r + 2) = \square$

Solution

a. Group the like terms. $(2r + 7) + (-5r) = [2r + (-5r)] + 7$

Combine like terms. $= r[2 + (-5)] + 7$

$= -3r + 7$

So $(2r + 7) + (-5r) = -3r + 7$.

b. Group the like terms. $(r + 4) + (-3r - 11) = [r + (-3r)] + [4 + (-11)]$

Combine like terms. $= r[1 + (-3)] + [4 + (-11)]$

$= -2r + (-7)$

$= -2r - 7$

So $(r + 4) + (-3r - 11) = -2r - 7$.

c. Distribute the 5. $5(r + 1) + (-8r + 2) = 5r + 5 + (-8r + 2)$

Group the like terms. $= [5r + (-8r)] + (5 + 2)$

Combine like terms. $= r[5 + (-8)] + (5 + 2)$

$= -3r + 7$

So $5(r + 1) + (-8r + 2) = -3r + 7$.

Key Concept

To **simplify an algebraic expression**, combine the like terms of the expression. Use the properties of operations to group the like terms. Then combine the like terms by adding their coefficients.

$$4x + 7y + (-6x) + 9y = [4x + (-6x)] + (7y + 9y)$$
$$= -2x + 16y$$

Part 3

Intro

The perimeter of a rectangle is the sum of the lengths of its four sides.

You can use this formula for the perimeter of a rectangle, where ℓ represents the length and w represents the width of the rectangle.

$$P = 2\ell + 2w$$

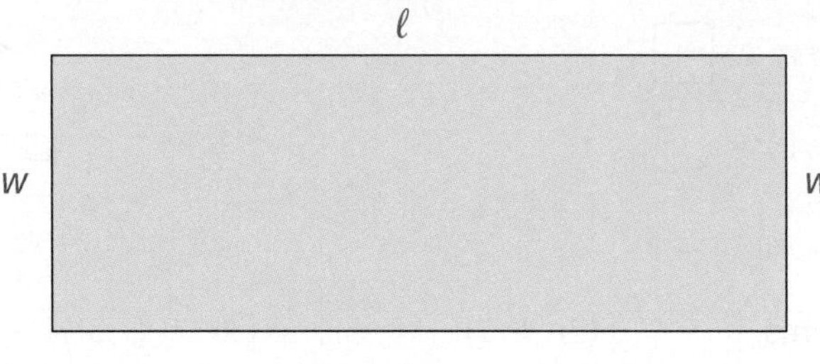

Example Writing Algebraic Expressions for Perimeter Problems

A rectangular frame for a flower bed is 9 feet longer than it is wide. Write and simplify an algebraic expression for the perimeter of the flower bed in terms of the width w of the flower bed.

Solution

The length ℓ of the flower bed is 9 feet more than its width w, so $\ell = w + 9$.

Use the formula for the perimeter.	$P = 2\ell + 2w$
Substitute $w + 9$ for ℓ.	$= 2(w + 9) + 2w$
Use the Distributive Property.	$= 2w + 2(9) + 2w$
Group like terms.	$= 2w + 2w + 18$
Combine like terms.	$= 4w + 18$

An expression for the perimeter of the flower bed is $P = 2(w + 9) + 2w$, which simplifies to $P = 4w + 18$.

Digital Resources   

1. Identify the number of terms in the expression $9m + 7$.
2. **a.** Identify all the coefficients of the expression $2 + 6a$.
   b. Identify all the constants of the expression $2 + 6a$.
3. List all the coefficients and constants of the following expression.
   $2 + \frac{b}{6} + 4 - y$
   a. The coefficient(s) of the expression is/are ■.
   b. The constant(s) of the expression is/are ■.
4. Add $(2a + 8) + (4b + 5)$. Simplify your answer.
5. Add $(8x - 7) + (6x + 8)$. Simplify your answer.
6. Frank is going to plant b vegetable seeds in one garden and $5b + 10$ vegetable seeds in another. How many seeds is Frank going to plant?
7. Nancy and Bill collect coins. Nancy has x coins. Bill has 5 coins fewer than five times the number of coins Nancy has. Write and simplify an expression for the total number of coins Nancy and Bill have. Simplify your answer.
8. **Error Analysis** On a math test a student, Sarah, has to identify all the coefficients and constants of the expression $4 + n + 7m$. Sarah says that 7 is a coefficient and 4 is a constant.
   a. Identify all the coefficients of the expression.
   b. Identify all the constants of the expression.
   c. What error might Sarah have made?
   A. Sarah did not include the constant 1.
   B. Sarah said 4 is a constant. It is actually a coefficient.
   C. Sarah said 7 is a coefficient. It is actually a constant.
   D. Sarah did not include the coefficient 1.
9. **a. Writing** Combine the like terms of the expression $(8 + 6x) + (-4 + 9c)$.
   b. Explain how you simplified the expression in each step.
10. **a. Reasoning** Find the sum $(8x + 2) + (-9x + 7)$.
    b. Explain how you know when to combine terms with variables.
11. **Estimation** Gabe goes to the mall. If k is the number of items he bought, the expression $14.74k + 24$ gives the amount he spent in dollars at one store. Then he spent 25 dollars at another store.
    a. Find the expression that represents the amount Gabe spent at the mall.
    b. Estimate how much Gabe spent if he bought 3 items.
12. A family is going on a road trip. On the first day the family traveled x miles. The following day the family went 52 miles more than three times the number of miles traveled on the first day. On the third day the family went 83 fewer miles than the first day. Write and simplify an expression for the total number of miles traveled.
13. **Design** An art class is making a mural for their school which has a triangle drawn in the middle. The length of the bottom of the triangle is x. Another side is 1 more than three times the length of the bottom of the triangle. The last side is 2 more than the bottom of the triangle. Write and simplify an expression for the perimeter of the triangle.
14. Find the sum $(8b + 7) + (6x - 4) + (5c + 8)$.
15. Combine like terms $(-3y - 5) + (5m + 7y) + (6 + 9m)$.

16. Think About the Process What should the expression $(8 + 8y) + (-3 - 2y) + (6 + 6y)$ look like after the like terms have been grouped together?

a. Which of the following expressions shows the like terms grouped correctly?

A. $(8y + (-2y) + 6y + 8) + (-3 + 6)$

B. $(8y + (-2y)) + (8 + (-3) + 6$

C. $(8y + (-2y) + 6y) + (8 + (-3) + 6)$

D. $(8 + 8y) + (-3 - 2y) + (6 + 6y)$

b. $(8 + 8y) + (-3 - 2y) + (6 + 6y) = \blacksquare$

17. Think About the Process A local store sells fences. The store has a standard sized fence and they also make custom fences. The store received an order for two different custom lengths. The buyer wanted one fence to be 5 feet fewer than 3 times x, where x is the length of the standard fence in feet. The buyer wanted the length of the second fence to be 8 feet more than 5 times x.

a. Which of the following is the correct expression for the total length of fence that was ordered before simplifying?

A. $(3x - 5) + (5x - 8)$

B. $(3x - 5) + 5x$

C. $3x + (5x + 8)$

D. $(3x - 5) + (5x + 8)$

b. What is the total length of fence that was ordered?

18. Challenge The width of a rectangle is $5x - 3$ feet and the length is $2x + 8$ feet. Find the perimeter of the rectangle.

19. Challenge A local middle school has x students. The school ran a survey to determine the students' favorite activity. Each student could only say one activity. The results showed that 25 more than one-tenth of the students said they enjoy dance, 20 fewer than three-tenths of the students said they enjoy soccer, and 21 more than one-tenth of the students said they enjoy baseball. Write and simplify an expression for the number of students who enjoy dance, soccer, and baseball.

7-4 Subtracting Algebraic Expressions

CCSS: 7.EE.A.1, 7.EE.A.2

Key Concept

When you subtract two algebraic expressions, you distribute the minus sign as you remove the parentheses.

Method 1 Subtract each term inside the parentheses. Remember that the subtraction sign inside the parentheses is the sign of the second term: $-7x$.

Subtract 2 | Subtract $-7x$

$$\begin{aligned}(x + 4) - (2 - 7x) &= x + 4 - 2 - (-7x)\\ &= x + 4 - 2 + 7x\\ &= x + 7x + 4 - 2\\ &= 8x + 2\end{aligned}$$

Method 2 Rewrite subtraction as addition.

$$\begin{aligned}(x + 4) - (2 - 7x) &= (x + 4) + (-1)(2 - 7x)\\ &= (x + 4) + (-1)(2) - (-1)(7x)\\ &= (x + 4) + (-2) - (-7x)\\ &= (x + 4) - 2 + 7x\\ &= x + 7x + 4 - 2\\ &= 8x + 2\end{aligned}$$

Part 1

Example Subtracting Two Algebraic Expressions

Rewrite each expression without parentheses.

a. $16m - (3 + 8m) = \blacksquare$

b. $\left(\frac{1}{3}p - 9\right) - \left(\frac{1}{4}p - 1\right) = \blacksquare$

c. $(-1.5h + 3) - 2(-0.5 + 4h) = \blacksquare$

Solution

a. Use Method 1.

Subtract each of the terms 3 and 8m. $16m - (3 + 8m) = 16m - 3 - 8m$

continued on next page >

Part 1

Solution continued

b. Use Method 1.

Subtract each of the terms $\frac{1}{4}p$ and -1. $\left(\frac{1}{3}p - 9\right) - \left(\frac{1}{4}p - 1\right) = \frac{1}{3}p - 9 - \frac{1}{4}p - (-1)$

Simplify. $= \frac{1}{3}p - 9 - \frac{1}{4}p + 1$

c. Use Method 2.

Rewrite subtraction as addition. $(-1.5h + 3) - 2(-0.5 + 4h)$
$= -1.5h + 3 + (-2)(-0.5 + 4h)$

Use the Distributive Property. $= -1.5h + 3 + (-2)(-0.5) + (-2)(4h)$

Multiply. $= -1.5h + 3 + 1 + (-8h)$

Simplify. $= -1.5h + 3 + 1 - 8h$

Part 2

Example Writing Steps for Subtracting Two Algebraic Expressions

The steps of subtracting two expressions are shown. Put the steps in order.

$3.5x + (-0.5x) + (-5.4)$

$3.5x + (-2)(2.7 + 0.25x)$

$3x - 5.4$

$3.5x + (-5.4) + (-0.5x)$

$3.5x - 2(2.7 + 0.25x)$

Solution

To put the steps in order, start with the subtraction of two expressions and end with the simplified expression.

Identify the initial expression. $3.5x - 2(2.7 + 0.25x)$

Rewrite subtraction as addition. $3.5x + (-2)(2.7 + 0.25x)$

Use the Distributive Property. $3.5x + (-5.4) + (-0.5x)$

Use the Commutative Property. $3.5x + (-0.5x) + (-5.4)$

Combine like terms. Rewrite addition of a negative as subtraction. $3x - 5.4$

Part 3

Example Writing and Subtracting Algebraic Expressions

Two friends shop for fresh fruit. Jackson buys a watermelon for \$7.45 and 3 pounds of cherries. Aaron buys a pineapple for \$3.50 and 2 pounds of cherries.

Using one variable, write expressions to represent the total amount of money each friend spent. Then write and simplify an expression to represent how much more one friend spent than the other.

Solution

Know	Need	Plan
Jackson: • Spent \$7.45 on watermelon • Bought 3 pounds of cherries **Aaron:** • Spent \$3.50 on pineapple • Bought 2 pounds of cherries	Expressions to represent: • the total amount each friend spent • how much more one friend spent than the other	• Write expressions for the total spent by each friend, in terms of the price per pound of cherries. • Subtract the expressions.

Choose a variable to represent the price per pound of cherries.

Let p = price, in dollars, per pound of cherries.

Write an expression for Jackson's total.

Words	cost of watermelon	plus	cost of 3 pounds of cherries

Expression	7.45	+	$3p$

An expression for Jackson's total is $7.45 + 3p$.

continued on next page >

Part 3

Solution continued

Write an expression for Aaron's total.

Words	cost of pineapple	plus	cost of 2 pounds of cherries
	to		
Expression	3.50	+	$2p$

An expression for Aaron's total is $3.50 + 2p$.

The watermelon costs more than the pineapple, and 3 pounds of cherries costs more than 2 pounds of cherries, so Jackson spent more than Aaron.

To write an expression to represent how much more, subtract the lesser total from the greater total.

Jackson's total − Aaron's total

$$\begin{aligned}(7.45 + 3p) - (3.50 + 2p) &= 7.45 + 3p - 3.50 - 2p \\ &= (7.45 - 3.50) + (3p - 2p) \\ &= 3.95 + p\end{aligned}$$

The expression $3.95 + p$ represents how much more Jackson spent than Aaron spent.

Digital Resources   

1. Rewrite the expression $14m - (5 + 8m)$ without parentheses.
2. Rewrite the expression $13m - (-9m - 4)$ without parentheses.
3. **a.** Write an equivalent expression of $8m - (5 + 2m)$ without parentheses.
   b. Simplify the result.
4. Subtract $7x - (9 + 5x)$.
5. A company has two manufacturing plants with daily production levels of $5x + 11$ items and $2x - 3$ items, respectively. The first plant produces how many more items daily than the second plant?
6. Two communications companies offer calling plans. With Company X, it costs 35¢ to connect and then 5¢ for each minute. With Company Y, it costs 15¢ to connect and then 4¢ for each minute.
   a. Which of these expressions represents how much more Company X charges than Company Y?
   A. $(35 + 4n) - (15 + 5n)$
   B. $35n - 5 - 15n - 4$
   C. $(35n - 4) - (15n - 5)$
   D. $(35 + 5n) - (15 + 4n)$
   b. Write and simplify an expression that represents how much more Company X charges than Company Y, in cents, for n minutes.
7. **Error Analysis** Tim incorrectly rewrote the expression $\frac{1}{2}p - \left(\frac{1}{4}p + 4\right)$ as $\frac{1}{2}p + \frac{1}{4}p - 4$.
   a. Rewrite the expression without parentheses correctly.
   b. What was Tim's likely error?
   A. He did not change the sign of the first term in the parentheses.
   B. He did not change the sign of the expression outside the parentheses.
   C. He did not change the sign of the second term in the parentheses.
   D. He multiplied each expression in the parentheses by $\frac{1}{2}p$.
8. **a. Writing** Rewrite the expression $\frac{1}{4}p - \left(1 - \frac{1}{3}p\right)$ without parentheses.
   b. Use a different method to rewrite the expression without parentheses.
   c. After rewriting the expression, what do you notice about each term inside the parentheses?
9. **a. Multiple Representations** Simplify the expression $10x - (-7 + 6x)$.
   b. Draw algebra tiles to represent the subtraction.
10. **Reasoning** Each month, a shopkeeper spends $5x + 11$ dollars on rent and electricity.
    a. If he spends $2x - 3$ dollars on rent, how much does he spend on electricity?
    b. For which value(s) of x is the amount the shopkeeper spends on electricity less than \$100? Explain how you found the value(s).
11. **Shopping** Two friends shop for fresh fruit. Jackson buys a watermelon for \$7.65 and 5 pounds of cherries. Tim buys a pineapple for \$2.45 and 4 pounds of cherries. Use the variable p to represent the price, in dollars, per pound of cherries. Write and simplify an expression to represent how much more Jackson spent.
12. Rewrite the expression without parentheses.
    $(1.6z + 4) - 4(-0.5 + 5z)$
    A. $1.6z + 4 + 2 - 20z$
    B. $1.6z + 4 - 2 - 20z$
    C. $1.6z + 4 - 2 + 20z$
    D. $1.6z + 4 + 2 + 20z$
13. Write an equivalent expression of $-2(1.5h + 5) - 4(-0.5 + 3h)$ without parentheses.

14. A rectangular garden has a walkway around it. The area of the garden is $6(6.5x + 3.5)$. The combined area of the garden and the walkway is $6.5(8x + 5)$. Find the area of the walkway around the garden as the sum of two terms.

15. Two friends from a band want to record a demo. Studio A rents for a fee of \$130 plus \$35 an hour. Studio B rents for a \$200 fee plus \$25 an hour.

a. What is the difference in renting Studio A for n hours rather than Studio B?

b. How many hours would they have to rent so the cost of renting Studio A is the same as renting Studio B?

16. Think About the Process Complete the following steps to simplify the expression $14m - 3(3 + 4m)$.

$14m - 3(3 + 4m)$

$=$ ■ Rewrite subtraction as addition.

$= 14m + (-9) + (-12m)$ ■

$= 14m + (-12m) + (-9)$ ■

$=$ ■ Combine like terms.

$=$ ■ Rewrite addition of a negative as subtraction.

17. Think About the Process A bag of mixed nuts contains only almonds and hazelnuts. The bag has $3x - 7$ hazelnuts, and $6x + 13$ nuts in all.

a. Which of these expressions represents the number of almonds in the bag?

A. $6x + 13 - (3x - 7)$

B. $3x - 7 - 6x + 13$

C. $6x + 13 - 3x - 7$

D. $3x - 7 - (6x + 13)$

b. There are ■ almonds in the bag.

18. Challenge Find the difference $\left(5x - 6\frac{1}{2}\right) - \left(-2x + 4\frac{2}{3}\right)$.

19. Challenge A family wants to rent a car to go on vacation. Company A charges \$50.50 and 8¢ per mile. Company B charges \$70.50 and 12¢ per mile. How much more does Company B charge for x miles than Company A?

7-5 Problem Solving

CCSS: 7.EE.A.1, 7.EE.A.2

Part 1

Example Writing Equivalent Algebraic Expressions

Write an expression that fits each description and is equivalent to $-6x - 30$.

a. A product of two factors

b. A difference of two expressions, each with two unlike terms

c. A sum that requires using the Distributive Property to simplify

Solution

Sample:

a. $-6(x + 5)$ is a product of two factors that is equivalent to $-6x - 30$.

b. $(-2x - 15) - (4x + 15)$ is a difference of two expressions, each with two unlike terms, that is equivalent to $-6x - 30$.

c. $-8(x + 2) + 2(x - 7)$ is a sum that requires using the Distributive Property to simplify and is equivalent to $-6x - 30$.

Check

a. $-6(x + 5) = -6x + (-6)(5)$ Use the Distributive Property.

$= -6x + (-30)$

$= -6x - 30$ ✓

b. $(-2x - 15) - (4x + 15) = -2x - 15 - 4x - 15$

$= -2x - 4x - 15 - 15$ Use the Commutative Property.

$= -6x - 30$ ✓

c. $-8(x + 2) + 2(x - 7) = -8x - 16 + 2x - 14$ Use the Distributive Property.

$= -8x + 2x - 16 - 14$

$= -6x - 30$ ✓

See your complete lesson at MyMathUniverse.com

Part 2

Example Using Algebraic Expressions to Solve Real-World Problems

A dog's owner wants to fence in a rectangular area for his dog, as shown in the diagram. Fencing costs $5.80 per foot.

a. Write and simplify an expression for the cost, in dollars, of the fencing.

b. The dog's owner has $200 to spend on fencing. Does he have enough money to have the length x be 8 feet?

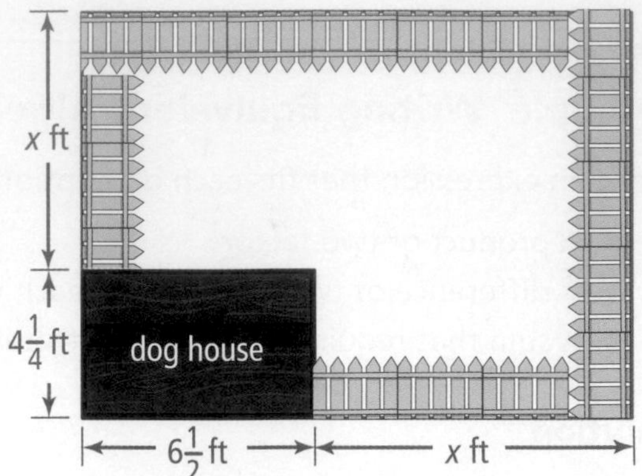

Solution

a. Step 1 Write an expression, in terms of x, for the total length, in feet, of the fence.

$6\frac{1}{2}$ ft + x ft

x ft

$4\frac{1}{4}$ ft + x ft

$4\frac{1}{4}$ ft

doghouse

$6\frac{1}{2}$ ft

x ft

$$\text{length} = \left(6\tfrac{1}{2} + x\right) + \left(4\tfrac{1}{4} + x\right) + x + x$$

$$= x + x + x + x + 6\tfrac{1}{2} + 4\tfrac{1}{4}$$

$$= 4x + 10\tfrac{3}{4}$$

The expression $4x + 10\frac{3}{4}$ represents the total length, in feet, of the fence.

continued on next page >

Part 2

Solution continued

Step 2 Write an equation for the cost, in dollars, of the fencing.

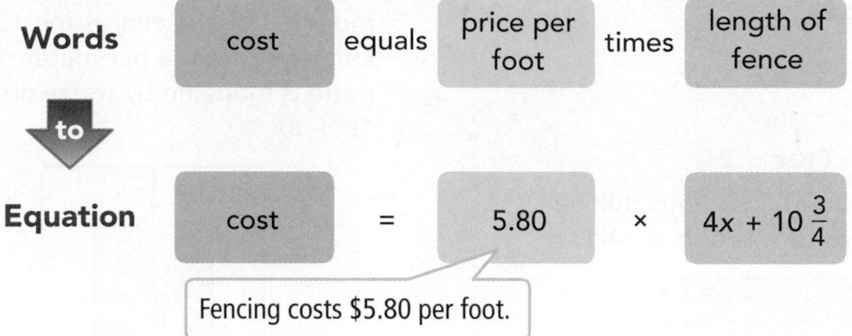

Fencing costs $5.80 per foot.

$$\text{cost} = 5.8\left(4x + 10\tfrac{3}{4}\right)$$

$= 5.8(4x + 10.75)$ To simplify, use the Distributive Property.

$= 23.2x + 62.35$

The expression $23.2x + 62.35$ represents the total cost, in dollars, of the fencing.

b. Use the cost expression that you wrote in part a to find the cost of the fencing when x is 8 feet.

Evaluate the cost expression $23.2x + 62.35$ when $x = 8$.

$$23.2(8) + 62.35 = 185.6 + 62.35$$
$$= 247.95$$

If x is 8 feet, the fencing costs $247.95 which is greater than $200. The owner does not have enough money to have the length x be 8 feet.

Digital Resources 

1. Which expression is the product of two factors and is equivalent to $-4x - 24$?
   A. $-4(x - 6)$
   B. $-4x - 3 - 21$
   C. $-4(x + 6)$
   D. $(6x - 3) - (10x - 21)$

2. Alexander is building a fenced-in pen in his backyard for his dog, as shown.

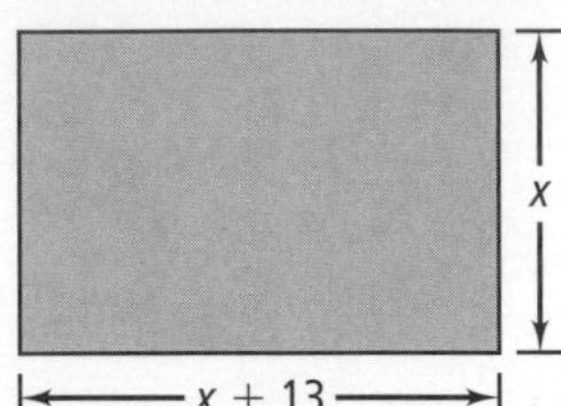

   a. Which expression represents the total amount of fencing, in feet?
      A. $2x + 13$ B. $2x + 26$
      C. $4x + 26$ D. $4x + 52$
   b. If the longer dimension of the rectangle is 28 feet, how many feet of fencing does Alexander need?

3. a. Which expression is a difference of two terms that is equivalent to $-6z + 13$?
      A. $(5z + 2) - (11z + 15)$
      B. $(11z + 2) - (5z + 15)$
      C. $(11z + 15) - (5z + 2)$
      D. $(5z + 15) - (11z + 2)$
   b. Which expression is a difference of two terms that is equivalent to $6z - 13$?
      A. $(5z + 15) - (11z + 2)$
      B. $(5z + 2) - (11z + 15)$
      C. $(11z + 15) - (5z + 2)$
      D. $(11z + 2) - (5z + 15)$

4. Write an expression equivalent to $9x - 11y - 59$ that is the difference of two products.
   $9x - 11y - 59 = \blacksquare$
   $(x + 2) - 11(y + \blacksquare)$

5. Jenna and Luis are building a patio around a flower bed, as shown. Jenna says that the perimeter of the patio is modeled by the expression $12 + 6x$. Luis says that the perimeter of the patio is modeled by the expression $18 + 8x$.

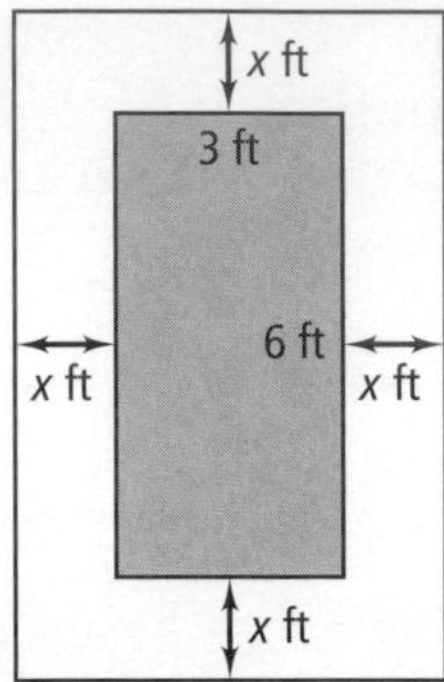

   a. Whose expression for the perimeter is incorrect?
      A. Jenna B. Luis
   b. What mistake could that person have made?
      A. The person did not completely simplify the expression.
      B. The person used the Distributive Property incorrectly.
      C. The person used the Commutative Property incorrectly.
      D. The person used the Associative Property incorrectly.
   c. If $x = 3$, what is the perimeter of the patio in feet?

6. A research ship lowers a probe into the ocean to explore an underwater trench. The probe starts on a crane 16 feet above the surface and is lowered at a rate of 9.2 feet per minute.
   a. Write an expression for the depth of the probe after m minutes.
   b. What is the depth after 90 minutes?

7. a. Write the expression $8x + 144 - 56$ as the product of two factors.
   b. Write at least three other equivalent expressions for the given expression.

See your complete lesson at MyMathUniverse.com

8. An art exhibit is made up of four panels, each with the same height. The width of each panel is shown.

Panel Areas

Panel	Width (ft)
A	5.58
B	6.02
C	4.42
D	3.98

a. Write an expression for the total area in terms of the height, h.

b. If each panel is 10 ft tall, what is the total area of the exhibit?

9. **a.** Write an expression equivalent to $\frac{5}{16}p + \frac{7}{12}$ that is the difference of two expressions with two unlike terms. The equivalent expression should be in the form $\frac{5}{16}p + \frac{7}{12} = \left(\blacksquare p + \frac{1}{3}\right) - \left(\frac{11}{16}p - \blacksquare\right)$.

b. Which properties of operations did you use to write your equivalent expression?

10. **Think About the Process**

a. Which properties of operations can you use to write a sum of two products that is equivalent to $16x + 39$? Select all that apply.

A. The Distributive Property

B. The Identity Property of Addition

C. The Commutative Property

D. The Zero Property of Multiplication

E. The Associative Property

b. Write a sum of two products equivalent to $16x + 39$.

$16x + 39 = \blacksquare(x + 2) + 7(x + \blacksquare)$

11. **Think About the Process** The square country of Squareland extends x km north, south, east, and west of the capital, Square City. Square City can be modeled by a square with side length y km.

a. Which expression represents the length of one side of Squareland?

A. $y + 2x$ **B.** $y + x$

C. $2y + x$ **D.** $2x - y$

b. If $x = 9$ and $y = 4$, the area of Squareland is $\blacksquare$ km^2.

12. **a. Challenge** Which expressions are equivalent to $-6x - 14$? Select all that apply.

A. $(-2x - 2) - (4x + 12)$

B. $-2(3x - 7)$

C. $(-2x - 2) + (4x - 12)$

D. $-2(3x + 7)$

E. $2(x - 1) + 4(x - 3)$

F. $-2(x + 1) - 4(x + 3)$

b. Could you use any of the equivalent expressions to help you find other equivalent expressions? Explain.

13. **Challenge** For a project, you cut a rectangle out of a large sheet of paper, as shown.

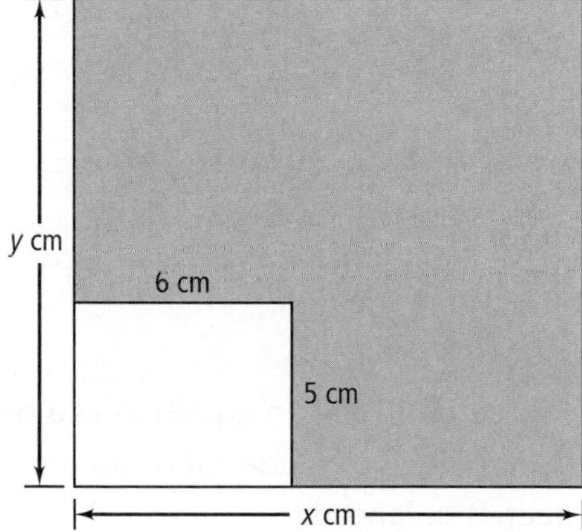

a. Write an expression for the area of the remaining paper in terms of width x and length y.

b. If $x = 42$ cm and $y = 40$ cm, how many more rectangles can you cut out of one sheet of paper?

8-1 Solving Simple Equations

Vocabulary
Addition Property of Equality, Division Property of Equality, isolate a variable, Multiplication Property of Equality, Subtraction Property of Equality

CCSS: 7.EE.B.4, Also 7.EE.B.4a

Key Concept

You can think of solving an equation as transforming the equation into a simpler equivalent equation. Your goal is to use inverse operations and the Properties of Equality to isolate the variable on one side of the equal sign.

Addition Property of Equality If you add the same number to each side of an equation, the two sides remain equal.

Arithmetic	**Algebra**
$6 = 3(2)$	If $a = b$, then
$6 + 5 = 3(2) + 5$	$a + c = b + c$
$11 = 11$	for all numbers a, b, and c.

Subtraction Property of Equality If you subtract the same number from each side of an equation, the two sides remain equal.

Arithmetic	**Algebra**
$9 = 3(3)$	If $a = b$, then
$9 - 2.5 = 3(3) - 2.5$	$a - c = b - c$
$6.5 = 6.5$	for all numbers a, b, and c.

Part 1

Intro

You can think of an equation as a balanced scale. When you do something to one side of an equation, you must do the same thing to the other side to keep it balanced.

Example Solving Addition Equations

Solve the equation.

$$3 + x = 11$$

continued on next page >

Part 1

Example continued

Solution

Method 1 Use a pan balance.

To get x by itself, first remove three 1–tiles from the left side of the pan balance. Then remove the same number of 1–tiles from the right side.

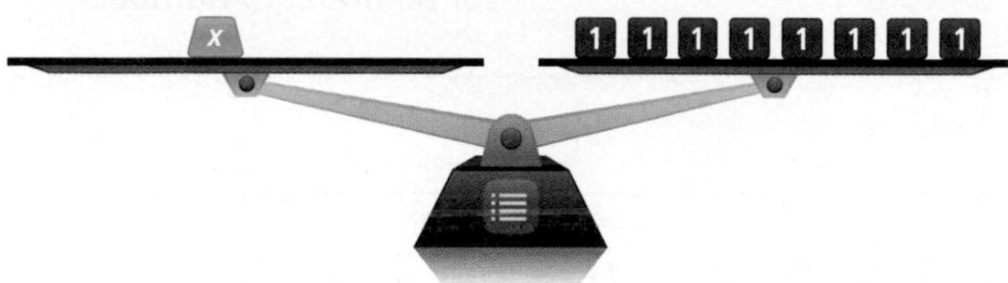

The solution is $x = 8$.

Method 2 Write an equivalent equation.

$$3 + x = 11$$

$$3 + x - 3 = 11 - 3$$

Undo addition using the Subtraction Property of Equality.

$$x + 3 - 3 = 11 - 3$$

$$x = 8$$

Check

$$3 + 8 \stackrel{?}{=} 11$$

$$11 = 11 \checkmark$$

Key Concept

Multiplication Property of Equality If you multiply each side of an equation by the same number, the two sides remain equal.

Arithmetic	Algebra
$\frac{10}{2} = 5$	If $a = b$, then
$\frac{10}{2} \cdot 4 = 5 \cdot 4$	$a \cdot c = b \cdot c$
$20 = 20$	for all numbers a, b, and c.

Division Property of Equality If you divide each side of an equation by the same nonzero number, the two sides remain equal.

Arithmetic	Algebra
$12 = 4(3)$	If $a = b$, then
$12 \div (-2) = 4(3) \div (-2)$	$a \div c = b \div c$
$-6 = -6$	for all nonzero numbers c.

Part 2

Example Solving Multiplication and Division Equations

Solve each equation. Check your answers.

a. $\frac{d}{-5} = 7.2$ **b.** $-2p = 1$

Solution

a. Write the original equation. $\frac{d}{-5} = 7.2$

Undo division using the Multiplication Property of Equality. $-5 \cdot \frac{d}{-5} = -5 \cdot 7.2$

Simplify. $d = -36$

b. Write the original equation. $-2p = 1$

Undo multiplication using the Division Property of Equality. $\frac{-2p}{-2} = \frac{1}{-2}$

Simplify. $p = -\frac{1}{2}$

Check

a. $\frac{d}{-5} = 7.2$

$\frac{-36}{-5} \stackrel{?}{=} 7.2$ Substitute -36 for d in the original equation to check the answer.

$7.2 = 7.2$ ✓

b. $-2p = 1$

$-2\left(-\frac{1}{2}\right) \stackrel{?}{=} 1$ Substitute $-\frac{1}{2}$ for p in the original equation to check the answer.

$1 = 1$ ✓

Part 3

Example Solving One-Step Equations

Three of the four equations have the same solution. Find the one equation that has a different solution.

a.

$$12n = 60$$
$$n - 3\tfrac{3}{4} = 1\tfrac{1}{4}$$
$$\frac{n}{1.25} = 4$$
$$n + 15 = 10$$

b.

$$\frac{3}{4} = w + \frac{1}{2}$$
$$3.5 = 14w$$
$$w - 0.75 = -1$$
$$5w = 1\tfrac{1}{4}$$

Solution

a.

$$12n = 60$$
$$\frac{12n}{12} = \frac{60}{12}$$
$$n = 5$$

Undo multiplication by dividing each side by 12.

$$n - 3\tfrac{3}{4} = 1\tfrac{1}{4}$$
$$n - 3\tfrac{3}{4} + 3\tfrac{3}{4} = 1\tfrac{1}{4} + 3\tfrac{3}{4}$$
$$n = 5$$

Undo subtraction by adding $3\frac{3}{4}$ to each side.

$$\frac{n}{1.25} = 4$$
$$1.25 \cdot \frac{n}{1.25} = 1.25 \cdot 4$$
$$n = 5$$

Undo division by multiplying each side by 1.25.

$$n + 15 = 10$$
$$n + 15 - 15 = 10 - 15$$
$$n = -5$$

Undo addition by subtracting 15 from each side.

The fourth equation is the one that is different. It is the only equation with a solution of $n = -5$.

b.

$$\frac{3}{4} = w + \frac{1}{2}$$
$$\frac{3}{4} - \frac{1}{2} = w + \frac{1}{2} - \frac{1}{2}$$
$$\frac{1}{4} = w$$

Undo addition by subtracting $\frac{1}{2}$ from each side.

$\frac{1}{4} = 0.25$

$$w - 0.75 = -1$$
$$w - 0.75 + 0.75 = -1 + 0.75$$
$$w = -0.25$$

Undo subtraction by adding 0.75 to each side.

$$3.5 = 14w$$
$$\frac{3.5}{14} = \frac{14w}{14}$$
$$0.25 = w$$

Undo multiplication by dividing each side by 14.

$$5w = 1\tfrac{1}{4}$$
$$5w = \frac{5}{4}$$
$$\frac{5w}{5} = \frac{5}{4} \div 5$$
$$\frac{5w}{5} = \frac{5}{4} \cdot \frac{1}{5}$$
$$\frac{5w}{5} = \frac{{}^{1}\cancel{5}}{4} \cdot \frac{1}{\cancel{5}_{1}}$$
$$w = \frac{1}{4}$$

Undo multiplication by dividing each side by 5.

Multiply by the reciprocal to divide.

The third equation is the one that is different. It is the only equation with a solution of $w = -0.25$.

See your complete lesson at MyMathUniverse.com

Digital Resources

1. Solve the equation $z + 18 = 27$.
2. Solve the equation $n - 19 = 13$.
3. Solve the equation $3x = 15$. Check your answer.
4. Solve the equation $\frac{x}{9} = 6$. Check your answer.
5. Select the three equations that have the same solution.
   A. $y + 3 = 4$
   B. $\frac{y}{1.75} = 4$
   C. $5y = 35$
   D. $22 + y = 29$
6. Which equation has the same solution as $6.5n = 45.5$?
   A. $4.97 + n = 11.97$
   B. $\frac{3}{4}n = 5\frac{1}{4}$
   C. Both A and B
   D. Neither A nor B
7. **a. Writing** Solve the equation $5 + y = 9$.
   b. Describe the properties you used to solve the equation.
   c. Write two more equations that you can solve using these same properties and solve them.
8. **a. Reasoning** Solve the equation $8x = -16$ and check your answer.
   b. Is it possible to solve the equation using multiplication? Explain your reasoning.
9. **Error Analysis** A teacher asked her students to solve the equation $t - 11 = 25$. One student incorrectly said that the solution is 14.
   a. What is the correct solution?
   b. What mistake might the student have made?
   A. The student applied the Addition Property of Equality instead of the Subtraction Property of Equality.
   B. The student applied the Subtraction Property of Equality instead of the Addition Property of Equality.
   C. The student applied the Multiplication Property of Equality instead of the Division Property of Equality.
   D. The student applied the Division Property of Equality instead of the Multiplication Property of Equality.
10. **Think About the Process**
    a. Which property of equality should you use to solve the equation for x?
    $$-3x = 21$$
    A. The Division Property of Equality
    B. The Subtraction Property of Equality
    C. The Addition Property of Equality
    D. The Multiplication Property of Equality
    b. The solution is ■.
11. **School Supplies** Matt bought notebooks at the store for \$1.07 each. He spent \$3.21 on the notebooks. Let x represent the number of notebooks Matt bought. Use the equation $1.07x = 3.21$ to find the number of notebooks he bought.
12. **a. Estimation** Estimate the solution to the equation $z - 5\frac{4}{5} = 6\frac{1}{9}$ by rounding each mixed number to the nearest whole number.
    b. Find the exact solution.
13. Solve and check the equation $x + 2\frac{2}{5} = 6$.

14. **Think About the Process**

a. What is the first step to solve the equation for x?

$$\frac{2}{11}x = 14$$

A. Multiply each side of the equation by the reciprocal of $\frac{2}{11}$.

B. Multiply each side of the equation by $\frac{2}{11}$.

C. Subtract $\frac{2}{11}$ from each side of the equation.

D. Add $\frac{2}{11}$ to each side of the equation.

b. The solution is ■.

15. Solve the equation $\frac{4}{7}x = \frac{12}{35}$.

16. Which of the following equations have the same solution? Select all that apply.

A. $w - 1\frac{1}{6} = 4\frac{5}{6}$

B. $23\frac{7}{9} + w = 17\frac{7}{9}$

C. $\frac{1}{4}w = 1\frac{1}{2}$

D. $\frac{w}{1.2} = 5$

17. **a.** Solve the equation $6.5z = -117$.

b. Which equation has the same solution?

A. $\frac{3}{4}z = -13\frac{1}{2}$

B. $11.16 + z = 29.16$

C. $\frac{z}{2} = -\frac{1}{36}$

18. **Challenge** Which equations have the same solution? Select all that apply.

A. $w - 4.95 = 2.30$

B. $15w = 103.75 + 5$

C. $25.4 + w = 23.25 + 9.4$

D. $\frac{w}{-0.25} = 14.5 + 14.5$

19. **a. Challenge** Solve the equation $0.14w = 0.70$ for w.

b. Which of these equations has the same solution?

A. $w - 12.76 = 7.76$

B. $w - 7.76 = 12.76$

C. $w + 12.76 = 7.76$

D. $w + 7.76 = 12.76$

20. **Think About the Process**

a. Which property of equality should you use to solve the equation for x?

$-9x = 45$

A. The Multiplication Property of Equality

B. The Addition Property of Equality

C. The Division Property of Equality

D. The Subtraction Property of Equality

b. The solution is ■.

21. **School Supplies** Jenny bought notebooks at the store for \$1.35 each. She spent \$8.10 on the notebooks. Let x represent the number of notebooks Jenny bought. Use the equation $1.35x = 8.10$ to find the number of notebooks she bought.

8-2 Writing Two-Step Equations

CCSS: 7.EE.B.4, Also 7.EE.B.4a

Part 1

Example Writing One-Step Equations

The length of an average toucan is about two thirds the length of an average blue-and-yellow macaw. Toucans are about 24 in. long. Write an equation to represent this situation.

Solution

Words length of toucan = $\frac{2}{3}$ of length of blue-and-yellow macaw

to

Let ℓ = the length of an average blue-and-yellow macaw.

Equation $24 = \frac{2}{3} \cdot \ell$

The equation $24 = \frac{2}{3} \cdot \ell$ represents this situation.

Part 2

Intro

A **two-step equation** is an equation that has two operations. Many real-world problems need more than one operation to describe the situation. Consider the photographer's situation.

A photography student wants to buy a digital camera that costs $269.95. She plans to make a down payment of $100 and pay the remainder in five equal monthly payments. Write an equation to represent this situation.

Given information:

- The cost of the camera: $269.95
- The amount of the down payment: $100
- The number of monthly payments: five

continued on next page >

Part 2

Intro continued

Words	cost	=	down payment	+	number of payments	•	amount of each payment

to

Let p = the amount of each payment.

Equation	269.95	=	100	+	5	•	p

The equation $269.95 = 100 + 5p$ represents this situation.

Example Writing Two-Step Equations

An orange grower ships oranges in boxes that weight 10 kg each. Each orange weighs 0.2 kg. The total weight of a box filled with oranges is 50 kg. Write an equation that you could use to find the number of oranges in each box.

Solution

Words	total weight	=	weight of box	+	weight of one orange	•	number of oranges

to

Let n = the number of oranges packed in each box.

Equation	50	=	10	+	0.2	•	n

The equation $50 = 10 + 0.2n$ represents this situation.

Part 3

Example Translating Words to Two-Step Equations

Match each equation to the situation it represents.

$2x - 17 = 7$ $\quad$ $2x - 7 = 17$ $\quad$ $2x + 17 = 7$ $\quad$ $2x + 7 = 17$

a. Seven more than twice a number is 17.
b. The product of 2 and a number increased by 17 is 7.
c. The difference between twice a number and 7 is 17.
d. Seventeen less than twice a number is 7.

continued on next page >

Part 3

Example continued

Solution

a.

Words	Seven	more than	twice a number	is 17.
to	Let x = the number.			
Equation	7	$+$	$2x$	$=$ 17

b.

Words	The	product of 2 and a number	increased by	17	is 7.
to	Let x = the number.				
Equation		$2x$	$+$	17	$=$ 7

c.

Words	The	difference	between	twice a number	and 7 is 17.
to	Let x = the number.				
Equation		$2x$	$-$		7 $=$ 17

d.

Words	Seventeen	less than	twice a number	is 7.
to	Let x = the number.			
Equation	$2x$	$-$	17	$=$ 7

Digital Resources 

1. Last night, 4 friends went out to dinner at a restaurant. They split the bill evenly. Each friend paid \$12.75. If *B* represents the total bill in dollars, what equation could you use to find the value of *B*?
   A. $B + 4 = 12.75$
   B. $4B = 12.75$
   C. $\frac{B}{4} = 12.75$
   D. $B - 4 = 12.75$

2. A farmer ships oranges in crates that weigh 6.1 lb each when empty. Each orange weighs 0.38 lb. The total weight of a crate filled with oranges is 63.1 lb. Write a word equation you could use to find the number of oranges packed in each crate.
   A. total weight = weight of crate + (weight of one orange) × (number of oranges)
   B. total weight = weight of crate + weight of one orange + number of oranges
   C. total weight = (weight of crate) × (weight of one orange) + number of oranges
   D. total weight = weight of crate − (weight of one orange) × (number of oranges)
   E. total weight = (weight of crate) × (weight of one orange) × (number of oranges)

3. At a graduation dinner, an equal number of guests were seated at each of 3 large tables, and 7 late-arriving guests were seated at a smaller table. There were 37 guests in all. If *n* represents the number of people seated at each of the large tables, what equation could you use to find the value of *n*?
   A. $3n - 7 = 37$
   B. $3n + 7 = 37$
   C. $7n + 3 = 37$
   D. $7n - 3 = 37$

4. Which answer shows the equation $7x - 18 = 17$ in words?
   A. Eighteen less than seven times a number is 17.
   B. Seven less than eighteen times a number is 17.
   C. Seven more than eighteen times a number is 17.
   D. Eighteen more than seven times a number is 17.

5. **Open-Ended**
   a. Write an equation to represent the following description.
   Fourteen more than three times a number is 12.
   A. $14x - 3 = 12$
   B. $3(x + 14) = 12$
   C. $3x + 14 = 12$
   D. $3x - 14 = 12$
   E. $14x + 3 = 12$
   b. Describe a real-world situation the equation could represent.

6. **a. Writing** You want to buy a pet iguana that costs \$48. You already have \$12 and you plan to save \$9 per week. If *w* represents the number of weeks until you have enough money to buy the iguana, what equation could you use to find the value of *w*?
   A. $9 - 12w = 48$
   B. $12w - 9 = 48$
   C. $9w + 12 = 48$
   D. $12 - 9w = 48$
   E. $9w - 12 = 48$
   F. $12w + 9 = 48$
   b. Explain how you could set up an equation to find the amount of money you should save each week if you want to buy the iguana in six weeks.

7. Banner One of the banners in a parade is one-third as tall as it is long. It is 5 feet tall. If L represents the length of the banner in feet, what equation could you use to find the value of L?

A. $\frac{1}{3} = 5L$ **B.** $5 = \frac{1}{3}L$

C. $5 = L \div \frac{1}{3}$ **D.** $L = 5 \cdot \frac{1}{3}$

8. Estimation A rectangle has length $3\frac{7}{8}$ inches and area $6\frac{15}{16}$ square inches. Round these measurements to the nearest integer. Let w represent the width of the rectangle in inches. Which of these equations correctly relates the rectangle's length and width to its area?

A. $4w = 6$ **B.** $4w = 7$

C. $w + 4 = 7$ **D.** $\frac{4}{w} = 7$

9. Last night, Mike bought four DVDs online. Each DVD cost the same amount. With a \$5.98 shipping charge included, the total cost came to \$79.94. Write a word equation you could use to find the cost of each DVD.

A. cost of one DVD = $\frac{\text{total cost} - \text{shipping charge}}{\text{number of DVDs}}$

B. cost of one DVD = $\frac{\text{total cost} + \text{shipping charge}}{\text{number of DVDs}}$

C. cost of one DVD = $\frac{\text{shipping charge} - \text{total cost}}{\text{number of DVDs}}$

D. cost of one DVD = (total cost + shipping charge) · (number of DVDs)

E. cost of one DVD = (total cost − shipping charge) · (number of DVDs)

10. Think About the Process A jar contains only pennies, nickels, dimes, and quarters. There are 15 pennies, 27 dimes, and 13 quarters. The rest of the coins are nickels. There are 67 coins in all.

a. How many of the coins are not nickels?

b. If n represents the number of nickels in the jar, what equation could you use to find n?

A. $n + 55 = 67$

B. $n - 54 = 67$

C. $n + 52 = 67$

D. $n + 54 = 67$

E. $n + 40 = 67$

F. $n - 52 = 67$

11. Think About the Process

a. Which of these word phrases represents the expression $19x$?

A. Nineteen times a number

B. Nineteen more than a number

C. Nineteen less than a number

D. Nineteen divided by a number

b. Which of these descriptions does the equation $19x + 5 = 9$ represent?

A. If nineteen more than a number is decreased by five, the result is 9.

B. If five is added to nineteen times a number, the result is 9.

C. If nineteen less than a number is increased by five, the result is 9.

D. If nineteen divided by a number is added to five, the result is 9.

12. Challenge If you decrease three times a number by six, you get 6.

a. Which equation represents the description?

A. $6x + 3 = 6$

B. $6x - 3 = 6$

C. $3(x - 6) = 6$

D. $3x + 6 = 6$

E. $3x - 6 = 6$

b. Is 4 a solution to the equation?

c. Show how to apply the same operation to each side of the equation to get an equivalent equation that has only one operation.

8-3 Solving Two-Step Equations

CCSS: 7.EE.B.3, 7.EE.B.4a, Also 7.EE.B.4

Part 1

Example Using Models to Solve Two-Step Equations

Write the modeled equation.
Then solve it.

Solution

Step 1 Represent the equation in algebra tiles.
$3x + 2 = 11$

Step 2 Add two -1 tiles to each side.

Step 3 On each side, the -1 and $+1$ tiles make two groups of zero pairs.

Step 4 Remove the zero pairs so there are three x tiles on the left and nine $+1$ tiles on the right.

continued on next page >

Part 2

Solution continued

Step 5 Each x tile is equal to three $+1$ tiles.

$x = 3$

Check

Substitute the answer, $x = 3$, into the original equation.

$$3x + 2 = 11$$

$$3(3) + 2 \stackrel{?}{=} 11$$

$$9 + 2 \stackrel{?}{=} 11$$

$$11 = 11 \checkmark$$

Key Concept

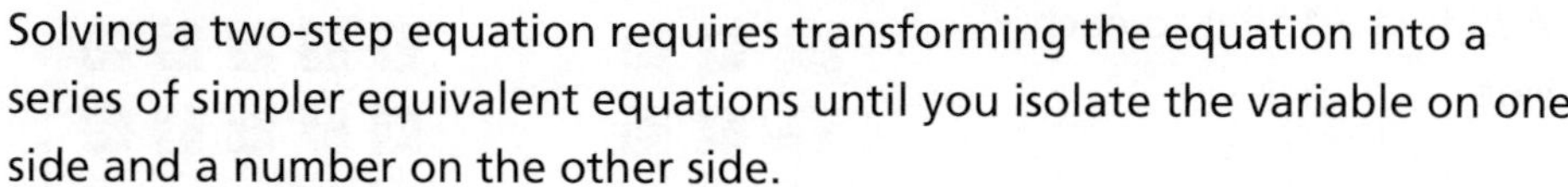

Solving a two-step equation requires transforming the equation into a series of simpler equivalent equations until you isolate the variable on one side and a number on the other side.

Step 1 Undo addition or subtraction. For many equations, you can undo addition or subtraction first.

Solve $\frac{x}{3} + 1.5 = 2.75$.

$$\frac{x}{3} + 1.5 = 2.75$$

$$\frac{x}{3} + 1.5 - 1.5 = 2.75 - 1.5$$

Undo addition by subtracting 1.5 from each side.

$$\frac{x}{3} = 1.25$$

continued on next page >

Key Concept

continued

Step 2 Undo multiplication or division. To isolate the variable, undo multiplication or division next. The coefficient of the variable should be 1.

Solve $\frac{x}{3} = 1.25$.

Undo division by multiplying each side by 3.

$$\frac{x}{3} = 1.25$$

$$(3)\left(\frac{x}{3}\right) = (3)(1.25)$$

$$x = 3.75$$

Step 3 Check your answer by substituting it into the original equation. Substitute 3.75 for x.

$$\frac{x}{3} + 1.5 = 2.75$$

$$\frac{3.75}{3} + 1.5 \stackrel{?}{=} 2.75$$

$$1.25 + 1.5 \stackrel{?}{=} 2.75$$

$$2.75 = 2.75 \checkmark$$

Part 2

Example Justifying Steps to Solve Two-Step Equations

Use the expressions below to write four steps for solving $5b - 3.75 = 26.25$.

6	$5b - 3.75 + 3.75$	$5b$	$\frac{30}{5}$
b	$\frac{5b}{5}$	30	$26.25 + 3.75$

Solution

$$5b - 3.75 = 26.25$$

$$5b - 3.75 + 3.75 = 26.25 + 3.75$$

$$5b = 30$$

$$\frac{5b}{5} = \frac{30}{5}$$

$$b = 6$$

Part 3

Example Writing and Solving Two-Step Equations

You are ordering concert tickets online. Each ticket costs \$39.95 and you have a processing fee of \$12.75. The total cost is \$212.50. Write and solve an equation to find the number of tickets ordered.

Solution

Words	total cost	=	cost per ticket	•	number of tickets	+	processing fee

to

Let n = the number of tickets ordered.

Equation	212.50	=	39.95	•	n	+	12.75

The equation is $212.50 = 39.84n + 12.75$.

Write the original equation. $212.5 = 39.95n + 12.75$

Undo addition using the Subtraction Property of Equality. $212.5 - 12.75 = 39.95n + 12.75 - 12.75$

Simplify. $199.75 = 39.95n$

Undo multiplication using the Division Property of Equality. $\frac{199.75}{39.95} = \frac{39.95n}{39.95}$

Simplify. $5 = n$

You ordered 5 tickets.

Digital Resources   

1. Use the algebra tiles to help you solve the equation $4x + 5 = 13$.

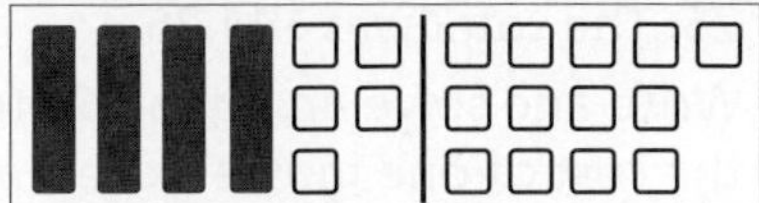

2. Use the algebra tiles to help you solve the equation $3x - 5 = 7$.

3. Complete the steps to solve the equation $6x + 16 = 58$.

a. Apply the Subtraction Property of Equality.

b. Apply the Division Property of Equality.

4. Complete the steps to solve the equation $-15x - 14 = -89$.

$-15x - 14 = -89$ Write the original equation.

$-15x = ■$ Apply the Addition Property of Equality.

$x = ■$ Apply the Division Property of Equality.

5. Solve the equation $7x - 7 = 56$.

6. When three times a number is decreased by 4, the result is 14.

a. Write an equation that you can use to find the number. Let n represent the number.

b. What is the number?

7. Multiple Representations Three times a number, added to 4, is 40.

a. Write an equation that you can use to find the number. Let n represent the number.

A. $4 - 3n = 40$

B. $3n - 4 = 40$

C. $4n + 3 = 40$

D. $4 + 3n = 40$

b. What is the number?

c. Draw a model of the equation.

8. In 2000, the number of federal hazardous waste sites in State X was 8 less than twice the number of sites in State Y. Suppose there were 34 such sites in State X. Write and solve an equation that represents the number of hazardous waste sites, n, there were in State Y.

9. a. Writing Solve the equation $3x + 2 = 17$ using algebra tiles.

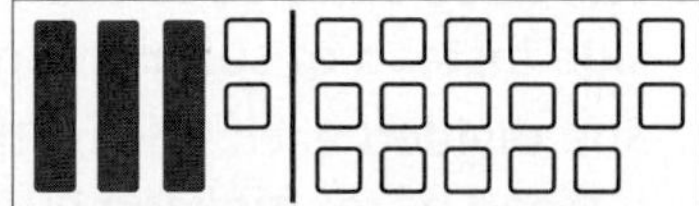

b. Describe a real world situation that could be modeled with the given equation and algebra tiles.

10. a. Reasoning Solve the equation $8x + 2 = 26$.

b. How is solving a two-step equation similar to solving a one-step equation?

11. Think About the Process Use the algebra tiles to help you solve the equation $4x - 12 = 16$.

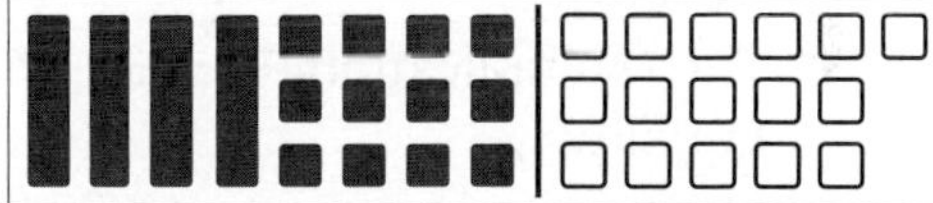

a. What is the first step in solving the equation using algebra tiles?

A. Divide each side of the model by 4.

B. Add 12 + 1 tiles to each side of the model.

C. Add 12 − 1 tiles from each side of the model.

D. Multiply each side of the model by 4.

b. The solution is ■.

12. Error Analysis A student solved the equation $2x + 4 = 10$ using algebra tiles. She incorrectly says the solution is 7.

a. Solve the equation.

b. What mistake might the student have made?

A. She multiplied each side by the 1's instead of dividing by them.

B. She added the 1's to the right side instead of subtracting them.

C. She divided each side by the 1's instead of multiplying by them.

D. She subtracted the 1's from the right side instead of adding them.

13. Think About the Process

a. What properties of equality do you need to use to solve the equation $4.9x - 1.9 = 27.5$? Select all that apply.

A. The Addition Property of Equality

B. The Subtraction Property of Equality

C. The Multiplication Property of Equality

D. The Division Property of Equality

b. The solution is ■.

14. Shopping While shopping for clothes, Tracy spent \$38 less than 3 times what Daniel spent. Tracy spent \$10. Write and solve an equation to find how much Daniel spent. Let x represent how much Daniel spent.

15. Mental Math Solve the equation $\frac{n}{10} + 7 = 10$.

16. a. Write the modeled equation.

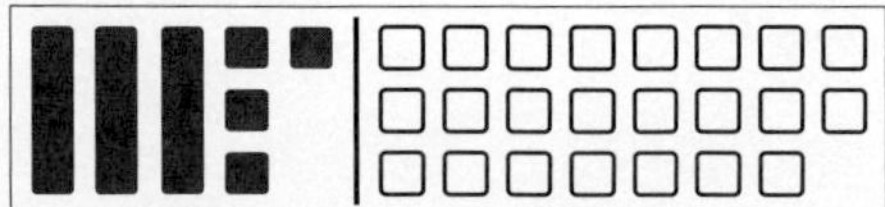

b. Use the algebra tiles to help you solve the equation.

17. Multiple Representations A group of 4 friends went to the movies. In addition to their tickets, they bought a large bag of popcorn to share for \$6.25. The total was \$44.25.

a. Write and solve an equation to find the cost of one movie ticket, m.

b. Draw a picture to model the equation.

18. Challenge A number n times 26, decreased by 126, is 238. A number m times 9, added to 112, is 265.

a. Choose an equation for n.

A. $26 - 126n = 238$

B. $26n - 126 = 238$

C. $126n - 26 = 238$

D. $126 - 26n = 238$

b. Solve the equation.

c. Choose an equation for m.

A. $112 - 9m = 265$

B. $112m + 9 = 265$

C. $112m - 9 = 265$

D. $112 + 9m = 265$

d. Solve the equation.

e. Compare n and m using a $<$, $>$, or $=$ symbol.

19. Challenge At a party, the number of people who ate meatballs was 11 less than $\frac{1}{3}$ of the total number of people. The number of people who ate meatballs was 5.

a. Write and solve an equation to find the number of people at the party. Let x represent the number of people at the party.

b. Write a one-step equation that has the same solution.

8-4 Solving Equations Using the Distributive Property

CCSS: 7.EE.B.3, 7.EE.B.4a, Also 7.EE.B.4

Part 1

Intro

You can use the Distributive Property to simplify the expressions $a(b + c)$ and $a(b - c)$, where a, b, and c are rational numbers.

$$a(b + c) = ab + ac \qquad a(b - c) = ab - ac$$

Some equations are easier to solve if you apply the Distributive Property first to simplify them.

Example Solving Two-Step Equations Using the Distributive Property

Solve the equation.

$$-8(x + 0.3) = 3.6$$

Solution

Method 1 Apply the Distributive Property first.

Write the original equation.	$-8(x + 0.3) = 3.6$
Apply the Distributive Property.	$(-8)(x) + (-8)(0.3) = 3.6$
Simplify.	$-8x - 2.4 = 3.6$
Add 2.4 to each side.	$-8x - 2.4 + 2.4 = 3.6 + 2.4$
Simplify.	$-8x = 6.0$
Divide each side by −8.	$\frac{-8x}{-8} = \frac{6.0}{-8}$
Simplify.	$x = -0.75$

Method 2 Undo multiplication first.

Write the original equation.	$-8(x + 0.3) = 3.6$
Divide each side by −8.	$\frac{-8(x + 0.3)}{-8} = \frac{3.6}{-8}$
Simplify.	$x + 0.3 = -0.45$
Subtract 0.3 from each side.	$x + 0.3 - 0.3 = -0.45 - 0.3$
Simplify.	$x = -0.75$

continued on next page >

Part 1

Solution continued

Check

Check your answer by substituting −0.75 for *x*.

$$-8(x + 0.3) = 3.6$$

$$-8(-0.75 + 0.3) \stackrel{?}{=} 3.6$$

$$-8(-0.45) \stackrel{?}{=} 3.6$$

$$3.6 = 3.6 \checkmark$$

Part 2

Intro

Analyzing an equation before you try to solve it is a good strategy. You can determine what operations you should use.

Example Identifying the Number of Steps Needed to Solve Equations

Group the equations based on whether the number of operations needed to solve them is one, two, or three.

$72 = m + 12$	$7(2x - 4) = 52$	$3a - \frac{1}{2} = 5\frac{1}{2}$
$18(9 + 4d) = 100$	$\frac{a}{2} = 10$	$6x + 13.9 = -10.1$

Solution

Needs One Operation

You need to use multiplication to solve $\frac{a}{2} = 10$.

You need to use subtraction to solve $72 = m + 12$.

Needs Two Operations

You need to use subtraction and division to solve $6x + 13.9 = -10.1$.

You need to use addition and division to solve $3a - \frac{1}{2} = 5\frac{1}{2}$.

Needs More than Two Operations

You need to apply the Distributive Property first, and then use subtraction and division to solve $18(9 + 4d) = 100$.

You need to apply the Distributive Property first, and then use addition and division to solve $7(2x - 4) = 52$.

Part 3

Example Writing and Solving Equations with Grouping Symbols

A family of six buys airline tickets online. Travel insurance costs $19 per ticket. The family is charged a total of $1,116. How much does one airline ticket cost if each airline ticket is the same price?

Solution

Know
- The number of tickets purchased
- The total cost

Need
An equation to represent the total cost of the tickets

Plan
- Define what the variable represents.
- Write an expression for the per ticket costs.
- Write and solve an equation to find the cost of one airline ticket.

Step 1 Define what the variable represents.

Let c = the cost of one airline ticket.

Step 2 Write an equation.

Words total cost = per ticket costs • number of tickets

Let c = the cost of one airline ticket.

Equation $1{,}116 = (c + 19) \cdot 6$

The equation $1{,}116 = 6(c + 19)$ represents this situation.

Step 3 Solve the equation.

$$1{,}116 = 6(c + 19)$$

$$1{,}116 = 6c + 114$$

$$1{,}116 - 114 = 6c + 114 - 114$$

Subtract 114 from each side to undo addition.

$$1{,}002 = 6c$$

$$\frac{1{,}002}{6} = \frac{6c}{6}$$

Divide each side by 6 to undo multiplication.

$$167 = c$$

One airline ticket costs $167.

8-4 Homework

1. Use the Distributive Property to solve the equation $-2(x + 5) = 4$.
2. Solve the equation $8(x - 4) = 16$ without using the Distributive Property.
3. A retired math teacher takes his niece shopping. He tells his niece that they can spend x dollars and $\frac{x}{19} = 3.3$. What operation does the niece need to use to find how much money they can spend?
   - **A.** Division
   - **B.** Subtraction
   - **C.** Addition
   - **D.** Multiplication
4. Which operations do you need to solve $3x - 8 = -2$?
5. Last season, a sports fan spent $5,248 to see her favorite team play 41 games. To see each game, the fan had to buy a ticket and pay $40 for parking. Let p represent the amount the fan paid for each ticket.
   - **a.** Which equation represents the total amount the fan paid?
     - **A.** $5{,}248 = 40p + 41$
     - **B.** $5{,}248 = 40(p + 41)$
     - **C.** $5{,}248 = 41p + 40$
     - **D.** $5{,}248 = 41(p + 40)$
   - **b.** A friend of the sports fan bought 5 tickets at the same price. How much did the friend spend?
6. **a. Writing** Which operation do you need to solve $\frac{x}{2.6} = 2$?
     - **A.** addition
     - **B.** multiplication
     - **C.** division
     - **D.** subtraction
   - **b.** Describe how you know which operation to use to solve any equation with one operation for the four basic operations.
7. **Reasoning** Kiera and Javier are grouping equations based on the number of operations needed to solve them. In order to solve the equation $-8(9 + x) = 111$, Kiera says that you need three operations. Javier says you need two operations. Their teacher says that they are both correct.
   - **a.** Which of the following would solve the equation in three operations?
     - **A.** First use the Distributive Property. Then use addition and division.
     - **B.** First use addition. Then use division and subtraction.
     - **C.** First use division. Then use addition and multiplication.
     - **D.** First use subtraction. Then use the Distributive Property and division.
     - **E.** First use the Distributive Property. Then use addition and multiplication.
   - **b.** Explain how you can use two operations to solve the equation. Which method do you prefer? Why?
8. What operations do you need to solve the equation $4(2x + 7) = 68$?
   - **a.** Which operation could you use first?
     - **A.** Addition
     - **B.** Subtraction
     - **C.** Division
   - **b.** What operation do you need to use next?
     - **A.** Addition
     - **B.** Subtraction
     - **C.** Multiplication
     - **D.** Division
   - **c.** What is the final operation you need to solve the equation?
     - **A.** Division
     - **B.** Subtraction
     - **C.** Multiplication
     - **D.** Addition

9. **Think About the Process** You are given the following equation.

$$6\left(\frac{d}{3} - 5\right) = 34$$

a. If you apply the Distributive Property first to solve the equation, what operation will you need to use last?

A. Division
B. Subtraction
C. Addition
D. Multiplication

b. If instead you divide first to solve the equation, what operation would you need to use last?

A. Division
B. Subtraction
C. Multiplication
D. Addition

10. **Error Analysis** The solution shown for the equation is incorrect.

$-3(6 - r) = 6$
$-18 - 3r = 6$
$-3r = 24$
$r = -8$

a. What is the correct solution?

b. What is the error?

A. The left side of the equation should be $-18 + 3r$ after distributing.
B. The right side of the equation should be -12 after subtracting -18 from each side.
C. The left side of the equation should be $-r$ after dividing each side by -3.
D. The right side of the equation should be 8 after dividing each side by -3.

11. **Sales** Fadil sells televisions. He earns a fixed amount for each television and an additional \$15 if the buyer gets an extended warranty. If Fadil sells 12 televisions with extended warranties, he earns \$900. How much is the fixed amount Fadil earns for each television?

12. **a. Multiple Representations** Use the Distributive Property to solve the equation $95.4 = 9(m + 2.2)$.

b. Draw a picture that represents the equation and shows the solution.

13. Use the Distributive Property to solve the equation $3.2 = \frac{4}{5}(b - 5)$.

14. **Think About the Process** Brianna buys hats for x dollars each. She then sells the hats for \$2.65 more than x. Brianna sells 39 hats for \$571.35.

a. Which equation represents the total amount Brianna receives for selling 39 hats?

A. $571.35 = 39(x + 2.65)$
B. $571.35 = 39x + 2.65$
C. $571.35 = 2.65x + 39$
D. $571.35 = 2.65(x + 39)$

b. What process should you use to solve this equation in three steps?

A. First apply the Distributive Property. Next subtract, and finally multiply.
B. First apply the Distributive Property. Next subtract, and finally divide.
C. First apply the Distributive Property. Next add, and finally divide.
D. First apply the Distributive Property. Next multiply, and finally subtract.

c. How much does Brianna pay for 51 hats?

15. Solve the equation $-9.2(x - 3.5) = 36.8$ without using the Distributive Property.

16. **Challenge** The ticket price for a concert at a historic music hall includes \$6.70 for the concert, \$4.20 for the program, and a hall restoration fee. The price for 19 tickets is \$223.25. How much is the restoration fee?

8-5 Problem Solving

Vocabulary
bar diagram, formula

CCSS: 6.NS.C.8, 6.G.A.3

Part 1

Intro

A bar diagram is a model that you can use to represent part-to-whole relationships. Consider the following situation:

A company has 5 samples to ship to a client. Each sample has the same weight. A box to ship them weighs 8 ounces before it is packed. The total weight of the shipment is 47 ounces.

You can make a bar diagram to represent this situation. Let g represent the weight of one sample.

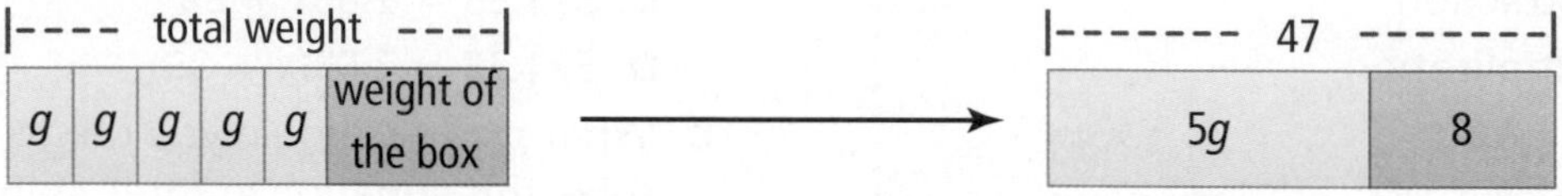

total weight					
g	g	g	g	g	weight of the box

→

47	
$5g$	8

total weight = weight of 5 samples + weight of the box

$47 = 5g + 8$

So you can represent this situation with the equation $5g + 8 = 47$.

Example Using Bar Diagrams for Two-Step Equations

You and your friend play online video games. You buy 1 software package and 3 months of game play. Your friend buys 1 software package and 2 months of game play. Each software package costs \$20. The total cost is \$115. Make a bar diagram to find the cost of one month of game play.

Solution

Let x = the cost of one month of game play.

115						
x	x	x	20	x	x	20

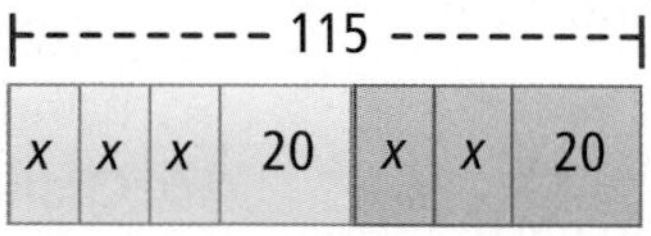

$$115 = 3x + 20 + 2x + 20$$
$$115 = 5x + 40$$

The equation is $115 = 5x + 40$.

continued on next page >

Part 1

Solution continued

$$115 = 5x + 40$$

$$115 - 40 = 5x + 40 - 40$$

Undo addition using the Subtraction Property of Equality.

$$75 = 5x$$

$$\frac{75}{5} = \frac{5x}{5}$$

Undo multiplication using the Division Property of Equality.

$$15 = x$$

The cost of one month of game play is $15.

Part 2

Intro

A formula is an equation that consists primarily of variables. Each variable in the equation represents an important part of the relationship expressed by the formula. Sometimes you need to rewrite or transform an equation to isolate a particular quantity to solve a problem.

The Celsius and Fahrenheit temperature scales are related by the formula $C = \frac{5}{9}(F - 32)$, where C represents degrees Celsius and F represents degrees Fahrenheit.

Solve the formula $C = \frac{5}{9}(F - 32)$ for F.

Write the original formula.	$C = \frac{5}{9}(F - 32)$
Multiply each side by $\frac{9}{5}$, the reciprocal of $\frac{5}{9}$.	$\frac{9}{5} \cdot C = \frac{9}{5} \cdot \frac{5}{9}(F - 32)$
Simplify.	$\frac{9}{5}C = F - 32$
Add 32 to each side.	$\frac{9}{5}C + 32 = F - 32 + 32$
Simplify.	$\frac{9}{5}C + 32 = F$

The new formula is $F = \frac{9}{5}C + 32$.

continued on next page >

Part 2

Example Solving the Distance Formula

The spacecraft *Magellan* space probe was launched on May 4, 1999. During its 463-day flight to Venus, it traveled about 806 million miles.

a. Solve the distance formula $d = rt$ for rate r.

b. Find *Magellan's* average speed in miles per hour. Round your answer to the nearest hundred.

Solution

a. Since you are looking for the speed, solve the distance equation for the rate r.

Write original equation.	$d = rt$
Divide each side by t.	$\frac{d}{t} = \frac{rt}{t}$
Simplify.	$\frac{d}{t} = r$

b. You are given the flight time in *days*, but you want to find the speed in miles per *hour*. Because there are 24 hours in each day, there are 463(24) hours in 463 days.

Time in hours, $t = 463(24)$ or 11,112 hours.

Substitute the given values into the new formulas.

$$r = \frac{d}{t}$$

$$= \frac{806{,}000{,}000}{11{,}112}$$

$$\approx 72{,}500$$

Magellan's average speed was about 72,500 miles per hour.

Part 3

Example Writing Problems for Equations

Write a baking problem that you can model with the equation $2\frac{1}{2}b = 3\frac{3}{4}$. Then solve the problem.

Solution

Sample answer: You make $2\frac{1}{2}$ batches of muffins and use $3\frac{3}{4}$ cups of flour.

How many cups of flour do you need for each batch?

continued on next page >

Part 3

Solution continued

Write the equation.	$2\frac{1}{2}b = 3\frac{3}{4}$
Write the mixed numbers as improper fractions.	$\frac{5}{2}b = \frac{15}{4}$
Multiply each side by $\frac{2}{5}$.	$\frac{2}{5} \cdot \frac{5}{2}b = \frac{2}{5} \cdot \frac{15}{4}$
Simplify.	$b = \frac{3}{2}$
Write as a mixed number.	$b = 1\frac{1}{2}$

You need $1\frac{1}{2}$ cups of flour per batch.

See your complete lesson at MyMathUniverse.com

Digital Resources

1. In a city, Building P is 405 feet taller than two times the height of Building Q. The height of Building P is 831 feet.

   a. Which diagram and equation represents the problem?

   A.

831	
q	405

$q + 405 = 831$

   B.

831		
q	q	405

$2q + 405 = 831$

   C.

405		
q	q	831

$2q + 831 = 405$

   b. What is the height of Building Q?

2. Find W if $A = LW$, $A = 12\text{ m}^2$, and $L = 4\text{ m}$.

3. a. Which situation could the equation $x + 11 = 47$ model?

   A. Susan has 47 dollars, 11 times as many as David.

   B. Michelle has 47 dollars, 11 more than Susan.

   C. David has 11 dollars, 47 dollars less than Rich.

   b. Solve for x and interpret your answer in the context of the correct situation.

4. **Reasoning** A traffic helicopter ascends 129 meters more than two times its original height. This is 879 meters above the ground. Let h be the original height of the helicopter.

   a. Write an addition equation to model the problem above.

   b. What was the original height h of the helicopter?

   c. Why would you use addition, instead of another operation, to model this situation?

5. Michelle says that you can use the equation $9 \times c = 981$ to find the number of calories burned jogging one mile if you burn 981 calories jogging 9 miles. Antoine says that you can use the given equation to find the total calories, c, burned if you jog 981 meters per minute for 9 minutes.

   a. Which friend is correct?

   A. Michelle is correct.

   B. Antoine is correct.

   C. Both Michelle and Antoine are correct.

   D. Neither Michelle nor Antoine is correct.

   b. What is the value of c?

   c. Interpret your solution in the context of the problem, and write several situations to which you could apply the equation.

6. How long will it take Kevin to drive 220 miles if he averages 40 miles per hour on the trip? Use the distance formula $d = rt$, where d represents distance, r represents rate, and t represents time, to find your answer.

7. The formula $A = LW$ represents the area of a rectangle.

   a. Solve the equation $\frac{7}{2}W = \frac{7}{8}$ for W to find the width of the rectangle in inches.

   b. Describe a situation when you could use this equation.

   c. What does the value of W represent in your problem?

8. **a.** Which question can you answer with the equation $2\frac{3}{4} = d \div 96$?

A. How many miles will an object travel in $2\frac{3}{4}$ hours if its speed is 96 miles per hour?

B. How many miles will an object travel in $2\frac{3}{4}$ hours if it has already gone 96 miles?

C. How long will it take an object to travel $2\frac{3}{4}$ miles if its speed is 96 miles per hour?

b. Solve for d and interpret your solution.

9. Substitute the values $A = 77$ mm^2, $b = 7$ mm, and $c = 4$ mm into the formula $A = \frac{1}{2}h(b + c)$ and solve for h.

10. A group of 5 friends each have x action figures in their collections. Each friend buys 11 more action figures. Now the 5 friends have a total of 120 action figures.

a. Which equation models the problem?

A. $5x + 11 = 120$

B. $11(x + 5) = 120$

C. $5(x + 11) = 120$

D. $x + 55 = 120$

b. Solve the equation. How many action figures did each friend start with?

11. **Think About the Process** Auditions for the next school play took place on Wednesday, Thursday, and Friday. Only 12 students can be in the play. Each day, t students tried out. The number of students who tried out but did not get a role is 60.

a. Which diagram and equation represent the problem?

A.

12	12	12

t	60

$3(12) + t = 60$

B.

t	t	t

12	60

$3t + 12 = 60$

C.

t	t	t

12	60

$3t - 12 = 60$

b. Solve the equation to find the number of students who tried out on Thursday.

12. **Think About the Process** The volume of the prism shown is 896 cm^3.

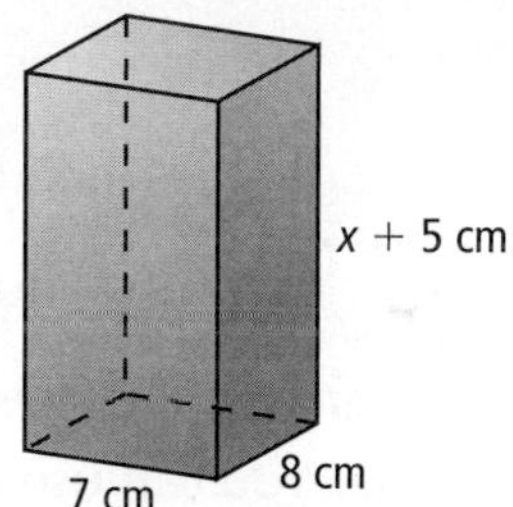

a. Write an equation for the volume V of the prism.

A. $V = 7 + 8 + x + 5$

B. $V = (7)(8)(x + 5)$

C. $V = (7)(7)(x + 5)$

D. $V = (7)(8)(x - 5)$

b. Solve the equation to find the value of x.

c. The height of the prism is ■ cm.

13. **Challenge** In 6 months, a shopkeeper spends $10,590 for rent, electricity, and water. Each month, he spends $1,500 for rent and $230 for electricity. How much does he spend for water each month?

a. Write an addition equation to model the problem.

b. Solve the equation.

9-1 Solving Inequalities Using Addition or Subtraction

CCSS: 6.NS.C.5, 6.NS.C.6a, Also 6.NS.C.6c

Vocabulary
Addition Property of Inequality, inequality, solution of an inequality, solution set, Subtraction Property of Inequality

Part 1

Intro

An **inequality** is a mathematical sentence that uses the $<$, $\leq$, $>$, $\geq$, or $\neq$ symbol to compare the values of two expressions. You will learn to recognize word phrases that indicate an inequality. For example, *is fewer than* indicates the symbol $<$.

Symbol	Meaning
$<$	less than
$\leq$	less than or equal to
$>$	greater than
$\geq$	greater than or equal to
$\neq$	not equal to

A **solution of an inequality** is any value of the variable that makes the inequality true. You can use a number line graph to indicate all of the solutions of an inequality with one variable.

The solutions of the inequality $x < 3$ are all numbers less than 3.

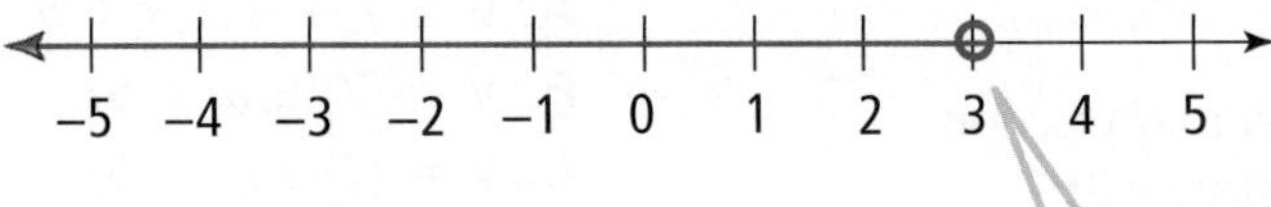

The open dot shows that 3 is *not* a solution.

The solutions of the inequality $x \leq 3$ are all numbers less than 3 or equal to 3.

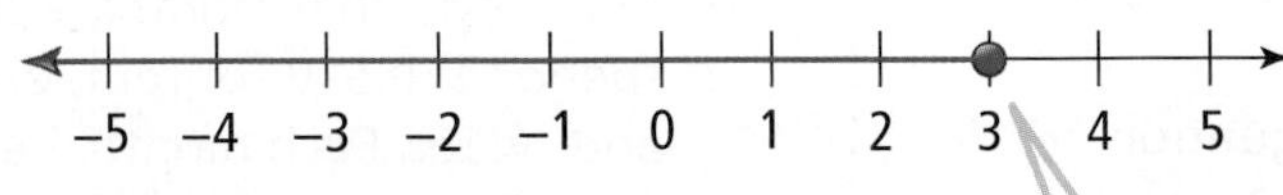

The closed dot shows that 3 *is* a solution.

See your complete lesson at MyMathUniverse.com

Part 1

Example Understanding Solutions to Inequalities

Three of the statements have the same solution. Find the one statement that has a different solution.

Round 1

- A number n is no more than 25.
- A number n is at most 25.
- You will work fewer than 25 hours this week.
- n is a legal speed to travel in a 25 mph zone.

Round 2

- The cost for Internet starts at $30 per month.
- You traveled more than 30 miles yesterday.
- 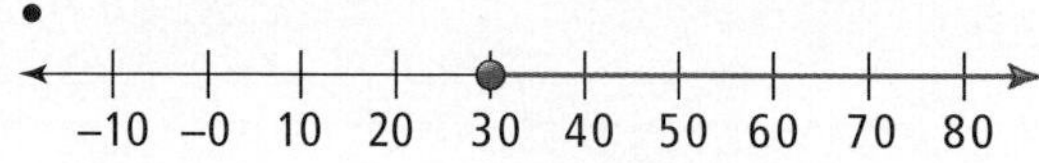

- A number n is at least 30.

Solution

Round 1

Statement	Reasoning	Inequality
A number n is no more than 25.	*No more than 25* indicates a number is not greater than 25. The number is less than or equal to 25.	$n \leq 25$
A number n is at most 25.	*At most 25* indicates that 25 is the greatest a number can be. The number is less than or equal to 25.	$n \leq 25$
You will work fewer than 25 hours this week.	*Fewer than 25* indicates a number is less than and not equal to 25.	$n < 25$
n is a legal speed to travel in a 25 mph zone.	A person can travel up to and including 25 mph in a 25 mph zone. Any speed over 25 mph is against the law.	$n \leq 25$

The statement *You will work fewer than 25 hours this week* is not like the others. The inequality that represents this statement is $n < 25$. The inequality that represents the other three statements is $n \leq 25$.

continued on next page >

Part 1

Solution continued

Round 2

Statement	Reasoning	Inequality
The cost for Internet service starts at $30 per month.	*Starts at $30* indicates that the cost can be equal to or greater than $30.	$n \geq 30$
You traveled more than 30 miles yesterday.	*More than 30* indicates that you traveled some number of miles greater than 30. 30 itself is not a solution.	$n > 30$
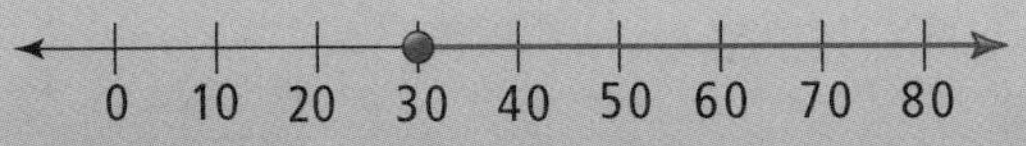	The closed dot at 30 with shading to the right indicates that any number greater than 30, and 30 itself, is a solution.	$n \geq 30$
A number n is at least 30.	*At least 30* indicates that 30 is the least a number can be. The number can be equal to 30 or any number greater than 30.	$n \geq 30$

The statement *You traveled more than 30 miles yesterday* is not like the others. The inequality that represents this statement is $n > 30$. The inequality that represents the other three statements is $n \geq 30$.

Key Concept

Addition Property of Inequality

If you add the same number to each side of an inequality, the relationship between the two sides does not change.

If $a < b$, then $a + c < b + c$ for all numbers a, b, and c.

$a < b$, so $a + c < b + c$

For example, let $a = 3$, $b = 7$, and $c = 2$.

$3 < 7$, so $3 + 2 < 7 + 2$

A number line can help show these relationships.

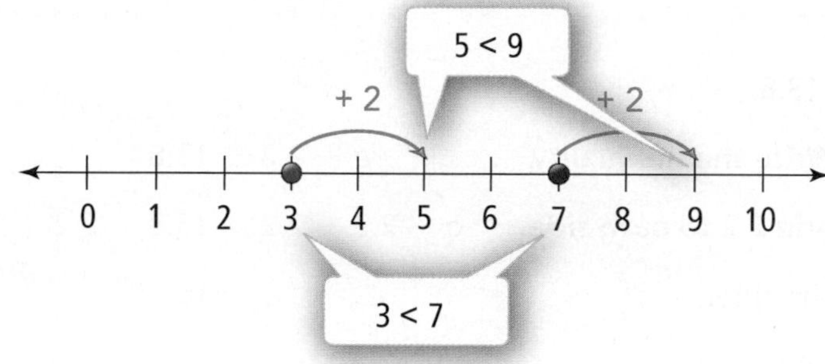

Similarly, if $a > b$, then $a + c > b + c$ for all numbers a, b, and c.

This property is also true for $\leq$ and $\geq$.

Subtraction Property of Inequality

If you subtract the same number from each side of an inequality, the relationship between the two sides does not change.

If $a < b$, then $a - c < b - c$ for all numbers a, b, and c.

$a < b$, so $a - c < b - c$

For example, let $a = 6$, $b = 10$, and $c = 9$.

$6 < 10$, so $6 - 9 < 10 - 9$

A number line can help show these relationships.

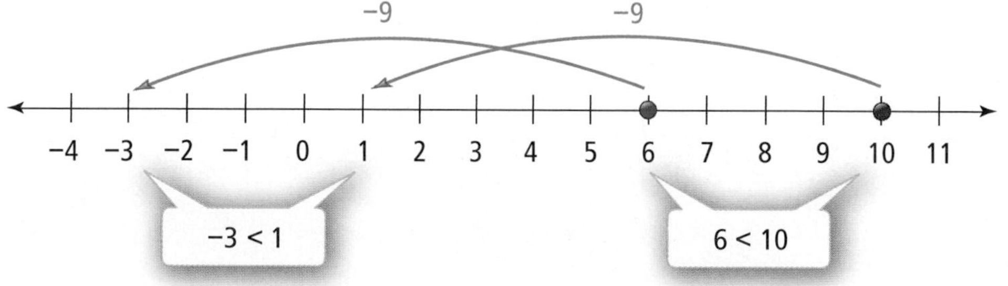

Similarly, if $a > b$, then $a - c > b - c$ for all numbers a, b, and c.

This property is also true for $\leq$ and $\geq$.

Part 2

Intro

To solve an inequality, use the properties of inequality to isolate the variable with a coefficient of 1 on one side of the inequality symbol. Then graph the solution on a number line to model the **solution set**, which contains all of the numbers that satisfy the inequality.

Example Solving Subtraction Inequalities

Solve $q - 2.2 > 13.8$. Graph the solutions.

Solution

Solve $q - 2.2 > 13.8$.

Write the inequality.	$q - 2.2 > 13.8$
Add 2.2 to each side.	$q - 2.2 + 2.2 > 13.8 + 2.2$
Simplify.	$q > 16$

Then graph the solutions.

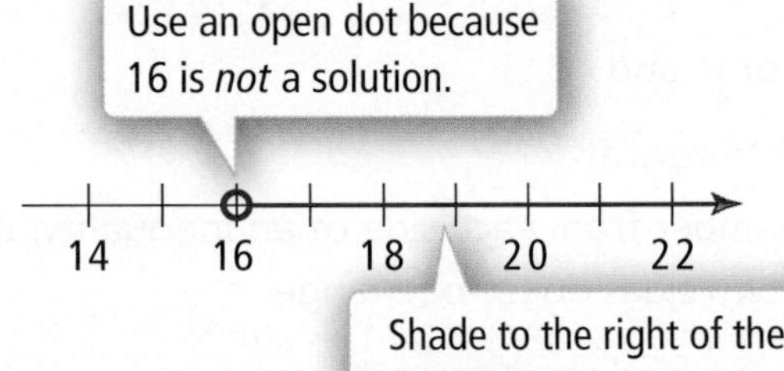

The number line shows that all numbers to the right of 16 are solutions of the inequality $q - 2.2 > 13.8$.

Part 3

Intro

When you solve an equation, you substitute your answer into the original equation to check your work.

When you solve an inequality, it is equally important to check your answer. However, inequalities often have an infinite number of solutions, so it's impossible to check each one.

Suppose you solve the inequality $s - 4\frac{1}{2} \geq 2\frac{1}{2}$ and get the solution $s \geq 7$.

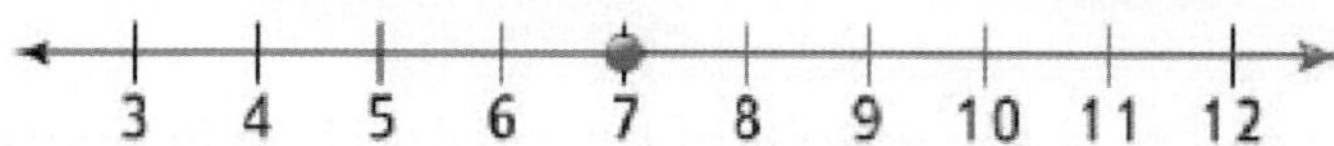

To check that $s \geq 7$is correct, first check that 7 is the solution of the related equation.

Then check the direction of the inequality symbol.

Step 1 Check the related equation.

Write the related equation. $s - 4\frac{1}{2} = 2\frac{1}{2}$

Substitute 7 for *s* in the related equation. $7 - 4\frac{1}{2} \stackrel{?}{=} 2\frac{1}{2}$

Simplify. $2\frac{1}{2} = 2\frac{1}{2}$ ✔

Step 2 Check the direction of the inequality $s \geq 7$.

To do this, choose a number that is greater than 7 and substitute it in the original inequality.

$s - 4\frac{1}{2} \geq 2\frac{1}{2}$

Substitute 10 for *s* in the original inequality. $10 - 4\frac{1}{2} \stackrel{?}{\geq} 2\frac{1}{2}$

Simplify. $5\frac{1}{2} \geq 2\frac{1}{2}$ ✔

Since both steps of the check are true, $s \geq 7$ is the solution of the inequality $s - 4\frac{1}{2} \geq 2\frac{1}{2}$.

Part 3

Example Solving Addition Inequalities

An airline restricts checked baggage to 80 lb per person. You pack one 42-lb bag. How much can your second bag weigh? Write and solve an inequality. Check your answer.

Solution

Words	weight of first bag	plus	weight of second bag	restricted to	80 lb

Let s = the weight of the second bag in pounds.

Inequality	42	+	s	$\leq$	80

$$42 + s \leq 80$$

$$42 - 42 + s \leq 80 - 42$$ Subtract 42 from each side.

$$s \leq 38$$

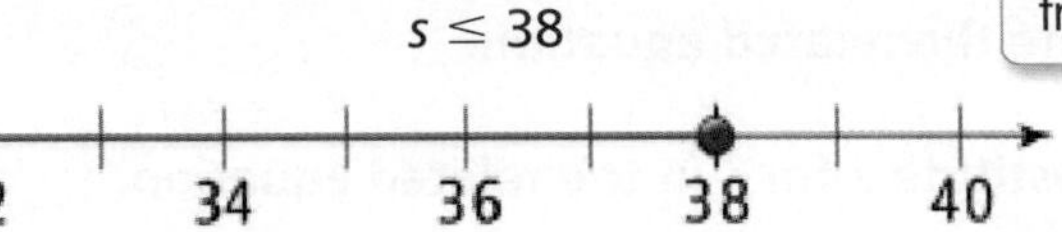

Check your answer.

Step 1 Check the related equation.

Write the related equation. $42 + s = 80$

Substitute 38 into the related equation. $42 + 38 \stackrel{?}{=} 80$

$80 = 80$ ✓

Step 2 Check the direction of the inequality.

$42 + s \leq 80$

Substitute 20 into the original inequality. $42 + 20 \stackrel{?}{\leq} 80$

$62 \leq 80$ ✓

You can substitute any number less than 38, such as 20.

So, $s \leq 38$ is the solution. Your second bag must weigh 38 lb or less.

9-1 | Homework

Digital Resources   

1. The number x is less than 78. Determine the inequality symbol needed for the situation.

2. A law clerk has earned more than \$20,000 since being hired. Define a variable and write an inequality to model the situation.

3. At school, the maximum number of students that can be in a classroom is 26. If there are 16 students signed up for the art class, how many more students can join the class?

4. Writing The number of flowers that will be planted in the yard will be fewer than 21.

a. Write an inequality for the situation.

b. Write other phrases that would also represent the inequality symbol from the situation.

5. Reasoning The number x is at most 25.

a. What is the appropriate inequality symbol for the situation?

b. When should you use a symbol that allows equality? Explain.

c. When should you use a symbol that does not allow equality? Explain.

6. Think About the Process Solve the inequality $x - 3 > 11$.

a. What are the solutions? Fill in the answer line to complete your choice.

A. $x \leq$ ■

B. $x <$ ■

C. $x >$ ■

D. $x \geq$ ■

b. How should the graph look?

A. The graph should have an open circle and the line should be shaded to the right.

B. The graph should have a closed circle and the line should be shaded to the left.

C. The graph should have an open circle and the line should be shaded to the left.

D. The graph should have a closed circle and the line should be shaded to the right.

c. Choose the correct graph below.

A. 14
0 5 10 15 20 25

B. 8
0 5 10 15 20 25

C. 14
0 5 10 15 20 25

D. 14
0 5 10 15 20 25

E. 11
0 5 10 15 20 25

F. 14
0 5 10 15 20 25

G. 8
0 5 10 15 20 25

H. 11
0 5 10 15 20 25

7. Think About the Process A number, x, plus 30 is greater than 46.

a. Which inequality represents this situation?

A. $x + 46 < 30$

B. $x + 30 < 46$

C. $x + 30 > 46$

D. $x + 46 > 30$

b. What are the solutions? Fill in the answer line to complete your choice.

A. $x \geq$ ■

B. $x <$ ■

C. $x >$ ■

D. $x \leq$ ■

8. Estimation There is a water tank behind a school. The school uses $5\frac{9}{10}$ gallons from the tank. There are more than $12\frac{4}{5}$ gallons left in the tank. Estimate the number of gallons in the tank before the school used the $5\frac{9}{10}$ gallons, and then find the exact solutions.

a. Which of the following is the best estimate for how many gallons were in the tank? Fill in the answer line to complete your choice.

A. There were more than ■ gallons in the water tank.

B. There were approximately ■ gallons in the water tank.

C. There were less than ■ gallons in the water tank.

b. What are the solutions? Fill in the answer line to complete your choice.

A. There were more than ■ gallons in the water tank.

B. There were less than ■ gallons in the water tank.

C. There were exactly ■ gallons in the water tank.

9. a. Challenge Find the solutions for the inequality $x + 29.4 \leq 54.5$.

b. Which graph shows the correct solutions?

A. 54.5
0 10 20 30 40 50 60 70 80 90 100

B. 25.1
0 10 20 30 40 50 60 70 80 90 100

C. 83.9
0 10 20 30 40 50 60 70 80 90 100

D. 25.1
0 10 20 30 40 50 60 70 80 90 100

E. 54.5
0 10 20 30 40 50 60 70 80 90 100

F. 83.9
0 10 20 30 40 50 60 70 80 90 100

G. 25.1
0 10 20 30 40 50 60 70 80 90 100

H. 25.1
0 10 20 30 40 50 60 70 80 90 100

c. Describe a situation for the inequality. Write three other inequalities using the other inequality symbols.

10. Solve $x + 10 \geq 14$, and then graph the solutions.

a. What are the solutions? Fill in the answer line to complete your choice.

A. $x \geq$ ■

B. $x >$ ■

C. $x \leq$ ■

D. $x <$ ■

b. Choose the correct graph below.

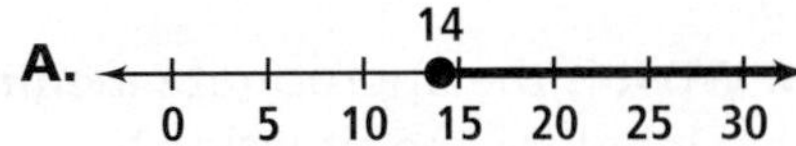

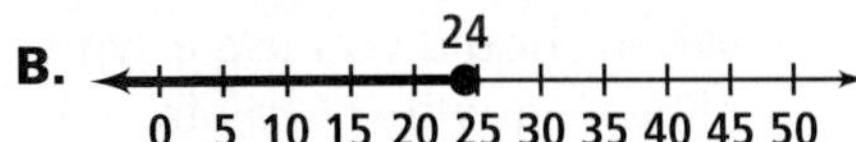

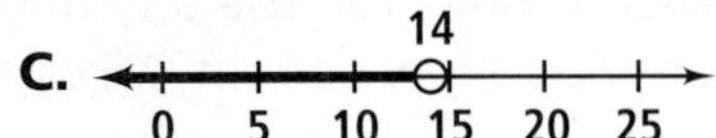

D. 4
0 5 10 15 20 25

E. 4
0 5 10 15 20 25

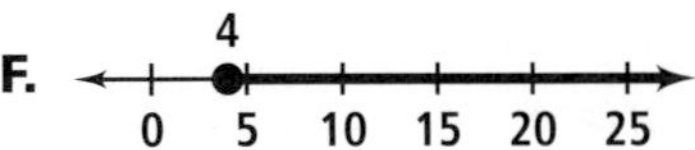

G. 24
0 5 10 15 20 25 30 35 40 45 50

H. 4
0 5 10 15 20 25

9-2 Solving Inequalities Using Multiplication or Division

Vocabulary
Division Property of Inequality
Multiplication Property of Inequality

CCSS: 7.EE.B.4, 7.EE.B.4b

Key Concept

Multiplication Property of Inequality Multiplying by a Positive Number

If you multiply each side of an inequality by the same positive number, the relationship between the two sides does not change.

If $a < b$, then $a \cdot c < b \cdot c$ for all numbers a, b, and c where $c > 0$.

For example, let $a = -5$, $b = 10$, and $c = 3$.

$$-5 < 10 \text{ so } -5 \cdot 3 < 10 \cdot 3$$

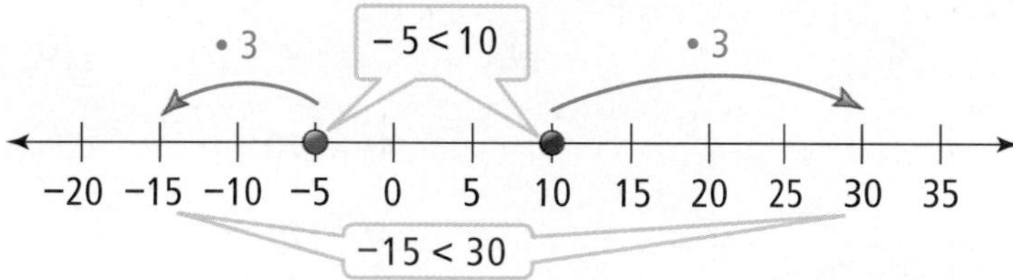

Similarly, if $a > b$, then $a \cdot c > b \cdot c$ for all numbers a, b, and c where $c > 0$. This property is also true for $\leq$ and $\geq$.

Division Property of Inequality Dividing by a Positive Number

If you divide each side of an inequality by the same positive number, the relationship between the two sides does not change.

If $a < b$, then $a \div c < b \div c$ for all numbers a, b, and c where $c > 0$.

For example, let $a = -6$, $b = 4.4$, and $c = 2$.

$$-6 < 4.4 \text{ so } -6 \div (2) < 4.4 \div (2)$$

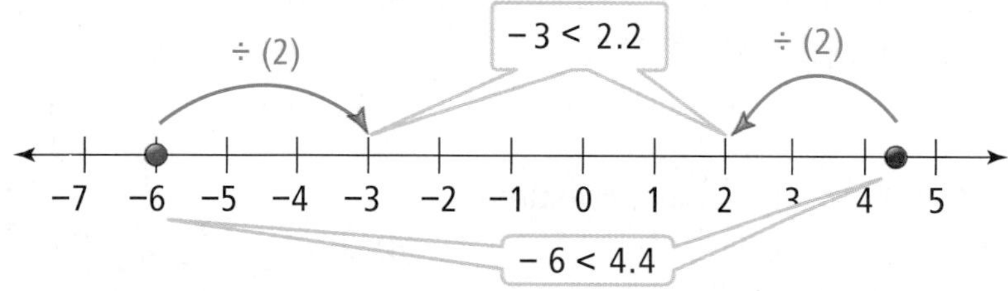

Similarly, if $a > b$, then $a \div c > b \div c$ for all numbers a, b, and c where $c > 0$. This property is also true for $\leq$ and $\geq$.

Part 1

Example Writing and Solving Multiplication Inequalities

An elephant drinks at least 70 L of water a day. Each trunkful holds 4 L of water. How many trunkfuls of water does the elephant drink in a day?

Write and solve an inequality.

Solution

Words	number of liters in one trunkful	times	number of trunkfuls per day	is at least	number of liters per day

Let t = the number of trunkfuls per day.

Inequality	4	•	t	≥	70

$$4t \geq 70$$

Divide each side by 4. $\frac{4t}{4} \geq \frac{70}{4}$

Simplify. $t \geq 17.5$

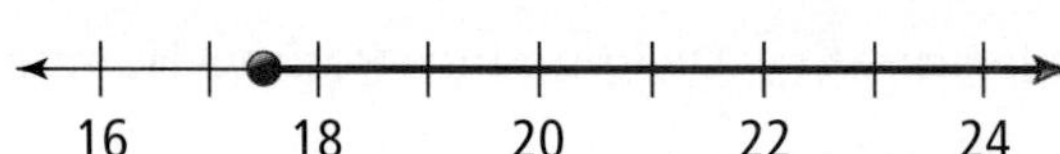

Check your answer.

Step 1 Check the related equation.

Write the related equation. $4t = 70$

Substitute 17.5 into the related equation. $4(17.5) \stackrel{?}{=} 70$

$70 = 70$ ✓

Step 2 Check the direction of the inequality.

$4t \geq 70$

Substitute 20 into the original inequality. $4(20) \stackrel{?}{\geq} 70$

$80 \geq 70$ ✓

You can substitute any number greater than 17.5, such as 20.

$t \geq 17.5$ is the solution of the inequality $4t \geq 70$. An elephant drinks at least 17.5 trunkfuls of water each day.

Key Concept

Multiplication Property of Inequality Multiplying by a Negative Number

If you multiply each side of an inequality by the same negative number, you must *reverse* the direction of the inequality sign to keep the relationship between the two sides from changing.

If $a < b$, then $a \cdot c > b \cdot c$ for all numbers a, b, and c where $c < 0$.

For example, let $a = -\frac{1}{2}$, $b = 3$, and $c = -2$.

$$-\frac{1}{2} < 3 \text{ so } -\frac{1}{2} \cdot (-2) > 3 \cdot (-2)$$

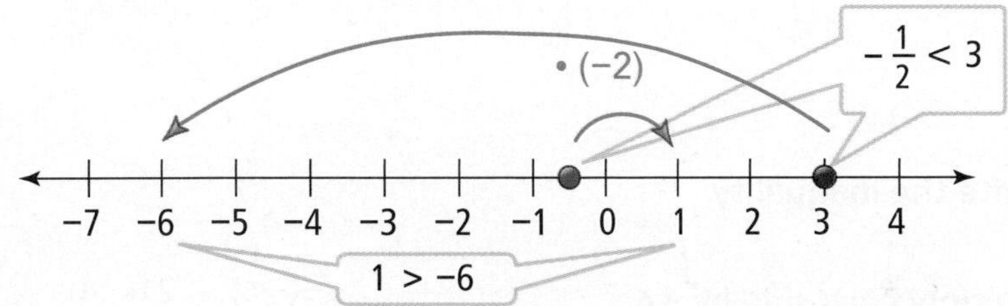

Similarly, if $a > b$, then $a \cdot c < b \cdot c$ for all numbers a, b, and c where $c < 0$. This property is also true for $\leq$ and $\geq$.

Division Property of Inequality Dividing by a Negative Number

If you divide each side of an inequality by the same negative number, you must *reverse* the direction of the inequality sign to keep the relationship between the two sides from changing.

If $a < b$, then $a \div c > b \div c$ for all numbers a, b, and c where $c < 0$.

For example, let $a = -8$, $b = 3$, and $c = -2$.

$$-8 < -6 \text{ so } -8 \div (-2) > -6 \div (-2)$$

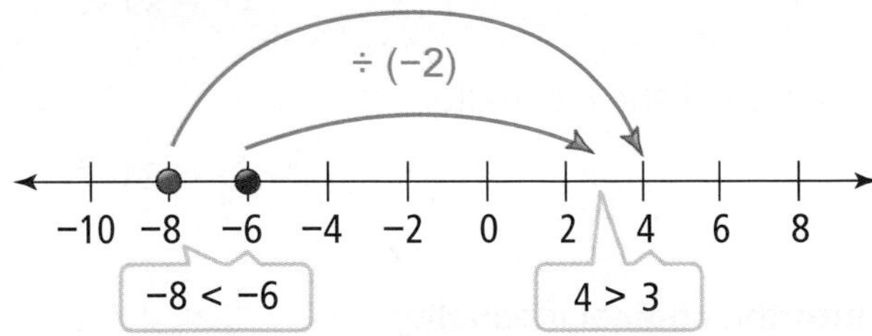

Similarly, if $a > b$, then $a \div c < b \div c$ for all numbers a, b, and c where $c < 0$. This property is also true for $\leq$ and $\geq$.

Part 2

Example Solving Division Inequalities

Fill in the missing symbols to solve.

$\cdot \quad = \quad \leq \quad \div \quad < \quad \geq \quad > \quad +$

$$\frac{k}{-4} < 21$$

$$\frac{k}{-4} \blacksquare (-4) \blacksquare 21 \blacksquare (-4)$$

$$k \blacksquare -84$$

Solution

Solve for k.

Write the inequality. $\frac{k}{-4} < 21$

Multiply each side by −4. $\frac{k}{-4}(-4) > 21(-4)$

Simplify. $k > -84$

When $\frac{k}{-4}$ is less than 21, k is greater than −84.

Check your answer.

Step 1 Check the related equation.

Write the related equation. $\frac{k}{-4} = 21$

Substitute −84 into the related equation. $\frac{-84}{-4} \stackrel{?}{=} 21$

$21 = 21$ ✓

Step 2 Check the direction of the inequality.

$\frac{k}{-4} < 21$

Substitute 0 into the original inequality. $\frac{0}{-4} \stackrel{?}{<} 21$

$0 < 21$ ✓

Part 3

Example Solving Multiplication and Division Inequalities

Match each inequality to its solution.

$a > -9$ $a < 9$ $a > 9$ $a < -9$

a. $3a < -27$ **b.** $3a < 27$ **c.** $-3a > 27$

d. $\frac{a}{3} > 3$ **e.** $\frac{a}{-3} < -3$

Solution

a. $3a < -27$

Divide each side by 3. $\frac{3a}{3} < \frac{-27}{3}$

Simplify. $a < -9$

$a < -9$ is the solution of the inequality $3a < -27$.

b. $3a < 27$

Divide each side by 3. $\frac{3a}{3} < \frac{27}{3}$

Simplify. $a < 9$

$a < 9$ is the solution of the inequality $3a < 27$.

c. $-3a > 27$

Divide each side by −3. $\frac{-3a}{-3} < \frac{-27}{-3}$

Reverse the inequality.

Simplify. $a < 9$

$a < -9$ is the solution of the inequality $-3a > 27$.

continued on next page >

Part 3

Solution continued

d. $\frac{a}{3} > 3$

Multiply each side by 3. $\frac{a}{3} \cdot 3 > 3 \cdot 3$

Simplify. $a > 9$

$a > 9$ is the solution of the inequality $\frac{a}{3} > 3$.

e. $\frac{a}{-3} < -3$

Multiply each side by −3. $\frac{a}{-3} \cdot -3 > -3 \cdot -3$ (Reverse the inequality.)

Simplify. $a > 9$

$a > 9$ is the solution of the inequality $\frac{a}{-3} < -3$.

Remember that you can check each solution by first checking the related equation and then checking the direction of the inequality.

Digital Resources    

1. You had a bag of fruit snacks that you shared with 5 friends. Each friend got no more than 3 fruit snacks. The inequality $x \div 6 \leq 3$ models this situation. Solve the inequality to find the number of fruit snacks that were in the bag.
2. Over the next 17 months you have to read more than 102 books. You have to read x books per month. The inequality $17x > 102$ represents this situation. Solve the inequality to find the number of books you have to read per month.
3. Solve the inequality $\frac{m}{-5} \geq 2$.
4. Solve the inequality $-7x > 56$.
5. A type of fish for your aquarium costs \$3 each. You can spend at most \$15.
   a. Let f be the number of fish you can buy. Which inequality models the problem?

      A. $f + 3 \geq 15$ **B.** $3f \leq 15$
      C. $f + 3 \leq 15$ **D.** $3f \geq 15$

   b. How many of these fish can you buy?
6. One-seventh of Julie's flowers fit in Richard's garden. Richard has at most 19 flowers in his garden. Write and solve an inequality to find the number of flowers in Julie's garden. Let x be the number of flowers in Julie's garden.
7. **Writing** Cynthia plans to build a tree house that is $\frac{1}{3}$ the size of Andrew's tree house. Cynthia plans to make the area of her tree house at least 13 square feet.
   a. Write and solve an inequality to find the area of Andrew's tree house. Let x be the area of Andrew's tree house.
   b. Describe how you know which tree house is larger without solving the inequality.
8. a. **Reasoning** Solve the inequality $-3x < 12$.
   b. Describe how you know the direction of the inequality sign without solving the inequality.
9. A teacher writes the inequality $x \div 6 < 12$ on the board. A student solves the inequality incorrectly and gets the result $x < 2$.
   a. What is the correct result?
   b. Why is the student's result incorrect?

      A. The student should have added, not divided.
      B. The inequality sign in the result should be $>$, not $<$.
      C. The student should have multiplied, not divided.
      D. The result should be an equation, not an inequality.
10. **Dog-Sitting** Your friend is watching your dog for the next 25 days. Your dog eats at most 50 treats every 25 days. Your dog eats x treats each day. The inequality $25x \leq 50$ models this situation. Solve the inequality to find the number of treats your friend should feed your dog each day.
11. **Mental Math** Solve the inequality $\frac{m}{-10} \leq 3$.
12. a. **Multiple Representations** Solve the inequality $-5.25x > 42$.
    b. Draw a model using algebra tiles to help solve the inequality.
13. **Multiple Representations** A group of 3 friends went to a play. The 3 tickets cost at most \$23.43. Each ticket to the play cost x dollars. The inequality $3x \leq 23.43$ represents this situation.
    a. Draw a model with algebra tiles to help solve the inequality.
    b. Solve the inequality. A ticket to the play costs at most \$ ■.

14. A container holds x ounces of lemonade. The serving size per person is 7 ounces. There is enough lemonade for at most 17 people. The inequality $x \div 7 \leq 17$ models the situation. Solve the inequality to find the amount of lemonade the container holds.

15. If $-\frac{1}{6}$ of a number n is no less than 34, what are the possible values of n?

a. Complete the inequality.

$-\frac{1}{6}n$ ■ 34

b. What are the solutions?

A. $n <$ ■

B. $n \geq$ ■

C. $n \leq$ ■

D. $n >$ ■

16. **Think About the Process** You want to solve the inequality $6z \geq 42$. What is the first step?

A. Subtract 6 from each side of the inequality.

B. Subtract $5z$ from each side of the inequality.

C. Add 6 to each side of the inequality.

D. Multiply each side of the inequality by 6.

E. Divide each side of the inequality by 6.

F. Divide each side of the inequality by z.

17. **Think About the Process**

a. To solve the inequality $4 \geq \frac{t}{-13}$ for t, what is the correct property of inequality to use?

A. The Multiplication Property of Inequality

B. The Addition Property of Inequality

C. The Subtraction Property of Inequality

D. The Division Property of Inequality

b. What are the solutions?

A. $t <$ ■ **B.** $t >$ ■

C. $t \geq$ ■ **D.** $t \leq$ ■

18. **Challenge** You have a bag of x peanuts. You share these peanuts with 6 of your friends. Each of you gets at least 21 peanuts. The inequality $21 \leq x \div 7$ models this situation. Which graph shows the correct solutions?

A.

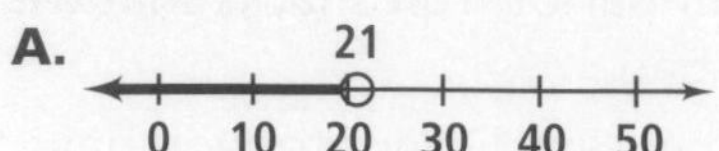

B. 3
0 2 4 6 8 10

C. 3
0 2 4 6 8 10

D. 147
0 40 80 120 160 200

E. 147
0 40 80 120 160 200

F. 147
0 40 80 120 160 200

G. 147
0 40 80 120 160 200

H. 21
0 10 20 30 40 50

9-3 Solving Two-Step Inequalities

Vocabulary
equivalent inequalities

CCSS: 7.EE.B.4, 7.EE.B.4b

Part 1

Example Representing Situations with Two-Step Inequalities

Match each inequality to the situation it represents.

$9n + 5.5 \leq 50$ $\quad\quad$ $50 - 5.5n < 9$ $\quad\quad$ $9 + 5.5n > 50$

a. A lunch special costs \$9. The Egyptology club can spend at most \$50. How many lunch specials can they order if they also share a dessert that costs \$5.50?

b. You read a 50-page chapter about the early Egyptians at the rate of $5\frac{1}{2}$ pages per minute. After how many minutes will you have fewer than 9 pages left?

c. 9 plus $5\frac{1}{2}$ times a number is more than 50.

Solution

a.

Words: cost of one lunch special times the numbers of specials ordered | plus | cost of one dessert | is at most | 50

to

Inequality

Let n = the number of lunch specials ordered.

$9n \quad + \quad 5.5 \quad \leq \quad 50$

b.

Words: number of pages in the chapter | − | 5.5 pages per minute | × | number of minutes spent reading | < | 9 pages

to

Inequality

Let n = the number of minutes spent reading.

$50 \quad - \quad 5.5 \quad \times \quad n \quad < \quad 50$

$5\frac{1}{2} = 5.5$

continued on next page >

Part 1

Solution continued

c.

Words	9	plus	$5\frac{1}{2}$ times a number	is more than	50
to	Let n = the number				
Inequality	9	+	$5.5n$	>	50

$5\frac{1}{2} = 5.5$

Key Concept

Equivalent inequalities are inequalities that have the same solution. You can solve an inequality by transforming it into a series of simpler, equivalent inequalities.

A two-step inequality involves two operations. To solve a two-step inequality, it is usually easier to perform the order of operation in reverse. So undo addition or subtraction and then undo multiplication or division.

Solve $\frac{x}{-3} + 12 < 28.9$.

Subtract 12 from each side. $\frac{x}{-3} + 12 - 12 < 28.9 - 12$

Simplify. $\frac{x}{-3} < 16.9$

Multiply each side by −3.
Reverse the inequality symbol. $-3\left(\frac{x}{-3}\right) > -3(16.9)$

Simplify. $x > -50.7$

Solution: $x > -50.7$

−60 −50 −40 −30 −20 −10 0 10

Key Concept

continued

Check

Step 1 Check the related equation.

Write the related equation.	$\frac{x}{-3} + 12 = 28.9$
Substitute −50.7 for *x* in the related equation.	$\frac{-50.7}{-3} + 12 \stackrel{?}{=} 28.9$
Simplify.	$16.9 + 12 \stackrel{?}{=} 28.9$
Add.	$28.9 = 28.9$ ✔

Step 2 Check the direction of the inequality.

Write the original inequality.	$\frac{x}{-3} + 12 < 28.9$
Substitute 0 for *x* in the original inequality.	$\frac{0}{-3} + 12 \stackrel{?}{<} 28.9$
Simplify.	$0 + 12 \stackrel{?}{<} 28.9$
Add.	$12 < 28.9$ ✔

When $\frac{x}{-3} + 12$ is less than 28.9, x is greater than −50.7.

Part 2

Example Writing and Solving Two-Step Inequalities

A magician's assistant makes $10.60 an hour. If he has already saved $53.70, how many hours must he work in order to save at least $165?

Write, graph, and solve an inequality.

Solution

Words	hourly wage	times	number of hours worked	plus	amount already saved	is at least	$165

Let h = the number of hours worked.

Inequality	10.60	×	h	+	53.70	≥	165

continued on next page >

Part 2

Solution continued

	$10.6h + 53.7 \geq 165$
Subtract 53.7 from each side.	$10.6h + 53.7 - 53.7 \geq 165 - 53.7$
Simplify.	$10.6h \geq 111.3$
Divide each side by 10.6.	$\frac{10.6h}{10.6} \geq \frac{111.3}{10.6}$
Simplify.	$h \geq 10.5$

The magician's assistant must work at least 10.5 hours to save at least $165.

Check

Step 1 Check the related equation.

Write the related equation.	$10.6h + 53.7 = 165$
Substitute 10.5 into the related equation.	$10.6(10.5) + 53.7 \stackrel{?}{=} 165$
Simplify.	$111.3 + 53.7 \stackrel{?}{=} 165$
	$165 = 165$ ✓

Step 2 Check the direction of the inequality. Select a number greater than 10.5 to substitute into the original inequality.

	$10.6h + 53.7 \geq 165$
Substitute 20 into the original inequality.	$10.6(20) + 53.7 \stackrel{?}{\geq} 165$
	$212 + 53.7 \stackrel{?}{\geq} 165$
	$265.7 \geq 165$ ✓

Part 3

Example Finding Solutions of Two-Step Inequalities

Three of the inequalities have the same solution. Find the inequality that has a different solution.

a. $2y + 15 > 6$

b. $6.8 + 27 > -3.6$

c. $-\frac{1}{3}y + 27 > 28\frac{1}{2}$

d. $-2y - 15 < -6$

continued on next page >

Part 3

Example continued

Solution

Solve each inequality.

a. $2y + 15 > 6$

Subtract 15 from each side.	$2y + 15 - 15 > 6 - 15$
Simplify.	$2y > -9$
Divide each side by 2.	$\frac{2y}{2} > \frac{-9}{2}$
Simplify.	$y > -4.5$

b. $6.8 + 27 > -3.6$

Subtract 27 from each side.	$6.8y + 27 - 27 > -3.6 - 27$
Simplify.	$6.8y > -30.6$
Divide each side by 6.8.	$\frac{6.8y}{6.8} > \frac{-30.6}{6.8}$
Simplify.	$y > -4.5$

c. $-\frac{1}{3}y + 27 > 28\frac{1}{2}$

Subtract 27 from each side.	$-\frac{1}{3}y + 27 - 27 > 28\frac{1}{2} - 27$
Simplify.	$-\frac{1}{3}y > 1\frac{1}{2}$
Multiply each side by −3.	$(-3) \cdot \left(-\frac{1}{3}y\right) < (-3) \cdot 1\frac{1}{2}$
Write the mixed number as a fraction.	$y < -3\left(\frac{3}{2}\right)$
Simplify.	$y < -\frac{9}{2}$
Write the fraction as a decimal.	$y < -4.5$

d. $-2y - 15 < -6$

Add 15 to each side.	$-2y - 15 + 15 < -6 + 15$
Simplify.	$-2y < 9$
Divide each side by −2.	$\frac{-2y}{-2} > \frac{9}{-2}$
Simplify.	$y > -4.5$

The inequality $-\frac{1}{3}y + 27 > 28\frac{1}{2}$ is not like the others. Its solution is $y < -4.5$, whereas the solution of the other three inequalities is $y > -4.5$.

Digital Resources    

1. A farmer has 28 bushels of apples and can harvest 24 bushels of apples each day. In how many days will he have more than 100 bushels to sell? What inequality represents this situation?

A. $24n - 28 \geq 100$

B. $24n + 28 \leq 100$

C. $100 - 24n < 28$

D. $24n + 28 > 100$

2. Which situation below does the inequality $9.65n + 38 \geq 175$ represent?

A. Your weekly paycheck is at least $175. You make $9.65 an hour. How many hours do you work each week if $33 is taken out for taxes and $5 is taken out for savings?

B. A ticket for a concert costs $38. There is a $6.65 tax and a $3 parking fee on the total order. How many tickets should you buy if you want to spend at most $175?

C. You need to save at least $175. You have $33 and a friend gives you $5. How many hours do you have to work if you make $9.65 an hour?

3. a. Solve the inequality $4x + 6 > 22$.

b. Solve the inequality $-3x + 20 < 8$.

c. Compare the solutions for $4x + 6 > 22$ and $-3x + 20 < 8$.

A. The inequalities have some common solutions.

B. The inequalities have the same solutions.

C. The inequalities have no common solutions.

D. The inequalities have one common solution.

4. Write, solve, and graph the inequality. 6 times a number plus 22 is greater than 7.

a. Which inequality models the statement?

A. $6x + 22 > 7$ **B.** $6x + 22 \leq 7$

C. $6x + 222 \geq 7$ **D.** $6x + 22 < 7$

b. Which inequality represents the solutions?

A. $x \geq \frac{5}{2}$ **B.** $x \leq -\frac{5}{2}$

C. $x > -\frac{5}{2}$ **D.** $x < \frac{5}{2}$

c. Which of the following is the graph of the solutions?

A.

−5/2

−10 −8 −6 −4 −2 0 2 4 6 8 10

B.

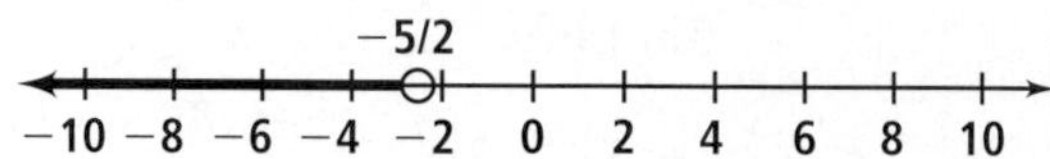

C.

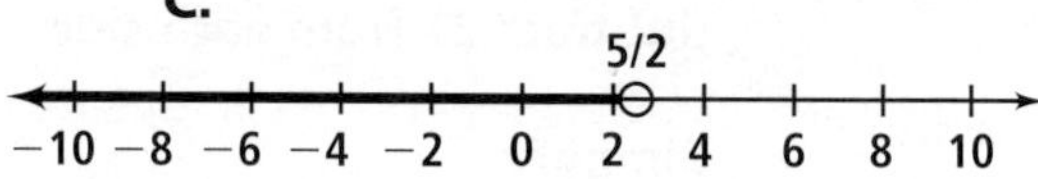

D.

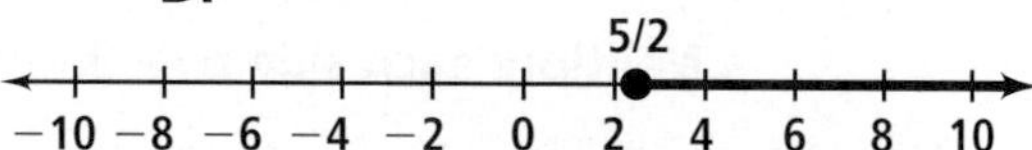

5. Writing The width of a rectangular garden is $\frac{1}{5}$ the length plus an additional 3 ft and can be no longer than 11 ft.

a. Which inequality can be used to find the possible lengths, *L*, of the garden?

A. $\frac{1}{5}L + 3 \geq 11$ **B.** $\frac{1}{5}L + 3 \leq 11$

C. $\frac{1}{5}L - 3 \leq 11$ **D.** $\frac{1}{5}L - 3 > 11$

b. Describe another situation where you can use the same inequality.

6. **Think About the Process** Mr. and Mrs. Sullivan have budgeted $1364 to go on vacation for 22 days. The hotel will cost $770 for the trip.

   a. How would you write an inequality to find the amount of money they can spend each day without going over budget?

   A. 770 subtracted from 22 times a number is at least 1364.

   B. 770 added to 22 times a number is at least 1364.

   C. 770 subtracted from 22 times a number is at most 1364.

   D. 770 added to 22 times a number is at most 1364.

   b. Which inequality represents this situation?

   A. $22x + 770 \geq 1364$

   B. $22x + 770 \leq 1364$

   C. $22x - 770 \geq 1364$

   D. $22x - 770 \leq 1364$

   c. Which graph represents the solutions?

   A.

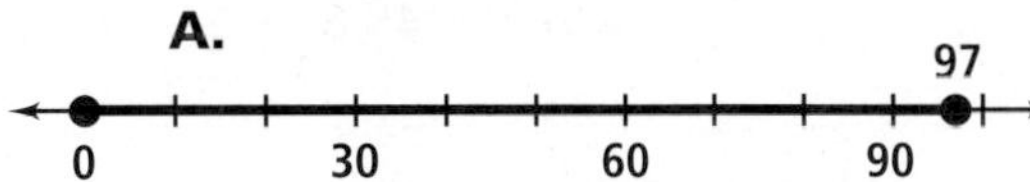

   B.

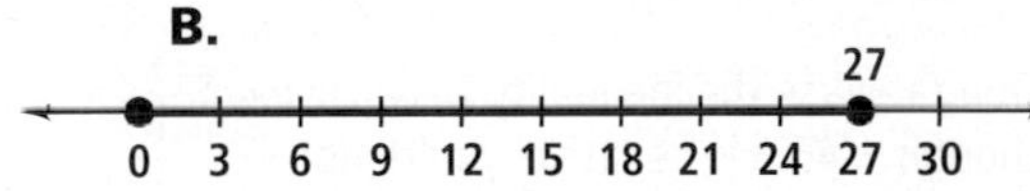

   C.

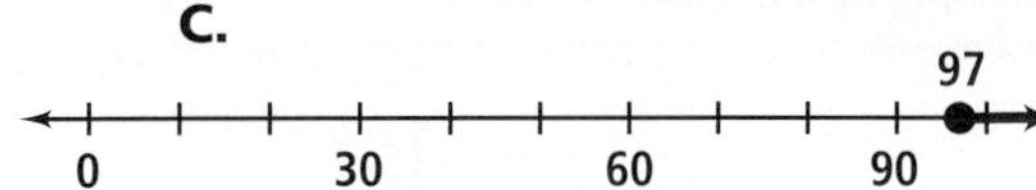

   D.

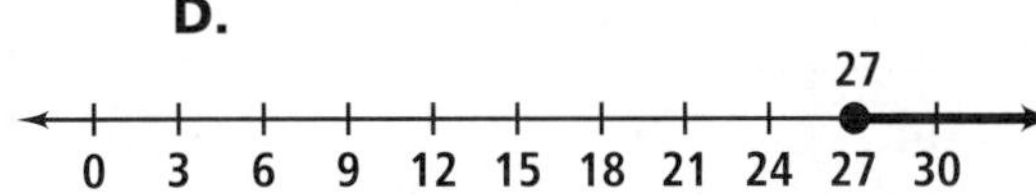

7. **Challenge** Which inequality has the opposite solutions of $\frac{1}{11}x - 5 < 1$?

   A. $-\frac{1}{11}x + 5 < -1$

   B. $-\frac{1}{11}x + 11 < 7$

   C. $12x - 48 > 576$

   D. $-12x + 48 > -576$

8. **a.** Solve the inequality $\frac{1}{2}x + 8 \leq 10$.

   b. Solve the inequality $-3x - 24 \leq -36$.

   c. Compare the solutions for $\frac{1}{2}x + 8 \leq 10$ and $-3x - 24 \leq -36$.

   A. The inequalities have no common solutions.

   B. The inequalities have one common solution.

   C. The inequalities have the same solutions.

   D. The inequalities have some common solutions.

   d. Explain how a number line is useful when comparing inequalities.

9. **Think About the Process** The inequalities $\frac{1}{5}x + 7 \leq 11$ and $-\frac{1}{5}x - 7 \geq -11$ share the same solutions.

   a. What are the solutions for $\frac{1}{5}x + 7 \leq 11$ and $-\frac{1}{5}x - 7 \geq -11$?

   b. How can you tell before performing the calculations that the inequalities have the same solutions?

10. $\frac{5}{7}$ times a number minus 9.4 is no more than 14.6.

   a. Which inequality represents this statement?

   A. $\frac{5}{7}n - 9.4 \leq 14.6$

   B. $\frac{5}{7}n - 9.4 < 14.6$

   C. $\frac{5}{7}n - 9.4 > 14.6$

   D. $\frac{5}{7}n - 9.4 \geq 14.6$

   b. Which inequality represents the possible solutions?

   A. $n \leq 33.6$

   B. $n > 33.6$

   C. $n \leq 7.3$

   D. $n < 7.3$

9-4 Solving Multi-Step Inequalities

CCSS: 7.EE.B.4, 7.EE.B.4b

Part 1

Intro

You can use the Distributive Property to simplify the expressions $a(b + c)$ and $a(b - c)$, where a, b, and c are rational numbers.

$$a(b + c) = ab + ac \qquad a(b - c) = ab - ac$$

Some inequalities are easier to solve if you apply the Distributive Property first to simplify them.

Example Solving Inequalities Using the Distributive Property

Solve $3(p + 5.8) \le -28.2$ and graph the solution.

Solution

$$3(p + 5.8) \le -28.2$$

Distribute 3 to each term in the parentheses. $3p + 3(5.8) \le -28.2$

Simplify. $3p + 17.4 \le -28.2$

Subtract 17.4 from each side. $3p + 17.4 - 17.4 \le -28.2 - 17.4$

Simplify. $3p \le -45.6$

Divide each side by 3. $\frac{3p}{3} \le \frac{-45.6}{3}$

Don't reverse the inequality, because even though −45.6 is negative, you're not dividing by a negative number.

Simplify. $p \le -15.2$

Graph $p \le -15.2$.

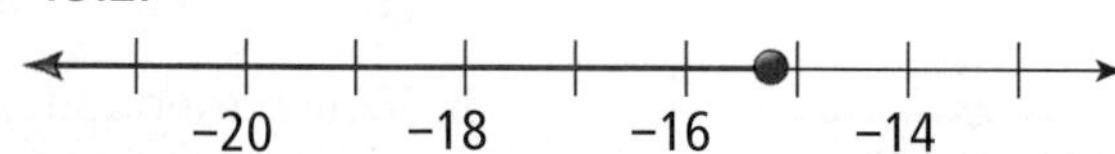

Check your answer.

Step 1 Check the related equation.

Write the related equation. $3(p + 5.8) = -28.2$

Substitute −15.2 into the related equation. $3(-15.2 + 5.8) \stackrel{?}{=} -28.2$

$$3(-9.4) \stackrel{?}{=} -28.2$$

$$-28.2 = -28.2 \checkmark$$

continued on next page >

Part 1

Solution continued

Step 2 Check the direction of the inequality.

$$3(p + 5.8) \le -28.2$$

Substitute −20 into the original inequality. $3(-20 + 5.8) \stackrel{?}{\le} -28.2$

$$3(-14.2) \stackrel{?}{\le} -28.2$$

$$-42.6 \le -28.2 \checkmark$$

So, $p \le -15.2$ is the solution of the inequality $3(p + 5.8) \le -28.2$.

Part 2

Intro

Some inequalities have more than one variable term on the same side of the inequality symbol.

To solve these inequalities, use the Distributive Property to combine like terms and simplify the inequality.

Example Solving Inequalities With Like Terms

A farmer harvests 25 bushels of McIntosh apples each day and 18 bushels of Granny Smith apples each day. In how many days will he have more than 100 bushels to sell?

Solution

Words	bushels of McIntosh per day	×	number of days	+	bushels of Granny Smith per day	×	number of days	is more than	100 bushels
Inequality	25	×	d	+	18	×	d	>	100

to: Let $d =$ the number of days.

$$25d + 18d > 100$$

Combine like terms. $(25 + 18)d > 100$

Add. $43d > 100$

Divide each side by 43. $\frac{43d}{43} > \frac{100}{43}$

Simplify. $d > 2.33$

continued on next page >

Part 2

Solution continued

Check your answer.

Step 1 Check the related equation.

Write the related equation.	$25d + 18d = 100$
Substitute 2.33 into the related equation.	$25(2.33) + 18(2.33) \stackrel{?}{=} 100$
	$58.25 + 41.94 \stackrel{?}{=} 100$
	$100.19 \approx 100$ ✓

Because 2.33 is rounded, the check will result in two numbers that are approximately equal.

Step 2 Check the direction of the inequality.

	$25d + 18d > 100$
Substitute 10 into the original inequality.	$25(10) + 18(10) \stackrel{?}{>} 100$
	$250 + 180 \stackrel{?}{>} 100$
	$430 > 100$ ✓

Since $d > 2.33$, the least whole number satisfying the inequality is 3. So, after 3 days, the farmer will have more than 100 bushels to sell.

Part 3

Example Solving Multi-Step Inequalities Correctly

Find, describe, and correct the error in the student work shown.

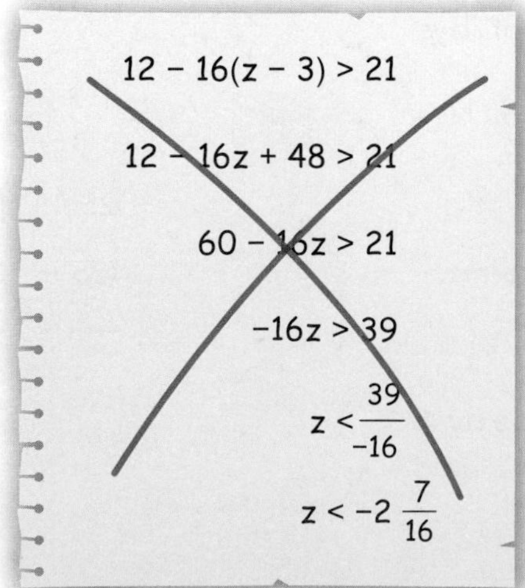

continued on next page >

Part 3

Example continued

Solution

Corrected Work

The student made an error when subtracting 60 from each side of the inequality. The fourth line should be $-16z > -39$ because $21 - 60$ is -39.

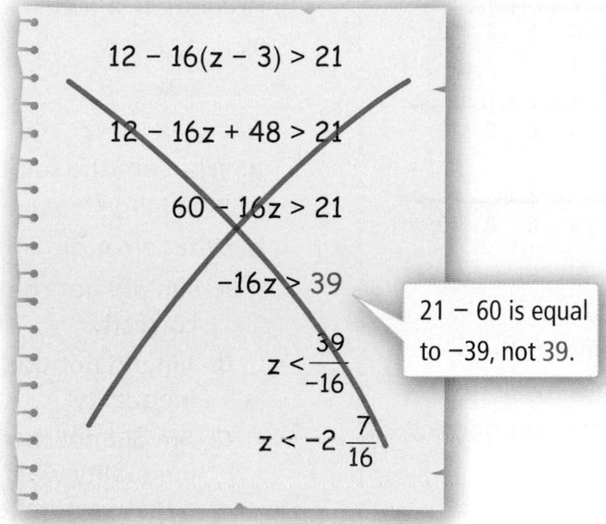

The rest of the problem is solved as follows.

$$-16z > -39$$
$$z < \frac{-39}{-16}$$
$$z < 2\frac{7}{76}$$

9-4 | Homework

Digital Resources   

1. a. Solve the inequality
$18 < -3(4x - 2)$.

b. Which graph shows the solutions of the inequality?

A.

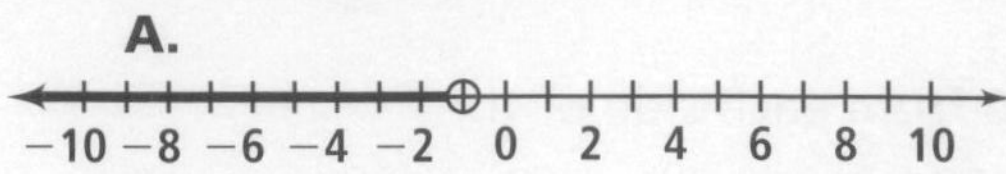

B.

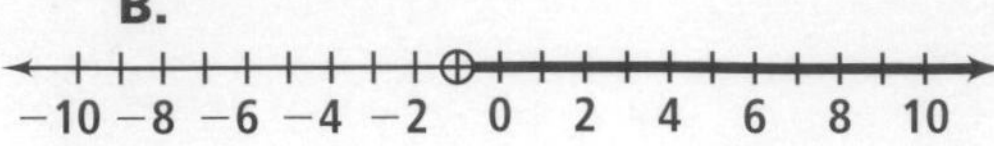

C.

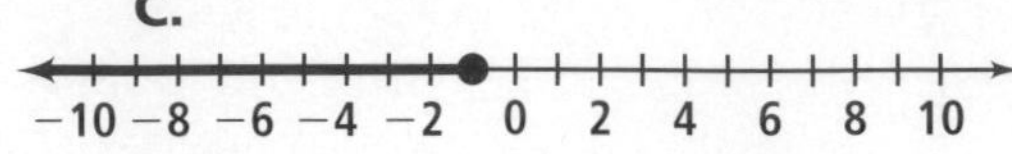

D.

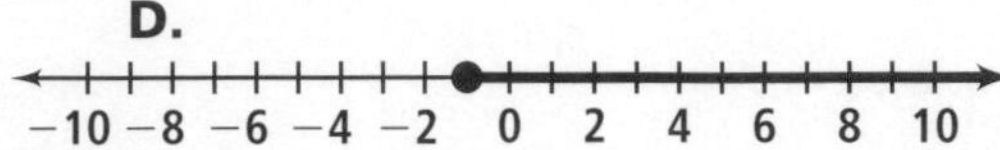

2. Solve the inequality.

$$4(z + 2) - 2z \leq 12$$

a. What are the solutions of the inequality?

b. Which graph shows the solutions of the inequality?

A.

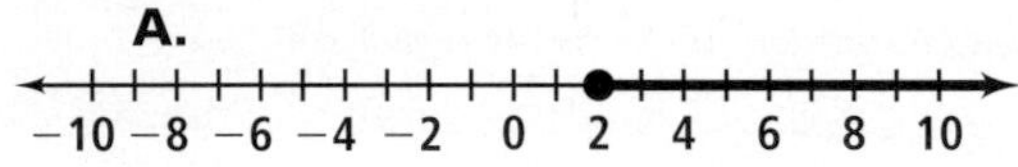

B.

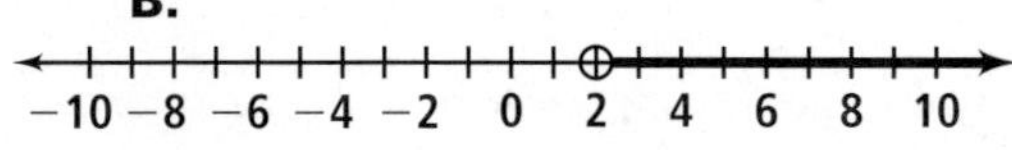

C.

−10 −8 −6 −4 −2 0 2 4 6 8 10

D.

3. Think About the Process You want to solve the given inequality for *y*.

$$3(5y - 7) \geq 9$$

a. After using the Distributive Property, what is the next step?

A. Subtract 7 from each side.

B. Subtract 21 from each side.

C. Add 7 to each side.

D. Add 21 to each side.

b. What are the solutions of the inequality?

4. Every hour, 90 people enter an office building, and 32 people leave. After how many hours will there be more than 348 people in the building? Use the inequality $90n - 32n > 348$ to solve the problem.

5. Jim says that the solutions to the inequality $9x - 12x \geq 6$ are $x \geq -2$. His work is shown.

$9x - 12x \geq 6$

$-3x \geq 6$

$x \geq -2$

a. What are the solutions of the inequality?

b. What error did Jim make?

A. Jim did not combine like terms correctly.

B. Jim did not use the correct given inequality.

C. Jim did not reverse the inequality when dividing by a negative number.

D. Jim did not use the Distributive Property correctly.

6. Think About the Process

a. Apply the Distributive Property to the right side of the inequality $12 \geq 6(12x + 2)$.

b. Solve the inequality.

c. What do you notice about the inequality that could help you solve it more easily?

7. a. Challenge What are the solutions of the inequality $4(2.3z + 2.25) > -27.8$?

b. What are the solutions of the inequality $2(1.2z + 1.5) \leq 12.6$?

c. Which of the inequalities have 7 as a solution?

A. inequality $2(1.2z + 1.5) \leq 12.6$ only

B. both inequalities

C. inequality $4(2.3z + 2.25) > -27.8$ only

D. neither inequality

8. Carefully examine Christina's and Natalia's work.

Christina	Natalia
$7 - 5(1 - x) \geq 4$	$7 - 5(1 - x) \geq 4$
$7 - 5 + 5x \geq 4$	$7 - 5 + x \geq 4$
$2 + 5x \geq 4$	$2 + x \geq 4$
$5x \geq 2$	$x \geq 2$
$x \geq \frac{2}{5}$	

a. Whose work is incorrect?

b. What error was made?

A. The Commutative Property was used incorrectly.

B. The Associative Property was used incorrectly.

C. The Distributive Property was used incorrectly.

D. The Addition Property of Inequality was used incorrectly.

9. **Farming** A farmer harvests 13 bushels of green peppers, 21 bushels of red peppers, and 15 bushels of yellow peppers every day. The farmer wants to know how many days, *d*, it will take to harvest more than 200 bushels of peppers.

a. Which inequality models the situation?

A. $13d + 21d + 15d > 200$

B. $13d + 21d + 15d < 200$

C. $200 > 13d + 21d + 15d$

D. $13d - 21d - 15d > 200$

b. How many days will it take to harvest more than 200 bushels of peppers?

10. **Estimation** Your friend says that the solutions of the inequality $1.9x - 4.9(x - 4) \leq 14.3$ are about $x \leq -2$.

a. Round each decimal to the nearest integer.

b. Use the estimated values to solve the inequality for *x*.

c. What mistake might your friend have made?

A. Your friend changed the sign of the answer and the inequality symbol.

B. Your friend changed the sign of the answer, not the inequality symbol.

C. Your friend rounded incorrectly.

D. Your friend used the Distributive Property incorrectly.

11. **a.** Solve the inequality $24 \geq 28 + 5(x - 3.8)$.

b. Which graph shows the solutions of the inequality?

A.

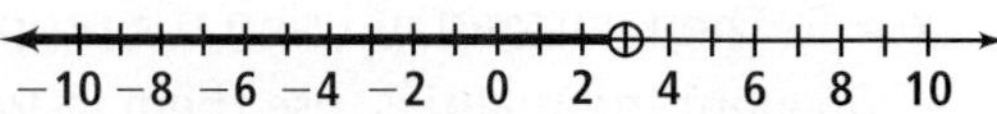

B.

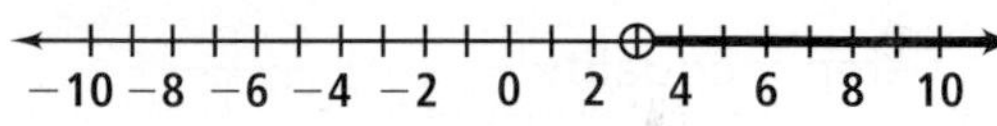

C.

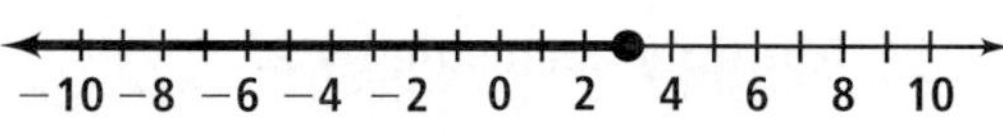

D.

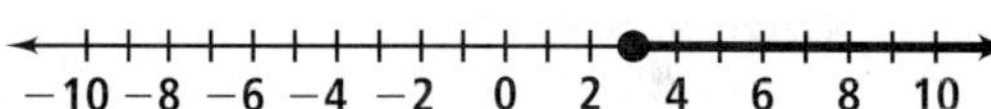

12. **a.** Solve $30 \geq 6\left(\frac{2}{3}z + \frac{1}{3}\right)$ for *z*.

b. Solve $15.6 < 2.7z - 3.3$ for *z*.

c. Are there any values of *z* that are solutions of both inequalities? Use a number line to support your answer.

13. For what values of *x* is the perimeter of the figure greater than 144 meters?

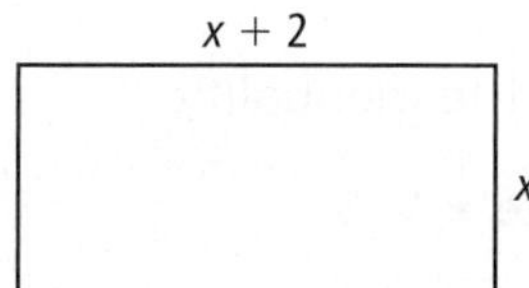

9-5 Problem Solving

Vocabulary
revenue, cost

CCSS: 7.EE.B.4, 7.EE.B.4b

Part 1

Example Writing 1- and 2-Step Inequalities

Write a 1-step inequality and a 2-step inequality that each have the solution $x > 5$.

To challenge yourself, include a word problem or a problem that involves reversing the inequality symbol.

Solution

To write a 1-step or 2-step inequality with the solution $x > 5$, start with $x > 5$. Then, instead of using the properties of inequalities to write *simpler* equivalent inequalities, use them to write *more complex* equivalent inequalities. Sample answers follow.

1-step inequality

Write $x > 5$.	$x > 5$
Multiply each side by 2.	$2x > 10$

2-step inequality

Write $x > 5$.	$x > 5$
Multiply each side by 3.	$3x > 15$
Add 6 to each side.	$3x + 6 > 21$

Word problem

Write $x > 5$ as a word sentence.	A number x is greater than 5.
Divide each side by 2.	A number x divided by 2 is greater than 2.5.
Write a real-world example.	Half a basket of apples weighs more than 2.5 lb. How much does a whole basket of apples x weigh?

Reverse the inequality

Write $x > 5$.	$x > 5$
Multiply each side by −3 and reverse the inequality.	$-3x < -15$

Part 2

Example Writing 2-Step Inequalities to Solve Problems

A salesperson has to decide whether to accept a job offer. The new job has a base salary of \$35,000 and a bonus of 18% of the money he makes in sales. His current job's salary is \$54,000.

How much money will he have to make in sales to earn more money in the new job?

Solution

Words: base salary plus bonus is more than current salary

to

Let s = the amount of money made in sales.

Inequality: $35{,}000 + 18\% \cdot s > 54{,}000$

The bonus is 18% of the money made in sales, or 18% • s.

$$35{,}000 + 18\% \cdot s > 54{,}000$$

Convert the percent to a decimal. $35{,}000 + 0.18s > 54{,}000$

Subtract 35,000 from each side. $35{,}000 - 35{,}000 + 0.18s > 54{,}000 - 35{,}000$

Simplify. $0.18s > 19{,}000$

Divide each side by 0.18. $\frac{0.18s}{0.18} > \frac{19{,}000}{0.18}$

Simplify. $s > 105{,}555.56$

Check your answer.

Step 1 Check the related equation.

Write the related equation. $35{,}000 + 0.18s = 54{,}000$

Substitute 105,555.56 into the related equation. $35{,}000 + 0.18(105{,}555.56) \stackrel{?}{=} 54{,}000$

$$35{,}000 + 19{,}000 \stackrel{?}{=} 54{,}000$$

$$54{,}000 = 54{,}000 \checkmark$$

continued on next page >

Part 2

Solution continued

Step 2 Check the direction of the inequality.

$$35{,}000 + 0.18s > 54{,}000$$

Substitute 110,000 into the original inequality. $35{,}000 + 0.18(110{,}000) \overset{?}{>} 54{,}000$

$$35{,}000 + 19{,}800 \overset{?}{>} 54{,}000$$

$$54{,}800 > 54{,}000 \checkmark$$

If $35{,}000 + 0.18s > 54{,}000$, then $s > 105{,}555.56$.

The salesperson would have to make more than $105,555.56 in sales to make more money in the new job.

Part 3

Intro

Revenue is the amount of money a company receives for goods sold or services provided.

Cost is the amount of money a company spends to produce those goods or provide those services.

To make a profit, revenue must be greater than cost.

Example Writing Multi-Step Inequalities to Solve Problems

An applesauce company's revenue is given by the equation $R = 7{,}000(u - 9) + 234{,}000$, where u is the number of units of applesauce sold.

The company's cost is $C = 5{,}204{,}000$.

For what values of u does the company make a profit?

Solution

Profit is made when Revenue is greater than Cost.

The company's revenue is $7{,}000(u - 9) + 234{,}000$, where u is the number of units of applesauce sold. The company's costs are $5,204,000. Write an inequality where Revenue > Cost.

continued on next page >

Part 3

Solution continued

Solve the inequality of u.

$$\text{Revenue} > \text{Cost}$$

$$7{,}000(u - 9) + 234{,}000 > 5{,}204{,}000$$

$$7{,}000(u - 9) + 234{,}000 > 5{,}204{,}000$$

Use the Distributive Property. $7{,}000(u) - 7{,}000(9) + 234{,}000 > 5{,}204{,}000$

Multiply. $7{,}000u - 63{,}000 + 234{,}000 > 5{,}204{,}000$

Simplify. $7{,}000u + 171{,}000 > 5{,}204{,}000$

Subtract 171,000 from each side. $7{,}000u + 171{,}000 - 171{,}000 > 5{,}204{,}000 - 171{,}000$

Simplify. $7{,}000u > 5{,}033{,}000$

Divide each side by 7,000. $\dfrac{7{,}000u}{7{,}000} > \dfrac{5{,}033{,}000}{7{,}000}$

Simplify. $u > 719$

$$7{,}000(u - 9) + 234{,}000 > 5{,}204{,}000$$

$$u > 719$$

When the company sells more than 719 units of applesauce they make a profit.

Check

Step 1 Check the related equation.

Write the related equation. $7{,}000(u - 9) + 234{,}000 = 5{,}204{,}000$

Substitute 719 into the related equation. $7{,}000(719 - 9) + 234{,}000 \stackrel{?}{=} 5{,}204{,}000$

$7{,}000(710) + 234{,}000 \stackrel{?}{=} 5{,}204{,}000$

Simplify. $4{,}970{,}000 + 234{,}000 \stackrel{?}{=} 5{,}204{,}000$

$5{,}204{,}000 = 5{,}204{,}000$ ✓

continued on next page >

Part 3

Solution continued

Step 2 Check the direction of the inequality.

$$7{,}000(u - 9) + 234{,}000 > 5{,}204{,}000$$

Substitute **720** into the original inequality.

$$7{,}000(720 - 9) + 234{,}000 \overset{?}{>} 5{,}204{,}000$$

$$7{,}000(711) + 234{,}000 \overset{?}{>} 5{,}204{,}000$$

$$4{,}970{,}000 + 234{,}000 \overset{?}{>} 5{,}204{,}000$$

$$5{,}211{,}000 > 5{,}204{,}000 \checkmark$$

1. Use the Division Property of Inequality and the number 9 to write a one-step inequality whose solution is $x > 3$. Then use the result with the Subtraction Property of Inequality and the number 6 to write a two-step inequality that has the same solution. What is the resulting inequality?
   A. $\frac{x}{9} + 6 > 6\frac{1}{3}$
   B. $9x + 6 > 33$
   C. $9x - 6 > 21$
   D. $\frac{x}{9} - 6 > -5\frac{2}{3}$
2. The initial cost to rent a bike is \$5. Each hour the bike is rented costs \$2.25. Liz is going to rent a bike and can spend at most \$11.75. Write and solve an inequality to find how long she can rent the bike.
3. Write and solve an inequality to find the values of x for which the perimeter of the rectangle is less than 120.

   $x + 4$

   x
4. A 150-pound person burns 5.1 calories per minute when walking at a speed of 4 miles per hour. While walking, this person eats a snack that has 50 calories. This snack subtracts from the calories burned while walking.
   a. How long must the person walk at this speed to burn at least 180 calories?
   b. Describe what values the person could change so that the amount of time spent walking would be less.
5. **Error Analysis** On a recent quiz, Greg needed to use the Division Property of Inequality and the number -8 to write a 1-step inequality whose solution is $x < 32$. Then he needed to use the result with the Subtraction Property of Inequality and the number 8 to write a 2-step inequality that has the same solution. Greg incorrectly said the resulting inequality is $-\frac{x}{8} - 8 < -12$.
   a. What is the correct resulting inequality?
   A. $-\frac{x}{8} + 8 < -12$
   B. $-8x + 8 < -248$
   C. $-8x - 8 > -264$
   D. $-\frac{x}{8} - 8 > -12$
   b. What mistake might Greg have made?
   A. Greg used the Multiplication and Addition Properties of Inequality.
   B. Greg did not reverse the direction of the inequality sign.
   C. Greg used the Division and Addition Properties of Inequality.
   D. Greg used the Multiplication and Subtraction Properties of Inequality.
6. A group of friends went out for lunch. Two people ordered soup. Two people ordered sandwiches. Each sandwich costs twice as much as a bowl of soup. Two people ordered burgers. Each burger cost three times as much as a bowl of soup. The total cost for their lunch was less than \$24.48. What was the price of a bowl of soup?
7. The cost of a car rental is \$30 per day plus 20¢ per mile. You are on a daily budget of \$94. Write and solve an inequality to find the greatest distance you can drive each day while staying within your budget.

8. The expression $4(133x + 139)$ represents the number of containers of juice sold in x days. How many days would it take to sell at least 3,216 containers of juice?

9. Use the Multiplication Property of Inequality and the number 5.3 to write a 1-step inequality whose solution is $10.6 > x$. Then use the result with the Addition Property of Inequality and the number 7 to write a 2-step inequality that has the same solution. What is the resulting inequality?

   A. $63.18 < 5.3x + 7$

   B. $9 > \frac{x}{5.3} + 7$

   C. $9 < \frac{x}{5.3} + 7$

   D. $63.18 > 5.3x + 7$

10. Andrew is making a bracelet and a necklace for himself and a bracelet for his friend. The necklace is going to be 4 times as long as each bracelet. Andrew only has 48 inches of string.

    a. The bracelets can be at most ■ inches long.

    b. The necklace can be at most ■ inches long.

11. **Think About the Process** Maria sells computer systems. Her annual base salary is \$34,000. She also earns a commission of 1.4% on the sale price of all computer systems that she sells. Maria wants her annual salary to be at least \$132,000.

    a. Let s = the total sales. Which inequality models this situation?

    A. $34{,}000s + 0.014 \geq 132{,}000$

    B. $34{,}000 + 0.014s > 132{,}000$

    C. $34{,}000 + 0.014s \geq 132{,}000$

    D. $34{,}000s + 0.014 > 132{,}000$

    b. Solve the inequality. Maria's annual salary will be at least \$132,000 if she sells at least \$ ■ worth of computer systems.

12. **Think About the Process** Ben bowled 139 and 211 in his first two games. He wants to bowl an average of at least 200 in three games. Let x be his score in the third game. Write an inequality for this problem.

    a. Which inequality symbol should you use for this situation if 200 is on the right side?

    A. $>$

    B. $\geq$

    C. $<$

    D. $\leq$

    b. Solve the inequality. Ben must bowl at least ■ in his third game in order to have an average of at least 200.

13. **Challenge** The number n is twice the sum of 3 and 2. Use the Multiplication Property of Inequality and the number 8 to write a one-step inequality whose solution is $x \leq n$. Then use the result with the Subtraction Property of Inequality and the number 6 to write a two-step inequality that has the same solution.

    a. What is the resulting inequality?

    A. $\frac{x}{8} + 6 \leq 7\frac{1}{4}$

    B. $8x + 6 \leq 86$

    C. $\frac{x}{8} - 6 \leq -4\frac{3}{4}$

    D. $8x - 6 \leq 74$

    b. Write about a real work situation that relates to the resulting inequality.

14. **Challenge** Andrea went to the store to buy a sweater. The sweater initially went on sale for 40% off the original price. It was then put on clearance at an additional 25% off the sale price. She also used a coupon that saved her an additional \$5. Andrea did not spend more than \$7.60 for the sweater. What are the possible values for the original price of the sweater?

English/Spanish Glossary

A

Absolute deviation from the mean Absolute deviation measures the distance that the data value is from the mean. You find the absolute deviation by taking the absolute value of the deviation of a data value. Absolute deviations are always nonnegative.

Desviación absoluta de la media La desviación absoluta mide la distancia a la que un valor se encuentra de la media. Para hallar la desviación absoluta, tomas el valor absoluto de la desviación de un valor. Las desviaciones absolutas siempre son no negativas.

Absolute value The absolute value of a number *a* is the distance between *a* and zero on a number line. The absolute value of *a* is written as $|a|$.

Valor absoluto El valor absoluto de un número *a* es la distancia entre a y cero en la recta numérica. El valor absoluto de *a* se escribe como $|a|$.

Accuracy The accuracy of an estimate or measurement is the degree to which it agrees with an accepted or actual value of that measurement.

Exactitud La exactitud de una estimación o medición es el grado de concordancia con un valor aceptado o real de esa medición.

Action In a probability situation, an action is a process with an uncertain result.

Acción En una situación de probabilidad, una acción es el proceso con un resultado incierto.

Acute angle An acute angle is an angle with a measure between 0° and 90°.

Ángulo agudo Un ángulo agudo es un ángulo que mide entre 0° y 90°.

Acute triangle An acute triangle is a triangle with three acute angles.

Triángulo acutángulo Un triángulo acutángulo es un triángulo que tiene tres ángulos agudos.

Addend Addends are the numbers that are added together to find a sum.

Sumando Los sumandos son los números que se suman para hallar un total.

English/Spanish Glossary

Additive inverses Two numbers that have a sum of 0.

Inversos de suma Dos números cuya suma es 0.

Adjacent angles Two angles are adjacent angles if they share a vertex and a side, but have no interior points in common.

Ángulos adyacentes Dos ángulos son adyacentes si tienen un vértice y un lado en común, pero no comparten puntos internos.

Algebraic expression An algebraic expression is a mathematical phrase that consists of variables, numbers, and operation symbols.

Expresión algebraica Una expresión algebraica es una frase matemática que consiste en variables, números y símbolos de operaciones.

Analyze To analyze is to think about and understand facts and details about a given set of information. Analyzing can involve providing a written summary supported by factual information, diagrams, charts, tables, or any combination of these.

Analizar Analizar es pensar en los datos y detalles de cierta información y comprenderlos. El análisis puede incluir la presentación de un resumen escrito sustentado por información objetiva, diagramas, tablas o una combinación de esos elementos.

Angle An angle is a figure formed by two rays with a common endpoint.

Ángulo Un ángulo es una figura formada por dos semirrectas que tienen un extremo en común.

Angle of rotation The angle of rotation is the number of degrees a figure is rotated.

Ángulo de rotación El ángulo de rotación es el número de grados que se rota una figura.

Annual salary The amount of money earned at a job in one year.

Salario annual La cantidad de dinero ganó en un trabajo en un año.

Area The area of a figure is the number of square units the figure encloses.

Área El área de una figura es el número de unidades cuadradas que ocupa.

English/Spanish Glossary

Area of a circle The formula for the area of a circle is $A = \pi r^2$, where A represents the area and r represents the radius of the circle.

Área de un círculo La fórmula del área de un círculo es $A = \pi r^2$, donde A representa el área y r representa el radio del círculo.

Area of a parallelogram The formula for the area of a parallelogram is $A = bh$, where A represents the area, b represents a base, and h is the corresponding height.

Área de un paralelogramo La fórmula del área de un paralelogramo es $A = bh$, donde A representa el área, b representa una base y h es la altura correspondiente.

Area of a rectangle The formula for the area of a rectangle is $A = bh$, where A represents the area, b represents the base, and h represents the height of the rectangle.

Área de un rectángulo La fórmula del área de un rectángulo es $A = bh$, donde A representa el área, b representa la base y h representa la altura del rectángulo.

Area of a square The formula for the area of a square is $A = s^2$, where A represents the area and s represents a side length.

Área de un cuadrado La fórmula del área de un cuadrado es $A = s^2$, donde A representa el área y l representa la longitud de un lado.

Area of a trapezoid The formula for the area of a trapezoid is $A = \frac{1}{2}h(b_1 + b_2)$, where A represents the area, b_1 and b_2 represent the bases, and h represents the height between the bases.

El área de un trapezoide La fórmula para el área de un trapezoide es $A = \frac{1}{2}h(b_1 + b_2)$, donde A representa el área, b_1 y b_2 representan las bases, y h representa la altura entre las bases.

Area of a triangle The formula for the area of a triangle is $A = \frac{1}{2}bh$, where A represents the area, b represents the length of a base, and h represents the corresponding height.

Área de un triángulo La fórmula del área de un triángulo es $A = \frac{1}{2}bh$, donde A representa el área, b representa la longitud de una base y h representa la altura correspondiente.

Asset An asset is money you have or property of value that you own.

Ventaja Una ventaja es dinero que tiene o la propiedad de valor que usted posee.

Associative Property of Addition For any numbers a, b, and c: $(a + b) + c = a + (b + c)$

Propiedad asociativa de la suma Para los números cualesquiera a, b y c: $(a + b) + c = a + (b + c)$

Associative Property of Multiplication For any numbers a, b, and c: $(a \cdot b) \cdot c = a \cdot (b \cdot c)$

Propiedad asociativa de la multiplicación Para los números cualesquiera a, b y c: $(a \cdot b) \cdot c = a \cdot (b \cdot c)$

Average of two numbers The average of two numbers is the value that represents the middle of two numbers. It is found by adding the two numbers together and dividing by 2.

Promedio de dos números El promedio de dos números es el valor que está justo en el medio de esos dos números. Se halla sumando los dos números y dividiendo el resultado por 2.

B

Balance The balance in an account is the principal amount plus the interest earned.

Saldo El saldo de una cuenta es el capital más el interés ganado.

Balance of a checking account The balance of a checking account is the amount of money in the checking account.

El equilibrio de una Cuenta Corriente Bancaria El equilibrio de una cuenta corriente bancaria es la cantidad de dinero en la cuenta corriente bancaria.

Balance of a loan The balance of a loan is the remaining unpaid principal.

El equilibrio de un préstamo El equilibrio de un préstamo es el director impagado restante.

Bar diagram A bar diagram is a way to represent part to whole relationships.

Diagrama de barras Un diagrama de barras es una forma de representar una relación de parte a entero.

Base The base is the repeated factor of a number written in exponential form.

Base La base es el factor repetido de un número escrito en forma exponencial.

English/Spanish Glossary

Base area of a cone The base area of a cone is the area of a circle. Base Area $= \pi r^2$.

Área de la base de un cono El área de la base de un cono es el área de un círculo. El área de la base $= \pi r^2$.

Base of a cone The base of a cone is a circle with radius *r*.

Base de un cono La base de un cono es un círculo con radio *r*.

Base of a cylinder A base of a cylinder is one of a pair of parallel circular faces that are the same size.

Base de un cilindro Una base de un cilindro es una de dos caras circulares paralelas que tienen el mismo tamaño.

Base of a parallelogram A base of a parallelogram is any side of the parallelogram.

Base de un paralelogramo La base de un paralelogramo es cualquiera de los lados del paralelogramo.

Base of a prism A base of a prism is one of a pair of parallel polygonal faces that are the same size and shape. A prism is named for the shape of its bases.

Base de un prisma La base de un prisma es una de las dos caras poligonales paralelas que tienen el mismo tamaño y la misma forma. El nombre de un prisma depende de la forma de sus bases.

Base of a pyramid A base of a pyramid is a polygonal face that does not connect to the vertex.

Base de una pirámide La base de una pirámide es una cara poligonal que no se conecta con el vértice.

Base of a triangle The base of a triangle is any side of the triangle.

Base de un triángulo La base de un triángulo es cualquiera de los lados del triángulo.

Benchmark A benchmark is a number you can use as a reference point for other numbers.

Referencia Una referencia es un número que usted puede utilizar como un punto de referencia para otros números.

English/Spanish Glossary

Bias A bias is a tendency toward a particular perspective that is different from the overall perspective of the population.

Sesgo Un sesgo es una tendencia hacia una perspectiva particular que es diferente de la perspectiva general de la población.

Biased sample In a biased sample, the number of subjects in the sample with the trait that you are studying is not proportional to the number of members in the population with that trait. A biased sample does not accurately represent the population.

Muestra sesgada En una muestra sesgada, el número de sujetos de la muestra que tiene la característica que se está estudiando no es proporcional al número de miembros de la población que tienen esa característica. Una muestra sesgada no representa con exactitud la población.

Bivariate categorical data Bivariate categorical data pairs categorical data collected about two variables of the same population.

Datos bivariados por categorías Los datos bivariados por categorías agrupan pares de datos obtenidos acerca de dos variables de la misma población.

Bivariate data Bivariate data is comprised of pairs of linked observations about a population.

Datos bivariados Los datos bivariados se forman a partir de pares de observaciones relacionadas sobre una población.

Box plot A box plot is a statistical graph that shows the distribution of a data set by marking five boundary points where data occur along a number line. Unlike a dot plot or a histogram, a box plot does not show frequency.

Diagrama de cajas Un diagrama de cajas es un diagrama de estadísticas que muestra la distribución de un conjunto de datos al marcar cinco puntos de frontera donde se hallan los datos sobre una recta numérica. A diferencia del diagrama de puntos o el histograma, el diagrama de cajas no muestra la frecuencia.

Budget A budget is a plan for how you will spend your money.

Presupuesto Un presupuesto es un plan para cómo gastará su dinero.

English/Spanish Glossary

C

Categorical data Categorical data consist of data that fall into categories.

Datos por categorías Los datos por categorías son datos que se pueden clasificar en categorías.

Center of a circle The center of a circle is the point inside the circle that is the same distance from all points on the circle. Name a circle by its center.

Centro de un círculo El centro de un círculo es el punto dentro del círculo que está a la misma distancia de todos los puntos del círculo. Un círculo se identifica por su centro.

Center of a regular polygon The center of a regular polygon is the point that is equidistant from its vertices.

Centro de un polígono regular El centro de un polígono regular es el punto equidistante de todos sus vértices.

Center of rotation The center of rotation is a fixed point about which a figure is rotated.

Centro de rotación El centro de rotación es el punto fijo alrededor del cual se rota una figura.

Check register A record that shows all of the transactions for a bank account, including withdrawals, deposits, and transfers. It also shows the balance of the account after each transaction.

Verifique registro Un registro que muestra todas las transacciones para una cuenta bancaria, inclusive retiradas, los depósitos, y las transferencias. También muestra el equilibrio de la cuenta después de cada transacción.

Circle A circle is the set of all points in a plane that are the same distance from a given point, called the center.

Círculo Un círculo es el conjunto de todos los puntos de un plano que están a la misma distancia de un punto dado, llamado centro.

Circle graph A circle graph is a graph that represents a whole divided into parts.

Gráfica circular Una gráfica circular es una gráfica que representa un todo dividido en partes.

Circumference of a circle The circumference of a circle is the distance around the circle. The formula for the circumference of a circle is $C = \pi d$, where C represents the circumference and d represents the diameter of the circle.

Circunferencia de un círculo La circunferencia de un círculo es la distancia alrededor del círculo. La fórmula de la circunferencia de un círculo es $C = \pi d$, donde C representa la circunferencia y d representa el diámetro del círculo.

Cluster A cluster is a group of points that lie close together on a scatter plot.

Grupo Un grupo es un conjunto de puntos que están agrupados en un diagrama de dispersión.

Coefficient A coefficient is the number part of a term that contains a variable.

Coeficiente Un coeficiente es la parte numérica de un término que contiene una variable.

Common denominator A common denominator is a number that is the denominator of two or more fractions.

Común denominador Un común denominador es un número que es el denominador de dos o más fracciones.

Common multiple A common multiple is a multiple that two or more numbers share.

Múltiplo común Un múltiplo común es un múltiplo que comparten dos o más números.

Commutative Property of Addition For any numbers a and b: $a + b = b + a$

Propiedad conmutativa de la suma Para los números cualesquiera a y b: $a + b = b + a$

Commutative Property of Multiplication For any numbers a and b: $a \cdot b = b \cdot a$

Propiedad conmutativa de la multiplicación Para los números cualesquiera a y b: $a \cdot b = b \cdot a$

Comparative inference A comparative inference is an inference made by interpreting and comparing two sets of data.

Inferencia comparativa Una inferencia comparativa es una inferencia que se hace al interpretar y comparar dos conjuntos de datos.

English/Spanish Glossary

Compare To compare is to tell or show how two things are alike or different.

Comparar Comparar es describir o mostrar en qué se parecen o en qué se diferencian dos cosas.

Compatible numbers Compatible numbers are numbers that are easy to compute mentally.

Números compatibles Los números compatibles son números fáciles de calcular mentalmente.

Complementary angles Two angles are complementary angles if the sum of their measures is 90°. Complementary angles that are adjacent form a right angle.

Ángulos complementarios Dos ángulos son complementarios si la suma de sus medidas es 90°. Los ángulos complementarios que son adyacentes forman un ángulo recto.

Complex fraction A complex fraction is a fraction $\frac{A}{B}$ where A and/or B are fractions and B is not zero.

Fracción compleja Una fracción compleja es una fracción $\frac{A}{B}$ donde A y/o B son fracciones y B es distinto de cero.

Compose a shape To compose a shape, join two (or more) shapes so that there is no gap or overlap.

Componer una figura Para componer una figura, debes unir dos (o más) figuras de modo que entre ellas no queden espacios ni superposiciones.

Composite figure A composite figure is the combination of two or more figures into one object.

Figura compuesta Una figura compuesta es la combinación de dos o más figuras en un objeto.

Composite number A composite number is a whole number greater than 1 with more than two factors.

Número compuesto Un número compuesto es un número entero mayor que 1 con más de dos factores.

Compound event A compound event is an event associated with a multi-step action. A compound event is composed of events that are the outcomes of the steps of the action.

Evento compuesto Un evento compuesto es un evento que se relaciona con una acción de varios pasos. Un evento compuesto se compone de eventos que son los resultados de los pasos de una acción.

Compound interest Compound interest is interest paid on both the principal and the interest earned in previous interest periods. To calculate compound interest, use the formula $B = p(1 + r)^n$, where B is the balance in the account, p is the principal, r is the annual interest rate, and n is the time in years that the account earns interest.

Interés compuesto El interés compuesto es el interés que se paga sobre el capital y el interés obtenido en períodos de interés anteriores. Para calcular el interés compuesto, usa la fórmula $B = c(1 + r)^n$ donde B es el saldo de la cuenta, c es el capital, r es la tasa de interés anual y n es el tiempo en años en que la cuenta obtiene un interés.

Cone A cone is a three-dimensional figure with one circular base and one vertex.

Cono Un cono es una figura tridimensional con una base circular y un vértice.

Congruent figures Two two-dimensional figures are congruent $\cong$ if the second can be obtained from the first by a sequence of rotations, reflections, and translations.

Figuras congruentes Dos figuras bidimensionales son congruentes $\cong$ si la segunda puede obtenerse a partir de la primera mediante una secuencia de rotaciones, reflexiones y traslaciones.

Conjecture A conjecture is a statement that you believe to be true but have not yet proved to be true.

Conjetura Una conjetura es un enunciado que crees que es verdadero, pero que todavía no has comprobado que sea verdadero.

Constant A constant is a term that only contains a number.

Constante Una constante es un término que solamente contiene un número.

Constant of proportionality In a proportional relationship, one quantity y is a constant multiple of the other quantity x. The constant multiple is called the constant of proportionality. The constant of proportionality is equal to the ratio $\frac{y}{x}$.

Constante de proporcionalidad En una relación proporcional, una cantidad y es un múltiplo constante de la otra cantidad x. El múltiplo constante se llama constante de proporcionalidad. La constante de proporcionalidad es igual a la razón $\frac{y}{x}$.

Construct To construct is to make something, such as an argument, by organizing ideas. Constructing an argument can involve a written response, equations, diagrams, charts, tables, or a combination of these.

Construir Construir es hacer o crear algo, como se construye un argumento al organizar ideas. Para construir un argumento puede usarse una respuesta escrita, ecuaciones, diagramas, tablas o una combinación de esos elementos.

Convenience sampling Convenience sampling is a sampling method in which a researcher chooses members of the population that are convenient and available. Many researchers use this sampling technique because it is fast and inexpensive. It does not require the researcher to keep track of everyone in the population.

Muestra de conveniencia Una muestra de conveniencia es un método de muestreo en el que un investigador escoge miembros de la población que están convenientemente disponibles. Muchos investigadores usan esta técnica de muestreo porque es rápida y no es costosa. No requiere que el investigador lleve un registro de cada miembro de la población.

Cost of attendance The cost of attendance of one year of college is the sum of all of your expenses during the year.

El costo de asistencia El costo de asistencia de un año del colegio es la suma de todos sus gastos durante el año.

Cost of credit The cost of credit for a loan is the difference between the total cost and the principal.

El costo de crédito El costo de crédito para un préstamo es la diferencia entre el coste total y el director.

Converse of the Pythagorean Theorem If the sum of the squares of the lengths of two sides of a triangle equals the square of the length of the third side, then the triangle is a right triangle. If $a^2 + b^2 = c^2$, then the triangle is a right triangle.

Expresión recíproca del Teorema de Pitágoras Si la suma del cuadrado de la longitud de dos lados de un triángulo es igual al cuadrado de la longitud del tercer lado, entonces el triángulo es un triángulo rectángulo. $a^2 + b^2 = c^2$, entonces el triángulo es un triángulo rectángulo.

Conversion factor A conversion factor is a rate that equals 1.

Factor de conversión Un factor de conversión es una tasa que es igual a 1.

English/Spanish Glossary

Coordinate plane A coordinate plane is formed by a horizontal number line called the *x*-axis and a vertical number line called the *y*-axis.

Plano de coordenadas Un plano de coordenadas está formado por una recta numérica horizontal llamada eje de las *x* y una recta numérica vertical llamada eje de las *y*.

Corresponding angles Corresponding angles lie on the same side of a transversal and in corresponding positions.

Ángulos correspondientes Los ángulos correspondientes se ubican al mismo lado de una secante y en posiciones correspondientes.

Counterexample A counterexample is a specific example that shows that a conjecture is false.

Contraejemplo Un contraejemplo es un ejemplo específico que muestra que una conjetura es falsa.

Counting Principle If there are m possible outcomes of one action and n possible outcomes of a second action, then there are $m \cdot n$ outcomes of the first action followed by the second action.

Principio de conteo Si hay m resultados posibles de una acción y n resultados posibles de una segunda acción, entonces hay $m \cdot n$ resultados de la primera acción seguida de la segunda acción.

Coupon A coupon is part of a printed or online advertisement entitling the holder to a discount at checkout.

Cupón Un cupón forma parte de un anuncio impreso o en línea que permite al poseedor a un descuento en comprueba.

Credit card A credit card is a card issued by a lender that can be used to borrow money or make purchases on credit.

Tarjeta de crédito Una tarjeta de crédito es una tarjeta publicada por un prestamista que puede ser utilizado para pedir dinero prestado o compras de marca a cuenta.

Credit history A credit history shows how a consumer has managed credit in the past.

Acredite la historia Una historia del crédito muestra cómo un consumidor ha manejado crédito en el pasado.

English/Spanish Glossary

Credit report A report that shows personal information about a consumer and details about the consumer's credit history.

Acredite reporte Un reporte que muestra información personal sobre un consumidor y detalles acerca de la historia del crédito del consumidor.

Critique A critique is a careful judgment in which you give your opinion about the good and bad parts of something, such as how a problem was solved.

Crítica Una crítica es una evaluación cuidadosa en la que das tu opinión acerca de las partes positivas y negativas de algo, como la manera en la que se resolvió un problema.

Cross section A cross section is the intersection of a three-dimensional figure and a plane.

Corte transversal Un corte transversal es la intersección de una figura tridimensional y un plano.

Cube A cube is a rectangular prism whose faces are all squares.

Cubo Un cubo es un prisma rectangular cuyas caras son todas cuadrados.

Cube root The cube root of a number, *n*, is a number whose cube equals *n*.

Raíz cúbica La raíz cúbica de un número, *n*, es un número que elevado al cubo es igual a *n*.

Cubic unit A cubic unit is the volume of a cube that measures 1 unit on each edge.

Unidad cúbica Una unidad cúbica es el volumen de un cubo en el que cada arista mide 1 unidad.

Cylinder A cylinder is a three-dimensional figure with two parallel circular bases that are the same size.

Cilindro Un cilindro es una figura tridimensional con dos bases circulares paralelas que tienen el mismo tamaño.

D

Data Data are pieces of information collected by asking questions, measuring, or making observations about the real world.

Datos Los datos son información reunida mediante preguntas, mediciones u observaciones sobre la vida diaria.

English/Spanish Glossary

Debit card A debit card is a card issued by a bank that is linked to a customer's bank account, normally a checking account. A debit card can normally be used to withdraw money from an ATM or to make a purchase.

Tarjeta de débito Una tarjeta de débito es una tarjeta publicada por un banco que es ligado la cuenta bancaria de un cliente, normalmente una cuenta corriente bancaria. Una tarjeta de débito puede ser utilizada normalmente retirar dinero de una ATM o para hacer una compra.

Decimal A decimal is a number with one or more places to the right of a decimal point.

Decimal Un decimal es un número que tiene uno o más lugares a la derecha del punto decimal.

Decimal places The digits after the decimal point are called decimal places.

Lugares decimales Los dígitos que están después del punto decimal se llaman lugares decimales.

Decompose a shape To decompose a shape, break it up to form other shapes.

Descomponer una figura Para descomponer una figura, debes separarla para formar otras figuras.

Deductive reasoning Deductive reasoning is a process of reasoning logically from given facts to a conclusion.

Razonamiento deductivo El razonamiento deductivo es un proceso de razonamiento lógico que parte de hechos dados hasta llegar a una conclusión.

Denominator The denominator is the number below the fraction bar in a fraction.

Denominador El denominador es el número que está debajo de la barra de fracción en una fracción.

Dependent events Two events are dependent events if the occurrence of the first event affects the probability of the second event.

Eventos dependientes Dos eventos son dependientes si el resultado del primer evento afecta la probabilidad del segundo evento.

Deposit A transaction that adds money to a bank account is a deposit.

Depósito Una transacción que agrega dinero a una cuenta bancaria es un depósito.

English/Spanish Glossary

Dependent variable A dependent variable is a variable whose value changes in response to another (independent) variable.

Variable dependiente Una variable dependiente es una variable cuyo valor cambia en respuesta a otra variable (independiente).

Describe To describe is to explain or tell in detail. A written description can contain facts and other information needed to communicate your answer. A diagram or a graph may also be included.

Describir Describir es explicar o indicar algo en detalle. Una descripción escrita puede incluir hechos y otra información necesaria para comunicar tu respuesta. También puede incluir un diagrama o una gráfica.

Design To design is to make using specific criteria.

Diseñar Diseñar es crear algo a partir de criterios específicos.

Determine To determine is to use the given information and any related facts to find a value or make a decision.

Determinar Determinar es usar la información dada y cualquier otro dato relacionado para hallar un valor o tomar una decisión.

Deviation from the mean Deviation indicates how far away and in which direction a data value is from the mean. Data values that are less than the mean have a negative deviation. Data values that are greater than the mean have a positive deviation.

Desviación de la media La desviación indica a qué distancia y en qué dirección un valor se aleja de la media. Los valores menores que la media tienen una desviación negativa. Los valores mayores que la media tienen una desviación positiva.

Diagonal A diagonal of a figure is a segment that connects two nonconsecutive vertices of the figure.

Diagonal La diagonal de una figura es un segmento que conecta dos vértices no consecutivos de la figura.

Diameter A diameter is a segment that passes through the center of a circle and has both endpoints on the circle. The term diameter can also mean the length of this segment.

Diámetro Un diámetro es un segmento que atraviesa el centro de un círculo y tiene sus dos extremos en el círculo. El término diámetro también puede referirse a la longitud de este segmento.

Difference The difference is the answer you get when subtracting two numbers.

Diferencia La diferencia es la respuesta que obtienes cuando restas dos números.

Dilation A dilation is a transformation that moves each point along the ray through the point, starting from a fixed center, and multiplies distances from the center by a common scale factor. If a vertex of a figure is the center of dilation, then the vertex and its image after the dilation are the same point.

Dilatación Una dilatación es una transformación que mueve cada punto a lo largo de la semirrecta a través del punto, a partir de un centro fijo, y multiplica las distancias desde el centro por un factor de escala común. Si un vértice de una figura es el centro de dilatación, entonces el vértice y su imagen después de la dilatación son el mismo punto.

Direct variation A linear relationship that can be represented by an equation in the form $y = kx$, where $x \neq 0$.

Dirija variación Una relación lineal que puede ser representada por una ecuación en la forma $y = kx$, donde x no iguale 0.

Distribution (of a data set) The distribution of a data set describes the way that its data values are spread out over all possible values. This includes describing the frequencies of each data value. The shape of a data display shows the distribution of a data set.

Distribución (de un conjunto de datos) La distribución de un conjunto de datos describe la manera en que sus valores se esparcen sobre todos los valores posibles. Eso incluye la descripción de las frecuencias de cada valor. La forma de una exhibición de datos muestra la distribución de un conjunto de datos.

Distributive Property Multiplying a number by a sum or difference gives the same result as multiplying that number by each term in the sum or difference and then adding or subtracting the corresponding products.
$a \cdot (b + c) = a \cdot b + a \cdot c$ and
$a \cdot (b - c) = a \cdot b - a \cdot c$

Propiedad distributiva Multiplicar un número por una suma o una diferencia da el mismo resultado que multiplicar ese mismo número por cada uno de los términos de la suma o la diferencia y después sumar o restar los productos obtenidos.
$a \cdot (b + c) = a \cdot b + a \cdot c$ and
$a \cdot (b - c) = a \cdot b - a \cdot c$

Dividend The dividend is the number to be divided.

Dividendo El dividendo es el número que se divide.

Divisible A number is divisible by another number if there is no remainder after dividing.

Divisible Un número es divisible por otro número si no hay residuo después de dividir.

Divisor The divisor is the number used to divide another number.

Divisor El divisor es el número por el cual se divide otro número.

Dot plot A dot plot is a statistical graph that shows the shape of a data set with stacked dots above each data value on a number line. Each dot represents one data value.

Diagrama de puntos Un diagrama de puntos es una gráfica estadística que muestra la forma de un conjunto de datos con puntos marcados sobre cada valor de una recta numérica. Cada punto representa un valor.

E

Earned wages Earned wages are the income you receive from an employer for doing a job. Earned wages are also called gross pay.

Sueldos ganados Los sueldos ganados son los ingresos que usted recibe de un empleador para hacer un trabajo. Los sueldos ganados también son llamados la paga bruta.

Easy-access loan The term easy-access loan refers to a wide variety of loans with a streamlined application process. Many easy-access loans are short-term loans of relatively small amounts of money. They often have high interest rates.

Préstamo de fácil-acceso El préstamo del fácil-acceso del término se refiere a una gran variedad de préstamos con un proceso simplificado de aplicación. Muchos préstamos del fácil-acceso son préstamos a corto plazo de cantidades relativamente pequeñas de dinero. Ellos a menudo tienen los tipos de interés altos.

Edge of a three-dimensional figure An edge of a three-dimensional figure is a segment formed by the intersection of two faces.

Arista de una figura tridimensional Una arista de una figura tridimensional es un segmento formado por la intersección de dos caras.

Enlargement An enlargement is a dilation with a scale factor greater than 1. After an enlargement, the image is bigger than the original figure.

Aumento Un aumento es una dilatación con un factor de escala mayor que 1. Después de un aumento, la imagen es más grande que la figura original.

Equation An equation is a mathematical sentence that includes an equals sign to compare two expressions.

Ecuación Una ecuación es una oración matemática que incluye un signo igual para comparar dos expresiones.

Equilateral triangle An equilateral triangle is a triangle whose sides are all the same length.

Triángulo equilátero Un triángulo equilátero es un triángulo que tiene todos sus lados de la misma longitud.

Equivalent equations Equivalent equations are equations that have exactly the same solutions.

Ecuaciones equivalentes Las ecuaciones equivalentes son ecuaciones que tienen exactamente la misma solución.

Equivalent expressions Equivalent expressions are expressions that always have the same value.

Expresiones equivalentes Las expresiones equivalentes son expresiones que siempre tienen el mismo valor.

Equivalent fractions Equivalent fractions are fractions that name the same number.

Fracciones equivalentes Las fracciones equivalentes son fracciones que representan el mismo número.

Equivalent inequalities Equivalent inequalities are inequalities that have the same solution.

Desigualdades equivalentes Las desigualdades equivalentes son desigualdades que tienen la misma solución.

Equivalent ratios Equivalent ratios are ratios that express the same relationship.

Razones equivalentes Las razones equivalentes son razones que expresan la misma relación.

Estimate To estimate is to find a number that is close to an exact answer.

Estimar Estimar es hallar un número cercano a una respuesta exacta.

English/Spanish Glossary

Evaluate a numerical expression To evaluate a numerical expression is to follow the order of operations.

Evaluar una expresión numérica Evaluar una expresión numérica es seguir el orden de las operaciones.

Evaluate an algebraic expression To evaluate an algebraic expression, replace each variable with a number, and then follow the order of operations.

Evaluar una expresión algebraica Para evaluar una expresión algebraica, reemplaza cada variable con un número y luego sigue el orden de las operaciones.

Event An event is a single outcome or group of outcomes from a sample space.

Evento Un evento es un resultado simple o un grupo de resultados de un espacio muestral.

Expand an algebraic expression To expand an algebraic expression, use the Distributive Property to rewrite a product as a sum or difference of terms.

Desarrollar una expresión algebraica Para desarrollar una expresión algebraica, usa la propiedad distributiva para reescribir el producto como una suma o diferencia de términos.

Expected family contribution The amount of money a student's family is expected to contribute towards the student's cost of attendance for school.

Contribución familiar esperado La cantidad de dinero que la familia de un estudiante es esperada contribuir hacia el estudiante es costado de asistencia para la escuela.

Expense Money that a business or a person needs to spend to pay for or buy something.

Gasto El dinero que un negocio o una persona debe gastar para pagar por o comprar algo.

Experiment To experiment is to try to gather information in several ways.

Experimentar Experimentar es intentar reunir información de varias maneras.

Experimental probability You find the experimental probability of an event by repeating an experiment many times and using this ratio: $P(\text{event}) = \frac{\text{number of times event occurs}}{\text{total number of trials}}$

Probabilidad experimental Para hallar la probabilidad experimental de un evento, debes repetir un experimento muchas veces y usar esta razón: $P(\text{evento}) = \frac{\text{número de veces que sucede el evento}}{\text{número total de pruebas}}$

Explain To explain is to give facts and details that make an idea easier to understand. Explaining can involve a written summary supported by a diagram, chart, table, or a combination of these.

Explicar Explicar es brindar datos y detalles para que una idea sea más fácil de comprender. Para explicar algo se puede usar un resumen escrito sustentado por un diagrama, una tabla o una combinación de esos elementos.

Exponent An exponent is a number that shows how many times a base is used as a factor.

Exponente Un exponente es un número que muestra cuántas veces se usa una base como factor.

Expression An expression is a mathematical phrase that can involve variables, numbers, and operations. See algebraic expression or numerical expression.

Expresión Una expresión es una frase matemática que puede tener variables, números y operaciones. Ver expresión algebraica o expresión numérica.

Exterior angle of a triangle An exterior angle of a triangle is an angle formed by a side and an extension of an adjacent side.

Ángulo externo de un triángulo Un ángulo externo de un triángulo es un ángulo formado por un lado y una extensión de un lado adyacente.

F

Face of a three-dimensional figure A face of a three-dimensional figure is a flat surface shaped like a polygon.

Cara de una figura tridimensional La cara de una figura tridimensional es una superficie plana con forma de polígono.

English/Spanish Glossary

Factor an algebraic expression To factor an algebraic expression, write the expression as a product.

Descomponer una expresión algebraica en factores Para descomponer una expresión algebraica en factores, escribe la expresión como un producto.

Factors Factors are numbers that are multiplied to give a product.

Factores Los factores son los números que se multiplican para obtener un producto.

False equation A false equation has values that do not equal each other on each side of the equals sign.

Ecuación falsa Una ecuación falsa tiene valores a cada lado del signo igual que no son iguales entre sí.

Financial aid Financial aid is any money offered to a student to assist with the cost of attendance.

Ayuda financiera La ayuda financiera es cualquier dinero ofreció a un estudiante para ayudar con el costo de asistencia.

Financial need A student's financial need is the difference between the student's cost of attendance and the student's expected family contribution.

Necesidad financiera Una necesidad financiera del estudiante es la diferencia entre el estudiante es costada de asistencia y la contribución esperado de familia de estudiante.

Find To find is to calculate or determine.

Hallar Hallar es calcular o determinar.

First quartile For an ordered set of data, the first quartile is the median of the lower half of the data set.

Primer cuartil Para un conjunto ordenado de datos, el primer cuartil es la mediana de la mitad inferior del conjunto de datos.

Fixed expenses Fixed expenses are expenses that do not change from one budget period to the next.

Gastos fijos Los gastos fijos son los gastos que no cambian de un período económico al próximo.

Fraction A fraction is a number that can be written in the form $\frac{a}{b}$, where a is a whole number and b is a positive whole number. A fraction is formed by a parts of size $\frac{1}{b}$.

Fracción Una fracción es un número que puede expresarse de forma $\frac{a}{b}$, donde a es un entero y b es un número entero positivo. La fracción está formada por a partes de tamaño $\frac{1}{b}$.

Frequency Frequency describes the number of times a specific value occurs in a data set.

Frecuencia La frecuencia describe el número de veces que aparece un valor específico en un conjunto de datos.

Function A function is a rule for taking each input value and producing exactly one output value.

Función Una función es una regla por la cual se toma cada valor de entrada y se produce exactamente un valor de salida.

G

Gap A gap is an area of a graph that contains no data points.

Espacio vacío o brecha Un espacio vacío o brecha es un área de una gráfica que no contiene ningún valor.

Grant A type of monetary award a student can use to pay for his or her education. The student does not need to repay this money.

Grant Un tipo de premio monetario que un estudiante puede utilizar para pagar por su educación. El estudiante no debe devolver este dinero.

Greater than $>$ The greater-than symbol shows a comparison of two numbers with the number of greater value shown first, or on the left.

Mayor que $>$ El símbolo de mayor que muestra una comparación de dos números con el número de mayor valor que aparece primero, o a la izquierda.

Greatest common factor The greatest common factor (GCF) of two or more whole numbers is the greatest number that is a factor of all of the numbers.

Máximo común divisor El máximo común divisor (M.C.D.) de dos o más números enteros no negativos es el número mayor que es un factor de todos los números.

English/Spanish Glossary

H

Height of a cone The height of a cone, h, is the length of a segment perpendicular to the base that joins the vertex and the base.

Altura de un cono La altura de un cono, h, es la longitud de un segmento perpendicular a la base que une el vértice y la base.

Height of a cylinder The height of a cylinder is the length of a perpendicular segment that joins the planes of the bases.

Altura de un cilindro La altura de un cilindro es la longitud de un segmento perpendicular que une los planos de las bases.

Height of a parallelogram A height of a parallelogram is the perpendicular distance between opposite bases.

Altura de un paralelogramo La altura de un paralelogramo es la distancia perpendicular que existe entre las bases opuestas.

Height of a prism The height of a prism is the length of a perpendicular segment that joins the bases.

Altura de un prisma La altura de un prisma es la longitud de un segmento perpendicular que une a las bases.

Height of a pyramid The height of a pyramid is the length of a segment perpendicular to the base that joins the vertex and the base.

Altura de una pirámide La altura de una pirámide es la longitud de un segmento perpendicular a la base que une al vértice con la base.

Height of a triangle The height of a triangle is the length of the perpendicular segment from a vertex to the base opposite that vertex.

Altura de un triángulo La altura de un triángulo es la longitud del segmento perpendicular desde un vértice hasta la base opuesta a ese vértice.

Hexagon A hexagon is a polygon with six sides.

Hexágono Un hexágono es un polígono de seis lados.

Histogram A histogram is a statistical graph that shows the shape of a data set with vertical bars above intervals of values on a number line. The intervals are equal in size and do not overlap. The height of each bar shows the frequency of data within that interval.

Histograma Un histograma es una gráfica de estadísticas que muestra la forma de un conjunto de datos con barras verticales encima de intervalos de valores en una recta numérica. Los intervalos tienen el mismo tamaño y no se superponen. La altura de cada barra muestra la frecuencia de los datos dentro de ese intervalo.

Hundredths One hundredth is one part of 100 equal parts of a whole.

Centésima Una centésima es 1 de las 100 partes iguales de un todo.

Hypotenuse In a right triangle, the longest side, which is opposite the right angle, is the hypotenuse.

Hipotenusa En un triángulo rectángulo, el lado más largo, que es opuesto al ángulo recto, es la hipotenusa.

I

Identify To identify is to match a definition or description to an object or to recognize something and be able to name it.

Identificar Identificar es unir una definición o una descripción con un objeto, o reconocer algo y poder nombrarlo.

Identity Property of Addition The sum of 0 and any number is that number. For any number n, $n + 0 = n$ and $0 + n = n$.

Propiedad de identidad de la suma La suma de 0 y cualquier número es ese número. Para cualquier número n, $n + 0 = n$ and $0 + n = n$.

Identity Property of Multiplication The product of 1 and any number is that number. For any number n, $n \cdot 1 = n$ and $1 \cdot n = n$.

Propiedad de identidad de la multiplicación El producto de 1 y cualquier número es ese número. Para cualquier número n, $n \cdot 1 = n$ and $1 \cdot n = n$.

Illustrate To illustrate is to show or present information, usually as a drawing or a diagram. You can also illustrate a point using a written explanation.

Ilustrar Ilustrar es mostrar o presentar información, generalmente en forma de dibujo o diagrama. También puedes usar una explicación escrita para ilustrar un punto.

English/Spanish Glossary

Image An image is the result of a transformation of a point, line, or figure.

Imagen Una imagen es el resultado de una transformación de un punto, una recta o una figura.

Improper fraction An improper fraction is a fraction in which the numerator is greater than or equal to its denominator.

Fracción impropia Una fracción impropia es una fracción en la cual el numerador es mayor que o igual a su denominador.

Included angle An included angle is an angle that is between two sides.

Ángulo incluido Un ángulo incluido es un ángulo que está entre dos lados.

Included side An included side is a side that is between two angles.

Lado incluido Un lado incluido es un lado que está entre dos ángulos.

Income Money that a business receives. The money that a person earns from working is also called income.

Ingresos El dinero que un negocio recibe. El dinero que una persona gana de trabajar también es llamado los ingresos.

Income tax Income tax is money collected by the government based on how much you earn.

Impuesto de renta El impuesto de renta es dinero completo por el gobierno basado en cuánto gana.

Independent events Two events are independent events if the occurrence of one event does not affect the probability of the other event.

Eventos independientes Dos eventos son eventos independientes cuando el resultado de un evento no altera la probabilidad del otro.

Independent variable An independent variable is a variable whose value determines the value of another (dependent) variable.

Variable independiente Una variable independiente es una variable cuyo valor determina el valor de otra variable (dependiente).

Indicate To indicate is to point out or show.

Indicar Indicar es señalar o mostrar.

Indirect measurement Indirect measurement uses proportions and similar triangles to measure distances that would be difficult to measure directly.

Medición indirecta La medición indirecta usa proporciones y triángulos semejantes para medir distancias que serían difíciles de medir de forma directa.

Inequality An inequality is a mathematical sentence that uses $<$, $\leq$, $>$, $\geq$, or $\neq$ to compare two quantities.

Desigualdad Una desigualdad es una oración matemática que usa $<$, $\leq$, $>$, $\geq$, o $\neq$ para comparar dos cantidades.

Inference An inference is a judgment made by interpreting data.

Inferencia Una inferencia es una opinión que se forma al interpretar datos.

Infinitely many solutions A linear equation in one variable has infinitely many solutions if any value of the variable makes the two sides of the equation equal.

Número infinito de soluciones Una ecuación lineal en una variable tiene un número infinito de soluciones si cualquier valor de la variable hace que los dos lados de la ecuación sean iguales.

Initial value The initial value of a linear function is the value of the output when the input is 0.

Valor inicial El valor inicial de una función lineal es el valor de salida cuando el valor de entrada es 0.

Integers Integers are the set of positive whole numbers, their opposites, and 0.

Enteros Los enteros son el conjunto de los números enteros positivos, sus opuestos y 0.

Interest When you deposit money in a bank account, the bank pays you interest for the right to use your money for a period of time.

Interés Cuando depositas dinero en una cuenta bancaria, el banco te paga un interés por el derecho a usar tu dinero por un período de tiempo.

Interest period The length of time on which compound interest is based. The total number of interest periods that you keep the money in the account is represented by the variable n.

Período de interés La cantidad de tiempo sobre la que se calcula el interés compuesto. El número total de períodos de interés que mantienes el dinero en la cuenta se representa con la variable n.

English/Spanish Glossary

Interest rate Interest is calculated based on a percent of the principal. That percent is called the interest rate (*r*).

Tasa de interés El interés se calcula con base en un porcentaje del capital. Ese porcentaje se llama tasa de interés, (*r*).

Interest rate for an interest period The interest rate for an interest period is the annual interest rate divided by the number of interest periods per year.

El tipo de interés por un período de interés El tipo de interés por un período de interés es el tipo de interés anual dividido por el número de períodos de interés por año.

Interquartile range The interquartile range (IQR) is the distance between the first and third quartiles of the data set. It represents the spread of the middle 50% of the data values.

Rango intercuartil El rango intercuartil es la distancia entre el primer y el tercer cuartil del conjunto de datos. Representa la ubicación del 50% del medio de los valores.

Interval An interval is a period of time between two points of time or events.

Intervalo Un intervalo es un período de tiempo entre dos puntos en el tiempo o entre dos sucesos.

Invalid inference An invalid inference is false about the population, or does not follow from the available data. A biased sample can lead to invalid inferences.

Inferencia inválida Una inferencia inválida es una inferencia falsa acerca de una población, o no se deduce a partir de los datos disponibles. Una muestra sesgada puede llevar a inferencias inválidas.

Inverse operations Inverse operations are operations that undo each other.

Operaciones inversas Las operaciones inversas son operaciones que se cancelan entre sí.

Inverse Property of Addition Every number has an additive inverse. The sum of a number and its additive inverse is zero.

Propiedad inversa de la suma Todos los números tienen un inverso de suma. La suma de un número y su inverso de suma es cero.

Irrational numbers An irrational number is a number that cannot be written in the form $\frac{a}{b}$, where a and b are integers and $b \neq 0$. In decimal form, an irrational number cannot be written as a terminating or repeating decimal.

Números irracionales Un número irracional es un número que no se puede escribir en la forma $\frac{a}{b}$ donde a y b, son enteros y $b \neq 0$. Los números racionales en forma decimal no son finitos y no son periódicos.

Isolate a variable When solving equations, to isolate a variable means to get a variable with a coefficient of 1 alone on one side of an equation. Use the properties of equality and inverse operations to isolate a variable.

Aislar una variable Cuando resuelves ecuaciones, aislar una variable significa poner una variable con un coeficiente de 1 sola a un lado de la ecuación. Usa las propiedades de igualdad y las operaciones inversas para aislar una variable.

Isosceles triangle An isosceles triangle is a triangle with at least two sides that are the same length.

Triángulo isósceles Un triángulo isósceles es un triángulo que tiene al menos dos lados de la misma longitud.

J

Justify To justify is to support your answer with reasons or examples. A justification may include a written response, diagrams, charts, tables, or a combination of these.

Justificar Justificar es apoyar tu respuesta con razones o ejemplos. Una justificación puede incluir una respuesta escrita, diagramas, tablas o una combinación de esos elementos.

L

Lateral area of a cone The lateral area of a cone is the area of its lateral surface. The formula for the lateral area of a cone is $\text{L.A.} = \pi r\ell$, where r represents the radius of the base and ℓ represents the slant height of the cone.

Área lateral de un cono El área lateral de un cono es el área de su superficie lateral. La fórmula del área lateral de un cono es $\text{A.L.} = \pi r\ell$, donde r representa el radio de la base y ℓ representa la altura inclinada del cono.

Lateral area of a cylinder The lateral area of a cylinder is the area of its lateral surface. The formula for the lateral area of a cylinder is L.A. $= 2\pi rh$, where r represents the radius of a base and h represents the height of the cylinder.

Área lateral de un cilindro El área lateral de un cilindro es el área de su superficie lateral. La fórmula del área lateral de un cilindro es A.L. $= 2\pi rh$, donde r representa el radio de una base y h representa la altura del cilindro.

Lateral area of a prism The lateral area of a prism is the sum of the areas of the lateral faces of the prism. The formula for the lateral area, L.A., of a prism is L.A. $= ph$, where p represents the perimeter of the base and h represents the height of the prism.

Área lateral de un prisma El área lateral de un prisma es la suma de las áreas de las caras laterales del prisma. La fórmula del área lateral, A.L., de un prisma es A.L. $= ph$, donde p representa el perímetro de la base y h representa la altura del prisma.

Lateral area of a pyramid The lateral area of a pyramid is the sum of the areas of the lateral faces of the pyramid. The formula for the lateral area, L.A., of a pyramid is L.A. $= \frac{1}{2}p\ell$ where p represents the perimeter of the base and ℓ represents the slant height of the pyramid.

Área lateral de una pirámide El área lateral de una pirámide es la suma de las áreas de las caras laterales de la pirámide. La fórmula del área lateral, A.L., de una pirámide es A.L. $= \frac{1}{2}p\ell$ donde p representa el perímetro de la base y ℓ representa la altura inclinada de la pirámide.

Lateral face of a prism A lateral face of a prism is a face that joins the bases of the prism.

Cara lateral de un prisma La cara lateral de un prisma es la cara que une a las bases del prisma.

Lateral face of a pyramid A lateral face of a pyramid is a triangular face that joins the base and the vertex.

Cara lateral de una pirámide La cara lateral de una pirámide es una cara lateral que une a la base con el vértice.

Lateral surface of a cone The lateral surface of a cone is the curved surface that is not included in the base.

Superficie lateral de un cono La superficie lateral de un cono es la superficie curva que no está incluida en la base.

Lateral surface of a cylinder The lateral surface of a cylinder is the curved surface that is not included in the bases.

Superficie lateral de un cilindro La superficie lateral de un cilindro es la superficie curva que no está incluida en las bases.

Least common multiple The least common multiple (LCM) of two or more numbers is the least multiple shared by all of the numbers.

Mínimo común múltiplo El mínimo común múltiplo (MCM) de dos o más números es el múltiplo menor compartido por todos los números.

Leg of a right triangle In a right triangle, the two shortest sides are legs.

Cateto de un triángulo rectángulo En un triángulo rectángulo, los dos lados más cortos son los catetos.

Less than < The less-than symbol shows a comparison of two numbers with the number of lesser value shown first, or on the left.

Menor que < El símbolo de menor que muestra una comparación de dos números con el número de menor valor que aparece primero, o a la izquierda.

Liability A liability is money that you owe.

Obligación Una obligación es dinero que usted debe.

Lifetime income The amount of money earned over a lifetime of working.

Ingresos para toda la vida La cantidad de dinero ganó sobre una vida de trabajar.

Like terms Terms that have identical variable parts are like terms.

Términos semejantes Los términos que tienen partes variables idénticas son términos semejantes.

Line of reflection A line of reflection is a line across which a figure is reflected.

Eje de reflexión Un eje de reflexión es una línea a través de la cual se refleja una figura.

Linear equation An equation is a linear equation if the graph of all of its solutions is a line.

Ecuación lineal Una ecuación es lineal si la gráfica de todas sus soluciones es una línea recta.

English/Spanish Glossary

Linear function A linear function is a function whose graph is a straight line. The rate of change for a linear function is constant.

Función lineal Una función lineal es una función cuya gráfica es una línea recta. La tasa de cambio en una función lineal es constante.

Linear function rule A linear function rule is an equation that describes a linear function.

Regla de la función lineal La ecuación que describe una función lineal es la regla de la función lineal.

Loan A loan is an amount of money borrowed for a period of time with the promise of paying it back.

Préstamo Un préstamo es una cantidad de dinero pedido prestaddo por un espacio de tiempo con la promesa de pagarlo apoya.

Loan length Loan length is the period of time set to repay a loan.

Preste longitud La longitud del préstamo es el conjunto de espacio de tiempo de devolver un préstamo.

Loan term The term of a loan is the period of time set to repay the loan.

Preste término El término de un préstamo es el conjunto de espacio de tiempo de devolver el préstamo.

Locate To locate is to find or identify a value, usually on a number line or coordinate graph.

Ubicar Ubicar es hallar o identificar un valor, generalmente en una recta numérica o en una gráfica de coordenadas.

Loss When a business's expenses are greater than the business's income, there is a loss.

Pérdida Cuando los gastos de un negocio son más que los ingresos del negocio, hay una pérdida.

M

Mapping diagram A mapping diagram describes a relation by linking the input values to the corresponding output values using arrows.

Diagrama de correspondencia Un diagrama de correspondencia describe una relación uniendo con flechas los valores de entrada con sus correspondientes valores de salida.

Markdown Markdown is the amount of decrease from the selling price to the sale price. The markdown as a percent decrease of the original selling price is called the percent markdown.

Rebaja La rebaja es la cantidad de disminución de un precio de venta a un precio rebajado. La rebaja como una disminución porcentual del precio de venta original se llama porcentaje de rebaja.

Markup Markup is the amount of increase from the cost to the selling price. The markup as a percent increase of the original cost is called the percent markup.

Margen de ganancia El margen de ganancia es la cantidad de aumento del costo al precio de venta. El margen de ganancia como un aumento porcentual del costo original se llama porcentaje del margen de ganancia.

Mean The mean represents the center of a numerical data set. To find the mean, sum the data values and then divide by the number of values in the data set.

Media La media representa el centro de un conjunto de datos numéricos. Para hallar la media, suma los valores y luego divide por el número de valores del conjunto de datos.

Mean absolute deviation The mean absolute deviation is a measure of variability that describes how much the data values are spread out from the mean of a data set. The mean absolute deviation is the average distance that the data values are spread around the mean. mean absolute deviation = $\frac{\text{sum of the absolute deviations of the data values}}{\text{total number of data values}}$

Desviación absoluta media La desviación absoluta media es una medida de variabilidad que describe cuánto se alejan los valores de la media de un conjunto de datos. La desviación absoluta media es la distancia promedio que los valores se alejan de la media. desviación absoluta media = $\frac{\text{suma de las desviaciones absolutas de los valores}}{\text{número total de valores}}$

English/Spanish Glossary

Measure of variability A measure of variability describes the spread of values in a data set. There may be more than one measure of variability for a data set.

Medida de variabilidad Una medida de variabilidad describe la distribución de los valores de un conjunto de datos. Puede haber más de una medida de variabilidad para un conjunto de datos.

Measurement data Measurement data consist of data that are measures.

Datos de mediciones Los datos de mediciones son datos que son medidas.

Measures of center A measure of center is a value that represents the middle of a data set. There may be more than one measure of center for a data set.

Medida de tendencia central Una medida de tendencia central es un valor que representa el centro de un conjunto de datos. Puede haber más de una medida de tendencia central para un conjunto de datos.

Median The median represents the center of a numerical data set. For an odd number of data values, the median is the middle value when the data values are arranged in numerical order. For an even number of data values, the median is the average of the two middle values when the data values are arranged in numerical order.

Mediana La mediana representa el centro de un conjunto de datos numéricos. Para un número impar de valores, la mediana es el valor del medio cuando los valores están organizados en orden numérico. Para un número par de valores, la mediana es el promedio de los dos valores del medio cuando los valores están organizados en orden numérico.

Median-median line The median-median line, or median trend line, is a method of finding a fit line for a scatter plot that suggests a linear association. This method involves dividing the data into three subgroups and using medians to find a summary point for each subgroup. The summary points are used to find the equation of the fit line.

Recta mediana-mediana La recta mediana-mediana es un método que se usa para hallar una línea de ajuste para un diagrama de dispersión que sugiere una asociación lineal. Este método implica dividir los datos en tres subgrupos y usar medianas para hallar un punto medio para cada subgrupo. Los puntos medios se usan para hallar la ecuación de la línea de ajuste.

Million Whole numbers in the millions have 7, 8, or 9 digits.

Millón Los números enteros no negativos que están en los millones tienen 7, 8 ó 9 dígitos.

Mixed number A mixed number combines a whole number and a fraction.

Número mixto Un número mixto combina un número entero no negativo con una fracción.

Mode The item, or items, in a data set that occurs most frequently.

Modo El artículo, o los artículos, en un conjunto de datos que ocurre normalmente.

Model To model is to represent a situation using pictures, diagrams, or number sentences.

Demostrar Demostrar es usar ilustraciones, diagramas o enunciados numéricos para representar una situación.

Monetary incentive A monetary incentive is an offer that might encourage customers to buy a product.

Estímulo monetario Un estímulo monetario es una oferta que quizás favorezca a clientes para comprar un producto.

Multiple A multiple of a number is the product of the number and a whole number.

Múltiplo El múltiplo de un número es el producto del número y un número entero no negativo.

Natural numbers The natural numbers are the counting numbers.

Números naturales Los números naturales son los números que se usan para contar.

Negative exponent property For every nonzero number a and integer n, $a^{-n} = \frac{1}{a^n}$.

Propiedad del exponente negativo Para todo número distinto de cero a y entero n, $a^{-n} = \frac{1}{a^n}$.

Negative numbers Negative numbers are numbers less than zero.

Números negativos Los números negativos son números menores que cero.

Net A net is a two-dimensional pattern that you can fold to form a three-dimensional figure. A net of a figure shows all of the surfaces of that figure in one view.

Modelo plano Un modelo plano es un diseño bidimensional que puedes doblar para formar una figura tridimensional. Un modelo plano de una figura muestra todas las superficies de la figura en una vista.

Net worth Net worth is the total value of all assets minus the total value of all liabilities.

Patrimonio neto El patrimonio neto es el valor total de todas las ventajas menos el valor total de todas las obligaciones.

Net worth statement Net worth is the total value of all assets minus the total value of all liabilities.

Declaración de patrimonio neto El patrimonio neto es el valor total de todas las ventajas menos el valor total de todas las obligaciones.

No solution A linear equation in one variable has no solution if no value of the variable makes the two sides of the equation equal.

Sin solución Una ecuación lineal en una variable no tiene solución si ningún valor de la variable hace que los dos lados de la ecuación sean iguales.

Nonlinear function A nonlinear function is a function that does not have a constant rate of change.

Función no lineal Una función no lineal es una función que no tiene una tasa de cambio constante.

Numerator The numerator is the number above the fraction bar in a fraction.

Numerador El numerador es el número que está arriba de la barra de fracción en una fracción.

Numerical expression A numerical expression is a mathematical phrase that consists of numbers and operation symbols.

Expresión numérica Una expresión numérica es una frase matemática que contiene números y símbolos de operaciones.

O

Obtuse angle An obtuse angle is an angle with a measure greater than 90° and less than 180°.

Ángulo obtuso Un ángulo obtuso es un ángulo con una medida mayor que 90° y menor que 180°.

Obtuse triangle An obtuse triangle is a triangle with one obtuse angle.

Triángulo obtusángulo Un triángulo obtusángulo es un triángulo que tiene un ángulo obtuso.

Octagon An octagon is a polygon with eight sides.

Octágono Un octágono es un polígono de ocho lados.

Online payment system An online payment system allows money to be exchanged electronically between buyer and seller, usually using credit card or bank account information.

Sistema en línea de pago Un sistema en línea del pago permite dinero para ser cambiado electrónicamente entre comprador y vendedor, utilizando generalmente información de tarjeta de crédito o cuenta bancaria.

Open sentence An open sentence is an equation with one or more variables.

Enunciado abierto Un enunciado abierto es una ecuación con una o más variables.

Opposites Opposites are two numbers that are the same distance from 0 on a number line, but in opposite directions.

Opuestos Los opuestos son dos números que están a la misma distancia de 0 en la recta numérica, pero en direcciones opuestas.

Order of operations The order of operations is the order in which operations should be performed in an expression. Operations inside parentheses are done first, followed by exponents. Then, multiplication and division are done in order from left to right, and finally addition and subtraction are done in order from left to right.

Orden de las operaciones El orden de las operaciones es el orden en el que se deben resolver las operaciones de una expresión. Las operaciones que están entre paréntesis se resuelven primero, seguidas de los exponentes. Luego, se multiplica y se divide en orden de izquierda a derecha, y finalmente se suma y se resta en orden de izquierda a derecha.

English/Spanish Glossary

Ordered pair An ordered pair identifies the location of a point in the coordinate plane. The *x*-coordinate shows a point's position left or right of the *y*-axis. The *y*-coordinate shows a point's position up or down from the *x*-axis.

Par ordenado Un par ordenado identifica la ubicación de un punto en el plano de coordenadas. La coordenada *x* muestra la posición de un punto a la izquierda o a la derecha del eje de las *y*. La coordenada *y* muestra la posición de un punto arriba o abajo del eje de las *x*.

Origin The origin is the point of intersection of the *x*- and *y*-axes on a coordinate plane.

Origen El origen es el punto de intersección del eje de las *x* y el eje de las *y* en un plano de coordenadas.

Outcome An outcome is a possible result of an action.

Resultado Un resultado es un desenlace posible de una acción.

Outlier An outlier is a piece of data that doesn't seem to fit with the rest of a data set.

Valor extremo Un valor extremo es un valor que parece no ajustarse al resto de los datos de un conjunto.

P

Parallel lines Parallel lines are lines in the same plane that never intersect.

Rectas paralelas Las rectas paralelas son rectas que están en el mismo plano y nunca se intersecan.

Parallelogram A parallelogram is a quadrilateral with both pairs of opposite sides parallel.

Paralelogramo Un paralelogramo es un cuadrilátero en el cual los dos pares de lados opuestos son paralelos.

Partial product A partial product is part of the total product. A product is the sum of the partial products.

Producto parcial Un producto parcial es una parte del producto total. Un producto es la suma de los productos parciales.

Pay period Wages for many jobs are paid at regular intervals, such a weekly, biweekly, semimonthly, or monthly. The interval of time is called a pay period.

Pague el período Los sueldos para muchos trabajos son pagados con regularidad, tal semanal, quincenal, quincenal, o mensual. El intervalo de tiempo es llamado un período de la paga.

Payroll deductions Your employer can deduct your income taxes from your wages before you receive your paycheck. The amounts deducted are called payroll deductions.

Deducciones de nómina Su empleador puede descontar sus impuestos de renta de sus sueldos antes que reciba su cheque de pago. Las cantidades descontadas son llamadas nómina deducciones.

Percent A percent is a ratio that compares a number to 100.

Porcentaje Un porcentaje es una razón que compara un número con 100.

Percent bar graph A percent bar graph is a bar graph that shows each category as a percent of the total number of data items.

Gráfico de barras de por ciento Un gráfico de barras del por ciento es un gráfico de barras que muestra cada categoría como un por ciento del número total de artículos de datos.

Percent decrease When a quantity decreases, the percent of change is called a percent decrease. percent decrease = $\frac{\text{amount of decrease}}{\text{original quantity}}$

Disminución porcentual Cuando una cantidad disminuye, el porcentaje de cambio se llama disminución porcentual. disminución porcentual = $\frac{\text{cantidad de disminución}}{\text{cantidad original}}$

Percent equation The percent equation describes the relationship between a part and a whole. You can use the percent equation to solve percent problems. part = percent · whole

Ecuación de porcentaje La ecuación de porcentaje describe la relación entre una parte y un todo. Puedes usar la ecuación de porcentaje para resolver problemas de porcentaje. parte = por ciento · todo

Percent error Percent error describes the accuracy of a measured or estimated value compared to an actual or accepted value.

Error porcentual El error porcentual describe la exactitud de un valor medido o estimado en comparación con un valor real o aceptado.

Percent increase When a quantity increases, the percent of change is called a percent increase.

Aumento porcentual Cuando una cantidad aumenta, el porcentaje de cambio se llama aumento porcentual.

Percent of change Percent of change is the percent something increases or decreases from its original measure or amount. You can find the percent of change by using the equation: percent of change $= \frac{\text{amount of change}}{\text{original quantity}}$

Porcentaje de cambio El porcentaje de cambio es el porcentaje en que algo aumenta o disminuye en relación a la medida o cantidad original. Puedes hallar el porcentaje de cambio con la siguiente ecuación: porcentaje de cambio $= \frac{\text{cantidad de cambio}}{\text{cantidad original}}$

Perfect cube A perfect cube is the cube of an integer.

Cubo perfecto Un cubo perfecto es el cubo de un entero.

Perfect square A perfect square is a number that is the square of an integer.

Cuadrado perfecto Un cuadrado perfecto es un número que es el cuadrado de un entero.

Perimeter Perimeter is the distance around a figure.

Perímetro El perímetro es la distancia alrededor de una figura.

Period A period is a group of 3 digits in a number. Periods are separated by a comma and start from the right of a number.

Período Un período es un grupo de 3 dígitos en un número. Los períodos están separados por una coma y empiezan a la derecha del número.

Periodic savings plan A periodic savings plan is a method of saving that involves making deposits on a regular basis.

Plan de ahorros periódico Un plan de ahorros periódico es un método de guardar que implica depósitos que hace con regularidad.

Perpendicular lines Perpendicular lines intersect to form right angles.

Rectas perpendiculares Las rectas perpendiculares se intersecan para formar ángulos rectos.

Pi Pi (π) is the ratio of a circle's circumference, *C*, to its diameter, *d*.

Pi Pi (π) es la razón de la circunferencia de un círculo, *C*, a su diámetro, *d*.

Place value Place value is the value given to an individual digit based on its position within a number.

Valor posicional El valor posicional es el valor asignado a determinado dígito según su posición en un número.

Plane A plane is a flat surface that extends indefinitely in all directions.

Plano Un plano es una superficie plana que se extiende indefinidamente en todas direcciones.

Polygon A polygon is a closed figure formed by three or more line segments that do not cross.

Polígono Un polígono es una figura cerrada compuesta por tres o más segmentos que no se cruzan.

Population A population is the complete set of items being studied.

Población Una población es todo el conjunto de elementos que se estudian.

Positive numbers Positive numbers are numbers greater than zero.

Números positivos Los números positivos son números mayores que cero.

Power A power is a number expressed using an exponent.

Potencia Una potencia es un número expresado con un exponente.

Predict To predict is to make an educated guess based on the analysis of real data.

Predecir Predecir es hacer una estimación informada según el análisis de datos reales.

Prime factorization The prime factorization of a composite number is the expression of the number as a product of its prime factors.

Descomposición en factores primos La descomposición en factores primos de un número compuesto es la expresión del número como un producto de sus factores primos.

Prime number A prime number is a whole number greater than 1 with exactly two factors, 1 and the number itself.

Número primo Un número primo es un número entero mayor que 1 con exactamente dos factores, 1 y el número mismo.

Principal The original amount of money deposited or borrowed in an account.

Capital La cantidad original de dinero que se deposita o se pide prestada en una cuenta.

Prism A prism is a three-dimensional figure with two parallel polygonal faces that are the same size and shape.

Prisma Un prisma es una figura tridimensional con dos caras poligonales paralelas que tienen el mismo tamaño y la misma forma.

Probability model A probability model consists of an action, its sample space, and a list of events with their probabilities. The events and probabilities in the list have these characteristics: each outcome in the sample space is in exactly one event, and the sum of all of the probabilities must be 1.

Modelo de probabilidad Un modelo de probabilidad consiste en una acción, su espacio muestral y una lista de eventos con sus probabilidades. Los eventos y las probabilidades de la lista tienen estas características: cada resultado del espacio muestral está exactamente en un evento, y la suma de todas las probabilidades debe ser 1.

Probability of an event The probability of an event is a number from 0 to 1 that measures the likelihood that the event will occur. The closer the probability is to 0, the less likely it is that the event will happen. The closer the probability is to 1, the more likely it is that the event will happen. You can express probability as a fraction, decimal, or percent.

Probabilidad de un evento La probabilidad de un evento es un número de 0 a 1 que mide la probabilidad de que suceda el evento. Cuanto más se acerca la probabilidad a 0, menos probable es que suceda el evento. Cuanto más se acerca la probabilidad a 1, más probable es que suceda el evento. Puedes expresar la probabilidad como una fracción, un decimal o un porcentaje.

Product A product is the value of a multiplication or an expression showing multiplication.

Producto Un producto es el valor de una multiplicación o una expresión que representa la multiplicación.

Profit When a business's expenses are less than the business's income, there is a profit.

Ganancia Cuando los gastos de un negocio son menos que los ingresos del negocio, hay una ganancia.

Proof A proof is a logical, deductive argument in which every statement of fact is supported by a reason.

Comprobación Una comprobación es un argumento lógico y deductivo en el que cada enunciado de un hecho está apoyado por una razón.

Proper fraction A proper fraction has a numerator that is less than its denominator.

Fracción propia Una fracción propia tiene un numerador que es menor que su denominador.

Proportion A proportion is an equation stating that two ratios are equal.

Proporción Una proporción es una ecuación que establece que dos razones son iguales.

Proportional relationship Two quantities *x* and *y* have a proportional relationship if *y* is always a constant multiple of *x*. A relationship is proportional if it can be described by equivalent ratios.

Relación de proporción Dos cantidades *x* y *y* tienen una relación de proporción si *y* es siempre un múltiplo constante de *x*. Una relación es de proporción si se puede describir con razones equivalentes.

Pyramid A pyramid is a three-dimensional figure with a base that is a polygon and triangular faces that meet at a vertex. A pyramid is named for the shape of its base.

Pirámide Una pirámide es una figura tridimensional con una base que es un polígono y caras triangulares que se unen en un vértice. El nombre de la pirámide depende de la forma de su base.

Pythagorean Theorem In any right triangle, the sum of the squares of the lengths of the legs equals the square of the length of the hypotenuse. If a triangle is a right triangle, then $a^2 + b^2 = c^2$, where a and b represent the lengths of the legs, and c represents the length of the hypotenuse.

Teorema de Pitágoras En cualquier triángulo rectángulo, la suma del cuadrado de la longitud de los catetos es igual al cuadrado de la longitud de la hipotenusa. Si un triángulo es un triángulo rectángulo, entonces $a^2 + b^2 = c^2$, donde a y b representan la longitud de los catetos, y c representa la longitud de la hipotenusa.

Q

Quadrant The *x*- and *y*-axes divide the coordinate plane into four regions called quadrants.

Cuadrante Los ejes de las *x* y de las *y* dividen el plano de coordenadas en cuatro regiones llamadas cuadrantes.

Quadrilateral A quadrilateral is a polygon with four sides.

Cuadrilátero Un cuadrilátero es un polígono de cuatro lados.

Quarter circle A quarter circle is one fourth of a circle.

Círculo cuarto Un círculo cuarto es la cuarta parte de un círculo.

Quartile The quartiles of a data set divide the data set into four parts with the same number of data values in each part.

Cuartil Los cuartiles de un conjunto de datos dividen el conjunto de datos en cuatro partes que tienen el mismo número de valores cada una.

Quotient The quotient is the answer to a division problem. When there is a remainder, "quotient" sometimes refers to the whole-number portion of the answer.

Cociente El cociente es el resultado de una división. Cuando queda un residuo, "cociente" a veces se refiere a la parte de la solución que es un número entero.

R

Radius A radius of a circle is a segment that has one endpoint at the center and the other endpoint on the circle. The term radius can also mean the length of this segment.

Radio Un radio de un círculo es un segmento que tiene un extremo en el centro y el otro extremo en el círculo. El término radio también puede referirse a la longitud de este segmento.

Radius of a sphere The radius of a sphere, r, is a segment that has one endpoint at the center and the other endpoint on the sphere.

Radio de una esfera El radio de una esfera, r, es un segmento que tiene un extremo en el centro y el otro extremo en la esfera.

Random sample In a random sample, each member in the population has an equal chance of being selected.

Muestra aleatoria En una muestra aleatoria, cada miembro en la población tiene una oportunidad igual de ser seleccionado.

Range The range is a measure of variability of a numerical data set. The range of a data set is the difference between the greatest and least values in a data set.

Rango El rango es una medida de la variabilidad de un conjunto de datos numéricos. El rango de un conjunto de datos es la diferencia que existe entre el mayor y el menor valor del conjunto.

Rate A rate is a ratio involving two quantities measured in different units.

Tasa Una tasa es una razón que relaciona dos cantidades medidas con unidades diferentes.

Rate of change The rate of change of a linear function is the ratio $\frac{\text{vertical change}}{\text{horizontal change}}$ between any two points on the graph of the function.

Tasa de cambio La tasa de cambio de una función lineal es la razón del $\frac{\text{cambio vertical}}{\text{cambio horizontal}}$ que existe entre dos puntos cualesquiera de la gráfica de la función.

Ratio A ratio is a relationship in which for every x units of one quantity there are y units of another quantity.

Razón Una razón es una relación en la cual por cada x unidades de una cantidad hay y unidades de otra cantidad.

English/Spanish Glossary

Rational numbers A rational number is a number that can be written in the form $\frac{a}{b}$ or $-\frac{a}{b}$, where a is a whole number and b is a positive whole number. The rational numbers include the integers.

Números racionales Un número racional es un número que se puede escribir como $\frac{a}{b}$ or $-\frac{a}{b}$, donde a es un número entero no negativo y b es un número entero positivo. Los números racionales incluyen los enteros.

Real numbers The real numbers are the set of rational and irrational numbers.

Números reales Los números reales son el conjunto de los números racionales e irracionales.

Reason To reason is to think through a problem using facts and information.

Razonar Razonar es usar hechos e información para estudiar detenidamente un problema.

Rebate A rebate returns part of the purchase price of an item after the buyer provides proof of purchase through a mail-in or online form.

Reembolso Un reembolso regresa la parte del precio de compra de un artículo después de que el comprador proporcione comprobante de compra por un correo-en o forma en línea.

Recall To recall is to remember a fact quickly.

Recordar Recordar es traer a la memoria un hecho rápidamente.

Reciprocals Two numbers are reciprocals if their product is 1. If a nonzero number is named as a fraction, , then its reciprocal is .

Recíprocos Dos números son recíprocos si su producto es 1. Si un número distinto de cero se expresa como una fracción, , entonces su recíproco es .

Rectangle A rectangle is a quadrilateral with four right angles.

Rectángulo Un rectángulo es un cuadrilátero que tiene cuatro ángulos rectos.

Rectangular prism A rectangular prism is a prism with bases in the shape of a rectangle.

Prisma rectangular Un prisma rectangular es un prisma cuyas bases tienen la forma de un rectángulo.

Reduction A reduction is a dilation with a scale factor less than 1. After a reduction, the image is smaller than the original figure.

Reducción Una reducción es una dilatación con un factor de escala menor que 1. Después de una reducción, la imagen es más pequeña que la figura original.

Reflection A reflection, or flip, is a transformation that flips a figure across a line of reflection.

Reflexión Una reflexión, o inversión, es una transformación que invierte una figura a través de un eje de reflexión.

Regular polygon A regular polygon is a polygon with all sides of equal length and all angles of equal measure.

Polígono regular Un polígono regular es un polígono que tiene todos los lados de la misma longitud y todos los ángulos de la misma medida.

Relate To relate two different things, find a connection between them.

Relacionar Para relacionar dos cosas diferentes, halla una conexión entre ellas.

Relation Any set of ordered pairs is called a relation.

Relación Todo conjunto de pares ordenados se llama relación.

Relative frequency relative frequency of an event $= \frac{\text{number of times event occurs}}{\text{total number of trials}}$

Frecuencia relativa frecuencia relativa de un evento $= \frac{\text{número de veces que sucede el evento}}{\text{número total de pruebas}}$

Relative frequency table A relative frequency table shows the ratio of the number of data in each category to the total number of data items. The ratio can be expressed as a fraction, decimal, or percent.

Mesa relativa de frecuencia Una mesa relativa de la frecuencia muestra la proporción del número de datos en cada categoría al número total de artículos de datos. La proporción puede ser expresada como una fracción, el decimal, o el por ciento.

Remainder In division, the remainder is the number that is left after the division is complete.

Residuo En una división, el residuo es el número que queda después de terminar la operación.

English/Spanish Glossary

Remote interior angles Remote interior angles are the two nonadjacent interior angles corresponding to each exterior angle of a triangle.

Ángulos internos no adyacentes Los ángulos internos no adyacentes son los dos ángulos internos de un triángulo que se corresponden con el ángulo externo que está más alejado de ellos.

Repeating decimal A repeating decimal has a decimal expansion that repeats the same digit, or block of digits, without end.

Decimal periódico Un decimal periódico tiene una expansión decimal que repite el mismo dígito, o grupo de dígitos, sin fin.

Represent To represent is to stand for or take the place of something else. Symbols, equations, charts, and tables are often used to represent particular situations.

Representar Representar es sustituir u ocupar el lugar de otra cosa. A menudo se usan símbolos, ecuaciones y tablas para representar determinadas situaciones.

Representative sample A representative sample is a sample of a population in which the number of subjects in the sample with the trait that you are studying is proportional to the number of members in the population with that trait. A representative sample accurately represents the population and does not have bias.

Muestra representativa Una muestra representativa es una muestra de una población en la que el número de sujetos de la muestra que tiene la característica que se estudia es proporcional al número de miembros de la población que tienen esa característica. Una muestra representativa representa la población con exactitud y no está sesgada.

Rhombus A rhombus is a parallelogram whose sides are all the same length.

Rombo Un rombo es un paralelogramo que tiene todos sus lados de la misma longitud.

Right angle A right angle is an angle with a measure of 90°.

Ángulo recto Un ángulo recto es un ángulo que mide 90°.

Right cone A right cone is a cone in which the segment representing the height connects the vertex and the center of the base.

Cono recto Un cono recto es un cono en el que el segmento que representa la altura une el vértice y el centro de la base.

Right cylinder A right cylinder is a cylinder in which the height joins the centers of the bases.

Cilindro recto Un cilindro recto es un cilindro en el que la altura une los centros de las bases.

Right prism In a right prism, all lateral faces are rectangles.

Prisma recto En un prisma recto, todas las caras laterales son rectángulos.

Right pyramid In a right pyramid, the segment that represents the height intersects the base at its center.

Pirámide recta En una pirámide recta, el segmento que representa la altura interseca la base en el centro.

Right triangle A right triangle is a triangle with one right angle.

Triángulo rectángulo Un triángulo rectángulo es un triángulo que tiene un ángulo recto.

Rigid motion A rigid motion is a transformation that changes only the position of a figure.

Movimiento rígido Un movimiento rígido es una transformación que sólo cambia la posición de una figura.

Rotation A rotation is a rigid motion that turns a figure around a fixed point, called the center of rotation.

Rotación Una rotación es un movimiento rígido que hace girar una figura alrededor de un punto fijo, llamado centro de rotación.

Rounding Rounding a number means replacing the number with a number that tells about how much or how many.

Redondear Redondear un número significa reemplazar ese número por un número que indica más o menos cuánto o cuántos.

S

Sale A sale is a discount offered by a store. A sale does not require the customer to have a coupon.

Venta Una venta es un descuento ofreció por una tienda. Una venta no requiere al cliente a tener un cupón.

Sales tax A tax added to the price of goods and services.

Las ventas tasan Un impuesto añadió al precio de bienes y servicios.

Sample of a population A sample of a population is part of the population. A sample is useful when you want to find out about a population but you do not have the resources to study every member of the population.

Muestra de una población Una muestra de una población es una parte de la población. Una muestra es útil cuando quieres saber algo acerca de una población, pero no tienes los recursos para estudiar a cada miembro de esa población.

Sample space The sample space for an action is the set of all possible outcomes of that action.

Espacio muestral El espacio muestral de una acción es el conjunto de todos los resultados posibles de esa acción.

Sampling method A sampling method is the method by which you choose members of a population to sample.

Método de muestreo Un método de muestreo es el método por el cual escoges miembros de una población para muestrear.

Savings Savings is money that a person puts away for use at a later date.

Ahorros Los ahorros son dinero que una persona guarda para el uso en una fecha posterior.

Scale A scale is a ratio that compares a length in a scale drawing to the corresponding length in the actual object.

Escala Una escala es una razón que compara una longitud en un dibujo a escala con la longitud correspondiente en el objeto real.

Scale drawing A scale drawing is an enlarged or reduced drawing of an object that is proportional to the actual object.

Dibujo a escala Un dibujo a escala es un dibujo ampliado o reducido de un objeto que es proporcional al objeto real.

English/Spanish Glossary

Scale factor The scale factor is the ratio of a length in the image to the corresponding length in the original figure.

Factor de escala El factor de escala es la razón de una longitud de la imagen a la longitud correspondiente en la figura original.

Scalene triangle A scalene triangle is a triangle in which no sides have the same length.

Triángulo escaleno Un triángulo escaleno es un triángulo que no tiene lados de la misma longitud.

Scatter plot A scatter plot is a graph that uses points to display the relationship between two different sets of data. Each point can be represented by an ordered pair.

Diagrama de dispersión Un diagrama de dispersión es una gráfica que usa puntos para mostrar la relación entre dos conjuntos de datos diferentes. Cada punto se puede representar con un par ordenado.

Scholarship A type of monetary award a student can use to pay for his or her education. The student does not need to repay this money.

Beca Un tipo de premio monetario que un estudiante puede utilizar para pagar por su educación. El estudiante no debe devolver este dinero.

Scientific notation A number in scientific notation is written as the product of two factors, one greater than or equal to 1 and less than 10, and the other a power of 10.

Notación científica Un número en notación científica está escrito como el producto de dos factores, uno mayor que o igual a 1 y menor que 10, y el otro una potencia de 10.

Segment A segment is part of a line. It consists of two endpoints and all of the points on the line between the endpoints.

Segmento Un segmento es una parte de una recta. Está formado por dos extremos y todos los puntos de la recta que están entre los extremos.

Semicircle A semicircle is one half of a circle.

Semicírculo Un semicírculo es la mitad de un círculo.

Similar figures A two-dimensional figure is similar to another two-dimensional figure if you can map one figure to the other by a sequence of rotations, reflections, translations, and dilations.

Figuras semejantes Una figura bidimensional es semejante a otra figura bidimensional si puedes hacer corresponder una figura con otra mediante una secuencia de rotaciones, reflexiones, traslaciones y dilataciones.

Simple interest Simple interest is interest paid only on an original deposit. To calculate simple interest, use the formula where I is the simple interest, p is the principal, r is the annual interest rate, and t is the number of years that the account earns interest.

Interés simple El interés simple es el interés que se paga sobre un depósito original solamente. Para calcular el interés simple, usa la fórmula donde I es el interés simple, c es el capital, r es la tasa de interés anual y t es el número de años en que la cuenta obtiene un interés.

Simple random sampling Simple random sampling is a sampling method in which every member of the population has an equal chance of being chosen for the sample.

Muestreo aleatorio simple El muestreo aleatorio simple es un método de muestreo en el que cada miembro de la población tiene la misma probabilidad de ser seleccionado para la muestra.

Simpler form A fraction is in simpler form when it is equivalent to a given fraction and has smaller numbers in the numerator and denominator.

Forma simplificada Una fracción está en su forma simplificada cuando es equivalente a otra fracción dada, pero tiene números más pequeños en el numerador y el denominador.

Simplest form A fraction is in simplest form when the only common factor of the numerator and denominator is one.

Mínima expresión Una fracción está en su mínima expresión cuando el único factor común del numerador y el denominador es 1.

Simplify an algebraic expression To simplify an algebraic expression, combine the like terms of the expression.

Simplificar una expresión algebraica Para simplificar una expresión algebraica, combina los términos semejantes de la expresión.

Simulation A simulation is a model of a real-world situation that is used to find probabilities.

Simulación Una simulación es un modelo de una situación de la vida diaria que se usa para hallar probabilidades.

Sketch To sketch a figure, draw a rough outline. When a sketch is asked for, it means that a drawing needs to be included in your response.

Bosquejo Para hacer un bosquejo, dibuja un esquema simple. Si se pide un bosquejo, tu respuesta debe incluir un dibujo.

Slant height of a cone The slant height of a cone, ℓ, is the length of its lateral surface from base to vertex.

Altura inclinada de un cono La altura inclinada de un cono, ℓ, es la longitud de su superficie lateral desde la base hasta el vértice.

Slant height of a pyramid The slant height of a pyramid is the height of a lateral face.

Altura inclinada de una pirámide La altura inclinada de una pirámide es la altura de una cara lateral.

Slope Slope is a ratio that describes steepness.

$$\text{slope} = \frac{\text{vertical change}}{\text{horizontal change}} = \frac{\text{rise}}{\text{run}}$$

Pendiente La pendiente es una razón que describe la inclinación.

$$\text{pendiente} = \frac{\text{cambio vertical}}{\text{cambio horizontal}}$$

$$= \frac{\text{distancia vertical}}{\text{distancia horizontal}}$$

Slope of a line slope =

$$\frac{\text{change in } y\text{-coordinates}}{\text{change in } x\text{-coordinates}} = \frac{\text{rise}}{\text{run}}$$

Pendiente de una recta pendiente =

$$\frac{\text{cambio en las coordenadas } y}{\text{cambio en las coordenadas } x}$$

$$= \frac{\text{distancia vertical}}{\text{distancia horizontal}}$$

Slope-intercept form An equation written in the form $y = mx + b$ is in slope-intercept form. The graph is a line with slope m and y-intercept b.

Forma pendiente-intercepto Una ecuación escrita en la forma $y = mx + b$ está en forma de pendiente-intercepto. La gráfica es una línea recta con pendiente m e intercepto en y b.

Solution of a system of linear equations A solution of a system of linear equations is any ordered pair that makes all the equations of that system true.

Solución de un sistema de ecuaciones lineales Una solución de un sistema de ecuaciones lineales es cualquier par ordenado que hace que todas las ecuaciones de ese sistema sean verdaderas.

Solution of an equation A solution of an equation is a value of the variable that makes the equation true.

Solución de una ecuación Una solución de una ecuación es un valor de la variable que hace que la ecuación sea verdadera.

Solution of an inequality The solutions of an inequality are the values of the variable that make the inequality true.

Solución de una desigualdad Las soluciones de una desigualdad son los valores de la variable que hacen que la desigualdad sea verdadera.

Solution set A solution set contains all of the numbers that satisfy an equation or inequality.

Conjunto solución Un conjunto solución contiene todos los números que satisfacen una ecuación o desigualdad.

Solve To solve a given statement, determine the value or values that make the statement true. Several methods and strategies can be used to solve a problem, including estimating, isolating the variable, drawing a graph, or using a table of values.

Resolver Para resolver un enunciado dado, determina el valor o los valores que hacen que ese enunciado sea verdadero. Para resolver un problema se pueden usar varios métodos y estrategias, como estimar, aislar la variable, dibujar una gráfica o usar una tabla de valores.

Sphere A sphere is the set of all points in space that are the same distance from a center point.

Esfera Una esfera es el conjunto de todos los puntos en el espacio que están a la misma distancia de un punto central.

Square A square is a quadrilateral with four right angles and all sides the same length.

Cuadrado Un cuadrado es un cuadrilátero que tiene cuatro ángulos rectos y todos los lados de la misma longitud.

English/Spanish Glossary

Square root A square root of a number is a number that, when multiplied by itself, equals the original number.

Raíz cuadrada La raíz cuadrada de un número es un número que, cuando se multiplica por sí mismo, es igual al número original.

Square unit A square unit is the area of a square that has sides that are 1 unit long.

Unidad cuadrada Una unidad cuadrada es el área de un cuadrado en el que cada lado mide 1 unidad de longitud.

Standard form A number written using digits and place value is in standard form.

Forma estándar Un número escrito con dígitos y valor posicional está escrito en forma estándar.

Statistical question A statistical question is a question that investigates an aspect of the real world and can have variety in the responses.

Pregunta estadística Una pregunta estadística es una pregunta que investiga un aspecto de la vida diaria y puede tener varias respuestas.

Statistics Statistics is the study of collecting, organizing, graphing, and analyzing data to draw conclusions about the real world.

Estadística La estadística es el estudio de la recolección, organización, representación gráfica y análisis de datos para sacar conclusiones sobre la vida diaria.

Stem-and-leaf plot A stem-and-leaf plot is a graph that uses the digits of each number to show the data distribution. Each data item is broken into a stem and into a leaf. The leaf is the last digit of the data value. The stem is the other digit or digits of the data value.

Complot de tallo y hoja Un complot del tallo y la hoja es un gráfico que utiliza los dígitos de cada número para mostrar la distribución de datos. Cada artículo de datos es roto en un tallo y en una hoja. La hoja es el último dígito de los datos valora. El tallo es el otro dígito o los dígitos de los datos valoran.

Stored-value card A stored-value card is a prepaid card electronically coded to be worth a specified amount of money.

Tarjeta de almacenado-valor Una tarjeta del almacenado-valor es una tarjeta pagada por adelantado codificó electrónicamente valer una cantidad especificado de dinero.

English/Spanish Glossary

Straight angle A straight angle is an angle with a measure of 180°.

Ángulo llano Un ángulo llano es un ángulo que mide 180°.

Student loan A student loan provides money to a student to pay for college. The student needs to repay the loan after leaving college. Often the student will need to pay interest on the amount of the loan.

Crédito personal para estudiantes Un crédito personal para estudiantes le proporciona dinero a un estudiante para pagar por el colegio. El estudiante debe devolver el préstamo después de dejar el colegio. A menudo el estudiante deberá pagar interés en la cantidad del préstamo.

Subject Each member in a sample is a subject.

Sujeto Cada miembro de una muestra es un sujeto.

Sum The sum is the answer to an addition problem.

Suma o total La suma o total es el resultado de una operación de suma.

Summarize To summarize an explanation or solution, go over or review the most important points.

Resumir Para resumir una explicación o solución, revisa o repasa los puntos más importantes.

Supplementary angles Two angles are supplementary angles if the sum of their measures is 180°. Supplementary angles that are adjacent form a straight angle.

Ángulos suplementarios Dos ángulos son suplementarios si la suma de sus medidas es 180°. Los ángulos suplementarios que son adyacentes forman un ángulo llano.

Surface area of a cone The surface area of a cone is the sum of the lateral area and the area of the base. The formula for the surface area of a cone is S.A. = L.A. + B.

Área total de un cono El área total de un cono es la suma del área lateral y el área de la base. La fórmula del área total de un cono es A.T. = A.L. + B.

Surface area of a cube The surface area of a cube is the sum of the areas of the faces of the cube. The formula for the surface area, S.A., of a cube is S.A. , where *s* represents the length of an edge of the cube.

Área total de un cubo El área total de un cubo es la suma de las áreas de las caras del cubo. La fórmula del área total, A.T., de un cubo es A.T. , donde *s* representa la longitud de una arista del cubo.

Surface area of a cylinder The surface area of a cylinder is the sum of the lateral area and the areas of the two circular bases. The formula for the surface area of a cylinder is S.A. L.A. 2*B*, where L.A. represents the lateral area of the cylinder and *B* represents the area of a base of the cylinder.

Área total de un cilindro El área total de un cilindro es la suma del área lateral y las áreas de las dos bases circulares. La fórmula del área total de un cilindro es A.T. A.L. 2*B*, donde A.L. representa el área lateral del cilindro y *B* representa el área de una base del cilindro.

Surface area of a pyramid The surface area of a pyramid is the sum of the areas of the faces of the pyramid. The formula for the surface area, S.A., of a pyramid is S.A. = L.A. + *B*, where L.A. represents the lateral area of the pyramid and *B* represents the area of the base of the pyramid.

Área total de una pirámide El área total de una pirámide es la suma de las áreas de las caras de la pirámide. La fórmula del área total, A.T., de una pirámide es A.T. = A.L. + *B*, donde A.L. representa el área lateral de la pirámide y *B* representa el área de la base de la pirámide.

Surface area of a sphere The surface area of a sphere is equal to the lateral area of a cylinder that has the same radius, *r*, and height 2*r*. The formula for the surface area of a sphere is S.A. = $4\pi r^2$, where *r* represents the radius of the sphere.

Área total de una esfera El área total de una esfera es igual al área lateral de un cilindro que tiene el mismo radio, *r*, y una altura de 2*r*. La fórmula del área total de una esfera es A.T. = $4\pi r^2$, donde *r* representa el radio de la esfera.

Surface area of a three-dimensional figure The surface area of a three-dimensional figure is the sum of the areas of its faces. You can find the surface area by finding the area of the net of the three-dimensional figure.

Área total de una figura tridimensional El área total de una figura tridimensional es la suma de las áreas de sus caras. Puedes hallar el área total si hallas el área del modelo plano de la figura tridimensional.

System of linear equations A system of linear equations is formed by two or more linear equations that use the same variables.

Sistema de ecuaciones lineales Un sistema de ecuaciones lineales está formado por dos o más ecuaciones lineales que usan las mismas variables.

Systematic sampling Systematic sampling is a sampling method in which you choose every nth member of the population, where *n* is a predetermined number. A systematic sample is useful when the researcher is able to approach the population in a systematic, or methodical, way.

Muestreo sistemático El muestreo sistemático es un método de muestreo en el que se escoge cada enésimo miembro de la población, donde *n* es un número predeterminado. Una muestra sistemática es útil cuando el investigador puede enfocarse en la población de manera sistemática o metódica.

T

Taxable wages For federal income tax purposes, your taxable wages are the difference between your earned wages and your withholding allowance. Your employer divides your withholding allowance equally among the pay periods of one year.

Sueldos imponibles Para propósitos federales de impuesto de renta, sus sueldos imponibles son la diferencia entre sus sueldos ganados y su concesión que retienen. Su empleador divide su concesión que retiene igualmente entre los períodos de paga de un año.

Tenths One tenth is one out of ten equal parts of a whole.

Décimas Una décima es 1 de 10 partes iguales de un todo.

Term A term is a number, a variable, or the product of a number and one or more variables.

Término Un término es un número, una variable o el producto de un número y una o más variables.

Terminating decimal A terminating decimal has a decimal expansion that terminates in 0.

Decimal finito Un decimal finito tiene una expansión decimal que termina en 0.

Terms of a ratio The terms of a ratio are the quantities *x* and *y* in the ratio.

Términos de una razón Los términos de una razón son la cantidad *x* y la cantidad *y* de la razón.

Theorem A theorem is a conjecture that is proven.

Teorema Un teorema es una conjetura que se ha comprobado.

Theoretical probability When all outcomes of an action are equally likely, $P(\text{event}) = \frac{\text{number of favourable outcomes}}{\text{number of possible outcomes}}$.

Probabilidad teórica Cuando todos los resultados de una acción son igualmente probables, $P(\text{evento}) = \frac{\text{número de resultados favorables}}{\text{número de resultados posibles}}$.

Third quartile For an ordered set of data, the third quartile is the median of the upper half of the data set.

Tercer cuartil Para un conjunto de datos ordenados, el tercer cuartil es la mediana de la mitad superior del conjunto de datos.

Thousandths One thousandth is one part of 1,000 equal parts of a whole.

Milésimas Una milésima es 1 de 1,000 partes iguales de un todo.

Three-dimensional figure A three-dimensional (3-D) figure is a figure that does not lie in a plane.

Figura tridimensional Una figura tridimensional es una figura que no está en un plano.

Total cost of a loan The total cost of a loan is the total amount spent to repay the loan. Total cost includes the principal and all interest paid over the length of the loan. Total cost also includes any fees charged.

El coste total de un préstamo El coste total de un préstamo es el cantidad total que es gastado para devolver el préstamo. El coste total incluye al director y todo el interés pagó sobre la longitud del préstamo. El coste total también incluye cualquier honorario cargado.

Transaction A banking transaction moves money into or out of a bank account.

Transacción Una transacción bancaria mueve dinero en o fuera de una cuenta bancaria.

Transfer A transaction that moves money from one bank account to another is a transfer. The balance of one account increases by the same amount the other account decreases.

Transferencia Una transacción que mueve dinero de una cuenta bancaria a otro es una transferencia. El equilibrio de un aumentos de cuenta por la misma cantidad que la otra cuenta disminuye.

Transformation A transformation is a change in position, shape, or size of a figure. Three types of transformations that change position only are translations, reflections, and rotations.

Transformación Una transformación es un cambio en la posición, la forma o el tamaño de una figura. Tres tipos de transformaciones que cambian sólo la posición son las traslaciones, las reflexiones y las rotaciones.

Translation A translation, or slide, is a rigid motion that moves every point of a figure the same distance and in the same direction.

Traslación Una traslación, o deslizamiento, es un movimiento rígido que mueve cada punto de una figura a la misma distancia y en la misma dirección.

Transversal A transversal is a line that intersects two or more lines at different points.

Transversal o secante Una transversal o secante es una línea que interseca dos o más líneas en distintos puntos.

Trapezoid A trapezoid is a quadrilateral with exactly one pair of parallel sides.

Trapecio Un trapecio es un cuadrilátero que tiene exactamente un par de lados paralelos.

Trend line A trend line is a line on a scatter plot, drawn near the points, that approximates the association between the data sets.

Línea de tendencia Una línea de tendencia es una línea en un diagrama de dispersión, trazada cerca de los puntos, que se aproxima a la relación entre los conjuntos de datos.

Trial In a probability experiment, you carry out or observe an action repeatedly. Each observation of the action is a trial.

Prueba En un experimento de probabilidad, realizas u observas una acción varias veces. Cada observación de la acción es una prueba.

Triangle A triangle is a polygon with three sides.

Triángulo Un triángulo es un polígono de tres lados.

Triangular prism A triangular prism is a prism with bases in the shape of a triangle.

Prisma triangular Un prisma triangular es un prisma cuyas bases tienen la forma de un triángulo.

True equation A true equation has equal values on each side of the equals sign.

Ecuación verdadera En una ecuación verdadera, los valores a ambos lados del signo igual son iguales.

Two-way frequency table A two-way frequency table displays the counts of the data in each group.

Tabla de frecuencia con dos variables Una tabla de frecuencia con dos variables muestra el conteo de los datos de cada grupo.

Two-way relative frequency table A two-way relative frequency table shows the ratio of the number of data in each group to the size of the population. The relative frequencies can be calculated with respect to the entire population, the row populations, or the column populations. The relative frequencies can be expressed as fractions, decimals, or percents.

Tabla de frecuencias relativas con dos variables Una tabla de frecuencias relativas con dos variables muestra la razón del número de datos de cada grupo al tamaño de la población. Las frecuencias relativas se pueden calcular respecto de la población entera, las poblaciones de las filas o las poblaciones de las columnas. Las frecuencias relativas se pueden expresar como fracciones, decimales o porcentajes.

Two-way table A two-way table shows bivariate categorical data for a population.

Tabla con dos variables Una tabla con dos variables muestra datos bivariados por categorías de una población.

U

Uniform probability model A uniform probability model is a probability model based on using the theoretical probability of equally likely outcomes.

Modelo de probabilidad uniforme Un modelo de probabilidad uniforme es un modelo de probabilidad que se basa en el uso de la probabilidad teórica de resultados igualmente probables.

English/Spanish Glossary

Unit fraction A unit fraction is a fraction with a numerator of 1 and a denominator that is a whole number greater than 1.

Fracción unitaria Una fracción unitaria es una fracción con un numerador 1 y un denominador que es un número entero mayor que 1.

Unit price A unit price is a unit rate that gives the price of one item.

Precio por unidad El precio por unidad es una tasa por unidad que muestra el precio de un artículo.

Unit rate The rate for one unit of a given quantity is called the unit rate.

Tasa por unidad Se llama tasa por unidad a la tasa que corresponde a 1 unidad de una cantidad dada.

Use To use given information, draw on it to help you determine something else.

Usar Para usar una información dada, apóyate en ella para determinar otra cosa.

V

Valid inference A valid inference is an inference that is true about the population. Valid inferences can be made when they are based on data from a representative sample.

Inferencia válida Una inferencia válida es una inferencia verdadera acerca de una población. Se pueden hacer inferencias válidas si están basadas en los datos de una muestra representativa.

Variability Variability describes how much the items in a data set differ (or vary) from each other. On a data display, variability is shown by how much the data on the horizontal scale are spread out.

Variabilidad La variabilidad describe qué diferencia (o variación) existe entre los elementos de un conjunto de datos. Al exhibir datos, la variabilidad queda representada por la distancia que separa los datos en la escala horizontal.

Variable A variable is a letter that represents an unknown value.

Variable Una variable es una letra que representa un valor desconocido.

Variable expenses Variable expenses are expenses that change from one budget period to the next.

Gastos variables Los gastos variables son los gastos que cambian de un período económico al próximo.

Vertex of a cone The vertex of a cone is the point farthest from the base.

Vértice de un cono El vértice de un cono es el punto más alejado de la base.

Vertex of a polygon The vertex of a polygon is any point where two sides of a polygon meet.

Vértice de un polígono El vértice de un polígono es cualquier punto donde se encuentran dos lados de un polígono.

Vertex of a three-dimensional figure A vertex of a three-dimensional figure is a point where three or more edges meet.

Vértice de una figura tridimensional El vértice de una figura tridimensional es un punto donde se unen tres o más aristas.

Vertex of an angle The vertex of an angle is the point of intersection of the rays that make up the sides of the angle.

Vértice de un ángulo El vértice de un ángulo es el punto de intersección de las semirrectas que forman los lados del ángulo.

Vertical angles Vertical angles are formed by two intersecting lines and are opposite each other. Vertical angles have equal measures.

Ángulos opuestos por el vértice Los ángulos opuestos por el vértice están formados por dos rectas secantes y están uno frente a otro. Los ángulos opuestos por el vértice tienen la misma medida.

Vertical-line test The vertical-line test is a method used to determine if a relation is a function or not. If a vertical line passes through a graph more than once, the graph is not the graph of a function.

Prueba de recta vertical La prueba de recta vertical es un método que se usa para determinar si una relación es una función o no. Si una recta vertical atraviesa la gráfica más de una vez, la gráfica no es la gráfica de una función.

Volume Volume is the number of cubic units needed to fill a solid figure.

Volumen El volumen es el número de unidades cúbicas que se necesitan para llenar un cuerpo geométrico.

Volume of a cone The volume of a cone is the number of unit cubes, or cubic units, needed to fill the cone. The formula for the volume of a cone is $V = \frac{1}{3}Bh$, where B represents the area of the base and h represents the height of the cone.

Volumen de un cono El volumen de un cono es el número de bloques de unidades, o unidades cúbicas, que se necesitan para llenar el cono. La fórmula del volumen de un cono $V = \frac{1}{3}Bh$, donde B representa el área de la base y h representa la altura del cono.

Volume of a cube The volume of a cube is the number of unit cubes, or cubic units, needed to fill the cube. The formula for the volume V of a cube is $V = s^3$, where s represents the length of an edge of the cube.

Volumen de un cubo El volumen de un cubo es el número de bloques de unidades, o unidades cúbicas, que se necesitan para llenar el cubo. La fórmula del volumen, V, de un cubo es $V = s^3$, donde s representa la longitud de una arista del cubo.

Volume of a cylinder The volume of a cylinder is the number of unit cubes, or cubic units, needed to fill the cylinder. The formula for the volume of a cylinder is $V = \pi r^2 h$, where r represents the radius of a base and h represents the height of the cylinder.

Volumen de un cilindro El volumen de un cilindro es el número de bloques de unidades, o unidades cúbicas, que se necesitan para llenar el cilindro. La fórmula del volumen de un cilindro es $V = \pi r^2 h$, donde r representa el radio de una base y h representa la altura del cilindro.

Volume of a prism The volume of a prism is the number of unit cubes, or cubic units, needed to fill the prism. The formula for the volume V of a prism is $V = Bh$, where B represents the area of a base and h represents the height of the prism.

Volumen de un prisma El volumen de un prisma es el número de bloques de unidades, o unidades cúbicas, que se necesitan para llenar el prisma. La fórmula del volumen, V, de un prisma $V = Bh$, donde B representa el área de una base y h representa la altura del prisma.

Volume of a pyramid The volume of a pyramid is the number of unit cubes needed to fill the pyramid. The formula for the volume V of a pyramid is $V = \frac{1}{3}Bh$, where B represents the area of the base and h represents the height of the pyramid.

Volumen de una pirámide El volumen de una pirámide es el número de bloques de unidades, o unidades cúbicas, que se necesitan para llenar la pirámide. La fórmula del volumen, V, de una pirámide es $V = \frac{1}{3}Bh$, donde B representa el área de la base y h representa la altura de la pirámide.

Volume of a sphere The volume of a sphere is the number of unit cubes, or cubic units, needed to fill the sphere. The formula for the volume of a sphere is $V = \frac{4}{3}\pi r^3$.

Volumen de una esfera El volumen de una esfera es el número de bloques de unidades, o unidades cúbicas, que se necesitan para llenar la esfera. La fórmula del volumen de una esfera es $V = \frac{4}{3}\pi r^3$.

W

Whole numbers The whole numbers consist of the number 0 and all of the natural numbers.

Números enteros no negativos Los números enteros no negativos son el número 0 y todos los números naturales.

Withdrawal A transaction that takes money out of a bank account is a withdrawal.

Retirada Una transacción que toma dinero fuera de una cuenta bancaria es una retirada.

Withholding allowance You can exclude a portion of your earned wages, called a withholding allowance, from federal income tax. You can claim one withholding allowance for yourself and one for each person dependent upon your income.

Retener concesión Puede excluir una porción de sus sueldos ganados, llamó una concesión que retiene, del impuesto de renta federal. Puede reclamar una concesión que retiene para usted mismo y para uno para cada dependiente de persona sobre sus ingresos.

Word form of a number The word form of a number is the number written in words.

Número en palabras Un número en palabras es un número escrito con palabras en lugar de dígitos.

Work-Study Work-study is a type of need-based aid that schools might offer to a student. A student must earn work-study money by working certain jobs.

Práctica estudiantil La práctica estudiantil es un tipo de ayuda necesidad-basado que escuelas quizás ofrezcan a un estudiante. Un estudiante debe ganar dinero de práctica estudiantil por ciertos trabajos de trabajo.

X

x-axis The x-axis is the horizontal number line that, together with the y-axis, forms the coordinate plane.

Eje de las x El eje de las x es la recta numérica horizontal que, junto con el eje de las y, forma el plano de coordenadas.

x-coordinate The x-coordinate is the first number in an ordered pair. It tells the number of horizontal units a point is from 0.

Coordenada x La coordenada x (abscisa) es el primer número de un par ordenado. Indica cuántas unidades horizontales hay entre un punto y 0.

Y

y-axis The y-axis is the vertical number line that, together with the x-axis, forms the coordinate plane.

Eje de las y El eje de las y es la recta numérica vertical que, junto con el eje de las x, forma el plano de coordenadas.

y-coordinate The y-coordinate is the second number in an ordered pair. It tells the number of vertical units a point is from 0.

Coordenada y La coordenada y (ordenada) es el segundo número de un par ordenado. Indica cuántas unidades verticales hay entre un punto y 0.

y-intercept The y-intercept of a line is the y-coordinate of the point where the line crosses the y-axis.

Intercepto en y El intercepto en y de una recta es la coordenada y del punto por donde la recta cruza el eje de las y.

Z

Zero exponent property For any nonzero number a, $a^0 = 1$.

Propiedad del exponente cero Para cualquier número distinto de cero a, $a^0 = 1$.

Zero Property of Multiplication The product of 0 and any number is 0. For any number n, $n \cdot 0 = 0$ and $0 \cdot n = 0$.

Propiedad del cero en la multiplicación El producto de 0 y cualquier número es 0. Para cualquier número n, $n \cdot 0 = 0$ and $0 \cdot n = 0$.

Formulas

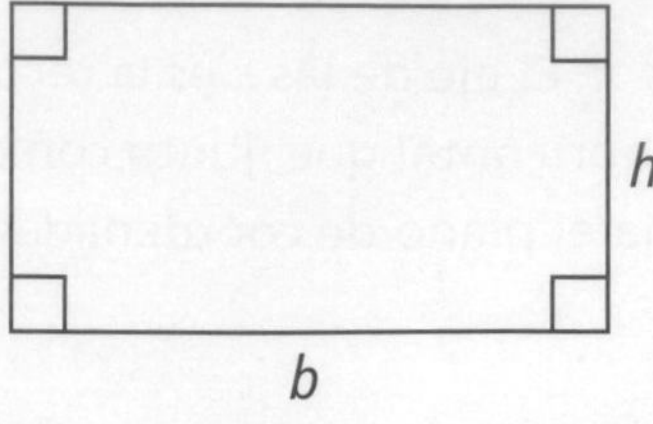

$P = 2b + 2h$
$A = bh$

Rectangle

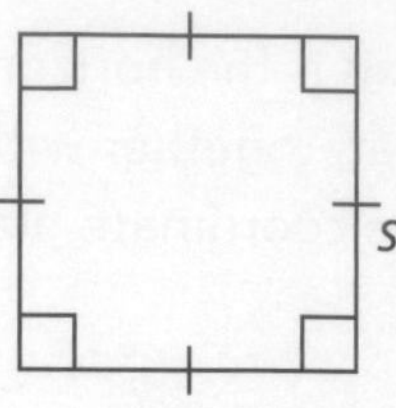

$P = 4s$
$A = s^2$

Square

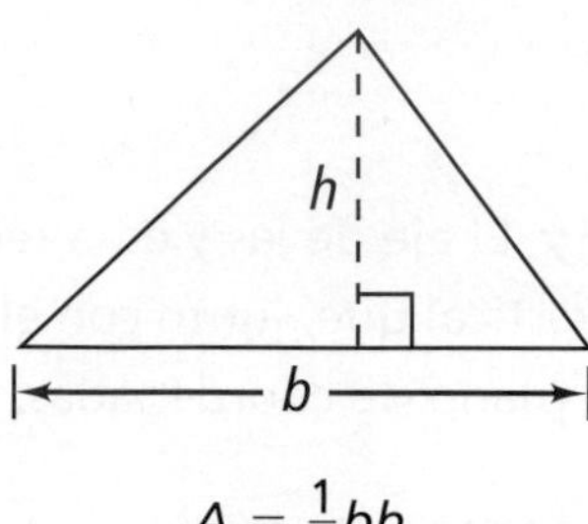

$A = \frac{1}{2}bh$

Triangle

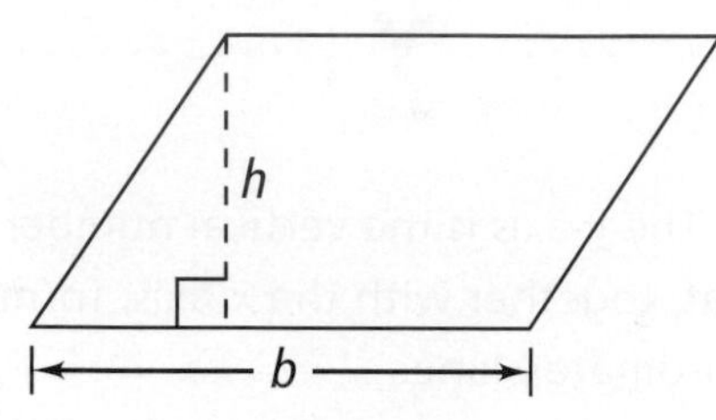

$A = bh$

Parallelogram

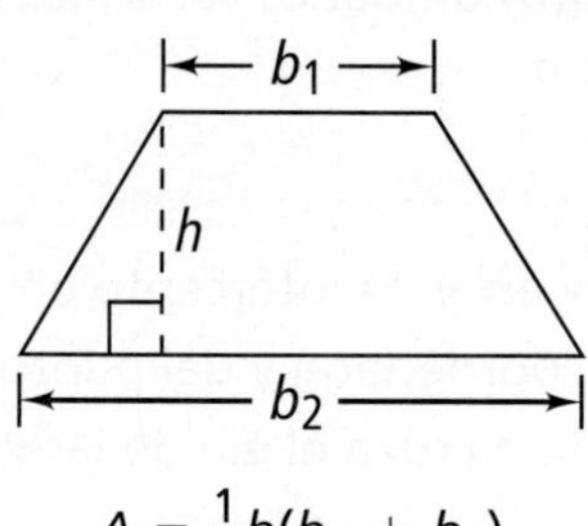

$A = \frac{1}{2}h(b_1 + b_2)$

Trapezoid

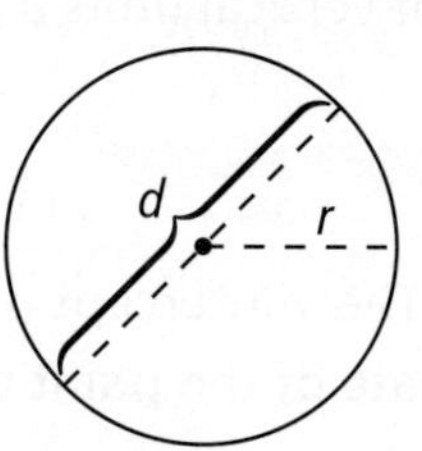

$C = 2\pi r$ or $C = \pi d$
$A = \pi r^2$

Circle

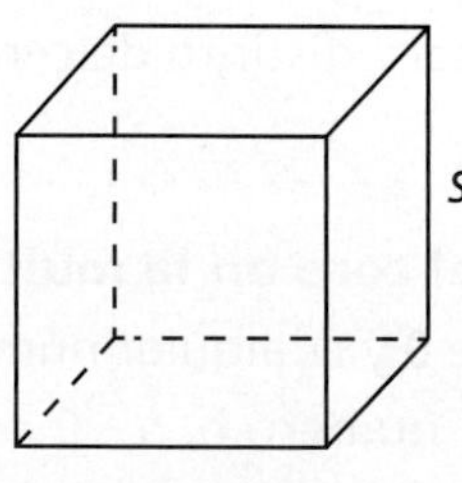

$S.A. = 6s^2$
$V = s^3$

Cube

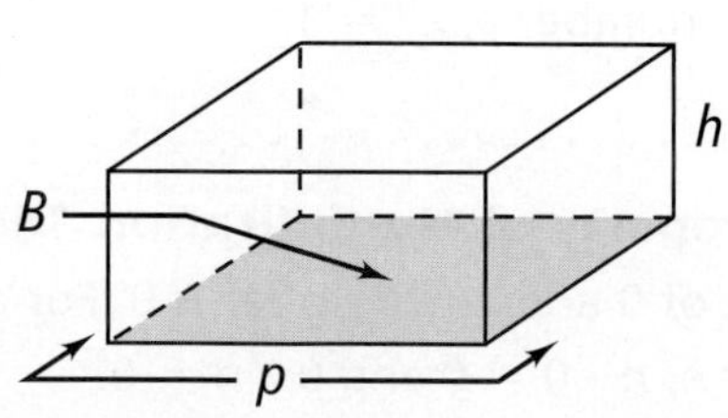

$V = Bh$
$L.A. = ph$
$S.A. = L.A. + 2B$

Rectangular Prism

Formulas

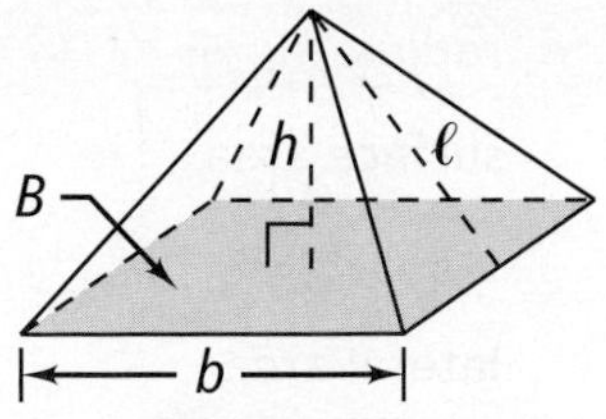

$V = \frac{1}{3}Bh$

L.A. $= 2b\ell$

S.A. = L.A. + B

Square Pyramid

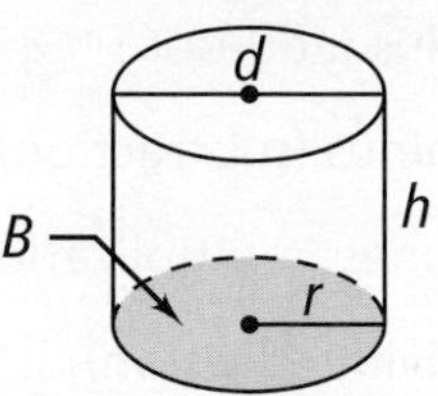

$V = Bh$

L.A. $= 2\pi rh$

S.A. = L.A. + $2B$

Cylinder

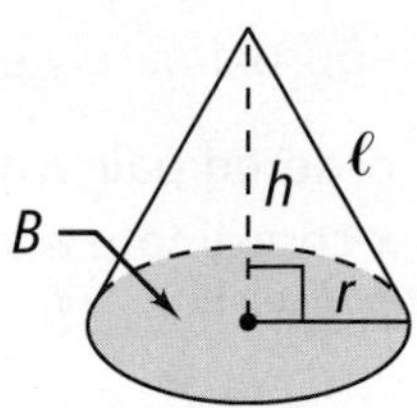

$V = \frac{1}{3}Bh$

L.A. $= \pi r\ell$

S.A. = L.A. + B

Cone

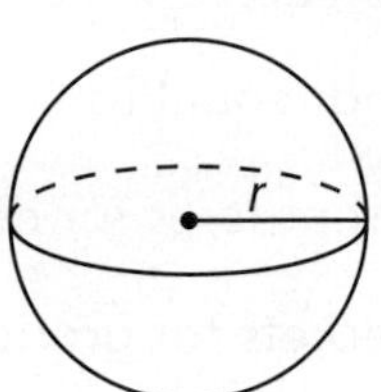

$V = \frac{4}{3}\pi r^3$

S.A. $= 4\pi r^2$

Sphere

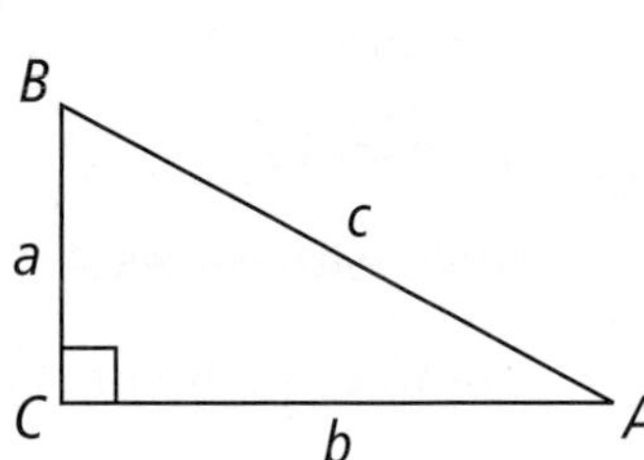

$a^2 + b^2 = c^2$

Pythagorean Theorem

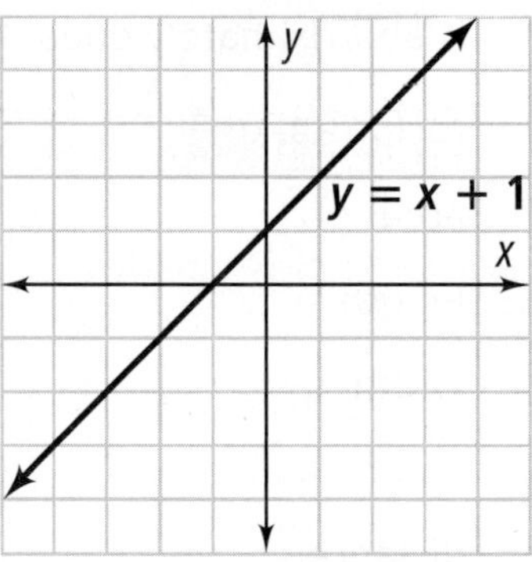

$y = mx + b$, where
m = slope and
b = y-intercept

Equation of Line

Math Symbols

Symbol	Meaning
$+$	plus (addition)
$-$	minus (subtraction)
$\times$, $\cdot$	times (multiplication)
$\div$, $\overline{)}$, $\frac{a}{b}$	divide (division)
$=$	is equal to
$<$	is less than
$>$	is greater than
$\leq$	is less than or equal to
$\geq$	is greater than or equal to
$\neq$	is not equal to
( )	parentheses for grouping
[ ]	brackets for grouping
$-a$	opposite of *a*
. . .	and so on
$^\circ$	degrees
$\lvert a \rvert$	absolute value of *a*
$\stackrel{?}{=}$, $\stackrel{?}{<}$, $\stackrel{?}{>}$	Is the statement true?
$\approx$	is approximately equal to
$\frac{b}{a}$	reciprocal of $\frac{a}{b}$
A	area
ℓ	length
w	width
h	height
d	distance
r	rate
t	time
P	perimeter
b	base length
C	circumference
d	diameter
r	radius
S.A.	surface area
B	area of base
L.A.	lateral area
ℓ	slant height
V	volume
a^n	*n*th power of *a*
$\sqrt{x}$	nonnegative square root of *x*
π	pi, an irrational number approximately equal to 3.14
(a, b)	ordered pair with *x*-coordinate *a* and *y*-coordinate *b*
$\overline{AB}$	segment *AB*
A'	image of *A*, *A* prime
$\triangle ABC$	triangle with vertices *A*, *B*, and *C*
$\rightarrow$	arrow notation
$a : b$, $\frac{a}{b}$	ratio of a to *b*
$\cong$	is congruent to
$\sim$	is similar to
$\angle A$	angle with vertex *A*
AB	length of segment $\overline{AB}$
$\overrightarrow{AB}$	ray *AB*
$\angle ABC$	angle formed by $\overrightarrow{BA}$ and $\overrightarrow{BC}$
$m\angle ABC$	measure of angle *ABC*
$\perp$	is perpendicular to
$\overleftrightarrow{AB}$	line *AB*
$\parallel$	is parallel to
%	percent
P (event)	probability of an event

Measures

Customary	Metric
Length	**Length**
1 foot (ft) = 12 inches (in.) 1 yard (yd) = 36 in. 1 yd = 3 ft 1 mile (mi) = 5,280 ft 1 mi = 1,760 yd	1 centimeter (cm) = 10 millimeters (mm) 1 meter (m) = 100 cm 1 kilometer (km) = 1,000 m 1 mm = 0.001 m
Area	**Area**
1 square foot (ft^2) = 144 square inches ($in.^2$) 1 square yard (yd^2) = 9 ft^2 1 square mile (mi^2) = 640 acres	1 square centimeter (cm^2) = 100 square millimeters (mm^2) 1 square meter (m^2) = 10,000 cm^2
Volume	**Volume**
1 cubic foot (ft^3) = 1,728 cubic inches ($in.^3$) 1 cubic yard (yd^3) = 27 ft^3	1 cubic centimeter (cm^3) = 1,000 cubic millimeters (mm^3) 1 cubic meter (m^3) = 1,000,000 cm^3
Mass	**Mass**
1 pound (lb) = 16 ounces (oz) 1 ton (t) = 2,000 lb	1 gram (g) = 1,000 milligrams (mg) 1 kilogram (kg) = 1,000 g
Capacity	**Capacity**
1 cup (c) = 8 fluid ounces (fl oz) 1 pint (pt) = 2 c 1 quart (qt) = 2 pt 1 gallon (gal) = 4 qt	1 liter (L) = 1,000 milliliters (mL) 1000 liters = 1 kiloliter (kL)

Customary Units and Metric Units	
Length	1 in. = 2.54 cm 1 mi ≈ 1.61 km 1 ft ≈ 0.3 m
Capacity	1 qt ≈ 0.94 L
Weight and Mass	1 oz ≈ 28.3 g 1 lb ≈ 0.45 kg

Properties

Unless otherwise stated, the variables a, b, c, m, and n used in these properties can be replaced with any number represented on a number line.

Identity Properties

Addition $n + 0 = n$ and $0 + n = n$

Multiplication $n \cdot 1 = n$ and $1 \cdot n = n$

Commutative Properties

Addition $a + b = b + a$

Multiplication $a \cdot b = b \cdot a$

Associative Properties

Addition $(a + b) + c = a + (b + c)$

Multiplication $(a \cdot b) \cdot c = a \cdot (b \cdot c)$

Inverse Properties

Addition

$a + (-a) = 0$ and $-a + a = 0$

Multiplication

$a \cdot \frac{1}{a} = 1$ and $\frac{1}{a} \cdot a = 1$, $(a \neq 0)$

Distributive Properties

$a(b + c) = ab + ac$ $\quad (b + c)a = ba + ca$

$a(b - c) = ab - ac$ $\quad (b - c)a = ba - ca$

Properties of Equality

Addition If $a = b$, then $a + c = b + c$.

Subtraction If $a = b$, then $a - c = b - c$.

Multiplication If $a = b$, then $a \cdot c = b \cdot c$.

Division If $a = b$, and $c \neq 0$, then $\frac{a}{c} = \frac{b}{c}$.

Substitution If $a = b$, then b can replace a in any expression.

Zero Property

$a \cdot 0 = 0$ and $0 \cdot a = 0$.

Properties of Inequality

Addition If $a > b$, then $a + c > b + c$. If $a < b$, then $a + c < b + c$.

Subtraction If $a > b$, then $a - c > b - c$. If $a < b$, then $a - c < b - c$.

Multiplication

If $a > b$ and $c > 0$, then $ac > bc$.

If $a < b$ and $c > 0$, then $ac < bc$.

If $a > b$ and $c < 0$, then $ac < bc$.

If $a < b$ and $c < 0$, then $ac > bc$.

Division

If $a > b$ and $c > 0$, then $\frac{a}{c} > \frac{b}{c}$.

If $a < b$ and $c > 0$, then $\frac{a}{c} < \frac{b}{c}$.

If $a > b$ and $c < 0$, then $\frac{a}{c} < \frac{b}{c}$.

If $a < b$ and $c < 0$, then $\frac{a}{c} > \frac{b}{c}$.

Properties of Exponents

For any nonzero number n and any integers m and n:

Zero Exponent $a^0 = 1$

Negative Exponent $a^{-n} = \frac{1}{a^n}$

Product of Powers $a^m \cdot a^n = a^{m+n}$

Power of a Product $(ab)^n = a^n b^n$

Quotient of Powers $\frac{a^m}{a^n} = a^{m-n}$

Power of a Quotient $\left(\frac{a}{b}\right)^n = \frac{a^n}{b^n}$

Power of a Power $(a^m)^n = a^{mn}$